POLITICS
ESSAYS IN TRIBUTE TO RANDHIR SINGH

Edited by
Dhananjay Rai

AAKAR

Politics: Essays in Tribute to Randhir Singh
Edited by Dhananjay Rai

First Published 2018

ISBN 978-93-5002-532-1 (HB)

Published by
AAKAR BOOKS
28 E Pocket IV, Mayur Vihar Phase I
Delhi 110 091 India
aakarbooks@gmail.com

Laser Typeset at
Arpit Printographers, Delhi 110 032

Printed at
Sapra Brothers, Delhi 110 092

Contents

Part III: Advancing the Domain

Part IV: Highlighting the Concern

Acknowledgements

I am thankful to Prof. Sudipta Kaviraj, and SAGE India for granting permission to reproduce two articles from *Perspectives on Capitalism: Marx, Keynes, Schumpeter, and Weber* (Editors: Krishna Bharadwaj and Sudipta Kaviraj, SAGE, Delhi, 1989) in this book: Sudipta Kaviraj, *On Political Explanation in Marxism* (pp. 132-175); Randhir Singh, *Politics—The Dialectics of Science and Revolution in Karl Marx* (pp. 176-184). I am also grateful to the *Economic and Political Weekly* for granting permission to include the following article in the book: Ajay Gudavarthy, *Brahmanism, Liberalism and the Postcolonial Theory* (*Economic and Political Weekly*, June 11, 2016, Vol. LI, No. 24, 15-17). This book would not have been possible without the extension of immense support from contributors who tolerated my never-ending mails. For comments on introduction and its present shape, I am highly indebted to my friends Abdul Rahman, Smruti Ranjan Dhal, Beryl Anand and Pavel Tomar. I extend my deepest gratitude to M.V. Kannan for his elaborate comments and sharp editing. Finally, I am also highly indebted to K.K. Saxena of Aakar Books, for his suggestions from time to time, constant help and the eagerness shown for completion of this book.

Introduction

Dhananjay Rai

Randhir Singh (1922-2016) envisioned an egalitarian world. This envisioning is not only antithetical to a simplistic ratiocination of capitalism along with pre-capitalistic continuation but also advancement of discernment by way of explanation of totality. For him, the explanation of totality becomes crucial for exhibition of innumerable instances of interconnectedness and mediations in it. This explanation of totality, however, does not remain a scholastic endeavour but conjoins with *politics*. Politics is not a super structural referential realm but the enablement of an agency for challenging and changing socio-economic formations. These two (explanation and politics) derive strength from Marxist weltanschauung (world view) and method which have, in turn, invited positional rejections by critics on two accounts: firstly and epistemologically, Marxist weltanschauung is a nonstarter to comprehend the complexities, and secondly thereafter, its method is reduced to historicism, determinism and teleology.

Related to this debate, Alain Badiou suggests three basic elements (a political one, a historical one and a subjective one) along with seamless synthesis between global and local yet universally transmittable truth to give new life to the ideal of communism in individual consciousness: "by combining intellectual constructs, which are always global and universal, with experiments of fragments of truths, which are local and singular, yet universally transmittable, we can give new life to the communist hypothesis, or rather to the idea of communism, in individual consciousness" (Badiou, 2010: 260). These are significant for outlining while begetting further questions: is the political epiphenomenon or agency empowering? Is it historical duplication or teleological? Is the subject determinist or autonomous? Some of these questions and concerns would be debated by way of discussing the world view and method in subsequent sections. Thereafter, Randhir Singh's contribution is delineated. This exercise, however, remains modest and not exhaustive. Towards the end, the summary of chapters is presented thematically.

Marxist Weltanschauung

Weltanschauung particularly of Marxism has been challenged on many occasions. There are three noteworthy interventions, *inter alia,* wherefrom Marxism is problematised concerning weltanschauung. Firstly, there is neutrality and the 'anti-ideological debate' wherefrom Marxism is treated as an enemy of freedom. Capitalism is the worldview. In this regard, discussion on 'end of ideology' and 'end of history' becomes crucially important vantage points. The veiled description and arrival of 'end of ideology' is nothing but in an allusion to the decline of Marxism and ascendancy of capitalism in the form of post-industrial society. Daniel Bell, Seymour Lipset, Edward Shils and Raymond Aron remain important theoreticians in this regard. Daniel Bell explicitly uses the term 'ideology' for the left and later on 'new left' was also included in the emergence of new language of revolutions. "I have applied the term largely to left-wing thought, and so restrict its scope. This is true. Yet, while there are "ideologies" of the "right" as well as of the "left,"—as there are now "ideologies" of economic development—one's historical contexts defines one's usage; and the word *ideology* was a product of the "left" and gained a distinctive resonance in that context. And this was the focus of my discussion" (Bell, 1988: 17).

In Bell's formulation, communism is reduced to a 'regulated living' for the hope of having a transforming moment which itself is an illusion. "The ideologist—Communist, existentialist, religionist—wants to live at some extreme, and criticises the ordinary man for failing to live at the level of grandeur. One can try to do so if there is the genuine possibility that the next moment could be actually, a "transforming moment" when salvation or revolution or genuine passion could be achieved. But such chiliastic moments are illusions. And what is left is the unheroic, day-to-day routine of living" (Bell, 1988: 302). Moreover, "[t]he point is that ideologists are "terrible simplifiers"" (Bell, 1988: 405). Once the rejection of an ideology qua Marxism gets completed, Bell proposes a post-industrial society within the framework of capitalism itself: vitality of service economy, professional class, theoretical knowledge, technology-led actions and intellectual technology (Bell, 1973). Social relations, production relations and accumulation become irrelevant. The attack is hereon organised protest and organised politics for transformation (aka Marxism).

Taking the argument further Francis Fukuyama presents his arguments in two stages. In the first stage, liberal democracy becomes the consensus model in terms of getting legitimacy. Herein, the end of history entails the final arrival of an ideological evolution of humankind and human government. The *sui generis* aspect of liberal democracy is being free from internal contradictions. The problem in modern liberal democracies like USA, France and Switzerland is not the principle per se but non-implementation of twin principles of liberty and equality. In the second phase, he proposes two underlying aspects of liberal democracy: economic and 'struggle for recognition'. Regarding economic, in contrast to Marxists *et al.*, Fukuyama says that "...liberal principles in economics—the "free market"—have spread, and have succeeded in producing unprecedented levels of material prosperity, both in industrially developed countries and in countries that had been, at the close of World War II, part of the impoverished Third World. A liberal revolution in economic thinking has sometimes preceded, sometimes followed, the move toward political freedom around the globe" (Fukuyama, 1992: xiii-xiv).

Regarding recognition, it should be given to all. Therefore, there is a defence of capitalism: "Capitalism is a dynamic force which constantly attacks purely conventional social relationships, replacing inherited privilege with new stratifications based on skill and education" (Fukuyama, 1992: 290). On the other hand, "the Marxist project sought to promote an extreme form of social equality at the expense of liberty, by eliminating natural inequalities through the reward not of talent but of need, and through the attempt to abolish the division of labor. All future efforts to push social equality beyond the point of a "middle-class society" must contend with the failure of the Marxist project" (Fukuyama, 1992: 293). Regarding recognition, he suggests that "Marxism, "modernisation theory," or any other theory of history based primarily on economics will be radically incomplete unless it takes account of the thymotic part of the soul, and of the struggle for recognition as a major driver of history" (Fukuyama, 1992: 204-205). Reading Hegel through Alexandre Kojève confirms universal citizenship in a homogeneous state which is liberal democracy for Fukuyama.

Secondly, worldview is fine but can Marxism as a worldview explain everything? This serious challenge comes from Sigmund Freud in his lecture on 'a philosophy of life' in 1932. According to him, *Weltanschauung...[is]...*an intellectual construction which gives a unified solution of all the problems of our existence in virtue of a comprehensive hypothesis, a construction, therefore, in which no question is left open and in which everything in which we are interested finds a place" (Freud, 1932). Thereafter, he suggests that the scientific worldview that is psychoanalysis must be upheld while rejecting non-scientific worldview. He also poses certain questions to Marxism while recognising the strength of Marxism through economic explanation: "The *unquestionable fact that different individuals, races and nations behave differently under the same economic conditions in itself proves that the economic factor cannot be the sole determinant*" (Freud, 1932).

These two positions reject Marxian worldview. There is a third dimension which is an anti-worldview postulation. This is primarily visible in Postmodernism. The theory is this: having a worldview is itself a problem. This has generated, *inter alia*, two core concepts: the absence of action, and the absence of organised mobilisation. This is due to the rejection of '*meta narrative*' or 'end of master' such as Marxism in Lyotard's *The Postmodern Condition* (1997). According to Perry Anderson,

> For Lyotard, the arrival of postmodernity was linked to the emergence of a post-industrial society—theorized by Daniel Bell and Alain Touraine—in which knowledge had become the main economic force of production in a flow bypassing national states, yet at the same time had lost its traditional legitimations. For if society was now best conceived, neither as an organic whole nor as a dualistic field of conflict (Parsons or Marx), but as a web of linguistic communications, language itself—'the whole social bond'—was composed of a multiplicity of different games, whose rules were incommensurable, and inter-relations agonistic. In these conditions, science became just one language game among others: it could no longer claim the imperial privilege over other forms of knowledge to which it had pretended in modern times. In fact, its title to superiority as denotative truth over narrative styles of customary knowledge concealed the basis of its own legitimation, which classically rested on the two forms of grand narrative itself. The first of these, derived from the French Revolution, told a tale of humanity as the heroic agent of its own liberation through the advance of knowledge; the second, descending from German Idealism, a tale of spirit as the progressive unfolding of truth. Such were the great justifying myths of modernity. The defining trait of the postmodern condition, by contrast, is the loss of credibility of these meta-narratives (Anderson, 1998: 24-25).

Marxian 'metanarrative' is not without action or mobilisation. The 'epistemic' rejection is thus the rejection of organised politics and actions. This is also visible in post-Marxism. Ernesto Laclau and Chantal Mouffe adhere to the floating signifier/empty signifier. "Every antagonism", they state, "left free to itself, is a floating signifier, a 'wild' antagonism which does not predetermine the form in which it can be articulated to other elements in a social formation" (Laclau and Mouffe, 2001: 171).

Laclau further suggests that "[a]n empty signifier is, strictly speaking, a signifier without a signified" (Laclau, 2007: 34). Despite sympathetic concern for and multiple use of Marx in their work, Michael Hardt and Antonio Negri (they make intervention through their concept 'multitude' which is, as asserted, 'inclusive' and 'contemporary' over 'people', 'masses', and 'working classes') remain ambiguous regarding concrete actions: "Keep in mind that this is a philosophical book. We will give numerous examples of how people are working today to put an end to war and make the world more democratic, but do not expect our book to answer the question, What is to be done? or propose a concrete program of action" (Hardt and Negri, 2004: xvi).

One of the outcomes, as Aijaz Ahmad points out, is atomisation of politics where resistance is seemingly everywhere but in effect nowhere: "The most far-reaching consequence of postmodernism in practical politics has been what I have called the atomisation of politics, the displacement of class politics by an amorphous entity called 'culture,' the further displacement of the politics of Equality by the politics of Identity, the fracture of the unity of the exploited and the oppressed into countless little oppositional claims, so that resistance seems to be everywhere but nowhere in particular" (Ahmad, 2011: 23).

Thus, some outlining of worldview of Marxism needs to be delineated in the context of three aforesaid positions. Worldview is not an intellectual construction but confluence of explanation of reality with the desired catapult which means that one suggests the 'operationality of reality' while making several propositions of the radical break. 'Operationality of reality' entails unbiased exhibition of reality. The reality must be explained in non-obtruded ways. The worldview cannot be a collection of realities. Thus, it has to be changed accordingly. A radical break is required. This radical break cannot be envisaged sans exhibition of operationality of reality. The radical break is *politics.*

Besides the operationality of reality and radical break, the Marxist worldview includes three core values and thus requires a categorical defence and elaboration. Firstly, relationality is an important component in the worldview. There are relations among components. It should be understood that relation between components must be seen dialectically, not causally. In other words, relations are crucial insofar as economic factors are concerned. The outcome, however, is not decided *merely* by economic factors. Secondly, this brings the concept of effectuality. The role of mediating factors, however, cannot be negated. There cannot be negation of multiple factors deciding outcomes. Randhir Singh talks about two errors: major empirical errors and minor holistic errors. The former is found in the right where grasping things through appearance, and in isolation, is the prevalent method. The latter is found in the left where richness of mediations constitute the whole is missed out. Thirdly, there is materiality of effectuality in place of 'externality in effectuality'. In other words, effectuality has materiality whereas externality in effectuality is described through unknown causes or forces. This makes the Marxian worldview real which is material without negating the mediations. This also brings the question of history to the fore.

History qua Method or Method which Includes History

After the worldview, history/method has invited incessant attention since Marxism and history have an inseparable relationship. Karl Popper criticizes Marxism from the vantage point of 'historicism'. He defines historicism for Marxism as follows: "The method of a science of society is the study of history, and especially of the tendencies inherent in the historical development of mankind" (Popper, 1945b: 303). According to Karl Popper, "[b]y describing Marxism as purest historicism, I have indicated that I hold the Marxist method to be very poor indeed" (Popper, 1945b: 80). Therefore, he stresses, the rejection of holistic approach for "Marx was the last of the great holistic system builders. We should take care to leave it at that, and not to replace his by another Great System. What we need is not holism. It is piecemeal social engineering" (Popper, 1945b: 123). The piecemeal social engineering formulation is a crucial one in contrast to historicism. He distinguishes between piecemeal social engineering and utopian social engineering to reject Plato. He, however, for the purpose of juxtaposing with historicism, uses social engineering. He uses social institutions to find out the contrast. The historicist perceives social institutions mainly from the vantage point of history; its origin is due to a definite design for definite ends. In contrast to it, the social engineer and technologist will not take into account the historical view or origin per se. The immediacy will be more important (Popper, 1945a: 18).

Maurice Cornforth rejects the charge of 'methodological essentialism' by Popper against Marx. He reminds him of Marx's statement from *The Eighteenth Brumaire of Louis Bonaparte* wherein both agency and circumstances become crucial components of change: "Men make their own history, but they do not make it just as they please; they do not make it under circumstances chosen by themselves, but under circumstances directly encountered and given and transmitted from the past". History is not a formula but description and explanation. Cornforth points out that "[o]bviously, so far as the past is concerned, history is not predicative but descriptive and explanatory (Cornforth, 1968: 137). "This descriptive-explanatory approach", he adds, "to the study of history does not represent history as the automatic consequence of the operation of inexorable "laws"—like, for example, a closed mechanical system in which a later state inexorably ensues from the earlier by the operation of the laws of mechanics" (Cornforth, 1968: 137). History is not used by Marx to find the superimposed pattern (Cornforth, 1968: 154).

Randhir Singh makes an important intervention. "The doctrine of Karl Marx is no determinist philosophy. There is no 'historicism' or 'historical inevitability' in Marx, nor any evolutionist metaphysics either" (Singh, 2011a: 104). For Marx, according to Singh, socialism is not "inevitable, it is something to be struggled for" (Singh, 2009a: 77). He cannot be called determinist. The conditional determinism gives importance to human praxis and revolutionary practices. "If attention was drawn to the economic-structural necessities underlying the historical processes, it was for enhancing the freedom for praxis, for not foreclosing but liberating human practice, for freer choices by humans, free not in some abstract or metaphysical sense, but in the only possible human sense of men and women choosing and acting with the fullest possible knowledge and consideration of the necessities of the objective material situation or circumstances. Such is the dialectics of freedom and necessity in Marx" (Singh, 2009a: 77). He further rules out the inevitability and certitude of victory. "Thus there are no inevitabilities in Marx and no guarantees of victory either, only alternatives" (Singh, 2009a: 77).

For this purpose, history becomes very important but it, itself, cannot become a method *ipso facto*. Method is important which includes history. Marx not only goes against 'consciousness' driven history of Hegel but also makes a significant departure from Ludwig Feuerbach. Consciousness has materiality and there is relationship between dialectics and history. "Feuerbach's analysis had been entirely ahistorical and non-dialectical: humans satisfy an emotional need through religion, but the origin of that need remains unexplained and unchanging whether satisfied by God or not. Marx sees the solution to this problem in material conditions. Human consciousness is critical in Marx's thought, but it can only be understood in relation to historical, social and material circumstances. In this way, Marx establishes a close relationship between dialectics and history, which would become a cornerstone of his own method. Consciousness is primarily determined by material conditions but these themselves evolve dialectically through human history" (Fine and Saad-Filho, 2004: 3-4).

Ben Fine and Alfredo Saad-Filho highlight five key features of Marx's method in Capital. Firstly, social phenomena exist. These can be understood only in their historical context. Understanding of these phenomena is not possible through trans-historical generalisations. Secondly, theory cannot be pushed beyond its historical and social limits; otherwise it will lose its validity. Thirdly, relationship between theory and history shapes the internal structure of Marx's analysis. In fact, this goes against Hegelian idealism where conceptual derivations are important. There is a serious problem in conceptual reasoning viz. changing reality cannot be reduced to concepts let alone determination. Fourthly, explanation of the concrete or outcomes is crucial. For this identification of several factors like key concepts, structures, relationships including the level of analysis are required. Fifthly, there has to be focus on historical changes (Fine and Saad-Filho, 2004: 5-8).

Despite making a difference between working class (exclusive concept) and multitude (inclusive concept) and prioritising the latter (Hardt and Negri, 2004: xii-xiv), Michael Hardt and Antonio Negri do take 'primary elements of Marx's method' to develop their own. These four elements are: the historical tendency, the real abstraction, antagonism, and the constitution of subjectivity (Hardt and Negri, 2004: 141). 'Tendency, abstraction, antagonism and constitution of subjectivity' do not define 'historicity'. Therefore, we can conclude that Marxism incorporates history in its method rather than making history as a method per se. Along with the 'anti-teleological' streak, not-historical generalisations, theory in historical and social limits, relationship between theory and history, not conceptual derivations, explanation of concrete and historical change are important aspects of the Marxist method. These are categorical components in the Marxist method.

Universe of Randhir Singh

Worldview and method in the intellectual universe of Randhir Singh remained linked with aforesaid debates. The materiality of worldview includes exhibition of operationality of reality, radical rupture, relationality, and materiality of effectuality. The worldview is not a scholastic endeavour. Regarding method, Randhir Singh incessantly emphasises on the anti-teleological method wherein the method includes history not otherwise. In other words, history is not historicism in Marxism and politics is consciousness of transformation and thus constitution of revolutionary subjectivity. The aforesaid dimensions are neatly available and structurally woven in Randhir Singh's *Reason, Revolution and Political Theory: Notes on Oakeshott's Rationalism in Politics* (1967), *Crisis of Socialism:Notes in Defence of A Commitment* (2006), *Of Marxism and Indian Politics* (1990), *Five Lectures in Marxist Mode* (1993), *Marxism, Socialism, Indian Politics: A View from the Left* (2008), *Contemporary Ecological Crisis—A Marxist View* (2009), *Indian Politics Today—An Argument for Socialism Oriented Path of Development* (2009), *On Nationalism and Communalism in India* (2010), *Struggle for Socialism:Some Issues* (2010), *The Right Lesson and the Wrong Conclusion* (2011), and *The World After the Collapse of the Soviet Union* (2011), *What was Built and What Failed in the Soviet Union* (2011). These were core concerns and reflected in Singh's academic and non-academic interventions. This part attempts modestly to map out some of the crucial concerns and realms of Randhir Singh. At the outset, this section explains why this book is titled as *Politics*. Thereafter, the primacy of politics, redefining the study of politics, universe of extended class, role of social sciences, semantic of academic freedom, explaining the crisis of socialism in USSR, environment and Marxism and the making of a life on the Left are expatiated.

Explaining the Title 'Politics'

Amidst the enormous range and contributions of Randhir Singh, a book christened as *Politics* in his memory needs an explanatory justification. Therefore, the epistemic task is not easy. Politics occupies a *sui generis* space in Randhir Singh in three crucial ways. Firstly, politics is a vantage point to understand inter-related processes. Politics is publicness and concerted effort. Politics is an arrival through the exercise of collectivity. Politics, being a form of engagement, thus becomes democracy. This is important in the context of two other categories, i.e. economics and social. The economic relation is conditioned by the ownership of means of production. The surplus is individualised. The alternative, in Randhir Singh's words, is 'politicisation of surplus utilisation'. Politics in both contexts plays a crucial role. In the former case, it *does* change the status quo. In the latter case, it *informs* constantly people's aspirations. Social relations which are constructed thus become ascriptive relations. The collective requires transformation from the ascriptive being to the ontological being. Secondly, thus, politics is/becomes spontaneity. It embodies not people's aspirations but it revels in contradictions constantly. The identification of contradictions and their immediate correction by way of spontaneity become a vital concern of politics. Thirdly, bringing politics into the forefront does not undermine the significance of other categories or relations. Politics adds the agency to people towards bringing change. In Randhir Singh, laws are not immutable. They can be changed and challenged *only* through invoking politics. Bringing politics into other realms is nothing but ensuing democracy.

The Primacy of Politics

Randhir Singh lays down a very complex yet extremely useful method to comprehend both politics (politics as a set of structure) and study of politics (discipline/subject) in one of his known essays *Politics—The Dialectics of Science and Revolution in Karl Marx* (1988). The detailed discussion of the essay becomes a *fait accompli* to understand the complexity and *sui generis* of politics/study of politics. According to him, to comprehend Marxism and politics, two positions in Marxism must be noticed. 'Marx's absolute Promethean conception of man' and 'his lifelong commitment to revolution' are not unrelated. The first position 'free, conscious activity is man's species character' can be fathomed in *Economic and Philosophical Manuscripts of 1844*. As defined by Engels ('Speech at the Graveside of Karl Marx'), he remains a man of science/a revolutionist in finality. This is crucial in both Marxism and Randhir Singh wherein a crucial understanding of politics is envisaged. While these positions are 'fully accommodated' in the Marxist framework, politics remains relatively open, undetermined and not entirely amenable to general laws (Singh, 1988a: 240).

For Singh, it is crucial in the Marxist project to understand society and overthrow it. It is a preparation for a communist society. The Marxist method is materialist dialectics. Herein, society is to be seen in totality shaped by economy, contradictions which decide dynamics and 'concrete over-determined historical development' (Singh, 1988a: 239-240). While production (economy) remains very significant to lay bare the motion of capitalism, "Marx aimed at achieving through 'successive approximations' from different perspectives, a 'mirrored' version of the concrete reality of capitalist social formation as a whole" (Singh, 1988a: 240). The understanding remains incomplete without understanding the whole/parts and their relationship. Hegel's epithet is apt, "the truth is whole" (*Phenomenology of Mind*) which is even extended by Marx: from the appearance to nature of things (*Capital*, Volume III), to avoid errors committed by, as earlier pointed out by David Goldway, who headed a Marxist Journal *Science & Society*, vulgar economist who takes appearance as real and metaphysicist wherein internal abstraction is only thing to be counted. "To deal with the most rigorous of abstractions and never to be metaphysical; to examine veritable mountains of minute detail and never to be empiricist- this is what makes *Capital* the great textbook of dialectical materialism" (Goldway, 1967: 444-445). This is "dialectical knowledge against positive science" (Singh, 1998a: 240).

Singh highlights two types of errors: major empiricist errors and minor holist errors. The major empiricist error is found in the Right wherein things are grasped only in appearance and isolation. The minor holist error is found in the Left as to missing out the significance of mediations. The mediations constitute the whole (Singh, 1988a: 240). Randhir Singh highlights complexities in a process between X and Y, in which Y cannot simply be treated as homologous to X. Politics requires attention as a form of 'politics', and not as a derivative alone. In other words, the political requires attention as an autonomous procedure (in itself), and not simply as a derivative of the economic. Marx, he asserts, gave us significant 'political writings': *Class Struggle in France, The Civil War in France* along with *The Eighteenth Brumaire of Louis Bonapart*. These are models of "treatment of politics in Marxism" (Singh, 1988a: 241).

Concerning 'relative autonomy of the state', he suggests that "...its value against economic and class reductionism apart, it could be more misleading than helpful in understanding or explaining politics in a given social formation; it easily tends to give rise to mutually reinforcing empiricist and liberal-reformist errors" (Singh, 1988a: 241). He adds two crucial components concerning autonomy of the state from a particular context while 'autonomy' is not from 'socio-economic condition'. Singh suggests that, as to the first, "'relative autonomy of the state' is a meaningful concept denoting as it does state's possible autonomy in a particular historical situation, from any given class or classes, economically dominant otherwise" (Singh, 1988a: 241). "However", as to the second, "the state is not autonomous from the socio-economic structure of a class-divided society which it serves. The state remains, always, the organizer of society in the interests of the class (exploitative) structure as a whole" (Singh, 1988a: 241). In other words, autonomy is significant in a particular context, not from socio-economic class.

According to him, scientific explanation and revolutionary politics in Marx are mutually reinforcing categories. Both put politics at the centre of social practice of contemporary time. Regarding primacy of politics, he suggests that the real basis can be changed only by revolutionary politics ergo becoming *sine qua non* in our analysis and practice.

> Given a Marxist understanding of the structured nature of the totality, and the crucial role of 'the economy' in it, any fundamental, revolutionary change in a society involves as a necessary, though not sufficient, condition, a changing of its economic structure, of its real basis, if I may, contrary to fashion and in a confession of 'orthodoxy' still use that much-maligned concept. Hence, the centrality of politics as revolution in Marx (Revolution is the highest form of class struggle'). In this sense, the sense in which 'Marx was before all else a revolutionist', politics, not economics, has primacy in Marxism. And the obvious corollary is that in the absence of this revolutionary politics

> changing the structural base of society the logic of this base shall assert itself, all politics will remain superstructural in its essential character and outcome. This is the basic, a determined and determining choice in politics, within which other, more or less important, choices occur. Such is the dialectics of the economy and politics in the social sciences of Karl Marx (Singh, 1988a: 241-42).

There is a promethean attempt in Singh to add an agency in 'politics'. There is no denying of the real basis. The alternative is possible only through changing it. This changing becomes possible through politics which is *ante* status quo. Remarkably, he not only delinks politics from economics in terms of changing later but also brings back the focus on economics. In other words, both are not homologous; also both are not delinked. 'Agency politics' is becoming a reality herein. Superstructural variations are possible. "... the supersturctural instances... are not some immediate or epiphenomenal manifestations of the economic-structural base" (Singh, 1988a: 242). Economy as a correspondence concerning variable is an important postulation in Singh.

Redefining the Study of Politics

Randhir Singh introduced interdisciplinarity in the discipline of politics (hereafter Politics). This not only enriched Politics but also completely metamorphosed it. There were three realms in which Politics used to be studied from post-independence till the seventies in India. The foremost realm was description of evolution of political institutions. Later on, constitutional studies and comparative constitutionalism were added. Secondly, voting behaviour and modernisation theses (input-output feedback) were an inescapable academic fad. The, third was a *desi* intervention and innovation in Politics. Herein, 'ancient wisdom in modern republic' had become a core 'non-heretical' formula. This formula accepted many uncritical and unexamined treatises and thinkers of the past as leading signifiers. Vulgar behaviouralism was reflected in the first two areas whereas unscientific 'reclamation of the past' echoed in the third area (Rai, 2016a and 2016b).

In these realms of Politics, Marxism was an anathema. Critical inquiries were pejorative and disinterred concerns. Poverty of Politics led to prosperity of other disciplines of social sciences. 'Historical materialism' was gifted to History whereas 'diamat' (dialectical materialism) was made part of Philosophy. Likewise, nationalism, colonialism and communalism became beacons of History. Marxism *became* sheer body-politic/ politics of subversion. Hence, Politics became bereft of politics (institutions, structures, conflicts etc.) leading to the truncation of its growth (Rai, 2016a and 2016b).

The arrival of Randhir Singh corresponded with the beginning of interpretation and challenge to trio-realms. His arrival, however, did not go uncontested by the mainstream. The significance was deviation and departure from 'mainstream'. There was hardly any challenge posed by the political scientist to behaviouralism, constitutionalism and ancient wisdom in the modern republic (Rai, 2016a and 2016b). A serious challenge was posed to settled serenity of Politics by Randhir Singh's *Reason, Revolution and Political Theory: Notes on Oakeshott's Rationalism in Politics* (1967). According to Singh, Michael Oakeshott's "book is significant, not only for what it says, and what it omits today, but also for how he says it" (Singh, 1988c: 7). Omission becomes a recognised inquiry in Politics.

Oakeshott disdained reason, rationality, Marxism and theory. His postulation was based on "twin principles of empiricism (to expose and demolish) and traditionalism (to defend and preserve and, perhaps build)" (Singh 1988c: 3). In Oakeshott, rationalism and its vice were the predicaments of European politics which could be removed from politics based on tradition. This itself was construed by Randhir Singh as against politics.

> He has been at work, using his undoubtedly brilliant powers to attack rationalism. And in the process he has developed a view of political philosophy which would virtually drive out all purposes from the study of politics and the subject itself from the universities (Singh 1988c: 7).

In Politics, primacy has been given to 'what to study' in place of 'why to study' (Rai 2014: 53-57). Likewise, Oakeshott also confirms this continuity. He theorises 'what to study' than 'why to study' at the university level. His treatment of Politics is also peculiar. In the first case, he reduces Politics to a kind of language and nothing more.

> In short, we have begun to recognise that 'politics' in a university is appropriately concerned with the study of a 'language' and with 'literatures' only as paradigms of this 'language' (Oakeshott, 1962: 326).

After reduction of Politics to a language, explanation is further envisaged, i.e. Politics *qua* explanation.

> An academic study appears only when an activity is isolated and when it is in a fit condition to be an occasion for explanatory modes of thought (Oakeshott, 1962: 332).

Randhir Singh gives equal importance to both philosophical and methodological realms of Politics, i.e. 'what to study' and 'why to study'. Therefore, there is an absolute rejection of Oakeshott (Rai, 2016a and 2016b). According to him, Oakeshott would, thus, purge 'the study of politics at a university of all moral and political purpose, and of all taint of truth or knowledge. Both as 'a philosophical study' and 'a historical study', it is the study only of concepts', 'words' and 'epithets' connected with it', of their 'ambiguity and confusion'. Its purpose lies only 'in disentangling the confusion which springs from merely crooked thinking', or 'in telling the story of the ambiguity and in making sense of it without the help of those adventitious aids, the categories of truth and error' (Singh, 1988c: 14).

"Why to Study' acquired primacy in 'wasteland' on its own terms. Mohit Sen points out that "into this wasteland *Reason, Revolution and Political Theory*, literally burst out, as a refreshing river" (Sen, 1967: 1251). In fact, the book covered the core of Politics. For many years, political scientists were teaching History to recognise it as Politics. Even the treatment of History was at the level of mere description. The casuality was contemporaneity which was given a miss. Randhir Singh did not reject History but catapulted it to the level of analysis and coevally brought in the significance of Politics. Contemporaneous issues started finding space in the syllabi of Politics (Rai, 2016a and 2016b).

His three particular interventions not only expanded the scope of Politics but also refreshed the entire domain. These constitute the study of communalism, extremist movements and democratic rights. Communalism is not an event-based description, an object of sheer empiricisation, and irreducible to a specific context of nationalism. Revivalism/fundamentalism and communalism need to be located in totality. In fact, criticism of these is criticism of society which not only gives birth to these but also makes both necessary and possible (Singh, 1990: 15). 'Totality' is answerable. He warns using religion as a noun before communalism (for example *Hindu* communalism) since it would obscure the source of communalism. Thus, the definition of communalism needs using the adjective of religion before communalism (for example *Hinduised* Communalism). It helps to identify location.

> Furthermore, with its implicit treatment of Hindus as one undifferentiated mass, this concept virtually makes a gift of all those who regard themselves as Hindus to the communal politics of the ruling classes (Singh, 1990: 20).

His study of Sikh extremism is crucial to highlight the structural problem. He rejects his friend Bipan Chandra's thesis on it while describing his line as "the Ribeiro-Girilal Jain-Bipan Chandra line" (Singh 1987: 1441). Singh's approach leads him to see the issue as a 'near total alienation of people', 'continuing fractured identity of the Punjabis and a nationality', and "virtual collapse of bourgeois politics' (Singh 1987: 1440-1442). With him, a systemic struggle against structural problem is being put forward. Communalism is a structural problem, not a 'law and order problem'. Along with it, democratic rights become extremely important in the backdrop of "a nation-wide 'selling of terrorism'" (Singh, 1992a: 285). Despite the availability of constitutional nationalism, legal democracy, sovereignty and legitimacy of the state, according to Singh, laws are implemented against the people but not against the State even if it violated democratic rights. There is an institution which implements laws while making itself free from laws.

> Whereas in a law-based State like India, there exists an elaborate code, an entire ensemble of laws, procedures, institutions and enforcing agencies to deal with private violence or lawlessness, there is nothing comparable, no genuine checks or controls, to take care of peaceful or violent lawlessness of the state, which is potentially and often in actual practice, the most powerful violator of democratic rights in society (Singh 1992a: 287).

Universe of Extended Class

Randhir was not the Randhir Singh we know of without his teaching classes. Two statements which became legends are: 'Randhir Singh said this on it' and 'I am his student'. The phrase 'teacher' conferred upon him an iconic status. The teacher and his teaching were both revolutionary. According to Manoranjan Mohanty, "Randhir Singh proved that teaching can also be a revolutionary activity" (Rai, 2016a and 2016b). After spending a long term at Delhi College (Zakir Husain National College, University of Delhi) and a brief term at the newly started Jawaharlal Nehru University, Singh joined Department of Political Science, University of Delhi as a professor of political theory in 1972. He retired from there in 1987, not before transforming the nature of classroom and its constituents. The class was the universe because it was a non-alienated life (Rai, 2016a and 2016b).

> For me, the comforting rationalising was that in our society, after 'revolution-making', teaching perhaps holds the maximum possibilities for a non-alienated life. Here, if you want, but only if you *want*, earning your living can be at the same time living your life. So teaching it was to be for me for the rest of my life (Singh, 1988c: iv).

The pedagogy was altered. Radical pedagogy was introduced. This universe, which was one of epistemic cosmopolitanism wherein diversity was an intrinsic feature, could be materialised because both the dialectical approach and the interdisciplinary approach became *sine qua non*. This invited and ensured pan-disciplinary participation. An otherwise 'dull subject' like Politics was rekindled due to epistemic plurality and the broken hierarchical relationship between teacher and students. This paved the way for the arrival of true social sciences wherein disciplines became reinforcing categories of each other (Rai, 2016a and 2016b).

> Students have come to my class from various other disciplines, even other universities at Delhi, from Economics and Sociology, Law and literature, Mathematics, even Chemistry and Physics (Perhaps Commerce and Business Management alone have been missing) (Singh,1988c: vi).

Students were the most crucial and defining aspect of his class. The epithet 'His students'—was both a claim and an assertion. This was followed by 'thy students'. The difference between official and non-official was shunned. All were his students; direct or indirect students were obsolete categories. He became the teacher of those who attended his classes, or of those who never attended classes but interacted and heard him without interactions. They all claim him as their teacher precisely because he was a thinking teacher who believed in communicating and not in educating. Classes were sites present both inside and outside the classrooms of universities. In these classes, a whole universe was present with everyone included.

> I will only add that what goes on within the discipline of Political Science or its classrooms, for that matter, within the universities and the social science institutes of this country, is only of marginal relevance to the problems and prospects of the Indian people's struggle for a better future. But this is where we work-teachers, students, scholars, all others. And it is axiomatic, for most of us, that we make our efforts where we work or we shall make no effort at all (Singh 1998c: viii).

Role of Social Sciences

The goal-oriented nature of Marxism is categorical. Marxism is social science for the people, the exploited and the oppressed. It is not for policy makers or for instrumentalist purposes.

Randhir Singh brings two crucial components in social sciences, i.e. 'knowledge of a social formation as a whole' and the need of the other necessity, of making revolution. To the extent of being a social science, "it seeks knowledge of a social formation as a whole, and recognises the decisive importance if its 'economic basis' or structural necessity, it carries with it the imperative, the other necessity, that Marxist political practice be revolutionary. It is not for nothing that Marx insisted: 'the working class is revolutionary if it is nothing'" (Singh, 1988a: 243).

Singh admits that Marxism as a social science has its own limitations like inadequacies, ambiguities and unfinished nature of a theoretical project in Marx. It, however, provides crucial understanding of social formations on both 'structure' and 'dynamics' along with recognition of 'growth' of human knowledge. He reminds us of unintended teleological tendencies within Marxism. For this, he blames pursuance of Marxism as a science which replaced revolutionary perspective with complacent 'historical necessity' (Singh, 1988a: 243). The historical necessity in Marxism was the dominant feature in the Second International. For Kautsky, as cited by Singh, "irresistible...natural necessity' having made socialism 'something inevitable' (Singh, 1988a: 243). Struggle for socialism became a side issue, i.e. a revolutionary struggle for socialism remained a non-starter. Lenin restored the original Marxian position while repudiating an evolutionist and deterministic metaphysics-led-Marxism. He also suggests that it is highly problematic to use the label 'historically progressive' perennially for some categories like 'progressive capitalism' and so on. Moreover, with Marx, taking a position in the ongoing war was crucial rather than reducing it to mere scientific -analysis-economic or social or historical (Singh, 1988a: 243-44). Singh, somewhere else, comments on historical determinism:

> The doctrine of Karl Marx is no determinist philosophy. There is no 'historicism' or 'historical inevitability' in Marx, nor any evolutionist metaphysics either... [H]istoricism, 'historical inevitability', 'stages of history', etc. in Marxism [as tendencies]

> ...surfaced as the dominant feature of the reformist mode of thinking in the Second International—Kautsky viewing socialism as 'something inevitable', so decreed by irresistible natural necessity', and Plekhanov declaring 'the victory of our program is as inevitable as tomorrow's sunrise'—to be questioned and rejected by Lenin and those who followed him in the authentic, revolutionary tradition of Marxism (Singh, 2011a: 104-105)

Regardless of the extreme and prevalent current of specialisation, professionalisation and vocationalisation of social sciences, commitment defines the *sui generis* aspect of Marx. Randhir Singh informs that when Marx was old, sick and dying, he was informed about having a theoretical impact in far-off Czarist Russia. Marx wrote to his daughter Laura Lafargue: "Nowhere is my success more delightful to me; it gives me the satisfaction that I damage a power which, besides England, is the true bulwark of the old society" (cited in Singh, 1988a: 247). Randhir Singh asks the following questions straightway: "Yes, damage is the word. How much of even Marxist scholarship can claim this quality for itself today?" (Singh, 1988a: 247).

Semantics of Academic Freedom

Randhir Singh provides us with an original formulation concerning academic freedom. Academic freedom, to him, is an important value/principle universally accepted. This has been primarily seen as an ethical question. Academic freedom is raised in absolute or abstract terms and defended for 'the nature of academic work', 'man's quest for truth', 'the spirit of free inquiry' and so on. Thereafter pragmatic and opportunistic concessions or departures are sought which violate the original principle. This is an important component of bourgeois ethical thought. The schism is created between bourgeois ethical thought and bourgeois ethical practice. The error committed is non-recognition of the ethical as a historical question. It is raised and resolved in concrete.

The most prevalent kind of such concessions or departures are sought in the name of 'the interest of society', 'academic's responsibility to society,' and 'social responsibility of social scientist'. Randhir Singh asks following questions: what or who is this society? Who defines 'the interest of society', this 'responsibility' or 'social responsibility'? These questions bring the whole nature of society and ruling classes to the fore. The conventional position, as taken by academicians, is to perceive academic and social science as 'intellect work' and 'social engineering' respectively while locating these two in safe boundaries.

Many do perceive the establishment as an actual threat to academic freedom thus maintaining a safe distance from it. This is extremely important to grasp the truth. The freedom is defined in terms of freedom from establishment. But this is not the complete picture. Randhir Singh here makes a very crucial intervention as to what is ignored or obscured: "...one's subjectively honest exercise of academic freedom, may yet, objectively, serve the same establishment, ruling classes of the powers that be...Thus it can happen that regardless of the absence of visible or direct external constraints on one's subjective sense of freedom, or even one's consciously held radical position as citizen, an academic's practice, a truly honest practice as a professional, as a 'free' social scientist, may yet make him, unconsciously and therefore all the more effectively, 'servant of the established power' as Loren Baritz once put it" (Singh, 1988b: 225).

What is the way out? Academic freedom is extremely important. Resolution of its problem lies in covering its two dimensions, i.e. the scientific dimension and the ethical dimension. Put differently, academic freedom by the academic must pursue the path of two commitments: commitments to truth and commitments to people. "Truth" and "People" are inescapable categories in academic freedom. Ruthless criticism and continuous confrontation of reality with reason not only serve the cause of people but also of expanding the horizon of truth. Ruling classes in the face of decline do not accept truth. The natural choice for them becomes mystifying, obscuring and concealing reality, i.e. sophisticated *apologetics*. Academic freedom is a dangerous luxury. Therefore, "those who would defend and assert the value of academic freedom in their practice of social or human sciences, need to cultivate not only the requisite skills or technique, but, above all, the virtue called *courage*" (Singh, 1988b: 226).

Explaining the Crisis of Socialism in USSR

There were two sets of questions (historical exhibition and explanatory exhibition) concerning the USSR. In the historical highlights, Randhir Singh focuses on 'what was built and what failed in the Soviet Union'. The *'build'* was enormous, and *failure* was colossal. There was a construction of a new society which achieved massive industrialisation without any help from capitalism. It helped to fulfil goals like giving employment to all or eliminating unemployment and envisaging radical socio-economic aka socialist transformation. Overthrowing the old regime led to enormous improvement of living conditions. The most crucial aspect was full employment and constitutional rights concerning job security. Singh tells us that despite various deviations in post-revolutionary era, this right could not be compromised which was almost an impossible goal in the capitalist world. Singh uses 'politicisation of the surplus utilisation process' to explain economic gains and substantive achievement regarding social security, i.e. education, health, housing, culture and leisure. In Singh, 'politicisation of the surplus utilisation process' acquires a distinct method wherefrom the difference with capitalism in which privatisation of surplus value takes place, can be commenced (Singh, 2011a: 386-462).

On this point, he reminds us what was it that failed in the USSR. He quotes Marx in this regard. Marx talks about the direct relationship of the owners of the condition of production to the direct produces. This is, according to Marx, is the innermost secret of the social structure. The contradiction that emerged in the USSR was pertaining to the ownership of condition of production and direct producers. Due to centralisation and bureaucratisation of decisions, workers remained politically and economically powerless while rendering surplus labour which led their alienation and finally the disintegration of the USSR. The situation was further aggravated by the introduction of 'laws of socialism' where economic issues were decided by a few, without popular intervention, thus abandoning the politics that is 'identification of public issues, making of choices, debating and deciding alternative paths of economic development, recognition of actual or potential conflict of interests, and correction of all mistakes in economic policy, planning and practice'. This politics was sacrificed for the arrival of 'laws of socialism' which was not Marx's scientific socialism (Singh, 2011a: 386-462).

The second is the explanatory exhibition concerning 'the right lesson and the wrong conclusion' regarding disintegration or in Singh's words, actual 'existing of socialism' in the Soviet Union. The right lesson is, he asserts, a *sine qua non* for making a complete assessment. Real socialism cannot be without democracy. In other words, a socialist society has to be fully democratic. The same also holds for economic necessity. These were absent in the USSR. In socialism, politics directs economy. Therefore, it becomes imperative for 'the politics of necessity' to be democratic. The contrast between capitalism and socialism is telling. In capitalism, market becomes a way of correction and indication whereas socialism makes people as a vantage point for guidance and corrections. The right lesson of failure of socialism in the USSR could be this: economic necessity for socialism has to be democratic. Along with the right lesson, the question of a wrong conclusion carries an equal concern. The wrong conclusion is treating the failure of 'actually existing socialism' as the triumph of capitalism over socialism. This needs an outright rejection (Singh, 2011b: 145-146). He finds a methodological error in this regard. "People have been encouraged to abandon history as a criterion for judgement and the notion of 'victory' substituting for facts or explanation..." (Singh, 2011b: 146). He sums up: "Despite its undoubted achievements, the system ultimately failed. But it is 'the Soviet System' and not socialism, that failed in the Soviet Union" (Singh, 2011a: 462).

Morality and Marxism

Randhir Singh, in his introduction to the Indian edition of William Ash's book *Workers' Politics: The Ethics of Socialism* (2010), outlines and exhibits the significance of morality in Marxism. I will be highlighting his two distinct contributions on morality. The first distinct contribution is the heterogeneity of epistemic resources to understand the subterranean aspects of morality. He uses numerous resources to highlight and formulate the principle of morality. The significant epistemic, besides Marx and Engels, resources are: James Petras (twine goals, political and economic) of the US cultural imperialism to capture market for selling cultural commodities and establishing hegemony through controlling popular consciousness, Michael Lowy (complete, absolute, undivided and unlimited sway over the whole world by capital), Hans Magnus Enzensberger ('secondary illiterates' for those who are products of mass media and require neither memory nor thinking/learning to sustain themselves), Carl Bernstein (true idiot culture as to mass media), C. Wright Mills (significance of 'answering back' in the context of enervation of civil society and its members), Jean Baudrillard (destruction of critical examination and reflections), John Lewis (imperative of morality), Eric Fromm (socialism aka overcoming alienation and freedom), Ernest Mandel (moral justification of opposing capitalism), Rosa Luxemburg (socialism or barbarism), Paul Baran (no defensibility of capitalism), István Mészáros (depressed continuum, i.e. survival of capitalism as a failed system), Wallerstein (non-negligence of short term defensive action including electoral election by an anti-systemic movement), and Paul Sweezy and Harry Magdoff (immortality of radical traditions to guide struggle) (Singh, 2010: ix-xliv).

The second distinct contribution is to highlight the significance of morality by way of three sets of observation. The first is the Marxist view on morality. According to Singh, alluding to Marxist view on morality, morality is intrinsic/natural to human beings. This natural is not transcendental, nor supported by abstract ideals, or a superhuman source or authority. The morality is natural in the sense of acquired as to fulfilling social needs and for human social existence. Moral or ethical principles, as theorised in the conventional realms, is good in and of itself. Singh rejects this view of 'good in and of itself'. Besides, moral or ethical principles are neither independent of nature and history in any way nor can they have origin in gods, goddesses, and scriptures. He emphasises on the naturalistic view of human and evolutionary process regarding morality. The naturalist view, which has been accepted by scholars of ethics, anthropologists, psychologists and scientists, claims that morality is a genuine phenomenon of living organisms. Since the evolutionary process has outgrown its sources, nature has caused humans to evolve morals, ideals and ethical principles. These morals are due to the requirement of social life and its validity lies in utility. He cites Engels to underline the fact that there is a commonality between feudal morality, bourgeois morality and proletarian morality due to exhibition of the representation of three different stages of similar historical development.

The second observation is related to morality and relativism (Singh, 2010: ix-xliv). As said by him, "...*relativism* ...is a staple of bourgeois social and moral theory, surfacing in it again and again in one form or another- the latest example being its centrality in the post-modernist theory" (Singh. 2010: xviii). I will come to this point in the succeeding paragraph. The third observation is regarding 'Marx's ethical-aesthetic critique of capitalism' for the arrival of better understanding of ethics of socialism. Singh quotes Marx extensively to highlight as to what is at stake. The *differentia specifica/ species being* (human) is stripped of freedom under capitalism. Capitalism is governed not only by accumulation but also by commodification. Socialism pertains to the *whole manner of being* that is not governed by production relations and commodification. "In other words, socialism is a society ensuring the 'free development of its members, 'the associated producers', enabling them to realise their human powers, needs and capacities in as rich, untrammelled and all round-manner as possible" (Singh, 2010: xxvii).

Singh highlights that Marx's ethical and aesthetic-cultural critique of capitalism is guided by deep concern for humanity, its present and future condition. Under capitalism, people are stripped of human essence, and human-to-human relations are being replaced by cash payment. All mental and physical senses are replaced by sense of *having*. It results in, as Marx says, *the more you have, the less you are.* For Marx, as quoted by Singh, communism is conscious and historically informed return of *social being* and therefore "[w]hat is avoided above all is the re-establishing of Society "as an abstraction *vis-à-vis* the individual. The individual is *the social being*". This turns Singh to suggest that "Marx is an individualist in the basic sense that his ultimate vision was a society where, as Marx himself put it, 'the freedom development of each is the condition for the free development of all'" (Singh, 2010: xxxi). Singh uses a brilliant summary of Ladislav Štoll concerning wealth of emotion in socialism and one single emotion in capitalism. Stoll states that "in place of many-sided, active, concrete appropriation of life and the world, through which the individual says not only "I see, I hear, I smell, I taste, I touch", but also "I work, I study, I love, I admire, I struggle for a happier tomorrow"—in place of all this wealth of emotion capitalism makes one single emotion supreme: "I *have*"" (Singh, 2010: xxxi). Singh via Marx underlines that transition to communism is transition from the realm of necessity to the realm of freedom (Singh, 2010: ix-xliv).

Therefore, morality in Marxism is the cynosure of social being wherein unbridled life is perceived for all by way of rejecting unequal production relationship and social hierarchies. The aforesaid passages highlight three important postulations in Randhir Singh concerning morality. Firstly, location and morality are interlinked. The morality question is inexplicable without unravelling the complexity of location. Location is both actual and factual. The structural cumbersome is answered while explicating morality. Secondly, location as actuality and factuality is not *eulogising differential moralism or relativism*. In fact, these are rejected therein. Locations explain origin of morality whereas relativism is perpetuation of *differentials* thus creation of insulated and isolated realms. Location-centric explanation informs that despite there being claims of different morality, all interface each other. Before interface and during interface, hierarchies are created and reinforced respectively. Thirdly, there is a need of people's morality. It has to be ontologically equal morality. It is not homogeneous but certainly against ontological superiority. Morality in Marxism is the recognition of humanness while striving for equality followed by freedom by way rejecting structural constrains and principles of homogeneity that is 'similarity'. Randhir Singh remains an important signifier vis-à-vis morality.

Environment and Marxism

Randhir Singh makes a substantive intervention concerning environment and Marxism. A careful reading makes a strong case for Marxism to address environmental concerns while rejecting the label of 'Prometheus' charge against Marxism while problematising the notion of 'productive'. According to him, "...to be effective 'green', it is necessary to be 'red' as well" (Singh, 2009: 84). The vantage point in the discourse remains two reminders of Carl Sagan: "Who speaks for the human species? Who speaks for Earth?" (Singh, 2009: 36). In other words, quintessential separation or sheer antagonism needs to be avoided. Randhir Singh problematises three terrains of environmentalism, i.e. population growth postulations, role of environmental NGOs, and the concept of sustainable development for ignoring capitalism. "World's growing ecological consciousness still fails to recognize that the 'pattern of development' it sees as the danger to the future of the planet has a name, capitalism- a system of production whose structural imperatives necessarily degrade the environment", he adds (Singh, 2009: 44).

There are four distinct contributions of Randhir Singh. These can be understood while addressing the four questions which are related to environmental movements and concerns. Firstly, is the environment question pertaining to or methodological return to the past, i.e. pre-modern return? Randhir Singh makes a categorical difference through alluding to earlier economic spheres of and not making any reference to culture spheres. He highlights that "...there was the transformation of agriculture from its natural complexity (and diversity of crops) to the simplicity of commodified agriculture" (Singh, 2009: 63). The environmental awareness is a result of immense destruction under capitalist development which was not the case earlier. "Environmental consciousness has grown with the growth of the environmental crisis" (Singh, 2009: 45).

Secondly, is environmentalism a celebration of communitarianism in the manner of 'local is special'? His answer is comprehensive in this regard. "The costs of cleaning up our environment must be met in the end by the community' is another platitudinous response, which in its evasion of the real issue not only provides an alibi to the established socio-economic system for its degradation of environment but also wants the people to pay—through cuts in their standard of living, etc.—to keep this system going by meeting the costs of 'environmental rehabilitation' as it is called. A characteristic of our times is post-modernism's contribution to contemporary green theory which refuses to see that the cause of ecological degradation lies not in modernity of science, as it contends, but in the capitalist mode of production" (Singh, 2009: 71). Environmental movement has to understand that this is also a *political* problem due to highly unequal control and utilisation of resources. He rejects bio-centric views for their binaries. Ecological radicalism (bio-centric) makes moral absolutism for natural beings against humans. "This 'bio-centric' view... is much muddled and even more evasive of real issues than the mainstream environmentalism... [and] fails to recognize the real enemy of all natural beings and environmental which is capitalism..." (Singh, 2009: 82). The dichotomy between of anthropocentrism and bi-centric is of no use for understanding *real* cause of environmental degradation. "Bio-centric environmentalism's eco-homo dualism is not only simply false, it is also politically suicidal in the sense that it labels the human race, the people as a whole, as the enemy, obscuring the real enemy which is the historically specific economic and social order in which we live and those who hold power in it" (Singh, 2009: 87).

Thirdly, does the production debate take cognisance of reconciliation between the human and the nature? To this, Randhir Singh suggests that reconciliation of the human and the nature is not possible in capitalism due to its constant emphasis on accumulation and commodification through resource depletion. In fact, he asserts that "... the environmental crisis, at its core, a crisis of capitalism" (Singh, 2009: 94). This assertion requires the rejection of 'productivism, even within Marxism. "Productivism", he states, "thus is no integral part of Marxism. As 'productive bias it was only a minor tendency within classical Marxism" (Singh, 2009: 106).

Fourthly, is environment-debate anti-people? Not by any means. Indeed, "...working classes, oppressed minorities, women, and the rural and urban poor worldwide who suffer most from both economic and ecological exploitation" (Singh, 2009: 60). Concerning location, there is prevalent environmental racism. "It is not surprising therefore to find heavily polluting operations at home located in poor neighbourhoods, where live the counterparts of the world poor within the rich countries... [And] most hazardous waste dumps in the US are located near poor African-American and Latino communities" (Singh, 2009: 60-61). This process has been an outcome of NIMBY (Not-In-My-Back Yard) phenomenon where hazardous and unstainable industries are shifted out (Singh, 2009: 62).

For Randhir Singh, the environmental question is a *question* of how to change the world and this change is envisaged through socialism where change is towards symmetrical relationship between nature and human while discarding accumulation and commodification that is capitalism.

Making of a Life on the Left

Marxism for Randhir Singh was an undeniable recognition of the universal/singular along with history and politics. These were *sine qua non* in his life world and everydayness. The worldview was for an egalitarian world and politics as a means to achieve it. History was to find continuity and discontinuity in social formations. Capitalism encompasses a slew of edifices. Economics informs social formation but politics provides opportunity to achieve it. Politics is an active agency to bring transformation. This activates the agency which is contrary to teleological schema. The egalitarian world is possible in post-capitalist world along with diminishing of pre-capitalist exploitation. The active agency is continuous political intervention. The active agency has to give primacy to politics to bring about changes at different levels. The politics cannot be suspended for *ipso facto* change at economic level. Randhir Singh's brilliant exhibition of operationality of reality and non-teleological assertion of method makes his intervention substantive.

These two are categorically visible and intrinsically linked with his life that is a communist life. There is hope and there is despair in it. Since autobiographies are written about both self and others, the life on the Left is also for self-positioning and outward analysis. In this regard, understanding Randhir Singh's *In Lieu of Biodata* is also an advancement of autographical writing. In autobiography, self is the centre wherefrom events are analysed. Randhir Singh's *In Lieu of Biodata* locates the self and the process together. Both are inseparable components. The self is not autonomous but located in the process.

In this regard, possibly the first serious attempt can be seen in the publication of *Lives on the Left*, edited by Francis Mulhern. The interviews of sixteen Marxist lives (Georg Lukács, Hedda Korsch, Jiri Pelikan, K. Damodaran, Ernest Mandel, Dorothy Thompson, Lucio Colletti, Luciana Castellina, Adolfo Gilly, Jean-Paul Sartre, Noam Chomsky, David Harvey, Joao Pedro Stedile, Asada Akira, Wang Hui and Giovanni Arrighi) also unravel both 'self' and 'process'. This is needed not only about explaining complexities of process but also evolution of 'agency'. For example, Lukács and Korsch and others were founders or associated with communist parties. There is also *'Franc Tireur'*, i.e. intellectuals who intervene on the basis of their own conscience without any benefit or constraining by the party. These are Chomsky, Sartre, Damodaran, and Harvey (Mulherm, 2011).

Returning to Randhir Singh, the active agency had witnessed two simultaneous processes: a national life (partition period, pre-liberalisation, communalisation phase and post 1991) (Singh, 1987, 1989a, 1990a, 1990b, 1992a, 1993, 2007, 2010a), and a life within or outside communist parties but not without it (Singh, 1989c, 1992b, 2007). Association with communist parties and simultaneous use of own intellectual recognisance make him an important Marxist theorist. As an active agency, there were two normative referential reminders. Firstly, 'where do you speak from'? Secondly, Goethe's rejoinder, 'one must, from time to time, repeat what one believes in, proclaim what one agrees with and what one condemns'. Singh spoke from the Marxist vantage point and asserted often its immense importance in ontological relevance of human beings.

Singh's activism included association with the CPI and CPI (M) as well as participation in the democratic rights movements and the publication of journals like *Enquiry, Socialist Digest, The Marxist Review* and so on. His contribution to the India's teachers' movement was unparalleled. According to Prabhat Patnaik, 'Professor Randhir Singh was not just a legendary teacher who inspired generations of students; he was also a Communist activist who played a stellar role in building up the progressive teachers' movement in Delhi University' (Rai, 2016a, 2016b: 490). This period in the intellectual history of Marxism was very crucial and can be called easily 'the Randhir Singh Phase'. He focused more on ontological questions rather than taking mere cognisance of appearances. He preferred the dialectics over the analytical in Marxism. In the post-USSR era, his writings on Marxism reflected not only his commitment but contained sharp insights on many crucial questions. His Marxism was weltanschauung—worldview—which had a historical responsibility to human emancipation.

His worldview included both scathing criticism of certain practices in the USSR and sanguinity about Marxism. Regarding the former, he called it the 'crisis of socialism' or 'betrayal in the post-Lenin era: "How come they failed to see what the poet [Bertolt Brecht], who was a communist, too, saw so early and so clearly, namely, the awesome alienation of the people from their rulers" (Singh, 1992b: 1625). His 'notes of commitment', however, remained sanguine about the future of Marxism : "You have to take only one quick look around to recognise the living presence of 'historical communism' in the enhanced awareness of humankind the world over concerning issues of human dignity, of justice and injustice, of equality, oppression and exploitation, in the voice and hope the poor and oppressed have come to acquire in our times, in the quality and spread, of their struggles for a better life and, above all, in their confidence, despite all the retreats and reverses that they can fight and win their emancipation" (Singh, 1992b: 1625). In other worlds, the grammar of contemporaneity is unthinkable without recognising the contribution of Marxism towards human dignity.

He, as an active agency, was also worried about the Left unity in India. He constantly stressed the need for Left unity. His three suggestions are important pointers in this regard. Firstly, "[p]eople will of course continue to fight. If they do not fight the right battles, they will fight the wrong ones—and this will be yet another tragedy for them and for the communist Left in India" (Singh, 2009a: 119). Second, "If we cannot do the impossible, we better prepare to face the unthinkable" (Singh, 2010a). Third, "Today, you have to establish your democratic credentials, otherwise you are making a gift of the people to dictatorship and capitalism" (Singh, 2013: 179). A truly ingrained Left unity and a robust Left struggle would be a befitting tribute to this dedicated intellectual-activist (Rai, 2016: 491) for envisaging and achieving an egalitarian world without compromising the politics. In the epistemic and praxis realms of Randhir Singh, politics remains supreme.

Structure of the Book

There are four sections of this book. The first section 'initiating the debate' exhibits a debate on the political explanation in

Marxism. The second section 'remembrance' consists of chapters regarding memoirs. Randhir Singh is being narrated in the form of both his role as a theoretician and the experiences of the narrators. The third section 'advancing the domain' highlights some of distinct contributions on particular issues which remain vital in everydayness. The fourth section 'highlighting the concern' emphasises the core concern of contemporary times and these chapters are dedicated to Randhir Singh. These chapters are included to reflect the concern on issues which are closer to Randhir Singh's practical and theoretical world.

Initiating the Debate

Sudipta Kaviraj (Chapter One: *On Political Explanation in Marxism*) opens up the most significant fulcrum as to 'political explanation' in Marxism amidst two opposite competing categories, i.e. determinism and pluralism. Kaviraj rejects both determinism and voluntarism attribution in Marx because the attempt by him was to break this dichotomy for the arrival of a coherent discourse. This also needs clarity on philosophical language in Marx. Like any other original thinker, Marx uses new thought in old language to make it understandable to the immediate audience. This commences a perpetual tension of deciphering meaning. The most important distinct contributions of Marx concerning modern social sciences are: the distinction in philosophy between idealism and materialism; in theories of science between positivism and hermeneutics; and in politics and social action, between determinism and indeterminism. Kaviraj says that Marx had to communicate these to an audience whose language was constructed in a determined manner. They would not have understood without a grid of concepts and pre-suppositions where dichotomies like materialism/idealism, voluntarism/determinism, and subjectivism/objectivism were used. Kaviraj searches for proof of non-determinism not by way of discovery of passage in Marxist texts but through logical workings of its concepts. Thus, the *logical proof not exegetic proof* is needed. Accordingly, he suggests to treat the relative autonomy of political as a logical concept, not a substantive political concept. Thereafter, Kaviraj elaborates the aforesaid complexity through 'filled and empty concepts', 'the problems of relative autonomy', 'autonomy as exception', 'autonomy as overdetermination', 'autonomy as underdetermination', 'determination and structure', 'explicit and abstract structure', and 'structure and agency'. Kaviraj says that 'reason or cause' dichotomies are redundant in Marx's model of political explanation. Reconstruction of Marx's theoretical project becomes crucial to see his attempt to transcend three dichotomies in explaining politics: between materialist and idealist philosophies, between positivist and hermeneutic notions of science, and between determinism and indeterminism (voluntarism).

Randhir Singh (Chapter Two: *Politics—The Dialectics of Science and Revolution in Karl Marx)* invites attention to two positions in Marxism which are related: absolute Promethean conception of man (free, conscious activity in human species), and commitment to revolution. Therefore, the following implication is inevitable: Marx's scientific project or the explanatory exercise accommodates these positions while leaving out different human activity including politics relatively open and unpredetermined. In other words, politics cannot be entirely amenable to *law-like* generalisation. Against the fragmented and surface studies of contemporary political science, Marxian explanation of politics is explanation of totality or whole through parts or interconnections, and movements. This also requires avoidance of the major empiricist error (grasping things in appearance and isolation by the right) and the minor holist error (missing the richness of mediations which constitute the whole by the left). 'Relative autonomy of politics' needs to avoid both errors. Relative autonomy of politics is the State's possible autonomy in a particular context from class or classes but it does not mean that the State becomes autonomous from social economic structure. In Marx, the scientific and the revolutionary are not only interconnected and growing together but also they put politics at the centre of social practices. The *real basis* needs to be changed to bring change in totality through *politics as revolution*. This gives primacy to politics, not economics, in Marxism. Singh unravels the complexity of overdetermination while referring to Marx: "The concrete is the product of many determinations".

Remembrance

Harbans Mukhia (Chapter Three: *In Punjab's Villages: A Week with Randhir Singh*) narrates a poignant trajectory of himself with his 'teacher and comrade'. Randhir Singh was also a political activist. He touched everyone's mind and heart irrespective of their personal backgrounds. Randhir Singh, Bipan Chandra and Harbans Mukhia were in Delhi University (Zakir Husain College, Hindu College and Kirori Mal College respectively; Mukhia subsequently joined Hindu College in 1967). Crumbling of old imperialist structure, augmentation of decolonisation and spreading of revolutionary ideas and thinkers, all set in 1950s and 1960s, had a lasting impact on that generation. The essay while remembering the context, ideas and people, brings out reminiscences of activism of Randhir Singh in villages of Punjab as a part of *Jatha* in which Mukhia was an intrinsic part. Randhir Singh's politics included, inter alia, his engagement with everydayness.

Chaman Lal (Chapter Four: *Randhir Singh—The Marxist Thinker, the Teacher, the Poet*) unwinds the trajectory of Randhir Singh who was a Marxist thinker, a teacher and a poet. The chapter vividly encapsulates his trajectory from birth, poetry, accidental choice of Political Science, beginning of full time activism at the tender age of seventieen, writing a poem to adore Lahore (*Lahore Nu Salam*), moving to Delhi and joining teaching, starting of journals and the arrival of the teacher and so on. Despite the reversal of socialism in various countries, he remained sanguine about it and was respected by all the left parties. His influence on Nepal was vital. He chose Indian publishers over international publishers for the simple reason as to making the availability of academic works at reasonable cost. He wrote profusely after retirement and spent time while giving public lectures in Punjabi, Hindi/Urdu. He also deserves to be remembered for his poetic expressions (his poetry collection: *Dust of the Paths)*. His poetic expression regarding Indian independence was: "*A Caravan has reached its destination/ and yet lost its way.*" He remains the model for the Indian Left, and his model was Paul Sweezy.

Savita Singh (Chapter Five: *In the Genre of an Intellectual Memoir: Randhir Singh as a Marxist Theorist and a Revolutionary Teacher*) dwells on two crucial elements of Randhir Singh: Teacher and Theorist. According to Savita Singh, accepting someone or someone becoming your teacher needs examination of the subjective and objective reality of your being. This invites new learning, possession, inner transformation and finally inner transformation. This further begets tensed moments along with new enchantment for accepting radical politics. Randhir Singh believed in the politics of taking stands. Savita Singh suggests or rather highlights the following components of his theory: non-determinism, ultimate determination (from Althusser), holism (*Influence of Anti Duhring*), openness of the future (from *Gotha Programme),* and reading Indian reality connectedly.

Manindra Nath Thakur (Chapter Six: *Of Marxism and Creative Theory: Engaging with Randhir Singh*) unravels, by way of collective memory, Randhir Singh's pedagogical practice which revolutionised both students and academic content and made a lasting impact. His lectures adopted a distinctive method of interpretation of Marxism. He highlighted through his interpretation 'Marxism of Marx'. Thakur focuses more on lectures and discussions with Randhir Singh than his writings, and privileges the former since it has an abiding influence in collective memories. Randhir Singh's pedagogical experiment had influenced Bertell Ollman and R.S. Sharma. Thakur highlights the need for a creative interpretation of Marxism in India's context which Randhir Singh attempted. For this, Thakur exhibits five important contributions of Randhir Singh: 'theoretical Importance of autobiographical anecdotes' (i.e. use of autobiographical anecdotes for effective pedagogical purposes), 'in defence of a commitment: question of the vantage point'(i.e. commitment towards knowledge in place of 'ideology'), 'unfinished project of Marxism and question of emergentism' (i.e. Marxism as unfinished project as to open knowledge for revolutionary purposes), 'Marxism, science, and positivism' (i.e. science aka commitment to growth of knowledge, critical self-reflection, continuous interaction with reality and critical thinking; it is a form of creative society ; science not as Newtonian model but creative realist model wherein 'regularity' is not vital), and 'Marxism and religion' (reading religion beyond the opium thesis and issue of continuity of alienation and related survival of religion). The 'creative theory movement' engages, due to the influence of Randhir Singh, Marxism to reflect reality at empirical, theoretical and philosophical levels.

Veena Ravikumar (Chapter Seven: *Randhir Singh – A Tribute to a Maverick Academic*) highlights his intervention as a *Teacher* and *Theorist*. Singh infused talent, freshness and research capacity into students. He simplified *Marxism* and complex political theoretical constructs. He inspired posterity to take up more challenging theoretical tasks. The award instituted in his name at the Department of Political Science, Lady Shri Ram College for Women, University of Delhi for students has inspired numerous young minds for taking these concerns to the wider level. His lectures on Hobbes, Locke and Marx were unparalleled. Nuances of Marxism were simplified, for example "the economy is doing good, the people are not". Singh engaged people from university to villages while underlining the significance of evolution in terms of the structural transformation of society. His political theory was located in the present global scenario.

Hilal Ahmed (Chapter Eight: *Commitments Never Die*) narrates his journey 'intellectually' and 'personally' along with Randhir Singh. By the time, Hilal joined Department of Political Science, University of Delhi for pursuing his Master's degree, Singh had retired. However, his classes, pedagogy, dream to change the world, and his belief that a better society can be formed and it is also feasible, had become the discourse and Randhir Singh had achieved the status of a legend. His understanding of politics was impeccable. The readymade module to understand politics is foolishness. It is important to understand the context wherefrom the popular meaning of politics comes out. That is why politics is called a realm of possibilities. Ahmed realises that this understanding of politics was not bookish but a delicate mixture of experience, struggle, and intellectualism. Through this understanding of politics, Ahmed felt that Singh was appealing to all of us that we must have our own sense of political choice. Moreover, according to Randhir Singh, in the context of Ahmed's interest to see Islam as a political movement, religion was a movement before modernity. Since a modern secular vocabulary was not available to these movements, they chose to express themselves through the language of religion. Randhir Singh believed that Marxist interpretation of Indian religion was not only possible but also desirable.

Advancing the Domain

Manoranjan Mohanty (Chapter Nine: *Dialectical Method and Creative Theory: Insights Offered by Randhir Singh*) underscores the significance of the dialectical method and the creative theory as elucidated by Randhir Singh. This approach of Randhir Singh, according to Mohanty, predicated all forms of theoretical knowledge on their capacity to explain concrete problems facing a society or a class or a group or an individual or the world. "Start from the concrete", "what is the problem that is bothering you?". These became part of the Randhir Singh folklore for two generations of students, friends and admirers. It challenged you not only to bring in high theory and detailed reading of classical texts for analysing the problem of study but also to identify gaps in the prevailing theories in their ability to explain new issues and guide action thereon. Be they philosophical problems such as rationalism and tradition, political problems in India such as the Emergency, the Sikh militancy, repression of people's movements, the question of nationalities, democratic rights movement, poverty, neo-liberal reforms or issues arising out of the collapse of the Soviet Union and other reversals in socialist systems, the concrete and the abstract were put together in political theory. The challenge was to seek fresh insights to analyse unanticipated developments, admit deficiencies in existing theories, including even the most persuasive among them, Marxism. The projection of the ability to mix scientific methods with philosophical enquiries was Randhir Singh's contribution towards the development of the creative threory.

Anand Teltumbde (Chapter Ten: *Furthering the Legacy of Randhir Singh*) makes an important intervention in the annals of Marxism. Marxism/dialectical materialism outlines a method for concrete explanation due to its basis on physical sciences. Dialectical materialism is impeccable in an unanimated world but its application needs utmost care due to, despite coherence in processes, infinite interactions with indeterminate outcomes in the animated world. The biggest strength of Marxism was its theoretical integrity. Therefore, its theoretical validity needs constant updating in the context of continual challenges. Teltumbde exhibits five challenges which need comprehensive attention by Marxists: 'conceptualization of classes relative to abstract modes of production whereas what obtain in reality are the hybrid modes of production' (i.e. recognition of heterogeneity in classes); 'the conception of the binary of reform and revolution and its associated baggage' (i.e. treatment of reform as advancing category than relapsing); 'the obsessive clinging by the Marxists to a metaphor of base and superstructure as though it was a basic tenet of Marxism'(i.e. binary has done more harm than good); 'huge theoretical rework prompted by the paradigmatic changes in technologies'(new technological development and its implications as to labour theory of value); and 'question of violence in revolution and construction of a model of post-revolution society'(need of ideological uprising of masses and mass organisations).

Ravi Kumar (Chapter Eleven: *The Radical Pedagogue Who Demolished the Meaningless Borderlines of Academia*) highlights the significance of a radical pedagogue. Randhir Singh personified the radical pedagogue. In the context of the rise of authoritarianism, attack on working class of politics and not sharpening of contradiction, Randhir Singh becomes extremely important for his praxis and thinking. Kumar asks: "What shall the teacher do?"; "What are the duties of a teacher?". The role of a teacher has to be seen in the context of the nature of production relations. Randhir Singh was a warrior in this regard. The academic world and social world relationship is crucial. Nowadays, there is a gross delinking taking place due to 'career' focused development in the form of Academic Performance Index etc. Randhir Singh, Kumar explains, rejects the delinking of relationship between an intellectual and social world in his own works. Radical pedagogy, as suggested by him as a political being, indicates the following features: 'knowledge is not qua mindless productions', teaching-learning evolves through social realities', and 'rather producing labour-power in classrooms, it has to be subverted', 'academic is important, not administrative idioms which kills creativity', and 'building of knowledge to reflect that classrooms are places of immense conflict needs constant awareness'.

Abdul Rahman (Chapter Twelve: *Environment, Green and Red)* explicates that Paul Burkett and John Bellamy Foster along with others have tried to create a link between Capitalism and environment degradation through exploring the writings of Marx and Engels. It is a well-known fact that accumulation, following the 'nature as a free gift' approach along with the exploitation of fellow human beings, without any consideration of future generations has been the sole reason of the destruction of the nature. Socialism, on the contrary, is an alternative to capitalist approach towards it. Socialism has promises of sustainable and egalitarian development of human kind with a 'paterfamilias' existence. Since Randhir Singh was a known critic of conventions, this essay makes an attempt to look into his writings, particularly his book *Contemporary Ecological Crisis: A Marxist View* to understand the long and rich history of Marxist writings on environmental crisis and his take on the issue.

Rityusha Mani Tiwary (Chapter Thirteen: *Communalism, Secularism and Socialism*) argues that of the various normative and methodological frameworks to understand communalism in India, Randhir Singh's theorisation from a Marxist perspective is significant and profound. In her chapter, communalism and its interconnections with economic base, ideology, culture, religion and politics is explored through secularism and socialism. The chapter begins with debates on communalism from various vantage points and moves on to focus on the present-day secularism as a strategy to deal with communalism. The various issues miring the discourse of secularism are explored to bring out its inadequacy for this purpose. The last part of the chapter focuses on the transformational politics in the form of socialism.

Pavel Tomar (Chapter Fourteen: *Reading '1917' as an Event: Randhir Singh avec Badiou*) points out that Randhir Singh's work '*What was Built and What Failed in Soviet Union*' has two aspects: its method of writing is akin to writing history with historical materialist theory and, its inverse, writing theory through writing its history. As an exercise in Marxist method, it rejects individualistic explanations and opts for a historical materialist reading of communism. The result is that while there is a bold acceptance of the failure of Marxist theory and Bolshevik practice, the status of the Revolution as an authentic liberating moment, an 'Event' in Badiou's sense of the term, is saved. In this process, not only the 'truth' of Marxist theory is saved, but also further strengthened by rejecting a certain limited understanding of its concepts.

Highlighting the Concern

Y.K. Alagh (Chapter Fifteen: *Sad Rural Stories*) sets the perspective at the outset, i.e. the futility of understanding rural poverty through numbers. In the context of MGNREGA and the Food Security Bill, it becomes important to visit villages to understand sustained agricultural and rural development growth as the basis of food security and to avoid distress. The village stories are included from Midnapur District (West Bengal) and some places in Gujarat. The complexities of village stories reveal the need of diversification and technological support in rural India. Alagh points out the diversification for income rise and thus the requirement of infrastructure and technology, including availability of better seeds. This is also true that higher wages cause technological changes in agriculture. The MGNREGA and food security remain necessary for marginal sections. Alagh offers a model in which Indian agriculture can meet the requirement of food security while diversifying itself (meeting of requirement of food security and diversification by the Indian agriculture; functioning in a rural-urban continuum; high employment growth rate). This will be feasible only if institutional support is available for technological and organisational and economic support in terms of pricing. He alludes to the missing of a chapter on the Perspective of the Economy in the Eleventh Five Year Plan under the Manmohan Singh Government. Since there is no planning commission, the effort of people outside the Government becomes more crucial concerning the country's future.

K.B. Saxena (Chapter Sixteen: *Democracy in Deep Crisis: Needs Mass Mobilisation for Reforms*) states that democracy in India is in deep crisis. This crisis is multidimensional. Its political manifestations lie in a polarised and conflicting vision of the polity on class lines with no seriousness to forge a harmonious vision at the policy level. Its other features include federalism under strain, creeping authoritarianism, narrow base of political participation, hollowing out of institutions and failure to deliver justice to the marginalised social groups. Its economic dimensions are reflected in the neoliberal globalised paradigm of development which has deprived a large number of rural poor of their productive assets and livelihood, intensified exploitation of workers and has provided neither decent jobs nor better quality of life but has sharpened and widened all types of inequalities. Its social dimensions are mirrored in persistence of a feudal society which resists change and a civil society which fails to take up causes of the poor and the weak and lacks assertion of autonomy vis-à-vis the Government and the corporates. Democracy has also failed to check the aggressive cultural assault on diversity with its ethno-majoritarian construct of the nation state, demonisation of minorities and enforcing 'Hindutva' values on people. The governance of the polity continues to be insensitive and unresponsive to the grievances of the poor, unleashes repression on protest movements and stubbornly refuses to engage in dialogue with various movements locked in conflict with the State. The emerging fascist tendencies which violate civil liberties and get covert support from State agencies are a cause of greater alarm. Only widest mobilisation of people-peasants, workers, marginalised groups, movements both violent and non-violent, and all secular and progressive persons on a mutually agreed agenda of social, economic and political transformation can salvage it from its continuing slide. The chances for such a movement emerging in the immediate future are bleak.

Atulan Guha (Chapter Seventeen: *Labour Under Stress in Gujarat?)* agues the condition of labour in the economic prosperity in Gujarat. Facts and contrasting facts are self-explanatory. The per capita income in Gujarat is higher than the all India average (1.38 and 1.51 times higher in 2004-05 and 2011-12 respectively). Unemployment rate in Gujarat is also higher than the all India average. Both conditions pave the way for higher wages and better living conditions for workers. Guha's studies reveal findings contrary to these two economic expectations. There are three possible factors for such denials: lack of bargaining power by workers, failures of the state labour department to safeguard the interest of workers, and the role of power structure of village communities in industries. Due to these, even higher output growth in farm and non-farm sectors failed to galvanise higher wage for working class. Highlighting the urban workers' earnings, barring the refinery sector, manufacturing sector has witnessed a decline along with not proportionate percolation of benefit of output growth to workers in the absence of bargaining power. There is an organisational inadequacy. Therefore, wage rates are going lower and profit rates are going up in comparison to the all India averages. The case study of Vithal Udyognagar (Vallav-Vidyanagar) GIDC in Anand reveals contractualisation of labour by big companies. The real wages are not linked to productivity due to the 'near absence of the workers' bargaining powers and the absence of implementation of labour laws. Regarding rural workers' earnings in Gujarat, workers' wages are lower in comparison to the all India average. Rural workers are denied benefits of agricultural growth causing a fast-growing inequality which is also higher than the national average inequality figures.

Ajay Gudavarthy (Chapter Eighteen: *Brahmanism, Liberalism and the Postcolonial Theory*) highlights the seamless 'commonality' between Brahmanism, liberalism and the postcolonial theory by way of focusing on the centrist tendency which encompasses two poles apart contradictory principles/ practices in the form of adjustment but not negation. Supposedly dismissive of each other, a closer reading of the triangular engagement informs us their operability into similar 'epistemic community'. The guiding glue remains 'politics of accommodation' and 'incremental and addictive change'. Bramhanism not only favours social hierarchies but also co-opt contradictions in the face of challenges. Liberalism accommodates dissent and does dialogue with radically challenging situations. In the post-colonial framework, a parallel 'engulf' situations are accommodated without challenge. Moreover, a category 'subaltern' may denote both a Dalit in ghettoised colony and a professor in the area studies department in the USA. In all three areas of study, microscopic changes are allowed, which suits the accommodative and centrist nature of the social that ignores larger structural changes. Moreover, 'ethnicisation of the subaltern' tantamounts to politics of patronage. Gudavarthy suggests that due to the emergence of multiplicity of contradictions and the emergent conflicts within subalterns at all levels, the binary of the east versus the west or subaltern versus elite do not render help.

REFERENCES

Ahmad, A. (2011). On postmodernism. *The Marxist, XXVII* (1), 4-38.

Anderson, P. (1998). *The origins of postmodernity.* London: Verso.

Aron, R. (1955/ 1962). *The opium of the intellectuals.* New York: Norton Library.

Badiou, A. (2010). *The communist hypothesis*. London: Verso.
Bell, D. (1960/1988). *The end of ideology: On the exhaustion of political ideas in the fifties*. Cambridge, Massachusetts: Harvard University Press.
Bell, D. (1973). *The coming of post-industrial society: A venture in social forecasting*. New York: Basic Books.
Cornforth, M. (1968). *The open philosophy and the open society: A reply to Dr. Karl Popper's refutations of Marxism*. London: Lawrence and Wishart.
Fine, B. and Saad-Filho, A. (2004). *Marx's Capital*. London: Pluto Press.
Freud, S. (1932). *Lecture xxxv: A philosophy of life*. Retrieved from https://www.marxists.org/reference/subject/philosophy/works/at/freud.htm
Fukuyama, F. (1992). *The end of history and the last man*. New York: The Free Press.
Goldway, D. (1967). Appearance and reality in Marx's "Capital". *Science & Society, 31* (4), 428-447.
Hardt, M. and Negri, A. (2004). *Multitude: War and democracy in the age of empire*. New York: The Penguin Press.
Laclau, E. (2007). *Emancipation(s)*. London: Verso.
Lyotard, Jean-Francois (1997). *The postmodern condition: A report on knowledge*. Minneapolis: University of Minnesota Press.
Mulhern, F. (ed.) (2011). *Lives on the left*. London: Verso.
Oakeshott, M. (1962). *Rationalism in politics and other essays*. London: Methuen & Co Ltd.
Popper, K. (1945a). *The open society and its enemies, volume I: The spell of Plato*. London: George Routledge & Sons, Ltd.
Popper, K. (1945b). *The open society and its enemies, volume II: The high tide of prophecy: Hegel, Marx, and the aftermath*. London: George Routledge & Sons Ltd.
Rai, D. (2014). Disappearance of the study of politics. *Economic and Political Weekly, xlix* (31), 53-57.
Rai, D. (2016a). Randhir Singh (1922-2016): The teacher who shaped posterity and the study of politics. *Social Scientist, 44* (March-April), 82-88.
Rai, D. (2016b). Professor Randhir Singh (1922–2016): Worldview of radical change. *Social Change, 46*(3), 486–491.
Sen, M. (1967). Revolutionary reason. *Economic and Political Weekly*, 2(28), 1251-1252.
Singh, R. (1987). Marxists and the Sikh extremist movement in Punjab. *Economic and Political Weekly*, 22 (34), 1440-1442.

Singh, R. (1988a). Politics — the dialectics of science and revolution in Karl Marx (appendix III). In *Reason, revolution and political theory*. Delhi: Ajanta Publications.

Singh, R. (1988b). On academic freedom (appendix 1). In *Reason, revolution and political theory*. Delhi: Ajanta Publications.

Singh, R. (1988c). *Reason, revolution and political theory*. Delhi: Ajanta Publications.

Singh, R. (1989a). Visions for the future one view. *Economic and Political Weekly, 24* (14), 723-725.

Singh, R. (1989b). The tradition of Marxism. *Economic and Political Weekly, 24* (43), 2421-2442.

Singh, R. (1990a): Communalism and the struggle against communalism: A Marxist view. *Social Scientist, 18* (8/9): 4-21.

Singh, R. (1990b). *Of Marxism and Indian politics*. Delhi: Ajanta Publications.

Singh, R. (1992a). Terrorism, state terrorism and democratic rights. *Economic and Political Weekly, 27* (6), 279-289.

Singh, R. (1992b). 'Crisis of Socialism': Notes in defence of a commitment. *Economic and Political Weekly, 27* (30), 1623-1627.

Singh, R. (1993). *Five lectures in Marxist mode*. Delhi: Ajanta Publications.

Singh, R. (2007). Future of Socialism. Retrieved from http://mrzine.monthlyreview.org/2007/singh291207.html.

Singh, R. (2009a). *Indian politics today: An argument for socialism-oriented path of development*. Delhi: Aakar Books.

Singh, R. (2009b). *Contemporary ecological crisis: A Marxist view*. Delhi: Aakar Books.

Singh, R. (2010a). A note on the current political situation. *Mainstream*, 48(34). Retrieved February 15, 2016, from http://www.mainstreamweekly.net/article2243.html.

Singh, R. (2010b). Introduction. In William Ash, *Workers' politics: The ethics of socialism*. Delhi: Aakar books.

Singh, R. (2011a). *What was built and what failed in the Soviet Union*. Delhi: Aakar Books.

Singh, R. (2011b). *The right lesson and the wrong conclusion*. Delhi: Aakar Books.

Singh, R. (2013). An interview with Prof. Randhir Singh by Rityusha Tiwary. In Manindra Nath Thakur & Dhananjay Rai (Eds.), *Democracy on the move: Reflections on moments, promises and contradictions*. Delhi: Aakar Books.

PART I

Initiating the Debate

1

On Political Explanation in Marxism

Sudipta Kaviraj

Marxist political analysis[1] seems forever threatened by two opposed types of imminent collapse–into determinism or pluralism. Critics of Marxism usually clam that it must necessarily reduce political occurrences into mere reflexes or corollaries[2] of economic events, and thus cannot say anything interesting or helpful about the way politics goes on.

Author's Note: The argument this paper offers is necessarily incomplete. It deals with three central political ideas of Marxist theory: relative autonomy, determination and structures of various kinds. But these ideas of course, depend on logical support from a host of other concepts in historical materialism. Traditional ways of reading their meaning may have been unsuggestive, but they certainly had the advantage of internal coherence. Any re-reading of their meaning, it follows, would have to redefine not only these three ideas, but all other implicated ones. Althusser's attempt to rework the meaning of some of these—particularly, causality and determination—led, necessarily, to a general reworking of explanatory concepts. Obviously, this rule also applies to the exercise presented in this paper, and because it cannot show how the surrounding concepts can be consistently reworked, it remains flawed. I have, however, tried the following method in presenting the argument here. In the course of my own argument on the three main concepts, I have tried to indicate points at which supporting demonstrations are required, though these are not provided here obviously. For example, both the reductionist and

This objection is made up of two distinct ideas. The first is (i) that a systematic reduction of political facts to any other order of facts, is, in principle, wrong, and explanatorily unhelpful. Its corollary is that although a political occurrence can have significant interconnections with occurrences of other kinds, these are not of a sort which can justify an a priori assumption of a single form of ordered relationship. The second proposition is that (ii) political analysis by Marxists must necessarily result in a reduction into the economy. To state this more fully: for an analysis to be Marxist, it must use some critically important concepts, and the logic of these concepts is such that the analysis must become reductionist as a necessary result of their use. These concepts, therefore, have the dual effect of rendering the analysis both Marxist and determinist. These offending concepts are well known–determination, structures, contradictions, and their various conceptual aliases. I shall refer to this cluster of ideas as the structure-related concepts of Marxist theory.

If this is a correct way of analysing the critical objection, then Marxists can answer this in two very different ways. A first response would contest statement (i) and accept statement (ii). In that case, instead of being seen as a weakness, reduction could be seen as a critical strength. It could then be claimed that like natural science, Marxism reduces the apparent disorder of the world of social facts into the convenience of a few general theorems. Marx's propositions would, then be a sort of equivalent in social thought of the unified field theory. This is a response sometimes adopted by Marxists–erroneously, in my

---

the redescriptive notions of an explanation involve some idea of a 'last instance' of explanation, a kind of 'rock bottom', after which, to call for more explanation would be meaningless. At a later point, it appears essential to me to disentangle two very different sets of meanings with which some Marxist propositions are used, because one set can lead to systematically misleading presentations, or even explanatory mistakes. For phrases, which can only be defended if they are seen as relating to consequences, are often apparently made about origins of social actions. Questions like these are merely indicated here.

view. To satisfactorily defend determinism as a model of social or cultural explanation is an impossible undertaking. On this view of the relation between the economic and the political. rather more than a narrow problem is at stake; the intellectual enterprise of treating a class of facts as political facts, preparatory to calling for a separate order of explanations for them, would then be condemned to redundancy. The Marxists' position would be very paradoxical indeed. For they would be saying in that case, that explanation of politics would be covered by the general thesis that politics does not need separate explanations.[3] The reductive case fails to make a case at all about how politics can be explained. It is no theory of politics, not even a bad one, as much as a statement that no theory is needed, is not a statement of a theory.

If, on the other hand, a Marxist does try to establish relative autonomy of the political level, and asserts that political events do have a logic which is not reducible into a corollary of the economic process, this must, it is argued, lead him to two falsehoods. Either he is reduced to making question-begging statements at crucial turns of his demonstration, hinting at reciprocal causation, which means that if he were really honest and not conceptually pre-committed, he would have confessed that he did not find any form of primacy or causality. He may have simply noted a 'structure' or a 'figure'; but simply to note a structure is not to establish causality. Alternatively, he would be led by his evidence so far away from his preferred model that he would turn into a pluralist with a bad conscience. Anyone who would deny that any kind of primacy can be ascribed to any level of social reality, or that such primacies are local and contingent, is a pluralist. But this pluralist would be in a very false position, for he would have pre-committed himself to a theory of primacy.

A Marxist is, thus, given the generous choice between a falsity of his empirical judgements, or a falsity in the use of his concepts. I wish to argue that the critical case may not be as decisive as it appears. Such conundra arise because of a misunderstanding of the conceptual logic of Marxism. I shall first examine some conceptual strategies by which Marxists have tried to escape a collapse into determinism, and then suggest some ways in which one can choose between them, effect a partial reconstruction, and, finally, render the entire structure of concepts logically coherent.

Some Remarks on Marx's Language

A kind of non-determinism of intentions in Marxist political theory is not difficult to establish hermeneutically, that is, in terms of the intended meanings of authors. Marxists normally take this particular route in their response to charges of determinism. Engels had written enough letters in his old age, when he was trying to protect Marxism from admirers who suspected that it had revelatory powers over history, to establish that this was their hermeneutic intent. Or, perhaps, what Engels intended then, they had intended earlier. Individual arguments, as structuralists often say, must be seen in context, as part of a structure of either a general discourse or of a particular controversy.What a particular idea means depends as much on its etymology as on what it is supposed to say or do to opposing ideas.- One useful test of meaning of theoretical statements is to study its opponents, a reconstruction of what it wished to say to them, rather than what its later adherents made of it in history. Paradoxically, in interpretation of polemical ideas, the character of the theory X wished to shoot down, constitutes a formal component of the context that determines the conceptual point of X's own doctrine.

To understand each particular brand of Marxism, therefore, one must understand its favourite enemy. A crucial element in the understanding of Gramsci is obviously an understanding of Bukharin, or, at least, what seemed to Gramsci to be the point of Bukharin's work. This spares us some agonising over Marx's logical sanity when, for instance, we come across statements with contradictory emphases. Some of Marx's statements on politics are evidently voluntaristic in their emphasis and stress that it is men who make history; some others are deterministic, and emphasise the limits underwhich they are obliged to make it. A simple solution to such elementary mysteries is to stick to Gramsci's judgement, that Marx was not trying to set up a theory which was voluntaristic or determinist in the usual sense, but to break the plane of that kind of discourse. His endeavour was to discover a level of coherent discourse which would be free from these presistent, and in his view, sterile, dichotomies.

But in order to say this one needs to clarify a point about the use of philosophical language in Marx. All discourse has to use pre-given constituted language, and cannot create an entire vocabulary all at once. Original thinkers are, thus, placed in a situation of paradox. They must use old concepts if they are to be understood by their audience; but they must press these concepts to express ideas that are new. Thus the concepts and their precise denotations exist in a kind of tension.[4] These concepts are the traditional vehicles of ideas which they now wish to displace. All original thinkers are, therefore, condemned to write in conceptual language which does injustice to the content of their thought. Sometimes authors try to underline the newness of content by explicitly putting together concepts which, under the pre-given rules of constituted descourse, could not conceivably be used jointly. By saying startling things, by saying things which are contradictions in terms by pre-given rules, they wish to convey that they are suggesting rules that are different. For, in cases of such statements which the rules do not permit, there are two possibilities: the first is that what is stated is a simple error; if not, this may indicate the need for a different set of rules. Apparent linguistic incongruity is meant to alert the reader to the fact that under shocking neologisms, what was being suggested was an unconventional and important thing. It is an incitement to alter fundamental definitions, and through them, gradually, the structure of the discourse itself.

I think this is what can truly be called a 'change of terrain', or breaking the plane of discourse. For every discourse is marked by its fundamental distinctions; those are what make it what it is. Breaking the plane of a discourse is to give it a new set of distinctions. It is usually forgotten, due to the general ahistoricity of discussions on social theory, that the term 'dialectical materialism'/'materialist dialectics' was a phrase of exactly this kind. Marx's theoretical revolution should be seen as a project of presenting the discourse of modern social science with a whole set of new distinctions, of which three are most significant: the distinction in philosophy between idealism and materialism; in theories of science between positivism and hermeneutics; and in politics and social action, between determinism and indeterminism. To say this term, and to mean it seriously, the normal philosophic discourse of the nineteenth century had to become incoherent, that is, get out its distinctions, or cross its normal frontiers. What is meant is not meaningless. It shows, rather, that the language used has become allegorical; it does not mean what it says, or it has invented new ways of saying things; or still further, it stretched the resources of the philosophic language to express thoughts which people did not know could be said with it. After all, ingenuity in its use is the only way a language and its world of meanings, can be stretched. Marx had to communicate with an audience whose discursive alphabet had been formed in determinate ways. They perhaps would not have understood an argument unless it was stated through a grid of concepts and pre-suppositions, which used dichotomies like materialism/idealism, voluntarism/determinism, subjectivism/objectivism.[5] Marx is evidently interested in overthrowing these dichotomies, in making them redundant. Yet, the only way in which he can attempt to do this is by using a language which presupposes them, and treats them as 'natural'. He uses it in a way which communicates with his audience, yet undermines it, much in the way of Wittgenstein's dispensable ladder.

Original thinkers are consequently in perpetual danger of being misunderstood. It is easy to see why this creates possibilities of slippage in interpretation. Those used to living within a constituted discourse, and translating every other into its own terms, can see in this not an invitation to think differently, and to alter fundamental distinctions, but merely positions that are indecisive, middling or contradictory. It is impossible to rigorously substantiate a view, that Marxist philosophy occupees a position midway between idealism and materialism, or a combination of some elements of both. For, both idealism and materialism are theories which have structures which do not allow this kind of a middle term to be coherent.[6]

Critics of Marxism argue that the existence of the letters of the late Engels is no proof that a non-deterministic political theory is possible, and that it can be coherent within the boundaries of Marxist theory. These may be simply acknowledgements by the ageing Engels that his theory did not work, and attempts to cover its breakdown. Indeed, the more the number of exceptions and attenuations suggested to the main propositions of economic determination, the more conceptually disingenuous the theory becomes. The proof of non-determinism would not lie in the discovery of passages in Marxist texts, but in the logical workings of its concepts. It needs, in other words, logical and not exegetic proof. This is what is attempted in the rest of this chapter.

Situations of choice, I shall argue, are not related to structures as exceptions to rules. It is not helpful to suggest that it is in exceptional cases that agency comes into play, by an uncharacteristic generosity of structures that choice becomes possible. Given this view, the whole of concrete history appears as an uninterrupted story of exceptions to this curious rule. It is odd, to say the least, to see the whole of history as a deviation. A rule should not be something that rarely happens. Complete determination of events by economic interests (pretending for the time that 'economic' and 'interests' are unambiguous ideas) rarely happens in real history, but determination as structural limitation happens all the time. That is why we can speak of a 'law' of determination only if it always, in principle, contains non-finalities and space for possible choice.

Marxist historians do not work with simple reductionist models of actual historical explanation. But formal adherence to reductionist propositions and actual non-reductionist analysis introduces a kind of internal incoherence in Marxist theory.

Usually, the way to avoid such threatened incoherence is thought to lie through some well- rehearsed evasive action.

Such evasive actions are, of course, well-known. A common one is to appeal to the notion of 'a relative autonomy of politics'. But the real nature of this concept is, in my view, very often misjudged.

There is some evident ambiguity in the ways in which the term is often used. Surely, Marxism is not a narrowly economic theory; it tries to provide a global theory of the historical process, in which economic explanations have a special place. Relative autonomy, it can be argued, is an economist's legitimate phrase to indicate what is, for him, a residue in analytical terms, to signalise formally that he does not feel entitled to expect a simple reduction of the oplitical order of things to easy explicability through analyses of the society's economy. It is a mark of his acceptance of the existence of areas in his global theory of society which his kind of analyses do not explain. That does not mean, however, that this in the only side from which social reality can be seen, even by Marxists.

Relative autonomy is, then, a primarily logical concept, not an explanatory concept in the ordinary sense, though one can argue that it is a precondition for the invention of explanatory concepts within Marxist theory. It explains the logical distinctions and hierarchies within Marxism, but nothing directly in the world. It describes the logical status of a class of facts–that they are not reducible to economic causalities. To say about a series of political occurrences that they demonstrate 'the relative autonomy of politics', is not to explain what happened and why it happened. It simply means that one should not expect a complete accounting for them by way of a reference to the economy and its necessary rhythms. Unfortunately, one finds too often that Marxists do take it as an explanatory concept, and believe that instead of calling for explanation, it actually does the explaining. This is to ask a wrong question of the concept, and to expect of it what it cannot do.

In my view, the idea of a relative autonomy of the political is a *logical* and not a substantive political concept. It indicates some logical qualities of the Marxist analysis of society; it does not say anything, as is often erroneously thought, about facts in the political world. Therefore, it is not a concept to be used directly in political analyses; it is, rather, something like a logical container in which political concepts of explanation, once formulated, can be conveniently stored. Relative autonomy is a summary name for processes which are not specified theoretically, but which must be. But to begin this argument, one must go back to the idea of two kinds of concepts in Marx's works.

Filled and Empty Concepts

Social theories are systems in two different senses. First, they are completed structures of propositions, which their authors presumably wished to arrange with internal consistency. Each of them is also, in a sense, an invitation to further elaboration. It is this quality of logical extendability which is suggested when some modern theories are designated as scientific. Some theories have an open conceptual space in and around their major propositions, to be filled in later, subject, of course, to consistency criteria. Scientific theories are open systems in this sense. It is to this corrigible form of openness to which Marxism aspires when it refers to itself as scientific. The author pointing out these areas in the general map, gives them provisional names and places in a definite hierarchy of significance, draws their boundaries, but places nothing or very little inside. These are conceptual vacant lots, empty spaces with names, with no theoretical occupants.

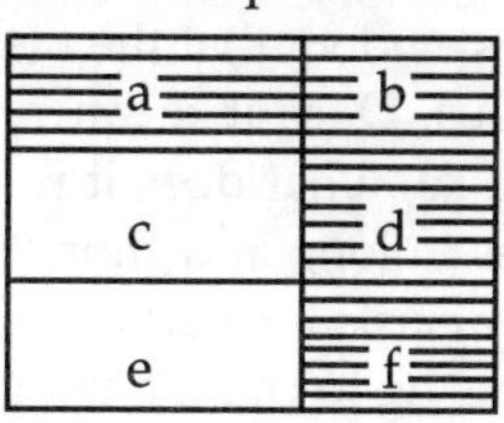

It is, of course, proverbially dangerous to use visual equivalents to logical relations, but the diagram points out roughly what I wish to assert about the internal unevenness in historical materialism. In a theoretical structure of this kind what are specified are not only *Rab*, but also *Rac*, even conceivably, *Rce*; or what are the necessary logical relations between statements that would fall in the areas c and e, even before these statements are, in fact, made. I shall call these 'filled' and 'empty' concepts.[7] The falling rate of profit, to take an example, is a filled concept. It does not merely demarcate the theoretical space this concept has to cover and analytically control, but it also provides detailed moves and arguments by which it can do so. Empty concepts only demarcate an area within the theory which must be covered if the theory is to be consistent, or live up to the criteria it has set for itself. But they do not provide the arguments with which to cover and control it. In a rather loose sense, concepts of the first kind provide answers, the second merely formulate questions (which, if they are taken as explanatory concepts, are mistaken for answers). Relative autonomy, therefore, designates an untheorised, or inadequated theorised logical space, rather than a theory of politics. It indicates the site on which a Marxist political theory would eventually be placed. It is not that theory but simply the announcement that a theory is necessary here. The accretion of metaphors makes this a particularly important idea to analyse with rigour, for metaphors are, after all, the unlit extremities of arguments.

The Problem of 'Relative Autonomy'

But strictly speaking, what exactly does the phrase mean? It is an autonomy relative to *what*?[8] And relative in what terms? Once such questions are asked, it becomes evident that the meaning of the idea is far from unambiguous. Does it mean relative autonomy in some terms of *time*? If so, what does it refer to? The distinction between possibilities in long and short terms? If this means that relative autonomy exists for part of the time in history, would not it be less confusing to call it a temporary or intermittent autonomy? Or does it mean relative autonomy in terms of the topological metaphor, that is, the 'base', the economy, determines its politics in a relative, not an absolute sense? But, where does the critical line between the relative and the absolute run? Or, is this again a different kind of reference to time? Does it mean that it does so for the 'normal' times, but not in abnormal times? Can time be distinguished after Hobbes's beautifully judged phrase, as 'high' and 'low':[9] In low times, the economy determines the political (absolutely?) and in high times, it is the other way round. This implies a privileged time, and privileged history makers who are inhabitants of these time zones (both, of course, determinable retrospectively), but other trespassers are prosecuted. Or, does it mean applying some criterion of significance? That is, in more important things the economy is in control; but politics too has small consolations to restore its pride. On less significant things, it often goes out of the economic prison on parole. Does this, alternatively, relate to the interesting but muted suggestion in some parts of Hegel's historical philosophy, that the process of history should be seen as a slow rising of humanity to consciousness, to reflexivity, tending to a self-reflexive resolution of the 'problem of history'– a gradual movement to a point of final transparency when what men do and what they think they are doing would become identical? This would imply, of course, that the rhythm and character of what is implied by determination has been changing over time. Through a vestigial extension of this idea into Marxism, one can argue that although the economy determined the polity in the earlier, 'unlit', forms, one should not be surprised if, after a socialist revolution, this gets reversed. This will be very similar to the ideas of the early Lukacs about the identical subject object of history.[10] But can one make sense of these jostling possible meanings of this 'enigmatically transparent'[11] idea, or reduce them into some kind of a reasonably ordered relation?

Political theory was given exactly this kind of logical treatment in Marx's mature works, specially in the high theoretical works like the *Grundrisse* and *Capital I*. Often, Marx refers to political events, occasionally in considerable detail. But it would be inattentive not to notice the discrepancy between the levels of generality on which the economic and the political explanations are placed! Both kinds of exercises do, of course, offer explanations, but the relations between them are asymmetric. The levels of abstraction are quite different. The time scales and rhythms are different, and the point at which an object crosses a threshold to become theoretically noticeable are different. *Capital*, for instance, takes an occasional glance at the political regimes under capitalism; it is ordinarily content to deal with forms of state in very abstract propositions. By contrast, the *Eighteenth Brumaire* does not consider the activities of even moderately ineffectual statesmen beneath its analytical attention. Capital seeks to explain the movement of capitalism from epoch to epoch–the *Class Struggle in France* follows the fortunes of French politicians literally from day to day. No doubt, days become epochs if one waits long enough. But unless one places one's faith in an unusually strong version of methodological individualism, one can hardly presume that statements about one would be convertible into reliable statements about the other. There is, thus, a lack of a sense of proportion in the suggestion that the political theory collateral to the socio-economic explanations of *Capital* can be found in Marx's writings about the historical short-term. It is plausible to suggest that we learn Marxian economics in Capital, and political theory from the *Eighteenth Brumaire*. But, in fact, the political analyses we get in one is not on the same scale and, therefore, not strictly comparable to the economics in the other. Of course, these have a vital interconnection in Marx's work, but it must be seen, I suggest, in a more complex fashion.

Autonomy as Exception

There is a general trend in current Marxist thought to look for non-reductive models of historical explanation. But there are logical variations between various non-reductive moves. Traditionally, Marxists often tried to open up some space for a 'play' or indeterminacy within the base-superstructure metaphor, by postulating a notion of weak reciprocity. But reciprocity is a relation, not a quality of which there can be more or less. Sometimes Marxists implied that the movement of politics was random, which would then mean that it will not be amenable to theoretical generalisation. As the purpose of theory is to map regularities, if politics excludes regularities by definition, all that theory can do is to ceremonially dissolve itself. This is not a frivolous suggestion. Marxist political literature shows recurrent examples of this sort. Individual political events are seen as framed in larger scenarios of slow-moving class forces which determine (wholly or positively) economic options and choices of basic social groups. But on the surface, above this deep level, there is the other plane on which everyday politics takes place, which demand detailed interpretation and commentary. Often, one finds an inverse relation between the large and the small analysis. Precisely because the 'large' analysis is done in such deterministic style, the political, as it were, takes its revenge. The 'small'analysis is done through a discourse which rarely refers to political forms which mediate class behaviour into history. Individuals are analysed either psychologically, or through a summary political ethics which can yield instant, and, therefore, necessarily changeable judgements about good and bad, or, progressive and reactionary. There are temporary traitors and heroes, because a twist in the immediate situation can turn one into the other, and they are fitted through their immediate political acts to the supposed longings of social classes.[12] An analysis of this kind, precisely because it has no patience for the problematic middle term, the political formations, oscillates violently between a language of teleological fatality, and a language of abusive psychologism.

A second familiar move is to declare that since Marxist theory is 'dialectical', all laws include the possibility of occasional reversals. This is bound to be unclear, because the initial task of theory was not only to specify regularities of behaviour, but also, preferably, specify conditions under which it can take particular turns. To say that something is probable, but the opposite of this is also equally probable, and not being able to specify conditions under which each is so, must reduce a theory's explanatory power. This is what Marx criticised younger Hegelians for: 'Yes becoming no, no becoming yes, and both yes and no becoming yes and no'.[13] But in more recent Marxist theory, some other interesting moves towards non-reductionism have been tried out. I should like to analyse one of them briefly.

Autonomy as Overdetermination

One of the most influential among these is Althusser's avoidance of determination. He observes the logical disingenuousness of the idea of an extenuating long term.[14] If law X is to hold over the long term, but the opposite of X can hold in the short run, this causes obvious difficulties, because the long term is composed of short ones. And this kind of relation can hardly obtain, unless it is stated why short runs of the non-X types cannot occur all the while, or methodologically, non-individualistic conditions are specified. Althusser tries to avoid these logical traps, yet retain the quality of non-determinism, which they impart to Marxist historical explanation. The two related concepts which enable us to do this in his thinking, are 'over-determination' and 'structural causality'. Even though the long term argument is a time argument, the last instance one is about the logical specification of causality. It is an idea of causality which has many layers, as it were. On some levels, the account closing falls due in a short period, and an economic level on which it takes a long time. Other levels of the social totality are allowed some room for play, subject, of course, to their coming back home at nightfall. But to analyse this literature is to witness the richness of metaphors, rather than a comparable richness of strictly conceptual moves.

The two concepts of contradiction and determination are integrally related; from different directions, they refer to the same qualities in historical events. The purpose of the concept of contradiction, like that of determination, is to show constraints on behaviour, to reveal underlying patterns, to reduce randomness, and exclude possibilities. In Marxist analyses, one must, of course, register the compulsions of 'pure' contradictions, like the one between the bourgeoisie and the proletariat. But in their pure form, these contradictions are merely heuristic devices, close to Weber's ideal types.[15] In history, one never comes across pure contradictions standing singly. Although it is analytically proper to characterise modes of production or social forms by their contradictions, actual conjunctures show the existence of many contradictions, not just the central one. No society is 'pure' in this sense. In fact, the notion of a conjuncture graphically suggests the plurality of contradictions at a point of time. I think Althusser's argument implies a subtle reworking of some concepts in Marxist social theory. Distinctions between central and incidental are not in terms of their significance; for, even the smallest element of the conjucture is necessary for it to have the effect it actually does. In making a conjuncture what it is, therefore, the primary and secondary contradictions are all equally necessary. They are meant to do quite different chores in the conceptual division of labour within the theory.

Significantly, there is a certain monochromic quality in Althusser's picture of contradictions, which is deliberate. Althusser is not introducing, as Gramsci and Sartre or Lukacs would in similar circumstances, other planes which intersect or qualify objective contradictions: interpretative or perceptual elements. Althusser's analysis is self-consciously distinct. All the complexities that Althusser carefully unravels exist on a single plane–the plane of objective contradictions, unmediated by interpretative aspects of meaning. An event happens all between contradictions. Both its structured and unstructured qualities can be deduced from the way structures are related. Any absence of rigidity or teleology occurs not because objectivities are crossed out or mitigated by other things, but due to the relations that obtain between these objectivities themselves. If contradictions are taken to be equivalent to structures (this diverges from Althusser's more scrupulous usage which reserves the term structure, only for the *global* structure, the structure in the 'structure-in-dominance'), each conjuncture is then a total effect of these. Structures that are analytically distinguishable always act in history through their conjoint effects. In history, there are no dark, lonely alleys in which groups or societies can be set upon by single, overwhelming structures. That is why there is not much point, in concrete historical explanations, in distinguishing between institutional structures like governments, and abstract ones like classes. Both types are historically present although Althusserians would surely admit that the sense in which they are 'present' must differ. When a structuralist Marxist speaks of 'the structure', the structure in this solemn singular is the combination, the conjunctural unity of all those structures that are analytically separable. (which, in structuralist terms, does not mean that they exist singly, like people in a crowded underground, each with a newspaper to his nose. Rather, no existence is part of their being; since in structuralism the character of an object is determined not by what it is in itself, but by the relations it has with objects in its surrounding world.)[16]

Each contradiction determines, has a logic of pressure on agents, and the actions they initiate and unintentionally cause. The totality of these effects gathered together in a conceptual unity, is the structure-in-dominance.[17] It is to this, in Althusser's view, that an adequate causality can be attributed. It is this structure which can fully explain a historical incident. Again, there is a subtle shift of implication. Traditional Marxism presupposed a traditional notion of what happened in an explanation, based on a strict distinction between explanation and description. For that tradition, therefore, to explain X was to refer it to Y. It would be inconceivable to refer X to X, and call it an 'explanation'. That would be disconcertingly similar to saying X is what it is because of the why it is.[18] But in Althusser's theory, to say this is not necessarily trite, or to beg the question. In words without a theatrical make-up, when we say something has been 'explained' in history, we simply indicate this whole complex of things. Theories of science, of course, have a very long tradition which asserts that a scientific explanation is a *reduction*–it referred an occurrence to another level of facts. To put it in a different, but related form, it reduced the chaos of concrete phenomena to the comparative manageability of general laws. Traditional Marxims exhibited fairly strong influence of the idea of explanation as a reduction. (Of course, there reduction does not have any derogatory implication. On the contrary, it suggests precision, economy, order and other similar scientific virtues.) Althusser's suggestion that causality is 'structural', or that it can be attributed only to the 'structure-in-dominance', obviously marks a sharp departure from the notion of explanation as reduction. It asserts, on the contrary, that in historical analysis, a reduction, evern in terms of the acknowledged central contradictions of a social form, is misleading. Modes of production are abstract analytical constructs; they map basic and minimal regularities, but they never have the richness of determinations of the concrete, to use a Hegelian phrase. To explain the concrete cannot be done by way of these. Reduction attenuates complexity. So, although there is an obvious Cartesian streak in Althusser's epistemology, central assertions about historical explanations in Althusser are, surprisingly similar to a Diltheyan construction, which presupposes a distinction in logical form in explanation in natural and historical sciences. Structure-in-dominance, if taken seriously, brings his theory of historical explanation quite close to some hermeneutic doctrines of history, despite the Cartesianism of his language. Structure-in-dominance is a structuralist's equivalent of situational uniqueness.

Althusser provides a clear account of the redescriptive nature of his category :

> In this complex whole containing many contradictions we cannot 'find' one contradiction that dominates the others as we might 'find' the spectator a head taller than others in the grandstand at the stadium. Domination is not an indifferent fact, it is a fact essential to complexity itself. That is why complexity implies domination as one of its essentials: it is inscribed in its structure. So to claim that this unit is not and cannot be the unity of a simple, original and universal essence, is not, as those who dream of that ideological concept foreign to Marxism, 'monism', think, to

> sacrifice unity on the altar of 'pluralism'–it is to claim something quite different; that the unity discussed by Marxism is the unity of the complexity itself, that the mode of organisation and articulation of this complexity is precisely what constitutes its unity. It is to claim that the complex whole has the unity of a structure articulated in dominance.[19]

This passage is full of interesting theoretical motifs, although it is not always easy to disentangle the conceptually suggestive in Althusser from the meretricious. Part of its attraction lies, perhaps, in this combination. But some of these are worth pursuing at a greater length.

Despite Althusser's declarations of hostility to Hegelianism, his argument shows an interesting similarity to Hegel's on one point: his belief that in explaining historical situations one should not ascribe analytical values *a priori*, but only *after* the event. Unilinear causality of the economy is normally an a *priori* ascription. We do not wait for an event to happen to know how it has been caused or can be explained; in a formal sense, we know in advance, through our commitment to a causality ascribed to the 'economic'. Althusser's approach to historical occurrences is more circumspect. Even among his jostling contradictions, one cannot decide any a *priori* hierarchy. In fact, he goes further to argue that any ascription of priority in a complex whole, which could not, in one's judgement, have been without all of its attendant circumstances, is itself inappropriate. Althusser's theory, therefore, avoids not only any *a priori* primacy, but the idea of primacy itself. And precisely because it avoids the idea of priority among the circumstances in thinking of historical causation, it becomes similar to an extended (though perhaps not unsuggestive) tautology or redescription. If it means that a historical conjuncture is what it is, because of the specific way its contradictions that constitute it are precisely mixed (that is, overdetermined), what is it saying really? It comes fairly close to saying that the historical situation is what it is (this is to put the language in a 'causal form'), because its elements are what they are, and they are related precisely the way they happen to be. The situation is what it is, because it is what it is. There is of course nothing, in principle, strange about this view of history, but it does require a drastic alternation in the notion of causality underlying most Marxist discourse. It raises the problem of the defining of an explanation in history; it implicitly faces us with the question of a explanation in history; it implicitly faces us with the question of a choice between two notions of what an explanation is. Is it primarily a *reduction*: a way of referring the apparent chaos of facts to the clarity of some essential laws and regularities, so that an explanation is 'simpler' in an epistemic sense, than a merely descriptive account of a historical occurrence? Or, is it a name for a redescription which tries precisely to preserve the complexity of the occurrence? Evidently, the two notions of explanations are opposed. In one, there is a clear line of demarcation between explanation and description, and an explanation is seen to be both more significant and economical than a descriptive account. In the other, it is this precise distinction that is formally questioned: an explanation is simply a description that is adequate to the complexity of the occurrence. the two theories arrange epistemic values differently. In one, simplicity is the value explanations would aim at; in the other, complexity. Surely, there are traditions in natural science theory which claim that there cannot be any clear line of difference between explanations and descriptions, just as in historical sciences there are theories which assert that the main epistemic preoccupation of historians should be to capture the unique complexity of occurrence. But Althusser's relation to either of these cannot be very straightforward. This shows that there could be an element of ambiguity in Marxism on this question.

If there had been one contradiction or one structure, it could have caused the event, that is, accounted for it in fullest detail. But since there are many of them, and this is necessarily the case, without reducing the claim of contradictions to determine fully, we can still derive a theory of underdetermined outcomes. The sufficiency of the cause lies in the specific manner in which these combine. Formal explanation is, thus, still left to the 'economic' in Althusser's Marxism, but effective explanation is given over to the 'structure'. 'Structure-in-dominance' is a significant and interesting concept, because it is supposed to provide one of the crucial solutions in Althusser's Marxism. It retains the theoretical injunction of 'determination by the economic in the last instance', but makes this kind of concrete instance historically unavailable. This means that the economic determined in the last instance, not in actual history, but in a particular kind of heuristic and idealising discourse.

Determination in history is made the joint work of multiple contradictions, and the strictly explanatory primacy of the economic is gently taken away. As an orthodox Marxist, Althusser feels obliged to show ritual reverence to the idea of determination in the last instance. But his sense of history, of how events actually occur, does not seem to offer much support to the idea of a deterministic causality. Indeed, he states quite explicitly about the feudal social form, that non- economic levels may, in fact, have dominance, because there is some scriptural support for this notion.[20] In explanation, therefore, the primacy of the economy is avoided,[21] but there is a kind of hollowly linguistic defence of the idea. This leads to the distinction between determination and dominance, and one can see how, in explanatory terms, dominance becomes the effective concept, and discretely pushes out determination. This leads to the curious paradox in the heart of Althusser's Marxism: a sort of division of sovereignty still lies with determination, but its function is unmistakably like that of British royalty. It simply stamps with formal approval what the effective concept of dominance decides to do.[22]

Autonomy as Underdetermination

This is attractive from the point of view of historical explanations, no doubt, but a more significant ambiguity seems to result from this. As the two concepts are rooted in two distinct notions of what historical explanation consists in, epistemic. propositions of Althusser's Marxism suffer from a fundamental ambiguity. Perhaps one can try to solve this problem by saying that one must, in reading Althusser, exercise an interpretative judgement about which idea is more significant or suggestive, and render his theory coherent by choosing one of them and qualifying the other. Clearly, the verdict in that case would go in favour of explanation as redescription, rather than reduction. Several aspects of Althusser's argument lend credence to this idea—the emphasis on complexity, opposition to what he considers to be Hegel's notion of a complexity reducible into simple essence, and his unwillingness to accept priorities between contradictions. Dominance has the dominance. But the compromise he arranges becomes suspect in logical terms, because the two notions of explanation are not only different, but in major ways, opposed. Using the language of one to argue for the other leads to recurrent and ineradicable ambiguity.

In Althusser's theory what happens is overdetermination, but what it causes or helps take place relative to each single contradiction is clearly underdetermination. But this is precisely what can be objected to. As this is a plausible model of social explanation, it is hardly surprising that most of the modern departures into political theory begin from Althusser's concepts (Poulantzas, Therborn, Laclau).[23] But conceptually, it is rather a waste to assert first that structures can determine if they exist singly, and then to say that (either normally or exceptionally) such instances never arise in history. From Althusser's point of view, it is a category mistake to expect to find them in history; they can exist only in a specific type of heuristic philosophical discourse. But it is simpler to say that it is in the nature of structures that exist in history to underdetermine their outcomes. This would be a simple alteration of conceptual meaning, which would preserve the explanatory advantages of Althusserian reasoning, but be free from its logical problems, besides doing it more practically and economically. In the social science discourse of Marxism, if not otherwise stated,' determination'—which is the constraining quality of structures over agency—is equal to underdetermination. It is an exclusion of possibilities, and not rendering one absolutely certain. I shall argue that this also creates some internal space in Marxism for interpretative concepts.[24]

Because of a strong element of objectivism in his thought, a persistent mistrust of all concepts of subjectivity, Althusser does not find the idea of complete determination implausible. But even on his own terms, since there is a reality to ideology, even though it may only interpolate individuals as subjects,[25] if a single individual turns round to answer, this would disturb the implicit symmetries of his entirely objectivist universe. It is simpler to admit the effectiveness of ideology, the latency of interpretative opportunities within human acts, and to make room for them within our concepts, rather than record their effects, a little disingenuously, by carefully arranging a stalemate between objective things.

In the conceptual reading suggested here, determination is the social process whose precise quality is to underdetermine events. This is not an indeterminacy at the cognitive level, resulting from there being one determination over another, so that one cannot see their lines of force clearly, or a joint causality unascribable to any one. Underdetermination is the quality of what Marxists refer to as historical determination—by classes, structures or stuations. This puts underdetermination in the heart of the concept of determination itself. It does not rule out choices, alternative possibilities, but restricts their range with greater or lesser severity. This makes options, or a certain order of indeterminacy, *internal* to the notion of determination, rather than an external condition to be arranged for logically, or attached by adhesive adjectives (like relative not absolute, etc.).

Let us now turn to the point which seems to bind the notions of necessity and determination. The idea of structures implicit in Marxism leaves room for subjectivity; indeed, it considers subjectivity, or agency, to be historically, crucial: problems sometimes arise in this regard from a confusion of tense problems in historical thinking. Obviously, historians and historical actors are placed on different planes, have different ontological relationships, dispositions to occurrences, and quite different orientations in terms of time. Actors live history prospectively; even the most dedicated followers of Dilthey or Collingwood are reduced to mere reconstructions of situations, which work under some limitations. At this level too, there can be hard fallacies to overcome for a reductivist theory of history. If understanding history is through reconstructing situations of actors, some of their dispositions would be unreconstructible. Actors' dispositions towards historical actions are determined by the fact that they do not know what will happen. A historian cannot reconstruct this, which by his own conceptual logic, would be a necessary condition of his enterprise. Reliving history, if taken beyond an allegorical phrase, is a misleading notion, bound to collapse, when pushed to extremes into incoherence. Indeed, this is the kind of the ontological bar that constitutes the first and the most fundamental point of the critique of relativist hermeneutic thinkers like Heidegger and Gadamer. Historians can do nothing about their ontological 'privilege' of knowing the future in advance. It is not a privilege they can drop out of. They cannot 'bracket' it in Husserl's sense, for, the need for bracketing itself would set him apart, and the entire artillery of Heidegger against the Husserlian 'epoche' would apply against his efforts. The gulf between the positions of actor and observer is unbridgeable. There is a certain residue which would always remain between the events and the knowledge-constructs of events, or as hermeneutic theorists would put it, between knowing and being.[26]

Determination can then be seen as a concept proper to the level at which history is lived, where the tense orientation is prospective; they go with time. Conversely, necessity is a concept proper to the level at which history is studied; it has a tense orientation that runs *against* time. Clearly, the sense in which there is room for agency in living history is quite different from the sense in which there can be an epistemic registration of the room that had once been there for a once-living agency in history which is now dead, that is, history as knowledge. To use a different metaphor (which may, in fact, compound our problems), what history as a discursive discipline encounters are traces of agency and subjective decisions having been taken, like fossils of non-compulsory decisions preserved in the strata of time. Room for agency is an idea which can apply realistically only to living history, to history as being. It cannot be applied the same way to the epistemic recovery of being, to history as reconstruction, because the uncertainty contained in the option would have already been spent. It is not the sort of uncertainty that attaches to an unmade choice, but a spent uncertainty of a choice that has been taken. Of course, although the choice has been made, for reasons which are still retrospectively specifiable, it is still, in principle, different from a situation in which no choice existed.

This is the meaning of determination: it asserts that events that have gone before (this can also come in a different form–of one kind of events exerting pressure on another), create pressures through the continuance of their effects on what is to happen. They restrict possibility and narrow down choice. It cannot be said at any point of historical time that anything can happen, if anything at all has happened before. Evidently, it is a significant part of the historian's enterprise to state what cannot happen, and different theories of history quarrel over which is the best way to know things which cannot take place. Marxists would assert that a detailed consideration of certain types of things, like the level of technology, the stable configuration of social interests, social relations arising out of production (which exerts similar pressure on other spheres of economic life, like circulation and exchange), are particularly and systematically suggestive in understanding excluded choices. Givens of all kinds restrict possibilities of what can happen, or what can be done, to a specific range. This is what is determined. This means that an individual choice, or an individual event is *underdetermined* by the logic of structures which form its context. Determination would never determine in a categorical fashion, what is going to happen. It refers, rather, to what cannot, in principle. This may look at first sight like an evasion. For, to say something about what cannot happen is only a recondite way of saying something about what can. But this accomplishes something which appears to me to be important. What is said about these two respects become asymmetric, logically. Saying something about what cannot happen categorically, is also saying something about what can, but much less definitely. It leaves open a range, a margin of occurrence. What can be extracted from a categorical statement about what cannot happen about what can, is precisely less categorical, and therefore, not open to similar kinds of logical or conceptual objection.

Determination in Marxism is, in this sense, a negative concept. To expect it to yield, or to extract from it, a positive outcome is to misconstrue its logical status; to ask it wrong questions, is to expect answers it is not equipped to provide. It fixes ranges of possible choice or outcomes. What we denote by determination is not the event, but the space allowed to the event; it is not what must take place, but the margin in which something must.

When a particular actor chooses, or a historical event takes place, this underdeterminant quality is lost. Of course, each exercised choice within this zone of specifiable indeterminacy would have a further set of reasons or causes. But these reasons cannot be inferred or read off from the initial conditions. These are genuinely underdetermined things. This can also be argued from another angle. A constraining or excluding idea of determination suggests specifying limits. But the idea of limits itself can be seen in two different ways. A more conventional one would say that the range of choice, or its limits, consists or a specifiable set or possibilities or state of affairs, say X or Y or Z; what comes to happen must be one of these. This introduces an indeterminacy of a certain kind. But it seems doubtful if historical possibilities can often be set out and stated in this form. A more suggestive way of talking of limits can be borrowed from linguistics, and its concept of combinatories or a generative structure. An alphabet ensures that only a certain range of things are possible with it: but its way of restricting is different from, and less restrictive than, a straightforward listing of possible outcomes. When Marxists speak of the interests of a class determining its actions or its discourse, the best construction of this idea would be something like this: the class acquires, through its historical experience, its specific alphabet of action or of thought. But what it decides to generate out of this alphabet is underdetermined.

If determination means a list of constraints and delimitation of choice, it can have only one tense mode–the present tense or the very near future. Its use is proper only when we refer to the historical actor, or an observer who is his contemporary, who is living history prospectively, where the actor's tomorrow is also the observer's. If the actor and analyst are related to the event asymmetrically, if the actor's tomorrow is the analyst's yesterday, the notion properly applicable is the second notion of necessity. Its mode is retrospective, it is a tense to which the owl of Minerva is eternally condemned, for it deals with dead choices, with the fossils of agency. It knows the future in advance; its problem is not underdetermined, but wholly determined.[27] Historians usually placed this way, can only try to separate out the space, or levels in the model in which determination and freedom of choice would have had their play. No doubt, in some cases of spent choice, this may be difficult to disentangle. Necessity is the concept used to denote the privileged observer's enterprise to understand what happened within the crucially underdetermined part of a historical event. This content of choice can be explained but not forecast. The language of necessity, the only language that Minerva's owl can speak, has no present tense. Determination is in prospective form what turns into necessity in retrospect.

Determination and Structures

Structures are usually considered to narrow down options. By contrast, the idea of a logic of a situation is often used to indicate a peculiar freedom which sometimes arises in history, which loosens up the stuffiness of structures somewhat, a freedom that is not illusory. It is natural to think of situations as intersections of structures or what results when structures meet, or as a result of a stalemate between two pure but contradictory tendencies. But a situation can act on structural logic in both ways.[28] It may narrow down options still more, but the idea generally is that when there are contradictory pulls, this tends to free political agents into a voluntaristic space, to do things much closer to the way they would like. If actors are particularly clever or lucky, they may be able to bring about, acting at the narrow openings that these immense things have between them, even the particular results they intended. Clashes between structures reduce the heteronomy of groups and individuals, if not enhance the autonomous space for political choice. Agents can, as it were, play these heteronomies against each other.

This, of course, is a familiar story in politics. Small states prefer to have two big neighbours instead of one. Western European statesmen, who would agree with the moral preferences of American administrations, would still prefer a bipolar world to one wholly dominated by the United States. Statesmen work out similar room for manoeuvre by saying that they have to be mindful of a proper trade-off between equally important principles, or claimants of distributive attention, or that they must be just in mediating between equally insistent interests. To be upholding two principles is less constraining than upholding one entirely unambiguous ideal. There is no reason why this should not apply to abstract things like structures as well. To be placed at the intersection of multiple structures may be less constraining than being swallowed up in one. After all, that is the lesson of Althusser's argument.

But structures are of different kinds, and it is important for the purposes of our argument to distinguish between the precise sense of determination proper to each one of them. For all structures determine, but not in the same way. One obvious distinction to make will be between explicit and abstract ones. In fact, the hazards of deterministic analysis can be traced to the tendency to drop the middle term in analysis, to go straight from an empirical state of facts to abstract things like classes. This is also exhibited in the tendency to think of these two types of propositions, not as things which are legitimate in their proper contexts, but as appearance and essence, in which a statement in terms of the essence would contain all possible true qualities of a statement in terms of appearance. But the distinction must not be seen in those terms.

The structure of imperialism, the structure of cabinet government, the bourgeois class, a political party, a situation–all these things do constrain, and all these would fit into some loose definition of structures. The concept of structure is, indeed, proper to all of them, because the fact that they are the way they are and not otherwise, exerts significant influence on agency. But they constrain in different ways, in different degrees, and these differences are worthy of some attention. I think three distinct implications come out if we analyse these examples. Determination implies somewhat different things when it is related to (i) explicit structures like institutions, (ii) abstract structures like classes, and (iii) situations which are seen as short term compulsions or freedoms. They are significant for political analysis, for politics always happens in the short term.

Explicit and Abstract Structures

The first two types restrict behaviour through complex arrangements of encouragement and sanction. But to speak of rewards and punishments in case of abstract structures, like classes, is naturally somewhat allegorical. This can lead to confusion and misplaced expectation if its qualifications are not specified. In case of explicit structures or institutions, this is unproblematic. A cabinet will dismiss a minister who disobeys rules of collective responsibility, but an individual will not long remain member of the capitalist class if his economic acts are dictated by motives of altruism. In both types of cases, it is common to say, colloquially, that the person has been 'thrown out'. But the second case is clearly different from the first. Evidently, there is a logic at work in the second case too, which supervises the internal coherence of the capitalist class, but it works through a latent structure like the market, which, though abstract, is obviously not ineffectual. Some of the stock arguments against Marxist social theory, that, for instance, it uses metaphysical concepts, are clearly disingenuous. If the concept of class has to be thrown out of the conceptual stock of rigorous social theory, so would the concept of the market. That too indicates merely a persistent configuration of effects of explicit acts and institutions. Markets do not exist in the sense in which firms do. Yet, one cannot make sense of a large, and probably the more significant part of the behaviour of firms, without recourse to a conceptual primacy of markets. These are no shadows; they indicate 'logics' which, indeed, compel and explain behaviour of institutions. After all, the distinction between actual and real is still not without its uses in social explanation. In social sciences, it is quite common to have to explain the activity of actual things, only by recourse to things which are real in this indirect way, which would always fail to answer an institutional roll-call.

Curiously, critics of market theory and its reductionist adherents often use similar moves in their thought, particularly in the ascription of political acts to abstract things. At one time, this was considered the fatal flaw of Marxist theory, that it tried to explain and understand the political world in terms of concepts which will fail to pass this most elementary of fitness tests. Goverments had a verifiable existence; states were simply metaphysical constructs. As Marxists insisted on the primacy of concepts like the state which could not be found, in Weldon's elegant condemnation, in the telephone directory, this was supposed to prove the ineradicable metaphysical content in Marxist analyses.[29] Arguments of this sort appear, in retrospect, particularly odd, because they are guilty of precisely the sort of category mistake that Ryle criticised so effectively.[30] The error about calling the concept of the state metaphysical is precisely of the same type as looking for an Oxford University beyond its colleges and other institutions; it is to mistake the two concepts as competitors or belonging to the same logical class. The state is real, a Marxist can argue, in the same sense in which the Oxford University is real.[31]

Institutional structures are transparent–entities like firms, governments and associations, with names, telephone numbers, explicit rules and clear boundaries. Their definitions are not subject to prior theoretical judgements. We are in no doubt about who are the members of a specific chamber of commerce, what are the rules of membership of a church, and when a person can be expelled from an association. But there are other structures, obviously related to these, but with a more elusive quality about them; a bourgeois class in relation to a chamber of commerce, a religion in relation to a church. Institutions in Marxist political analysis, are not simply embodied versions of classes; they have a more complex relationship. the definition of a bourgeoisie, of the delineation of the ideas which form the core of a religious system, are largely theory-dependent affairs. So, the second type of structures depend on, one can almost say they are brought into existence, by, definitional constructs; at least their boundaries certainly are.[32] Rules of institutions are explicit, if not always entirely public. Consequently, the systems of reward and punishment which they work are either well-known or empirically recoverable. At this level, the use of a language of decision is, therefore, appropriate. A person truly decides whether he will become a member of an association; this decision is not previously dictated by the rules of the organisation; his behaviour of course will be, only if he does join. But it is a necessary quality of determination of abstract structures that it is latent, and can be masked from the person whose behaviour is being determined. At least, seeing that they exist is not a condition for making use of the alphabets they provide.

Although there is often a great difference between what institutions profess and what they actually do, this relation is unmysterious and accessible. But when we use the ordinary verbs of action in relation to abstract structures, it is done *faute de mieux*, and an ambiguity tends to creep into our language.[33] Ascription of actions to surface structures does not give a complete account of acts in social life; for the world is made up of these other more insidious structures too, and they condition and constrain the actions at the institutional level. And here the distinction between 'surface' and 'deep' structures is of a kind that a deep account does not make a surface account redundant. Just as the concept of firm does not invalidate the use of a concept of market, use of categories like parties or political formations does not close off the logical space for using the notion of class. To argue against this is, paradoxically, a common point between vulgar Marxism and conventional anti-Marxism. Both believe that the conceptual space in political explanation can be occupied by only one set of categories. Thus, the use of explicit concepts closes off the use of abstract ones, or vice versa.

Of course, this implies that the sense in which we use the terms 'surface' and 'deep' is not the conventional dichotomy between appearance and reality. Rather, they should be thought of as describing reality at different levels, although the distinction must imply that one considers one group more basic. In explanations of politics there is a kind of reciprocal dependence between them as categories. Both types of descriptions are necessarily incomplete, and the nature of this incompleteness hints at the existence of the counterpart. What categories of the first level can capture, those of the second cannot, and vice-versa. This guards against the common trend towards a sort of class substitutionism in political and cultural analysis in Marxism,[34] in which the class takes over directly from political actors or utterers of discourse. In reductive Marxism, surface and deep concepts are taken in the sense of being high/low, inclusive/exclusive, or appearance/reality. In this view, they are supposed to take in conceptually quite different qualities of the social process, or more precisely, perhaps, qualities which exhibit themselves at different levels of generality.[35]

Abstract structures have their effects only in the longer term, for they constrain indirectly. This is why their logic should be seen as statistical; their effects intensify and wane over long periods. If a businessman violates formal laws of company behaviour, his actions will be punished by his government. If he disobeys the subtler but no less insistent laws of the capitalist market, say by excessive altruism, it will restrain him more indirectly. Other things being equal, this will result in his financial ruin and a consequent alteration of his social role. These are laws of large numbers and long periods. When we talk of determination of individual actions by classes, we are using a shorthand, a convenient abbreviation; we are talking not of a single-remove determination, but a double-remove one. In politics, classes do not constrain individuals directly, but through the alphabets of political formations to which these individuals belong. Political formations need not be directly aligned to particular classes or fractions; they still show instances of class politics because they work on an alphabet of decisions whose range is determined by class in a language-like way. In culture, I think Marxists must offer a largely parallel argument, in which determination acts through patterns of discourse, through which thoughts of individuals are coordinated with acts and thoughts of others.

Political formations always exist on the level we have called explicit and they are always the proximate sources of political action. Indeed, actual politics happens on this plane, through relations between agents of this sort. Constraints to which individual agency is subject can be traced to them. Classes and other deep structures do not figure on the political stage as actors; in culture they do not act as actual utterers of discourse. They exist as references to the general alphabet of which discourses are historically formed. It is wrong to refer discourses, or actions, or similar meaning-related things to classes.[36] It is proper, and logically quite a different thing, to refer to them as 'creators' of intellectual resources.

Class causes, it may be said, would be condemned to live in a state of suspended animation until they find their way into somebody's reasons. Explanations of revolutions are normally structured in this form. The cost of being fundamental is to have only indirect results. Fundamental structures have always to be 'represented' or mediated (a term not wholly free of ambiguity), and the logic of this representation relation is not one of exact homology between real and perceived interest and between interest and acts. It is through this conceptual space/gap–between class interest and concrete action–that interpretative explanations come to assume great significance in Marxist theory. It is due to this non-homologous relation that the presumptions of reductionism are false. For representation is not a relation of expressiveness, as if representatives of classes are related to them the way spokemen at news conferences are related to parties. Nor is it that the 'representatives' cannot make up their minds until the class does. The relation between them, on the contrary, goes the other way round. It is basically an area of a critical overlap between individual decisions that is called a class's mind on a particular issue. Classes rarely take decisions in a simple sense, and what is called its mind is something that can only be retrospectively posited. Structures are, then, the names we give to the regularities of relations and effects which the actual behaviour of men and institutions exhibit in history.

Those who analyse politics often find, however, that the complexities of actual situations are not analysable through these two types of determining structures. They still leave an analytical residue. They are cut through by what are called the 'logic of situations'. The precise way in which historical circumstances combine, of course, have an effect on how cleanly the logic of determination can work: But what are called situations, can work in two ways. They can close off options which under normal circumstances, would have been open to actors; or, contrarily, open up choices that normally would not have existed. Thus, if the structual pressures are seen as being statistical, the way situations behave can be conceptualised through something like game theory.[37] Structural tendencies take long periods to mature or decline, but situational opportunities open and close.

Consequently, it is critical in political activity, not only to be right about what Marxists call the 'political line'—that is, a mapping of these structural tendencies with reference to one's place and preferences within it—but also about timing, that is, not to miss opportunities. A right line means a correct picture of the way structures are tending to move; right timing is to understand circumstantial openings of opportunities, which, if spurned, will soon close off. Compulsions of imperialist control over the rest of the world tend to weaken over time. Classes crystallise or decline in Braudelian long rhythms. Situational logic, critical for both political enquiry and political action, is the realm of opportunities, response and anticipated response. It is the understanding of this that is called statesmanship, and historical materialism does not stop its adherents from distinguishing between statesmen and ordinary politicians with higher rates of mortality. Use of structure-related notions, therefore, does not rule out the use of judgements about opportunities. These cannot assume the conceptual functions of one another. In Gramsci's prison notes in particular, one finds an implied suggestion that to be complete, a Marxist political theory must supplement an analysis of structures by analyses of situations—a suggention that has been little explored.[38] Reductivism implies, on the contrary, that one can deduce political acts from structural horizons. This is misleading, and utterly impoverishes the conceptual complexity of the political theory of Marxism. From the identification of a mode of production, the stage of growth of a social form, the extent of coalescence of the economic-corporate life of classes, from a reference to what Gramsci calls 'refractory realities', it is possible to infer not the actions which must follow, but the range in which they are most likely to happen. The language is not one of imperatives. The logic of determination is a logic of probability.

Structures and Agency

Political analysis within Marxism can take two very different forms. One form, the one that I prefer, would use this probabilistic concept of determination symmetrically, as holding between all levels of social or political reality. And it would naturally follow that if this is the relation between classes and parties, it would admit of a similar relation between individual agents and structures of various kinds. By going for a harder order of determination, out of positivistic delusions, reductionism slides into indefensible generalisations about historical or political causality. The entire point of the foregoing critique of Althusser, however, was to clear some room for reintroduction of some concepts of intentionality within Marxist political theory.

Once more, this is not something new, only not adequately remembered. I have argued before that this was precisely Marx's project, to transcend the sterile dichotomy between positivistic and hermeneutic notions of a social science. This project is clearly announced in the critical *Theses on Feuerbach*, which is the true 'work of the break' in Marx. *The German Ideology*, as Althusser observes, shows the first results of the philosophical reconstitution of his problematic. But it is the *Theses on Feuerbach*, which shows Marx at the experiment. After all, the reason for the preference of underdetermination over overdetermination was that this helped avoid objectivist notions of contradiction (or structures), and made room for interpretative origins of individual acts. It places the concept of interpretation *within* the concept of determination. If determination in history is underdetermination, that is, a combination of constraints which agents in history do not necessarily register (but these are not non-violent things. If actors do not register them, they wreak their vengeance by arranging to ruin the actors' projects), it allows us to reintroduce a concern for agency, and as its precondition, interpretation.

Collective actions are often averages made out of individual actions, but these are what Durkheim called 'social facts'. All qualities of individual actions are not transferable to collective acts; what these lack is precisely the immediacy of meanings that individual projects have. Perhaps, the main distinction between individual actions and what we regard as a collective endeavour is that one cannot attribute simple intentionalities to them. Meanings always attach, to use a Diltheyan phrase, to the 'insides' of actions, and only individual acts can properly be said to have an 'inside'. To go further, one might say that meanings are proper not to acts, but to projects, if acts are taken to denote a stage in the life of the project at which it has already moved out into the world, from the precincts of a purely private intentionality. Meanings, in this sense, can never be unintended. It is useful to deploy Goldmann's distinction between meaning and significance, to indicate the difference between what the author meant to do, and what others took him to have meant, or did with his actions. So, while speaking of class action at the level of institutions or structures, it is misleading to use meaning- related terms. Class actions cannot have meanings, only objectives that can be ascribed to them, after prefacing this by a sufficiently complex argument about structural coincidence of interests. Collective actions are real (because it does not follow from the argument above, that having meanings is the only mode of an action's being real), and they bear significance. The analytic unification that the concept of significance achieves, is external, through somebody else's criteria and act of judgement (ususlly *ex post*), not the actor's own. Actions carry meanings for their subjects, and significance for all others including historians. But significance does not make meanings dissolve; in my view, they simply do not compete as concepts. They occupy two different floors in the explanatory model for social action.[39]

The logic of both kinds of structures is mediated by interpretative acts, through the peculiarly individual faults of individual craftsmanship of meanings by way of which men arrange their relations with the political world. It is in this sense that one must admit an irreducibility of the acts of individual agents, if Marxist analysis of either politics or culture is to be realistic, and not to legislate how the worlds of politics or culture ought to be. Of course, it is men who act, and who must act before classes and other abstractions can act through them. Since these august entities must depend on them, individual actions must assume some priority in the simple sense that these must happen before we can say that through them other more complicated things can. In quite the same way, reasons can claim priority over causes. The other things simply have no way of happening by themselves, but can happen only through these happenings. In politics, men react not to objectively given situations, but to what they consider their situations to be, by means of options which they think are open to them. At both levels, there can be suboptimal decisions. Individuals may have faulty pictures of the way they are placed, or correct pictures of their location but faulty notions of what this entails. They may have a picture of their options that is larger or narrower than what they really are. Practical options are, as a rule, narrower than logical ones, but they are hardly ever so narrow that the analyst (historian) can legitimately bracket interpretative considerations altogether, and can say that whatever way the act came into existence, we shall study only what came of it–its 'after', not its 'before'. It is my general contention that projects are constitutive of acts; they are not things which easily allow such subtracting operations without altering their conceptual values in critical ways. The abbreviation does not really imply that we set out to study. The abbreviation alters it subtly, and gives us something which looks exactly like what we set out to study, but actually is not.

The only way interests can translate themselves into acts is through interpretative understanding, through purposes men posit and meanings men confer on their actions. In this sense, the bifurcation of meanings and interests, and the widespread belief that an explanation in terms of interests can displace one in terms of meanings, appears rather odd. For, it is precisely interests which implicate the sphere of meanings; a pre-interpreted interest is an extraordinarily unhelpful concept. This does not take away from some of the durable distinction between real and perceived interests. People's judgement about their own interests can be shown occasionally to be faulty, but as they remain, nonetheless, real judgements observers of society have to take account of them and make sense of them. They must be given at least as much explanatory significance as the others, for here, paradoxically, it is the 'correct' judgements which have the status of counter-factuals.[40] It is not very suggestive, for instance, to say that Hobbes 'failed' to articulate a bourgeois theory of the state on points X or Y, lacking a prior demonstration of his manifest obligations to have done so. But it does make sense to say that on points X or Y, Hobbes advanced ideas which did not fit into the 'ideal discourse' that can be ascribed (in Lukac's terms, 'imputed') to the bourgeois class, or the real discourse of liberalism which it came to develop historically.

What is thus called an ideal discourse may not square with any actual discourse of an actual bourgeoise. Yet, in a sense, it can be more significant than actual ones, because it can plot the common ground covered by all of them–something close to Foucault's discursive unconscious, or Dilthey's alphabet. By its very nature, this is something that can be seen by the historian, a kind of judgement that can only be made *ex post*. On this argument, Hobbes' theories would be seen as contributing to the conceptual or argumentative alphabet (= resources), through which the bourgeoisie was later to 'think' about the state and allied problems of power, to undermine feudal political discourse, to justify its own claims to legitimate political authority, to try to circumscribe and limit dissidence, by constructing around its social position the astonishingly resilient of ideas. Hobbes, or Locke. or Harrington, did not 'reflect' a mystical thing called the bourgeoisie's views about the state. What they proposed, individually, as reasonable ways of looking at political power, coincide with the parts of the ideal discourse, and helped fashion the rising bourgeoisie's intellectual resources. Instead of the bourgeoisie constituting their discourse, they should be seen as constituting through their theories, the discourse-like thing which we can ascribe to the bourgeoisie.

A possible objection to this argument could be that since social analysis is about behaviour of collectivities–groups, classes, institutions, etc., and as these are all subject to what Lange called the law of large numbers, individual interpretative nuances must cancel each other out statistically. Thus, it could be claimed, it is possible to return to a non-interpretative case. On this view, interpretative aspects of actions would not be denied, but rendered epistemically unimportant. Through the refinements of the notion of over-determination, Althusser achieves this kind of a 'softening' of structural rigidities. A different and preferable way would turn Althusser's argument round on this point as well: to state that intentionalities give rise to actions, which slip out of the agents' control, and give rise through their unintended consequences over a long term, to what we abstractly term structures. These, grown strange and external, constrain further intentional acts, even of positing intentions. Structures and intentions are then seen as being internally related.

Sartre correctly saw the origin of all human acts in intentionality, but wrongly concluded that the conceptual problem this gave rise to could be solved by inserting into a Marxist theory of the social process, unreconstructed hermeneutic notions taken from Heidegger's philosophy. But here, Althusser's objection that transfer of a concept from one context to another must alter its meaning, would apply. The very act of taking them out of historicist phenomenology must do something to their conceptual values. It is proper to try to generate within Marxism, concepts which could cover the same ground, to cover the phenomenologists' concerns. What this requires is not a theory of intentionality. Of course, this will deal with those things in the world with which the phenomenologist of the hermeneutic theorist deals, but not the way he does. This is not to graft the solutions offered by hermeneutics to the quite other solutions of Marxism, a kind of federalism of philosophies. Historically, both hermeneutics and Marxism grew out of the decline of Hegelianism, their common precondition. Consequently, the two traditions share common concerns, reflected in a crucial overlap between their concepts: superstructure and objective mind; ideology/hegemony and collective representations; underlying structures and alphabets. As concepts, they are not interchangeable, for they presuppose very different assumptions. But they refer, from within different theoretical traditions, to similar areas of social reality.

Although a Marxist cannot accept the hermeneutic theorists' solutions, he cannot afford to neglect his problems.

One advantage of the Marxist theory is in its conception of itself as a science, and the room that it provides for internal conceptual experiments—an idea rooted in both the 'emptiness' of some of its concepts, and the corrigibility implicit in the claim to being a science. It has an ability to subsume within itself, critical hypotheses generated within other traditions, without losing its internal coherence. In political analysis, one can use both notions of causes and reasons, or meaning and significance, instead of looking for a dissolution of either of these.

Do revolutions happen through a convergence of reasons, or of causes? It would appear odd to suggest that a historian can do systematically without one of these two notions in his business of explaining actual events in history. The idea of 'class consciousness', particularly of the type that can come only 'from outside', implies that it is of some importance to supply people with reasons to act for, or acquiesce in, a revolutionary initiative. But that does not stop Marxists from believing, entirely without contradiction, that revolutions happen due to the operation of causes; that existence of those causes make men prone to accept the reasons. Causes, again, would stand in the row of second order concepts. The two concepts are not exclusive or contradictory. The notion of reasons captures features of political life, which the notion of cause cannot. Conversely, the idea of cause is not merely a statistical average of the reasons men have, or their simple accumulation.

It is a common experience of those who look for political explanation that both voluntarist and determinist models soon run into difficulty. Their difficulties tend to come from opposite directions. Objectivist models of political explanation, in trying to account for crucial decisions–their forms and timing–have to admit that intentionality is often of critical significance in historical occurrences. No historical law obliged the Bolshevik party to decide to attempt a revolution on the dawn of exactly the seventh of November. Though it was just as true, that this took place within a causal horizon. Agency makes possible the translation of objective possibility into an actual occurrence. Conversely, attempted accounts of history, in purely rational terms, must get involved in problems of the reverse type. For history is, in large part, an unintended story, or intentions gone out of control. Every unintended consequence must, however, have as its logical counterpart an intended occurrence which failed to come off. Historical accounts may justifiably transcend these intents in the larger process of explaining, but they must begin from them.

I wish to suggest that Marx's model of political explanation, properly understood, tries to render this dichotomous discourse of political theory redundant. I think it is crucial for a reconstruction of Marx's theoretical project to see the three dichotomies he tried to transcend. These were: the dichotomies between materialist and idealist philosophies; between positivist and hermeneutic notions of science; and between determinism and indeterminism (voluntarism) in explaining politics. These dichotomies are mutually connected.

Among the modern forms of political theory, the Leninist form of Marxism tries, most tenaciously, to avoid a relapse into traditional dichotomies. Part of the reason for this lies in the peculiar structure of this theory, the dual role in which it places its adherents. Marxists try to combine in themselves the roles other theorists ususlly keep distinct–the roles of observer and actor. Thus, the criterion of praxis holds such a central place in Marxist social epistemics. As historians, Marxists cannot ignore the rather well-known fact that intentions have a way of eluding the control of actors, and becoming, through unintended consequences, remarkably like natural occurrences. As actors in history with strong preferences, they must work against this eventuality, and try to stop history from doing what they know it usually does. They must try to arrange one of those rare occurrences in which intentions, of at least some actors, will bear a reasonably symmetric relation with outcomes; or in which the collective intention of a particular group can adjust effectively to this fugitive quality of events, so that even though they are not mechanically in control, they still have a general grasp over its drift. Eventually, of course, they may be in control in the mildly paradoxical sense that they may have made a revolution, but not the one they wanted. 'Successful' revolutions seem to happen that way, and 'making' them with whatever premediation, must involve a grasp of the contending logics of a variety of structures—of what they disallow, of what they leave open, of how the opportunities in the short term open and close.

This is one way of arranging an adequation between the

way events occur and the conceptual structure of Marxist political theory. Events happen through a process which arranges, orders, restricts, narrows, hurries, delays–but never quite excludes choice. The agony of the choice between determinism and indeterminism is avoided if we simply refuse to make it–by sticking, instead, to a relatively simple conceptual point. Structure scan determine the agency without destroying it, and the agency can exist without laws of history collapsing all around us, if determination is seen as underdetermining outcomes, as an excluding, negative concept. This would save us from sliding into the two counter-intuitive worlds which constantly threaten political analyses–a world which knows no structures, or a world which knows of no choice.

ENDNOTES

1. Recently, several forms of this move have peen tried out. One of the most influential was Althusser's views about structural causality and overdetermination, a theory discussed below. The other significant move is presented in G.A. Cohen's *Karl Marx's Theory of History: A Defence*, Oxford, 1978. Some of the issues arising out of this work were discussed in reviews by Elster and a reply by Cohen in Political Studies, 1980, I. A more pessimistic view is held out in Terrell Carver, *Marx's Social Theory*, Oxford, 1983, who regards the thesis of determination in the last instance as nothing more than a research hypothesis. This seems to me weaken the proposition too much, while the real need is for a reworking of its common reading. A similar statement is found in Ralph Miliband, *Marxism and Politics*, Oxford, 1977, p. 8. 'There remains', according to Miliband, 'in Marxism an insistence on the "primacy" of the "economic base" which must not be understated. This "primacy" is usually taken by Marxists, following Engels, as meaning that the "economic base" is decisive, or determining, "in the last instance". But it is much more apposite and meaningful to treat the "economic base" as a starting point, as a matter of the first instance.' This, of course, is possible; and Miliband's interpretation makes it more likely by suggesting that 'Marx's own cast of mind was strongly anti-determinist.' On this reading, the matter becomes identical with treating the thesis as a research hypothesis, in Carver's terms.

(Terrell Carver *Marx's Social Theory*, Oxford, 1983.) But there seems to be one in appositeness to this procedure. Statements about the last instance, right or wrong, are presumably about the way things happen in history; the first instance proposition, must, however, be a matter of explanation, of how these things are sought to be understood. Surely, in the first case, there is a latent expectation of symmetry between the structure of the historical process and the structure of the explanatory form. But it seems difficult to take the second (the first instance proposition) as about the historical process.

2. I have used these terms here advisedly. Of course, causes have consequences, not corollaries, But this is to indicate an oddity that lies inside deterministic Marxism. Political events may indeed be seen as being caused by economic ones; but this, taken in a strict sense leads to paradoxes. 'Hard' uses of the base-superstructure idea tend to see political events as something close to corollaries. For economic causes have economic effects too, and political consequences must be seen as being more secondary in some sense. Strictly speaking, therefore, deterministic Marxism contains an ambiguity about the relation between the economic and the political behind its appearance of decisiveness and clarity. Ironically, however, this apparent clarity is the main reason behind its appeal. What appears clear when it is allowed to talk in metaphor, appears much less so when a clear logical account is asked for.
3. All this still does not open up the endlessly contentious question, what kind of creatures are what we term 'the economic, the political', etc.? Surely, this is not a trivial question. The entire philosophic tradition of Marxism is implicitly divided on this question. Some regard the concept of totality in Marxism as a structure stretched over planes and levels; others, like Korsch and Lukacs deny that the dialectical category of totality can be so split. except according to the shifting contingencies of argument. Despite Lukacs's well-known hostility to Weber, his view on this question seems fairly close to Weber's discussions in *Methodology of the Social Sciences*, New York, 1949.
4. I do not pretend that this question can be solved in the simplified manner in which it is presented here. Here, only those minimal propositions are presented which are necessary for making my case.
5. After he announced his intention of developing a transcending

discourse in the *These on Feverbach* (1845), Marx consistently pursued it. But in later discussions this is implied, rather than stated in such dramatic declarations of intent.

6. I think it can be argued that what is true about political statements is also true about doing things in politics. The bureaucratic and occasionally tyrannical deformations of the socialist idea that one finds in the real world, and the usual rationalisations of such systems are results of doing or seeing political life through such fragmented categories. It is particularly due to the fact that the values of equality and liberty are allowed to be seen in zero-sum terms. This relation is implied not only by conventional critics of say Soviet society, but equally by its conventional defenders. Marxists often go into disputes about moral questions, and take up and defend their positions in a language that does not allow them to do it properly, because the theoretical and value syntax of this discourse is different and uncongenial. Consequently, they are obliged to misrepresent their ideal in the very act of defending them. Too often Marxists, in debating moral evaluation of societies, allow themselves to be put a question like: Which do you hold primary: liberty or equality? Which obliges them to answer 'equality'. They ought to say in such cases that the question ought to be reconstituted, and given an historical form. If they answer that question in that form, they make a tactical mistake, giving their critics an ineradicable advantage. Historically, of course, it is clear that the two contending societies are not amenable to such simple moral descriptions. Capitalist societies are not realms of untramelled freedom; just as there are obvious limits to equality in historical socialist societies. Indeed, the best course in such debates seems to be the one Marx suggests in the *Critique of the Gotha Programme* (1875)—to register the deformities in socialist societies, but retaining a historical optimism about their correction. The defence then has to be done in quite other terms. Instead of pretending, or what is worse, believing that these societies are perfect, one believes that they are historically perfectible.
7. This is similar to the sense in which philosophers use the terms. To use an example from Husserl: looking at a row of houses at the end of a field, one can specify the determinate characteristics of the front of the second house from the left: but one's idea of its back must remain empty. One knows that a house must have a back, with specific determinations, but it must remain

unspecified.

8. Althusser pursued some of these ambiguities in the 'Appendix' to 'Contradiction and Overdetermination', *For Marx*, London, 1969, pp. 117-28.
9. This refers to that wonderful passage at the start of *Behemoth*, in which, instead of introducing a metaphor of fast and slow, which is inherently confusing when used about time, Hobbes uses the deliberately inappropriate metaphor of high and low. The first is confusing because time, or time consciousness, can be said to be fast or slow. Use of the other metaphor, since time cannot be naturally high or low alerts one to the metaphorical status of the reasoning. One wishes all metaphors in social discourse were used with such discretion, so scrupulously or that such little danger signals,were built into all of them.
10. *History and Class Consciousness*, London, 1968.
11. Althusser's phrase, used about the concept of alienation.
12. As an Indian, I find one example irresistible. After Indian Independence, Soviet Marxists dismissed Nehru as an agent of imperialism and a representative of a comprador bourgeoisie. After a few years he came to be celebrated as a heroic builder of non-capitalist society, a change unrelated to any major alterations of policy on Nehru's part. It was a purely conceptual revolution.
13. Marx, *Poverty of Philosophy*, Moscow, 1973.
14. *For Marx*, op. cit., 117 ff.
15. Max Weber, *Methodology of the Social Sciences*, op. cit., pp. 41-46 and 92ff, which makes the suggestion that 'Marxian laws are ideal-typical'.
16. Althusser, 'On the Materialist Dialectics', *For Marx*, op. cit.
17. Ibid., p. 202.
18. This involves an interesting problem, but one too large to be taken up here. The language of the 'last instance' implies a reference to an idea which is more often discussed in non-Marxist literature. Can one say, with some kind of explanation, that one has reached a kind of rock bottom, that this explanation cannot be further explained? Charles Taylor associates this with pre-Galilean science, and demarcates the natural science theories from social science theories of purpose by this division. Natural science theories from social science theories of purpose by this division. Natural science explanations always leave room for further possible explanations of the same phenomenon, by reference to a finer, or still more basic, element. What

distinguishes explanations by purpose is that after such an explanation is given, it leaves no room for anything more to be said. The two notions of explanation underlying the two types of Marxist theory, ironically make very similar claims to the effect that nothing can be said after these. But they do it in very different ways. The last instance idea, obviously, hints at this; but because it believes social reality can be divided between levels, and because, in its view, no more fundamental level can be dicovered than the economic level. Althusser's redescriptivism also implies that there cannot be a more basic explanation, because a condition for an explanation must be a complete account. And if it is complete, nothing could be added to it. See the discussion in Charles Taylor, *Explanation of Behaviour*, London, 1964, pp. 21-25.

19. *For Marx*, op. cit., p. 202.
20. Althusser and Balibar, *Reading Capital*, London, 1970, pp. 178-81.
21. Ibid; Chapter 9 *passim.*
22. It is significant that some of Althusser's followers have been pushed by his arguments (or perhaps certain readings of it) into declaring finally that there cannot be any predeterminate primacy that can be ascribed to any single level of the social totality. Hindess and Hirst, *Mode of Production and Social Formation*, London, 1977, p. 5. It is of course difficult to ascertain what these post-Althusserians believe about any serious question, due to the frequency of their autocritiques.
23. Nicos Poulantzas. *Political Power and Social Classes*, London, 1973: Goran Therborn, *What Does the Ruling Class Do When It Rules*, London. 1978; Ernesto Laclau, *Politics and Ideology in Marxist Theory*, London, 1978.
24. I do not mean that concepts from interpretative sociology should be grafted on to Marxist theory, but that Marxists ought to try to generate concepts which would be able to take in interpretative elements of behaviour, instead of trying to bracket them.
25. Althusser. *Lenin and Philosophy and Other Essays*, London, 1971.
26. The most powerful contemporary argument against this is, of course, Gadamer, *Truth and Method*, London, 1975.
27. E.H. Carr's exposition of 'determinism' in history is exactly in these terms, though he is not interested in doing it formally. *What is History*?, New York, 1962.
28. Althusser observes this point in *For Marx*, op. cit., p. 106.

29. T.D. Weldon, *Vocabulary of Politics*, Harmondsworth, 1953.
30. Gilbert Ryle, *The Concept of Mind*, 1949 (1980), pp. 18 ff.
31. Ibid., pp. 17-18.
32. This does not imply that classes do not exist if they are not registered in a conceptual definition. Rather, what the concept of class would include, and what it can do in explanation, would depend substantially on how it is defined.
33. This is related to the point made at the beginning of the paper– about some untidiness of expression in Marxist political analyses. This kind of unclarity may be called, after Ryle, 'systematically misleading' expressions. Ryle says:

    > There are many expressions in non-philosophical discourse which, though they are perfectly clearly understood by those who use them and those who hear or read them, are nevertheless couched in grammatical or syntactical forms which are in a demonstrable way improper to the states of affairs they record (or the alleged states of affairs which they profess to record).

    Many political propositions of Marxism would fall under this kind of stricture. However, Ryle's belief that those who read them understand them perfectly, seems to me rather optimistic: Often they lead to confusion, ambiguity or misleading consensus (that is, when two people believe that they agree because they have supported the same proposition, but actually they hold different versions of it). A recent controversy in Indian Marxist historiography comes to mind. Two historians of peasant politics disagreed about the extent of 'autonomy' of peasant political action. Actually, however, the debate remained unclear eventually, because it was not clear whether they differed about terms or about facts of history. It appears that Chatterjee means by dominance a consequence proposition, while Alam means by the same term, a characterisation of origin. Quite often, standard Marxist propositions about politics can be interpreted very differently. For instance, when we say class is dominated, or class X undertakes an act, what we mean (or should mean) is not that the class is the direct actor, but that it is the principal beneficiary. From this point of view, then, to treat these propositions as relating to origins of acts is misleading: they can be suggestive only if they refer to consequences, but sometimes their grammatical form may indicate a reference to origins. It follows from this, however, that the consequences of this sort of 'error' may not be as innocuous as Ryle thought.

34. The debates about C.B. Macpherson's interpretation of English political thought of the 17th century brought out some of these points quite clearly. Some of the basic objections raised by John Dunn against Macpherson's procedures appear to me to be justified, as also Quentin Skinner's more general objections to reductionist Marxism. Their criticism against Macpherson is right, but against Marxism wrong. For, in much of their criticisms they assume that Marxist interpreters of political thought must ascribe discourses to collective entities like classes, while this seems to be not necessarily true. The work of Lucien Goldmann on Pascal and Racine follows methodological rules and even research procedures that are fairly comparable to their own (except of course a more indirect ascription to class). Clearly, their criticism of prolepsis in interpretation is closely parallel to Althusser's discussions on how to study the philosophy of the young Marx. In my view, their criticisms of Macpherson are well judged, but their view of what Marxist theory allows to an interpreter is too restrictive and wrong. Cf. John Dunn, *The Political Thought of John Locke*, Cambridge, 1968; Quentin Skinner, 'Meaning and Understanding in the History of Ideas', *History and Theory*, 1969; Lucian Goldmann. *The Hidden God*, London, 1964; Althusser, *For Marx*, op. cit.
35. On the view presented here, Locke does not have the responsibility of thinking the bourgeoisie's thoughts for it. One can retain all the specific peculiarities of Locke's ideas, ranging from ontology to toilet training, and still relate it to the 'discourse' in history of particular classes. In fact, here too it might be a case of what can be plausible as a statement about consequences becoming vulnerable when made about intent.
36. This is, stated another way, the central problem about Macpherson's interpretation of English political thought of the 17th century. It is worth noting that his argument about liberal democracy, since it is about an aggregate and not an individual doctrine, has drawn fewer criticisms of inappropriateness. Two types of objections were being made about his procedure. 1. It was doubted whether such direct relations could be established between ideas and behaviour of large groups. 2. It was objected that such general discourses, related to stable interests (that is assuming that the answer to the first question is positive), could not be attributed to individuals. Individuals create theories with meanings; these may come to have a different kind of historical

significance. One way of solving this problem can be Goldmann's suggestion of using the two concepts of meaning and significance, as being proper to individual and collective subjects. Goldmann, *Lukacs and Heidegger*, London, 1974; and *Cultural Creation*, Oxford, 1977.

37. This obviously does not mean that game theory will be able to provide miraculous explanations of political processes, but simply that, within the interstices of long-term and large-scale analyses, there can be room for a purely formal account of how strategies can be worked out. Quite often, the mistrust of Marxists against formal techniques is misplaced. The fault usually lies not with the techniques, but of too large expectations placed on them. There is something very odd about the view that something must be wrong about the techniques rather than the way they are used.
38. Antonio Gramsci, *Selections from Prison Notebooks*, London, 1971, p. 181.
39. Goldmann, *Lukacs and Heidegger*, op. cit., Chapter 4 passim.
40. Though this manner of speaking is quite common in Marxist analyses of culture, I think it is misleading to say that someone failed to represent the views of a social class. The idea of being a 'faulty', or incomplete representative, actually gives the argument away. It implies, first, that the worldview of a class is an existent in a straightforward sense. It does not state that this is necessarily a logical posited idea, something that can be, or needs to be created by the synthesising imagination of the historian. The oddity of the argument lies in the suggestion of something like a prior obligation of a theorist to represent some class which, still more oddly, possesses clear and decisive cultural preferences, such that the theorists can reflect them. On most of these points, Dunn's criticism of Macpherson is suggestive. However, it is not necessarily the case that when a Marxist refers to an author as bourgeois, he is one the Marxist 'greatly dislikes'. Cf. Dunn, *Political Thought of John Locke*, op. cit., p. 205. On the contrary, the ideas they contain are, more often than not, seen as progressive ideas in their age. Consequently, the author is given a kind of approval, if somewhat patronisingly.

2

Politics—The Dialectics of Science and Revolution in Karl Marx

Randhir Singh

Taking off from the specific and limited, but very rigorously argued exercise of Sudipta Kaviraj's paper, I shall confine my hurried response to making a few points very briefly on the interrelated issues of Marxism, politics and 'explaining politics'. Nothing original and necessarily general in nature, these points can still bear being restated here for their relevance, albeit a bit rambling, to the theme of this seminar and also to certain 'empty spaces', as it were, in Kaviraj's argument.

Let me state at the very outset that, the finer points of his argument apart, I am in sympathy with Kaviraj's main position, though I would have preferred to have it expressed in a more direct and straightforward manner. However, his is essentially an analytical, or clarificatory exercise, which offers but limited *substantive* help towards sorting out the problem of what he has chosen to describe as 'political explanation in Marxism.' (I am not even sure if this is a happy phrasing of the problem, from a strictly Marxian standpoint.)

Now, in whatever manner one describes or phrases this problem, a discussion in this area needs—among other considerations like the unfinished nature of Marx's theoretical work (especially as it affects politics), the intellectual ethos of his time, what he was arguing with or against, etc.—to take notice of two positions in Marxism, which are also integral to each other. These are Marx's absolute Promethean conception of man ('free, conscious activity is man's species character')[1] and his lifelong commitment to revolution (a 'man of science ...Marx was before all else a revolutionist'–Engels).[2] One implication is obvious. Marx's scientific project, the explanatory exercise, I suggest, fully accommodates these positions and thus leaves different areas of human activity, including politics, that are often loosely defined as 'non-economic' or 'non-material', relatively open and unpredetermined, in a manner as to be not entirely amenable to *lawlike* generalisations, to *scientific explanation* as it is properly understood.

Marx's scientific project was focused on understanding the society he wanted to overthrow. It is a reconstruction of the way capitalism as a system arises, functions and develops, and prepares the necessary, though not sufficient, objective conditions for the transition to a higher, more rational form of society, a communist society. In this scientific/explanatory enterprise, Marx's method is a model of the practice of materialist dialectics. Thus, the key concepts in his social-scientific theory involve viewing society as a whole, as a *totality* (complex and differentiated, a historically specific structured interdependence of parts), which is marked by the predominance, in the long run, of one part within it, the economy ('the mode of production', and more precisely, the *economic structure*), and which is characterised by *contradictions* (principal or structural, and other equally specific secondary ones within and between the various parts), that account for its dynamics, its concrete *over-determined* historical development. Even as he emphasised the special role of the economy, 'the direct relationship of the owners of the conditions of production to the direct producers... which holds the innermost secret, the hidden foundation of the entire social structure'[3]—without which Marxism would be theoretically indistinguishable from any other 'sociology'–and, more specifically, sought to lay bare 'the economic law of motion' of capitalism. Marx aimed at achieving through 'successive approximations' from different perspectives, a 'mirrored' version of the concrete reality of capitalist social formation as a whole. It is part of the story of

Marx's unfinished project that, concerned with all of capitalism, he lived long enough to view it only from the vantage point of capitalist economics (even that incompletely).

A fuller version or understanding would require that it be viewed from the vantage points of other parts also, of capitalist politics, ethics, culture, etc. Therefore, Marxian explanation of politics requires that, as against the fragmented and surface studies of contemporary political science, the problems of this area be handled in such a way as to illuminate the character of the capitalist system (including its politics) as a whole, in all its structured interconnections and movements—the whole shaping and expressing itself through the parts, and the parts—even as they represent and bear the signature of the whole—constituting, in their inter-relatedness, the specific unity that makes it a whole, *the* whole and no other. This goes for the study of any given social formation. For Marxism 'the truth is the whole',[4] as Hegel put it; and in Marxism, as Marx insisted, one seeks to move from 'appearance' to 'the nature of things'.[5] Such is the cardinal methodological thrust behind Marxism's social scientific enterprise, its search for dialectical knowledge as against positivist science.

This Marxist approach or perspective avoids the major *empiricist error* and the minor *holist error* characterising most contemporary writing on politics within the discipline of political science and outside. The former error, found typically on the Right, lies in grasping things only in their appearance and isolation, while the latter error, found typically on the Left, lies in missing out on the richness of the mediations that constitute the whole. Though not written as exercises in social science scholarship, one could draw attention in this connection to what are now rightly recognised as the *political* writings of Karl Marx: *The Class Struggles in France, The Civil War in France*, etc., and above all, *The Eighteenth Brumaire of Louis Bonaparte* which is a model, as it were, of the treatment of politics in Marxism. Here we have, along with a wealth of other insights, Marx's. full recognition and masterly exposition, in a Marxian perspective, that is, within the objective conditions structurally constituted by the prevalent mode of production, of the realm of the political, of the class struggle at the level of politics– at a particular juncture in the history of France. Though one must add that just as Marx's proposed work on the state never came to be written, Marx's treatment of politics, as of the realm of the non-economic in general, remained largely *untheorised* by him.

In this context, the phrase 'relative autonomy of politics', its value against economic and class reductionism apart, could be more misleading than helpful in understanding or explaining politics in a given social formation: it easily tends to give rise to mutually reinforcing empiricist and liberal-reformist errors. On the other hand, 'relative autonomy of the state' is a meaningful concept, denoting as it does the state's possible autonomy in a particular historical situation, from any given class or classes, economically dominant or otherwise. However, the state is not autonomous from the socio-econoimic structure of a class-divided society which it essentially serves. The state remains, always, the organiser of society in the interests of the class (exploitative) structure as a whole.[6]

Marx's scientific and revolutionary projects are not merely interconnected, they grow into each other, and together they put politics at the centre of social practice for our times. At least that is how Marx understood it, and one may legitimately note a divergence between Marxism as Marx himself practised it, and a certain kind of contemporary Marxist scholarship. Given a Marxist understanding of the structured nature of the totality and of the crucial role in it of 'the economy', any fundamental, revolutionary change in a society involves as a necessary, though not sufficient, condition, a changing of its economic structure, of its real basis—if I may, contrary to fashion and in a confession of 'orthodoxy' still use that much-maligned concept. Hence the centrality of politics as revolution in Marx. ('Revolution is the highest form of class struggle'.)[7] In this sense, the sense in which 'Marx was, before all else, a revolutionist', politics, not economics, has primacy in Marxism. And the obvious corollary is that in the absence of this revolutionary politics changing the structural base of society, the logic of this base shall assert itself, all politics will remain superstructural in its essential character and outcome. This is the basic, a determined and determining choices occur. Such is the dialectics of the economy and politics in the social science of Karl Marx.

Viewed thus, the political as a whole is the realm of the contingent, of historical conjunctures and changing balance of social forces, a realm of *real* choices and possibilities; and for that very reason devoid of the certainties and predictabilities that politics as 'social science' seeks. Yet, as suggested earlier, these choices and possibilities arise and exist *within* the necessities and constraints of the given objective situation, above all, the economic-structural situation, which sets their context, outer limits and parameters. The economic defines, as it were, the terrain, the 'conditions of existence', and the horizon of the non-economic. including the political. Though, it must again be stressed, it does not in a direct, or reductionist manner determine it. This determination, insofar as we must use the term, is far more complex and problematic, achieved through any number of mediations, horizontal, vertical and across each other. To put the argument differently, the superstructural instances, these parts or levels of the uneven and differentiated unity that a social formation is, along with the contradictions that characterise them, are not some immediate or epiphenomenal manifestations of the economic-structural base. On the contrary, they have, each one of them, an autonomous, irreducible, and historically specific existence. But this is an existence of dialectical, determined and determining, relationship to each other and the whole. And the dynamics of this existence, the working out of their contradictions, is ultimately and most decisively conditioned by the structural logic of the given mode of production, and the basic contradiction that constitutes it. Thus, whatever happens, every complex historical effect or outcome, is 'overdetermined' in the Althusserian sense. As Marx himself put it: 'The concrete is the product of many determinations.'[8] Furthermore, for Marxism the working out of the structural necessity, the determination by the economic, is not unique. It is essentially a correspondence and, therefore, variable, For example, speaking of 'the political form of the sovereignty-dependency relationship', that is, 'the specific form of the state', Marx wrote: '...due to innumerable different empirical circumstances, natural conditions, relationships among races (tribes, & c.), outside historical influences, etc., the same economic basis– same in terms of the main conditions–can show endless variations and gradations in the phenomenon, which can be made out only by analysis of these empirically given circumstances.'[9]

It needs to be emphasised that Marxism is social science not for peers or for policy-makers; it is social science at the service of the people, the exploited and the oppressed. And, insofar as it seeks knowledge of a social formation as a whole, and recognises the decisive importance of its 'economic basis' or structural necessity, it carries with it the imperative, the other necessity, that Marxist political practice be revolutionary. It is not for nothing that Marx insisted: "The working class is revolutionary or it is nothing".[10]

It is true that there are problems with the theory and practice of Marxism as social science. But it is also true that most critiques of Marxism in this area are simply nihilistic. Notwithstanding the limitations and inadequacies, even ambiguities, and the unfinished nature of his theoretical work, Marx did open up the continent of social science. And Marxism has provided better knowledge concerning the structure and dynamics of social formations, particularly the capitalist social formation, than anything bourgeois social science has to offer. Equally important is Marxism's explicit assumption about the *growth* of human knowledge. As Engels put it: "The generations which will put us right are likely to be far more numerous than those whose knowledge we... are in a position to correct... The stage of knowledge which we have now reached is as little final as all that have preceded it."[11]

Pursuit of Marxism as 'science', especially during certain phases of historical development; does tend to produce a loss of revolutionary perspective, its replacement by a complacent concern with 'the historical necessity' at work in the social process. Such, for example, was the Marxism dominant in the Second International; 'irresistible'... natural necessity' having made socialism 'something inevitable, (Kautsky),[12] it simply turned its back on the other necessity, which is yet a free choice, namely, a revolutionary struggle for socialism. Lenin's repudiation of this Marxism was in the authentic tradition of Marx himsilf whose political theory and, still more, political practice throughout his life, never countenanced such deformation of Marxism into an evolutionist, deterministic metaphysics. At other times, a valid, Marxist recognition of the 'historically progressive' character of certain phenomena (men/women, movements, economic developments, etc.) has been deemed excuse enough to eulogise and extend support to them, in a manner as to go soft on the exploiting classes, even to the point of rallying behind them in the name of Marxism. Marx would have none of such political opportunism either. It was on this issue that he, along with Engels, broke publicly with the Lassalleans in Germany and later (1881), apropos Russia, spoke with unconcealed scorn of 'Russian capitalism admirers'.[13] (Apropos India, we may today well speak of 'Indian capitalism admirers', the apologists for 'progressive capitalism', 'independent capitalist development', 'self-reliant economic growth', 'independent economic/national development', etc.) Marx was always allergic to and contemptuous of such doctrinaire or, shall we say, 'scientific' Marxism. If Marx sought to discover the necessity underlying contemporary sociohistorical process, it was to establish the objective context or terrain of his political struggle, and to define its revolutionary thrust. And when he recognised the historical progressiveness of certain roles or developments, it was as *fait accompli*, without approval but with all their advantages and drawbacks, so as to make the best possible use of the new starting points or opportunities provided by them for the prosecution of his own political purpose, his uncompromising struggle aimed at overthrowing the system of exploitation and oppression that is capitalism—'progressive' or any other. In this sense, Marx's practice of science was always subject to the logic of his political position, of the choice he had already made in the fight between the people, and those who oppress and exploit them. And he had chosen to stand by the people. A political position for Marx was not a matter of scientific analysis—economic, or social, or historical. It was, always and above all, taking of sides in the ongoing class war.

To put the argument in more general terms, Marxism as science, seeks knowledge of the necessity underlying the historical process for enhancing the freedom for praxis, for not foreclosing but liberating human practice, for free choices by men, free not in some abstract or metaphysical sense, but in the only possible human sense, of men choosing and acting with the fullest possible knowledge and consideration of this necessity, the objective situation or circumstances. Such is the dialecties of men and science in Karl Marx. Moreover, it is of the nature of the structured and changing character of the social process that the relation between freedom and necessity, the ratio between them, varies from one period to another in the development of society. And taking everything into consideration, it seems to me that ours is preeminently an age of freedom, of revolutionary praxis. The alternative is mankind's rapid descent into another age of barbarism.

Within the framework of the reasonably adequate scientific generalisations that Marxism provides about the structure and dynamics of society (and which encompass State and politics also), and within the more limited range of the necessities and the possibilities of revolutionary and non-revolutionary practice of politics respectively, we can, given the requisite data and delicacy of analysis, still make more or less valid, historically specific, explanatory statements about what is generally seen and understood to be *politics*. (Incidentally, 'political scientists' are still having a lot of problems with defining the object of their learned attentions.) But this latter exercise possibly cannot add up to anything that can be legitimately called *science*. I have already suggested as much earlier on. To phrase it a little differently, in politics as elsewhere, men and their choices, all the diverse factors, elements, variables constituting, as it were, the subjective dimension of society, always a most vital part of social reality, are yet not calculable as the objective dimension is. In a famous passage, Marx himself drew attention to the *differing* amenability of the levels of base and *superstructure* in society to scientific treatment. Speaking of the historical transformations set off by the conflict between 'the material productive forces of society' and 'the existing relations of production', and involving 'the economic foundation' and 'the entire immense superstructure', Marx wrote: "In considering such transformations a distinction should always be made between the material transformation of the economic conditions of production, which can be determined with the precision of natural science, and the legal, political, religious aesthetic or philosophic—in short, ideological forms in which men become conscious of this conflict and fight it out."[14] Obviously, this fight and its outcome cannot be determined 'with the precision of natural science.' Elsewhere, even as he insists that 'the history of all hitherto existing society is the history of class struggle', Marx immediately points out that this struggle 'each time ended, either in a revolutionary reconstitution of society at large, or in the common ruin of the contending classes.'[15] There are, thus, no promises of inevitability or guarantees of victory in Karl Marx's politics, only *real* possibilities and *strong* probabilities. Men and women choose and act, but the outcome, the outcome of concrete historical class struggles, is not predetermined, cannot be predicted in advance, least of all with the certainty of natural science. Thus understood, the historical process, in a most meaningful sense, remains open, relatively undetermined. It shall be *ultimately* determined by the activity of men in pursuit of *their* purposes, an activity in which men continually seek to materialise their freedom. And it is quite possible and probable that some time, in ths course of this determination, politics itself shall wither away and with it, the need for explaining politics, scientifically or otherwise.

All this may sound rather dismal to those in the profession who, subject to the 'functional rationality' permeating the discipline, are committed to the search for 'a science of politics'.

But do we really want it to be otherwise? I think not. Especially so if freedom is indeed 'the essence of man' and if our prime commitment is for man, as indeed was the proud and passionate commitment of Marx, who spoke of "the categorical imperative to overthrow all conditions in which man is a humiliated, enslaved, despised and rejected being",[16] who laughed at 'the so-called "practical" men with their wisdom', and wrote: "If one chose to be an ox, one could turn one's back on the sufferings of mankind and look after one's own skin",[17] who, writing to an old friend, expressed his contempt for the philistines who 'consider people like you and me immature fools who all this time have not been cured of their evolutionary fantasies',[18] and who, even as he argued that while "people make their own history... they do not make it just as they please",[19] and always warned against utopianism and Blanquism in the movement, yet stood up magnificently in defence of the Paris communards for "storming heavens",[20] and scorned the socialists who "keep themselves within the limits of the logically presumable and of the permissible by the police..."[21]

I would like to conclude by pointing out, for whatever it is worth at this stage of the extreme 'specialisation', 'professionalisation' and 'vocationalisation' of the social science disciplines, that it is this commitment that gives its special quality to the scholarship of Karl Marx. Typical of this 'man of science', is his response to the news of the great run his theories were then having in Czarist Russia. On December 14, 1882, Karl Marx, old, sick and dying, wrote thus to his daughter Laura Lafargue: "Nowhere is my success more delightful to me; it gives me the satisfaction that I *damage* a power which, besides England, is the true bulwark of the old society" (italics added).

Yes, *damage* is the word. How much of even Marxist scholarship can claim this quality for itself today?[22]

REFERENCES

1. Karl Marx, *Economic and Philosophic Manuscripts of 1844*, Moscow, no date.
2. Frederick Engels, 'Speech at the Graveside of Karl Marx', in Franz

Mehring, *Karl Marx: The Study of His Life*, London, 1951.
3. Karl Marx, *Capital*, Vol. III, Chicago, 1909.
4. G.W.F. Hegel, *The Phenomenology of Mind*, Preface, London, 1949.
5. Karl Marx, *Capital*, op. cit.
6. See Hal Draper, *Karl Marx's Theory of Revolution*, Vols. I, II, III +, New York, 1977 +. This is possibly the most outstanding work to date on Marx's political theory, including his theory of the state.
7. Karl Marx. *The Poverty of Philosophy*, London, 1941.
8. Karl Marx. *Grundrisse*, Introduction, Harmondsworth, 1973.
9. Karl Marx, *Capital*, op. cit.
10. Karl Marx's letter to Frederick Engels, February 18, 1865.
11. Frederick Engels, *Anti-Duhring*, Moscow, 1965.
12. Quoted by Lucio Colletti in 'Bernstein and the Marxism of the Second International', *From Roussau to Lenin*, London, 1972.
13. Marx-Zasulich Correspondence in Teodor Shomin, *Late Marx and the Russian Road*, Part II, London, 1984.
14. Karl Marx, *A Contribution to the Critique of Political Economy*, Preface, Calcutta, no date.
15. Karl Marx and Frederick Engels, *Manifesto of the Communist Party*, Moscow, 1948.
16. Karl Marx, A Contribution to the Critique of Hegel's Philosophy of Right, Introduction, in *Early Writings*, London, 1975.
17. Karl Marx's letter to S. Meyer, April 30, 1867.
18. Karl Marx's letter to J.P.Becker, February 26, 1862.
19. Karl Marx, *The Eighteenth Brumaire of Louis Bonaparte*, Moscow, 1948.
20. Karl Marx's letter to L. Kugelmann, April 12, 1871; *The Civil War in France*, Moscow, 1971.
21. Karl Marx, *Critique of the Gotha Programme*, Moscow, 1947.
22. It is part of the sociology of Marxism that in recent years, so often, it has come to be reduced to a subject for academic study in the universities with strong fragmentist, scholastic and theoreticist deformations, or, as in the countries of 'actually existing socialism' and even elsewhere, to a legitimising ideology.

PART II
REMEMBRANCE

3

In Punjab's Villages: A Week with Randhir Singh

Harbans Mukhia

Perhaps in 1968 or thereabout in a village in Punjab: Professor Randhir Singh addressing the audience. Sitting (from left) unidentified, Comrade Sat Pal Dang, Bipan Chandra and Harbans Mukhia. Poster in the background: Shahid Bhagat Singh Samaroh. Source: Personal collection of Professor Singh's daughter, Professor Priyaleen Singh.

A great deal has been said and written about the towering intellectual stature of my teacher and comrade, Professor Randhir Singh as well as the inspiring mode of communicating his very radical ideas about the State and society to his students and whoever came in contact with him. I for one intend to focus here in this brief memoir on Professor Singh as a political activist, true to his lessons in the class. I happen to have been his student for a course on Political Theory, one of the eight papers for the M A degree in History at the University of Delhi in 1958-60. I had enrolled for the B A (Hons) and M A programmes at the Kirori Mal College where the abiding influence of the over-powering presence of the great historian and eminent Communist, Dr K M Ashraf, had already rubbed off on me deeply as it did on several generations of students. I was therefore all the more receptive to the lectures on Political Theory by Professor Singh. But Professor Singh touched everyone's mind and heart irrespective of their personal backgrounds.

Within a couple of months of obtaining my M A degree in 1960 with just about reasonable percentage, I was lucky to have landed a teaching position in my own K M College, a position incidentally vacated by Dr Ashraf who had gone on leave to be at Humboldt University in the then East Germany as a Visiting Professor. Thus began my entry into the teaching profession which was to last forty-four years. As a teacher, it brought me in closer interaction with Professor Singh and other renowned left faculty members of various Colleges and Institutes of Delhi University. While a motley group of leftist and even pretender leftist teachers was active, my association with Professor Singh and Professor Bipan Chandra was to last a long time. Professor Singh was at that time in Delhi College (Zakir Husain College) and Bipan Chandra was at the Hindu College. I too moved to Hindu College in 1967.

It is worth remembering that the period 1950s to 70s were remarkable in the global milieu when old imperialist structures were rapidly crashing to the forces of decolonisation, when new major 'revolutions' were seizing spaces as projected alternatives to the status quo regimes, and when superhuman figures like Gandhi and Mao Zedong and later on awe-inspiring leaders like Fidel Castro, Che Guevara and above all Ho Chi Minh were all inspirations of hope and change for a better, a more just world. The ideal of socialism as the end of exploitation of human beings for accumulation of more and more private profit had captured the imagination of the youth around the world. Movements of protest led by students on the campuses of the most advanced capitalist countries like the US and France had galvanised youth everywhere. There were high ideals in the air we breathed.

India had never been a socialist regime at any point of time, some measures of state control of the economy being projected as 'socialism' or the 'socialistic pattern' notwithstanding. For the twenty years or so after Independence, it had established a fairly stable regime of parliamentary politics, multi-party elections and a slow-growing economy. This was a remarkable achievement considering the long drawn freedom struggle and the trauma of Partition and displacement of several millions of people. But near the end of two decades, cracks and cleavages were beginning to show. A certain restlessness with the pace of growth and its inability to meet the growing needs of the people was finding utterance. The last straw came with the sudden price rise of daily necessities. Interestingly, protests originated at the India Coffee House located in the centre of Connaught Place in New Delhi, perhaps where the Palika Bazar is now located. This was where the Capital's intelligentsia, whose volubility was always in inverse relationship with the money in their pockets, hit by a suddenly announced raise in the price of coffee, formed a PRRM, Price Rise Resistance Movement. This was just a trigger. The movement began to spread wide and went far beyond the cup of coffee and the leisurely coffee drinkers. Soon it acquired an unorganised and uncoordinated political shape in anticipation of the elections which were due.

In 1967, with Indira Gandhi in power, the Congress lost all elections 'from Punjab to West Bengal' as it was salaciously proclaimed then, though of course the Congress was able to retain the Centre. The widespread popular anger against the Congress spread out a message to all on the other side that India was ready for a massive change. This was how the message was received by us on the Left. This is where the Naxalite experiment with the violent overthrow of the regime also had its origins. Some of the brightest students from the highest echelons of society, studying in the crème de la crème of elite institutions, Presidency College in Calcutta and St Stephen's in Delhi, were willing to forego their careers and even their lives for what for them constituted a high ideal of seeking to establish an egalitarian regime.

Professor Randhir Singh and Professor Bipan Chandra enthusiastically joined the CPI-M and apart from their teaching and research preoccupations were inspired to 'do more' for the revolution which appeared to be knocking on the door. I had an earlier Party Card (a real small sized red card) first from the (undivided) CPI and after its split in 1964 from the CPM. The three of us, two as the mentors and I as a junior disciple, decided to take our message to the villages of Punjab. Sometime in the summer of 1968 we made plans to visit some villages where one or another communist was the sarpanch. In the perhaps three villages that we visited the sarpanch belonged to the CPI. What lent enormous charm and memorable experience to it all was that Comrade Gursharan Singh, the legendary street corner theatre artist and his group also came along and it became an occasion for great bonhomie and camaraderie, almost a celebration. Gursharan Singh happened to be Professor Randhir Singh's brother-in-law, his wife's brother. Comrade Sat Pal Dang of the CPI also joined us. It was here that the legendary Punjabi poet Pash also became part of what earned the delightful epithet of our 'jatha'. Let me mention here that Professor Randhir Singh was also a poet of the Punjabi language and in his youth had even published a collection of poems, and then forgot all about it. But the readers didn't and recently another respected Punjabi poet, Lâltu, has translated the collection into Hindi; it is ready for publication with the title *râhon kî dhûl.* Aakar Books, who have published most of Professor Singh's books, have undertaken the publication of this one too.

We spent four or five days and nights in the villages, talking to the poorest sections and mostly listening to them. There were also some functions organised to enable the senior ones among us to speak to an audience. It was a delight to hear Professor Singh speak in simple but fluent Punjabi. No one could link the tensions of one's daily life, like for example, health, to the exploitative class character of the system as convincingly as him. The simplicity of his language hid a very deep understanding of Marxist theory. Comrade Sat Pal Dang was of course an established public speaker. Professor Bipan Chandra was not as used to speaking in Punjabi, but nonetheless his enthusiasm overrode his hesitation. They explained in very simple language the class nature of state and of politics and the need to change the system not by voting for one party or another, but for an alternative regime altogether. A vision of the future was being unveiled.

I cannot vouch for how much the villagers learnt from us, for very often their off the cuff remarks showed that they were fully aware of the class nature of the State and polity, but what we learnt from them was far more durable for us, at least for me. They told us that in the village they voted for the CPI (*Sajja dhada and Khabba Dhada?* Right group and Left group, is how they distinguished between CPI and CPM) because that was the only option available on the Left, but for the Assembly and Parliament elections they chose the Congress. That came as a bit of a surprise to us but they had an astounding explanation for it. In face to face conversations while we would turn to the levels of poverty to which they had been reduced, their concern was more with the fight for human dignity and they attributed the restoration of this dignity to the Congress. In one such conversation that stayed on in my mind for ever, a very poor landless labourer in a truly rustic description said to us: "Time was when we would go to a dhaba and ask for a cup of tea. The tea would be served to us at a distance in broken vessels in which dogs had pee'd; now we sit along with you people on the same bench and have tea in the same cups as you do." I realised how misleading our exclusive preoccupation with the economic issues had led us to ignore the equally vital issues of human life even at the lowest levels of economic existence. We did try to explain to them that their poverty was the cause of even their humiliation, but our voices had somehow lost some of the vigour and confidence. One major lesson I took back was of humility.

Within a year or two, the euphoria created by the electoral defeat of the Congress had evaporated and the regime was back in the comfort zone. The realisation of how in our enthusiasm we had misread the tensions within the system as signs of an impending revolution was a little dampening for us. That is obviously putting it a bit mildly. Indeed a sad reminder of it all was perhaps either the title or the opening line of a lesser known Punjabi poet (whose name slips my mind) who had also become part of our *jatha* in the villages: *Oye, krânti tûn aundî kyon nahîn!* (O Revolution, why do you not arrive?). Succinctly and in the raw, it evoked the angst and the desperation of us all.

By 1970-71 we were back to the classrooms where we really belonged and decided to mainly focus on teaching, research, publishing and speaking whenever a cause beckoned, but our circle was the familiar one of fellow academics, students and at best those few outside the campus willing to listen to us. By 1973 or so, I had quietly withdrawn from the CPM by simply not renewing membership mainly because of the restrictions the party discipline imposed on developing one's own understanding of history, although I never turned against the Party. Professor Bipan Chandra began to drift away from not only the Party but even from the ideals it stood for and began to move closer to the Congress in his thinking, writings and relationship. However, to the best of my knowledge, he never joined the Congress as a member; nor was he required to. I do not know if Professor Singh ever snapped ties with the Party, but he remained firmly committed to the cause of socialism/ communism right to his last breath. His several books written and published post-retirement bear testimony to his assertive commitment to the ideals, even as he was never a blind follower of either the Party diktat or even of Marxist theory, which was never a single entity for him.

Some two or three months before his demise, my friends and old students of Professor Singh, Arjun Dev, Zahoor Siddiqi and I learnt of the very sad state of Professor Singh's health from a picture, Shamsul Islam, a courageous and uncompromising fighter against communalism and of course a former student of Professor Singh, had circulated on the email. The three of us went to see Professor Singh at his daughter, Priyaleen Singh's official residence in New Friends Colony in New Delhi. It was sad to see the indefatigable, energetic, tall and both physically and intellectually towering revolutionary confined to the wheel chair, unable to see or speak and barely able to hear. He was yet able to recognise all three of us, for he whispered our names when Priyaleen asked him. She told us that he sometimes indicated the book he would like her to read out to him. His mind was clearly alert, though his body, ninety, had given way. What gave us comfort was that Priyaleen had soundly inherited his indefatigable spirt and was looking after him and her mother, in no better condition, in her house with utmost care and love with not a trace of resentment on her face. Her own multifarious engagements as a Professor in the prestigious School of Planning and Architecture in New Delhi did not in the least affect her commitment to her parents' welfare.

Some months after our visit we learnt of the passing away of a legend of our life time. It is one of my rare privileges to have had a long association with Professor Singh as his student, friend and comrade. I hope the next generation will be fortunate to have another one like him in their midst to learn from, to admire and be inspired by.

4

Randhir Singh—The Marxist Thinker, the Teacher, the Poet

Chaman Lal

Early in the night of January 31, 2016, Randhir Singh, known in India as Professor Randhir Singh breathed his last at the ripe age of ninety-four. Up to the age of ninety years, he remained fully active, travelling, delivering lectures, writing and interacting with his family/friends, comrades and admirers. The last four-five years he was mostly confined to home, though coming out once in a while, as he did to JNU, New Delhi on May 3, 2013 to release a book *'Understanding Bhagat Singh'* (of this author), on his childhood favourite hero–Bhagat Singh. His magnum opus-*Crisis of Socialism—Notes in Defence of a Commitment* was published a decade earlier, which was released by another notable Marxist thinker Aijaz Ahmad in Delhi. Since then he published a few more collections—one was Indian Communist Revolutionary T Nagi Reddy memorial lectures in book form—*Indian Politics Today: An Argument for Socialism—Oriented Path of Development (2009)* and another book, a collection of his early essays *On Nationalism and Communalism in India* (2010). He could not fulfil his wish to write on his most favourite hero from childhood—Bhagat Singh, for which he had collected lot of material, but his health and age did not permit him to complete the task, nor could he write on Gandhi and draw a comparison between Bhagat Singh's and Gandhi's perceptions of Indian society. He began his writing career at the age of twenty-three years with a major publication on—*'Ghadar Heroes:*

A Forgotten Story of the Punjab Revolutionaries of 1914-15', published in 1945 by People's Publishing House Bombay, with an introduction by Ajay Ghosh, a comrade of revolutionary Bhagat Singh and later General Secretary of Communist Party of India for long years. In fact, it was part of a larger writing—the biography of legendary Ghadar party hero, Baba Gurmukh Singh, which was never completed or at least published. At that time, Randhir Singh was on the editorial staff of CPI's Punjabi weekly *'Jang-i-Azadi'*. This book was published in Punjabi from Lahore in 1946. It was the time, when Randhir Singh was an activist using Punjabi language with his mass of work; he was writing even poetry in Punjabi at this point of time and his poetry collection *'Rahan Di Dhudh'*-'Dust of the Paths' was published in 1950 in partitioned India. This was a collection of his twenty-five selected poems out of many, the exact number not mentioned, written during 1947-49 about the painful partition and post-partition conditions. The poetry was highly acclaimed by literary critics of that time, but Randhir Singh never took to writing poetry again.

Randhir was born on January 9, 1922 in Moga district of Punjab. His father was an idealist and a doctor/Civil Surgeon by profession. As per Randhir Singh, his father was a deadly combination of Gandhi and Lenin in his head and was a believer in religion. Randhir Singh was a good student, and so qualified for a medical degree, but he opted for arts in which he was very good as per his teachers, and which was proved by his topping the Masters in Political Science from Panjab University, Lahore, though he was an activist at that time and even had had a one year stint in Lahore jail, which was one of the *'happiest periods'* of Randhir's life as per his *'In Lieu of a Bio-data'* that was because as he spent time with his hero Bhagat Singh's comrades like Kishori Lal in the 'Terrorist Ward', where Bhagat Singh was incarcerated earlier! Randhir Singh had become a full time activist of Communist Party of India in 1939 at the age of seventeen years, first as an activist of All India Students' Federation (AISF), of which Satya Pal Dang was the leader at that time. He remained underground as well, reaching out to peasants in rural area, remained part of editorial staff of the party journal in Punjabi and translated the *Communist Manifesto* and some other works of Karl Marx in Punjabi in those early days. Lahore was the headquarters of his activities prior to the 1947 partition of India, when it went to Pakistan. It was painful for Randhir, who really loved Lahore and he wrote many poems expressing the pangs of partition and particularly feeling the pinch of leaving Lahore on which he wrote a beautiful poem-*'Lahore Nu Salam'*—Salute to Lahore.

Randhir Singh was twenty-five plus at the time of partition and after moving to Delhi, he started teaching refugees from Pakistan at the Camp College. His first class first master's degree in Political Science came in handy at this critical time and he got a lecturer's job in Political Science in Delhi University's famous Delhi College, where his colleagues and friends like Bhisham Sahni, eminent progressive Hindi author and historian Bipan Chandra taught in the same or nearby colleges. With Bipan Chandra, he would distribute the issues of *'Enquiry'* in those days, apart from other leftist journals of the world. He continued to be part of the CPI, but was critical of its 'revisionist' policies. With the split of the party in 1964, he went along with the CPI (Marxist) for a few years. This was the period, he was viciously attacked by 'official' Communists. He was removed from the editorship of CPI's theoretical Punjabi journal *'Sada Jug'* (Our Age), charged with 'individualism and intellectual arrogance', as he refused to publish B.T. Randive's criticism of Mao Tse-tung. In such days of crisis, teaching was a relief and pleasure for Randhir Singh. After spending nearly two decades in Delhi College and a brief stint in Jawaharlal Nehru University (JNU), he was finally invited by the Delhi University to become a Professor in Political Science department in 1972, from where he retired in 1987. In between, his PhD thesis was rejected; he published only one book in 1967—*Reason, Revolution and Political Theory—A Critique of Michael Oakeshott's Rationalism in Politics.* But just this one book earned him laurels as a political theorist. His other publications came much later in life, mostly after retirement.

Even though he did not write or publish much, Randhir Singh earned laurels as a teacher. In fact, he became legendary as The Teacher. His political science class would attract students from History, Philosophy, Sociology, Economics, Literature and many other disciplines. Sometimes students used to stand outside his classroom to listen his lecture, as the classroom was full. He was advised many times 'not to teach subversion', he was denied permission to teach Marx and instead given Plato to teach but he would teach Marx through Plato! Randhir Singh termed his teaching as 'Robinhooding'! Despite facing harassment and acts of humiliation from organised groups, Randhir Singh's 'Robinhooding' went on very well, though he was conscious of the fact that this was 'within the system' and even lent legitimacy to the system, many would get 'co-opted' in the system by such liberalism. Yet Randhir Singh was made of a different mould, he did not confine himself to teaching alone; he remained active on the teachers' union front as well. Though he did not contest any election, he remained an active supporter of Delhi University Teachers' Association (DUTA), which fought many battles to protect teachers' interests. Randhir Singh's personality came out more expressively in his writings and public activities in his post-retirement period after 1987.

When the Political Science department of Delhi University wished to bring out a memorial volume of 'Teaching Politics' in his honour, he was requested to send his bio-data and he penned down his now famous *'In Lieu of Bio-data'*, which was not only published in the volume edited by Sushila Kaushik as-*History, Politics and Theory: Essays in Honour of Randhir Singh* in 1988. *Monthly Review* also published this and it brought him in close relationship with the *Monthly Review* and its editors—Paul Sweezy and Harry Magdoff. Randhir Singh was in touch with Marxist theory and practice the world over and with various strands of thoughts, but he found himself most comfortable in the *Monthly Review* tradition of Marxist scholarship, as he himself mentions in his Preface to his Magnum Opus—*Crisis of Socialism—Notes in Defence of a Commitment.*

> It is the journal I have felt most comfortable with, intellectually and politically, over the past fifty odd years, and my debt here is

> writ large over several important parts of this book. For Marxist theory and sustained revolutionary commitment, there has been indeed nothing else like *Monthly Review*. Its authentic Marxist analysis of development across the globe, easily accessible yet sophisticated in the best sense of the word, its unwavering commitment to the cause of socialism and principled support to revolutionary struggles everywhere, have educated, encouraged and inspired socialists and radicals throughout the world. Paul Sweezy and Harry Magdoff have been a constant source of enlightenment and inspiration. For me personally, Paul Sweezy was and remains a model of what a Marxist intellectual should be in our times. In recent years, I have much benefited from the wide ranging work of Ellen Meiksins Wood and John Bellamy Foster's writings on ecology.

Perhaps Randhir Singh was not informed of the passing away of Ellen Meiksins Wood a few weeks earlier. The above quote is from his Preface written in March 2004.

After retirement, Randhir Singh was offered two national fellowships—one by Indian Council for Social Sciences Research (ICSSR) and another by Indian Institute of Advanced Studies Shimla, which was terminated midway inexplicably. He was invited to deliver Moin Shakir Memorial Lecture in Marathwada University, Aurangabad in 1991, which prompted Randhir Singh to develop it into the 1080-page book—*Crisis of Socialism*, which came out in 2006. A series of six books were further brought out from this very book. These were

- *The World After the Collapse of the Soviet Union*
- *What was Built and What Failed in the Soviet Union*
- *Marxism, Socialism, Indian Politics: A View from the Left*
- *The Right Lesson and The Wrong Conclusion*
- *Contemporary Ecological Crisis: A Marxist View*
- *Struggle for Socialism: Some Issues.*

In between, he wrote the introduction to Bertell Ollman's Indian publication *Marxism: An Uncommon Introduction* in 1989. He also wrote an introduction to the Nepal Maoist leader Baburam Bhattrai's book *Monarchy vs. Democracy: The Epic Fight in Nepal,* published in 2005. In addition, Randhir Singh wrote an introduction to the Indian edition of William Ash's book-*Workers' Politics: The Ethics of Socialism,* published in 2007.

One can see from all his publications that Randhir Singh, throughout his life, was concerned about socialism and the building of socialism in the Soviet Union and China and after the fall of Soviet Union. He was a fearless critic of Stalinism and all such tendencies inside Communist parties which crushed their internal democratic structure. He was not a pessimist or a disillusioned man despite failures of socialist societies particularly in the Soviet Union and China. He kept alive his optimism, seeing the different kinds of changes being brought about in Latin America, particularly in Cuba. Nepali Maoist movement leaders kept close contact with him and both Prachanda and Baburam Bhattrai used to seek his advice; he was also very enthusiastic about Nepali people's struggles to bring down the feudal king. Crisis of Socialism is aptly dedicated to—*The Memory of Che Guevara and Countless Known and Unknown Martyrs of the Communist Movement*.

Despite the shabby treatment meted out to him in mid-sixties by the CPI, all Left parties and groups came to respect him a lot, including CPI. Randhir Singh was not just an armchair intellectual; he took firm stands on issues of state repression and in support of democratic movements, joining the processions as well. His house was open to all Leftist activists. During Nepal's Maoist underground movement, Hisila Yami, Central Committee member of Nepal Maoist party, and later minister in Prachanda-led Nepal Government, and wife of the Nepal Prime Minister, Baburam Bhatrai, could find a safe place in Randhir Singh's house for her medical treatment. The leaders and activists of CPI, CPM, CPI-ML and different factions joined the celebration of his life and work in Delhi on February 5, 2016 in large numbers and earlier on his cremation on February 1. They were joined by a galaxy of scholars/academicians as well like Romila Thapar, Prabhat Patnaik, Manoranjan Mohanty, Manager Pandey and more.

Despite having an international stature as a Marxist thinker and the possible availability of international publishers like

Oxford University Press, Penguin, Harper and Collins, Routledge, etc. or even left wing publishers like Verso, Monthly Review Press or more, Randhir Singh never felt tempted to get his books published by big publishing houses. His earliest two books were published by the People's Publishing House of CPI, later books by Ajanta Publications, Delhi and lastly by Aakar Books, Delhi. Probably he never wished to earn any royalty from publishers, and desired that the prices of books be kept reasonable in order to ensure their accessibility to the Indian middle class readers. Ajanta Publications published his *Of Marxism and Indian Politics* in 1990 and *Five Lectures in Marxist Mode* in 1993 and *Crisis of Socialism* in 2006. It also brought out the enlarged edition of *Reason, Revolution and Political Theory* in 1988. Aakar Books took out six books from *Crisis of Socialism* and two more publications in 2009 and 2010 as mentioned earlier.

After retirement, Randhir Singh delivered a number of lectures at various places in India, but never abroad. Some of his lectures got into book forms. He would ask for a minimum of two hours for his lecture time, but it used to go on for several hours. In some cases he spent even nights. In fact from his early activist life, he got used to addressing Communist Party schools, which used to continue for days and nights together. Randhir Singh's style of delivering lectures was of party schools. He wished to train his audience in Marxism theory and practice. Desh Bhagat Yadgar Halls in Jalandhar, Patiala, Chandigarh, Delhi were his favourite places of delivering lectures, and so were those in Shimla and Aurangabad. He used Punjabi and Hindi/Urdu languages for his public lectures, though he was more comfortable with English. Many of his books have been published in Hindi and Punjabi translations. Along with his brother-in-law and the well known People's Theatre personality Gursharan Singh, who published his books in Punjabi, they became iconic figures in Punjab. Gursharn Singh predeceased him five years earlier in 2011, though younger in age.

For six long decades Randhir Singh stormed the Bastille of rightist conservative ideas by his subversive radical Marxist thought and none in the Right was able to face him. Randhir Singh though combative was always courteous and refined in debates and paid due attention to his adversaries arguments, before demolishing them through counterarguments.

Lastly, he should be remembered for his poetic expressions from the collection—Dust of the Paths, about Indian independence in 1947 with and the Partition which he phrased as—*A Caravan has reached its destination/And yet lost its way.*

In contrast the around, same time, he welcomed Chinese Revolution of 1949-

> Red springs have bloomed
> In Asia's 'peaceful' desert
> Where extreme slavery got distributed
> Now rebellions shall meet there (Translated from Punjabi)

Paul Sweezy was the model for Randhir Singh and Randhir Singh is the model for Indian Left intelligentsia, but it is something that is difficult to emulate!

5

In the Genre of an Intellectual Memoir: Randhir Singh as a Marxist Theorist and a Revolutionary Teacher

Savita Singh

> We do not set ourselves up against the world in doctrinaire fashion with a new principle: Here is the truth! Here you must kneel! We develop new principles for the world out of the principles of the existing world...
>
> It is the great advantage of the new movement that we do not seek to anticipate the new world dogmatically, but rather to discover it in the criticism of the old ... It is not our task to build up the future in advance and to settle all problems for all time; our task is ruthless criticism of everything that exists, ruthless in the sense that the criticism will not shrink either from its own conclusions or from conflict with the powers that be...
>
> Karl Marx (cited in Singh, 1989: 2421)

> Marxism retains its validity and viability as a tradition of social theory within which it is possible not only to do social science-, that is, identify real causal mechanisms and understand their consequences- but also do it as an emancipatory project for our times, which remains a socialist project
>
> Randhir Singh (Singh, 2008: 40)

Randhir Singh, a Marxist theorist and an influential teacher who believed in the primacy of revolutionary politics, had chosen to teach in Delhi University—a challenging task which he thought was the most non-alienating thing to do next to making revolution. Although the life in Delhi University was full of potholes for him, it is here that he practised his theory creatively, engaging himself with the radical politics of the university. To figure out his theoretical posture, or rather position within Marxism or Marxist praxis which has wavered historically from critical to orthodox to critical, requires at this moment a speculation into the dialectics of his life and time. Randhir Singh had himself figured out his intellectual space within the university system dialectically. Reading his early writings, particularly, his *Five Lectures in Marxist Mode,* makes the complexity of his being amply clear which was, in effect, situated both within the body of Marxist theory and his immediate personal context, that is, India and the contradictions of its social reality. In fact, in later endeavours to explore the possibility of writing on Indian political theory, one constantly returned to Randhir Singh for one could find a critical interpretation of Marxism, not a mere replication of Western Marxism or Western Political Theory. The real test of his theoretical understanding lay in its theoretical praxis, which meant, an interpretation of Marxist understanding in an unorthodox manner, achieved within the Indian context. Consequently, he could assert that it is not economics that primarily determines the nature of the social, but revolutionary politics as the latter transforms the former.

In the process of carving out a space for himself within Marxist social theory which he could make sense of in his own historical context, Randhir Singh went to Marx's writings first. He wanted to understand it without being excluded from the process of understanding Marx. He thought that Marxism as praxis demanded locating him within one's own context as without this basic mediation, mere theory would prove vacuous. He figured out, that an orthodox, or a replicated understanding, would be untenable. For an understanding to be effective and correct, it must simultaneously be applicable, as it is understood. In other words, to understand the contradiction of Indian society, in its postcolonial form, one would need a creative application of Marxist theory. To him thus, Marxism meant a theory of revolutionary politics as its telos was a transformation of existing reality. The ultimate nature of this theory was emancipatory and helping to create a socialist society—one that will satisfy human needs fairly, in the process unleashing unknown freedoms.

To elaborate for Randhir Singh, Marxism as revolutionary politics was an ongoing project of human imagination and emancipation—an unfinished project of human struggle to create a more equal and freer society. On the second page of the first lecture of *Five Lectures in Marxist Mode* he clearly distances himself from the positivist interpretation of Marxist theory which tries to establish it as a scientific theory, a theory that is unrevisable and accomplished in a final sense. By doing this he counts himself out of any closed reading of Marx and dissociates himself from the Marxist politics that is based on this sort of understanding. Stating his position on this issue, Singh writes, "Marx was not a system builder, nor his Marxism a positivist science. And it needs to be remembered that his theoretical work is, in a most important sense, an 'unfinished project'. So much of what Marx expressly wished to write to ensure a clearer or fuller understanding of his ideas—for example, on philosophy (Hegel), or political theory (the state), or at least 'two or three printer's sheets' on method (Dialectics), and much else- remained simply unwritten. Part of the explanation lies in the inescapable, near exclusive, concern of the mature Marx with his work on economics, as he called it, which yet remained unfinished... More specifically, Marx's treatment of politics, ethics, literature, culture, in fact, of the realm of non-economic in general, remains largely untheorized by him" (Singh, 1993: 2). So how could it be a closed project, that is to say a complete theory?

To him, even though, Marx opened up a new continent of social sciences for all, it was up to others to understand their realities dialectically. As one can figure out, with this method of thinking and understanding, one arrives at different understandings in different historical situations. This method itself would not generate one universal understanding or an outcome or result. The politics of revolutionary Marxism must grasp the dynamic of existing reality. Any orthodoxy that pertains to this mode of understanding could easily give wrong results; the test of theory lies in its practice in a dialectical sense. The nondemocratic practices in the name of socialism have resulted in their failure precisely because their creative reinterpretations were suppressed as Marxism was confusedly understood as science in a positivist sense. Randhir Singh was critical in his teaching and writings about the ideological closure of Marxist Social Theory in the name of its scientificity. In fact, he often argued that Marxism has suffered historically in terms of its revolutionary politics because of this treatment of Marxist theory. It is this lack of theoretical openness that Marxist Social Theory has missed out on many moments of creative inclusion of movements that arose outside its theoretical suppositions. To get the inner struggle of his own positioning within Marxism, let me quote him again as he articulates it in his *Of Marxism of Karl Marx*,

> In understanding Marxism, it helps to remember that Marx was not a professional philosopher, a system builder, offering us, in the tradition of Plato or Hobbes or Hegel, a more or less complete system of thought. Nor was Marxism ever intended to be a 'positive science', or an assortment of statements about past and present facts, a set of predictions about the shape or timing of future events. Not a 'philosopher' or a 'social scientist', Marx was by vocation a revolutionary, 'before all else a revolutionist', as Engels described him. The major thrust behind his systematic theoretical work (pre-eminently represented by Capital) was born of his urge to understand the capitalist social order, the system he wanted to overthrow, and most of his other writings was done as part of his revolutionary, that is, Marxist practice of politics. Insofar as his work claims to be scientific, it was never science for science's sake or for peers of policy-makers. It was his commitment to the liberation of working class that drove Marx to gather together the theoretical and factual knowledge that he could muster at the time into a scientific understanding of history in general and capitalist society in particular, and put it at the service of the emancipatory struggle of his time, which remains our struggle today (Singh, 2008: 44).

It is in the sense of struggle remaining 'our today' that Marxism in India, taking into account its own historical social contradiction, must be made sense of. Randhir Singh attended to this task most seriously and interpreted Marx accordingly. His practice of Marxist social theory is informed by this realisation. Later, in his *Of Marxism of Karl Marx* he reasons out why a more contextually flexible reading must be chosen to understand Marx. First of all, because one has to take it forward to understand one's own material reality in its politics and economics, and secondly, because otherwise one would end up practising a distorted understanding developed by later Marxists. In Singh's one to one admonitions and advices to his students he would insist on reading Marx's original texts first. As here one would develop an understanding of what he was actually doing. In fact, when he goes to Marx's entire oeuvre one finds the words, "which have come down to us scattered and translated over a long period of time," (Singh, 2008: 44) and these include all kinds of writings, articles written under immediate pressure of events, weekly columns, "as Marx said of his famous *The Eighteenth Brumaire*, unpublished and unpublishable mice-nibbled manuscripts in finished, unfinished or fragmentary form, numerous articles and other journalistic, and even hack pieces as Marx called them" (Singh, 2008: 46). This was to point out the realities of Marx's life as a revolutionary, to give a perspective on Marx as a mortal being, not as a deity who supplied formulae for system building (Singh, 2008: 46). He writes in his *Of Marxism*:

> The point is that all of Marx's writings cannot be treated on par in terms of their theoretical importance and significance. There is always the need for utmost caution in determining their precise nature and theoretical status in each case for purposes of understanding and assessing Marxism-a caution generally observed in the breach by the critics who have preferred to take every liberty with the texts of Marx, and often degraded even by many of the professed followers of Marx himself, . 'If people could only read', Marx used to say; we may well add, they also need to know' how not to quote him' (Singh, 2008: 47).

The above analysis should be enough for us to surmise that Randhir Singh tried to open up theoretical space for further theoretical articulation and practice by unburdening Marx of the responsibility of having thought of for the posterity in any prophetic manner or sense. It would amount to expecting Marx of possessing suprahuman capabilities. It is important for any theorising within Marxist framework to understand Marx himself being the child of his own time, and to that extent also limited in his analysis for,

> Marx was, of course, very much-as much as anybody else- a 'child of his time' (to borrow an expression from Hegel).. Of course there is a continuous growth and development in the thinking of Marx. But obviously he was not some sort of supra historical genius who would be always fully consistent in what he said or wrote; and what needs to be recognized is that, revision of earlier positions or perspectives apart, there are different and indeed sometimes inconsistent strands in his writing, in those belonging to different periods and even to the same period. .one of the gravest of them, for example, could appeal to many statements in the thought of Marx particularly in popular or propagandist or polemical writings which either articulated an economistic view or can be interpreted in economistic manner, the most famous being Marx's frequently quoted formulation of the doctrine of historical materialism in the preface to his *Critique of Political Economy* (Singh, 2008: 48).

Reading Marx in the context of his own oeuvre, Randhir Singh found himself placed differently within the dominant Marxist practices of his own time. Marx's creative endeavours to theorise revolutionary politics was indeed a complex task It demanded dialectical understanding through and through to save it from future ossifications. Randhir Singh tried this form of theorising himself by being on the side of Marx. He struggled against the economistic interpretation of Marx which, which in view, ultimately normalised politics and put power in the hands of those who distorted it putting an end to revolutionary politics. It was an attempt to make metaphysics of Marxism. And ultimately it led to the closure of Marxist Social Theory.

Reflecting on the justification of economistic formulation of Marx by his followers, he tried to reason it out by saying, that they "came to be emphasized and exaggerated, and thus misinterpreted by the followers in the half a century after his death, as part of the justificatory ideology and political theory of the reformist working class movement, which grew up in the industrialized West in the period of emerging monopoly capitalism. Such emphasis excluded other more representative and more important tendencies in his thought, and simply overlooked the overall dialectical orientation of his thinking to which any kind of factorization of social life is alien. Marx and Engels rejected the metaphysical mode of thought as the latter called it, which is 'one sided, limited, abstract' studies of things' in isolation, detached from the whole, vast interconection of things, and thus, cannot see the woods for the tree. "For Marx, as with Hegel, 'the truth is the whole" (Singh, 2008: 48).

Rejecting the scientistic, economistic orthodoxy within Marxism, Randhir Singh practised Marxist social theory in the space released by his critique of other interpretations. Though he did not define it as Creative Political theory, later on, however, some of his students took it up seriously, characterizing the praxis of Marxist theory as critically creative. This does not mean that one has eschewed Marxism's alternative view of scientific analysis as the necessary path to understand society for Randhir Singh himself writes in a discerning manner about this complex issue. He writes:

> To question scientism in Marxism, the scientistic emasculation or mangling of Marxism, by both its supporters and detractors, is not to deny the scientific credentials of Marxism but to assert them by focusing on how precisely it claims to be scientific, what indeed it has to offer as a critical science of society, with careful attention to certain long standing misuses of the word. Marxism is, and needs to be scientific in its philosophical foundation and commitment to criticism and continuing verification and development of its main principles, postulates and conclusions" (Singh, 2008: 57). In this sense, "it is a living and creative theory that continuously interacts with the reality of the world around it and with the rest of contemporary thought and grows with the

growth of scientific and historical knowledge (Singh, 2008: 57).

It is in this space that a creative Marxist Social Theory has been practised by some of us who studied under him. There are clear indications in his writing that this space if worked upon could bear valuable fruits as Singh writes, "Marxism has its limitations and inadequacies, its ambiguities and silences', or empty spaces'; there are many loose threads, the argument often yielding large questions rather than providing neat answers. This indeed is as it should be" (Singh, 1993: 3). These loose ends provide the intellectual space to interpret it further from within one's own location. His analysis of Indian economy, nationalism, communalism and terrorism bears it out. In fact, in his *Five Lectures in Marxist Mode*, except the first chapter, the rest of the book is about understanding Indian social and economic reality only. Some of these issues were analysed in their incipient form in his *Of Marxism and Indian Politics* published in 1990.

This intellectual attention to his theory and praxis that made his teaching in the classroom so exciting and him as an influential teacher. His classrooms used to be his political field where he practised Marxism in all its revolutionary seriousness. In his lectures after rejecting an economistic interpretation of Marx, he would insist on paying attention to dialectical method to understand the nature of bourgeois social science. This social science based on natural science method of positivism needed to be transformed as much as the reality it claims to understand, he would argue. It is this delicate weaving of theory and practice that his teaching method used to bring forth in his classes; discussions following after each lecture as a necessary part of the lecture producing the impact it used to: radicalisation of young minds and formation of the initial ground of sound scholarship. The primacy of revolutionary politics over economism in all its forms used to align him to his students like ants to molasses. He himself became an expression of his own understanding of Marxism. It was from here that the power or the effect of his teaching used to emanate.

We can get a clue as to how he prepared himself for this role of a Marxist theorist and a revolutionary teacher by reading the first few pages of his article, 'Concerning Marxism', the first article of the *Five Lectures in Marxist Mode*. When I say prepared, it actually means, each lecture would be informed by the relationship worked out between theory and radical politics applicable to the reality of Indian society. Another way of putting it is to call it 'an interpretation that is self-applicative'- a creative political theory which ensures the adequacy of theory in its application. In his lectures he would draw distinctions; acknowledge differences to bring clarity to the specificity of Marxist Social Science and what it was supposed to have achieved in all its permutations and combinations in different historical settings through revolutionary politics. For example he writes:

> It is not merely that Marx's combination of insights and method permanently altered the manner in which reality would thereafter be perceived, as Heilbrooner has argued more recently; it is that none has provided, so far, a better method of understanding this reality, the reality of society in a historical process. Marxism has gained for us knowledge of the structure and dynamics of social formations, past and present, particularly the contemporary dominant capitalist social formation, better than anything bourgeois social sciences has to offer (Singh, 1993: 3).

The fact that the bourgeois social sciences based on the liberal principles of individualism and positivism generate a one-sided view of reality through the method of deduction and induction, categorised as scientific, Singh would take pains to interpret Marxist method as scientific in its non-positivistic dialectic presupposition. Any acceptance of the bourgeois view of science, he argued would limit understanding to its procedural method only. It is here that he used to join the debate within the Marxist discourse as to what finally determines the transformation of a particular reality or mode of production. He would argue along the lines of intervention in the discourse that stayed away from economism. He would prioritise revolutionary politics over the economic determinism in his explanation of how reality moves and gets transformed. Just to concretise the content of his lecture let me quote him as he expressed later in his writings:

> As Marxism views it, society is not merely an aggregate or random togetherness of parts, factors, levels or instances. It is a social whole, or totality, a historically specific structured interdependence of parts, with an economic structural base and loaded with contradictions that account for its dynamics, its concrete over-determined historical development. In other words, the determination, insofar as we must use the term, is neither unique, nor is it to be understood in any economic and class reductionist manner; it is something far more complex and problematic, realized on an economic base, but through any number of interactions and mediations. The important point is that the parts, aspects or instances generally referred to as superstructure, along with their contradictions, are not some epiphenomenal manifestations of the economic base. On the contrary, they may and often do have an autonomous, irreducible, historically specific existence of their own. But this is an existence of dialectical, determined and determining, relationships to each other and to the social whole (Singh, 1993: 3).

Deepening the analysis of the processes of understanding and change, he would say that dynamics of their existence, the working out of their contradictions, the structural logic may be decisively conditioned by the basic economic contradictions, and "one might add, it is only within the necessities and constraints of the given objective, economic-structural situation, within 'this determination by the economic in the first instance', that whatever happens, including a revolutionary transformation of the economic structure itself, is ultimately these choices and possibilities arise and exist within the necessities and constraints, which sets determined by the activity of men in pursuit of their ends..."(Singh, 1993: 3) even though "their contexts, outer limits and parameters... The economic defines, as it were, the terrain, the 'condition of existence', the horizon of the non-economic, including... the political" (Singh, 1993: 3). For "without this emphasis on the role of the economy, Marxism would be theoretically indistinguishable from any other sociology" (Singh, 1993: 18).

He kept on expanding the realm of politics by giving the widest possible interpretation of the determining role of economics, of a structure which is like a system that limited the role of freedom in making revolutionary choices. He would work on the notion of agency as he thought it led to the formation of a free and humane society. The working men and women need a new society achieved by revolutionary transformation of the earlier one, he would argue. To get to hear his voice more on this complex issue as to how one's theory must inform one's practice in a non-deterministic manner so that it generates a transformative politics he would quote extensively from Marx himself. This was reflected in his writings later. In his *Five Lectures in Marxist Mode*, for example, he writes, "... in politics as elsewhere, men and their choices, all the diverse factors, elements and variables, constituting as it were the subjective dimension of society, always a most vital part of social reality, are yet not calculable of the objective dimensions. There are thus no promises of inevitability or guarantees of victory in Karl Marx's politics, only strong probabilities and real possibilities. Men and women choose and act, but the outcome of concrete historical class struggle, is not predetermined, cannot be predicted in advance, least of all with the certainty of the natural science. Thus understood, the historical process in a most meaningful sense remains open and relatively undetermined. It shall be ultimately determined by the activity men in pursuit of their purpose, an activity in which men continuously seek to materialize their freedom. It is not for nothing that Marx insists: the working class is revolutionary or its is nothing" (Singh, 1993: 5).

Most emphatically then, Randhir Singh had arrived at a point in his theoretical journey through his teaching and writings where he could say that "Marx's scientific and revolutionary project are not merely interconnected, they grow into each other and together they put politics at the centre of social practice for our times. (At least that is how Marx understood it and one may legitimately note a divergence between Marxism as Marx himself practised it and a certain kind of contemporary Marxist scholarship). There is the centrality of 'politics as revolution' in Marx. 'Revolution is the highest form of class struggle'. In this sense, the sense in which Marx was before all else a revolutionist', politics, not economics, has the primacy in Marxism. And the obvious corollary is that in the absence of a revolutionary politics changing the economic-structural base of society, the logic of its economic structure shall assert itself, all politics will remain superstructural in its essential nature and outcome..Such is the dialects of economy and politics in the social sciences of Karl Marx..." (Singh, 1993: 20).

In his *Of Marxism of Marx* he interprets it by linking it to the Marxist notion of freedom where he argues that "economism was not the dominant thing in Marx, ever. It is not just his insistence that 'the proletariat needs his dignity more than he needs bread' or that 'the realm of freedom' truly human freedom for him lay beyond the sphere of actual material production (where) begins that development of human energy which is an end in itself'. Marxism accords primacy not to economics but politics; politics is the cutting edge of the social revolution it argues for. Very early on, Marx saw the weakness of Feuerbach's preoccupation with philosophy in that 'it refers too little to politics'. For Marx philosophy had to be realized through politics. This conviction remained central to Marx's lifelong practice as a revolutionary" (Singh, 2008: 49).

When I came to Delhi University to pursue M.A. in Political Science, Randhir Singh had been teaching in the department of Political Science for over a decade. In his rather unique autobiographical note, 'In Lieu of a Bio-data', Randhir Singh pens down his own process of arriving at the revolutionary politics and his theoretical struggles within the corpus of Marxist writings. His life itself appears to be a story of Indian Marxism unfolding itself historically. And this is also the story of him becoming a teacher of enormous influence in the university. The process of how one becomes someone's teacher, the momentousness of its becoming and the fact that it actually becomes or happens, may demand reflection on one's own situatedness in both subjective and objective manners. As a newly arrived student in Delhi University to do M.A. in Political Science, I learned from Randhir Singh something that was new in its intention and content. It became a personal 'something' in its novelty, setting me on the path of inner transformation. Learning from him in the classroom, hearing him deliver his influential lectures on Hobbes, Locke and Rousseau, for these were the political thinkers he used to teach then, opened up a way to understand radical politics. Its enchantment was deep. He had well worked out his theoretical position, carefully, I should say, by understanding the relationship of theory to praxis in an academic setting. His lectures would keep one bound to his renderings. Each day would be another day of personal calibration of 'who one is and where one needs to go'. Slowly and gradually most of us, the M.A. class, began to accept the intellectual shift within ourselves. We shifted to his side.

That meant reading a lot more and discussing with him issues in the next class that began to emerge in our minds. We discussed most of it, though, post-lecture, after the class, that is. There would be another class after the main lecture almost regularly. He would be surrounded by students as he would come out. He would be answering, chiding, joking- teaching literally in the most interesting manner one can think of. Then there would be a few whom he would ask to stay longer, have tea with him, and see him off by walking with him up to his car. He used to have a red Maruti car, a beautiful machine to look at that point of time—a sleek, small, beautiful, red bodied, enticing, enviable piece of automobile. The most enticing thing was not this car though, but what used to be transferred to us as students while walking up to this machine with him—each time a new piece of knowledge one got introduced to. He would share a bit of politics of the university, content of a new article that had just appeared or some incident that took place in Indian politics. He would be frank and honest in his statement about something that bothered him in the department and the university. He would be politicising every issue he took up for discussion urging us to take positions and speak about what appeared correct. I had my own Socratic moments with him, and many in number, I must say.

Now when I reflect on the phenomenon of Professor Randhir Singh, a Marxist theorist and my teacher of formative years in academia, and ask as to how he became my teacher in the way he did, I have many memories of his generosity and compassion. Apart from the reasons I have already elaborated above, I think it is also important to mention that a teacher does have a special relationship with truth no matter how one would like to define it in the postmodern age today. I think he became my teacher because of his earnestness to examine every situation and accept what emerged as truthful. Who would be your teacher if he or she did not have a primary relationship with truth or who didn't have the ability to tell what he or she thinks truth is, or what it looks like? Truth does not only discipline you through its discourses but expands you, even if one wants to miss its 'enlightenment' moment as vilified today. Randhir Singh would often say in his own Marxist sense "What appears is not the reality, it is what lies beneath it."

One had one's first lesson in understanding the nature of appearances, ideology, to be precise, in this way only—just walking with him. To get to truth, he would say, "You need a particular method. Learn to think dialectically. Find where the contradictions are. The one that you can spot first is in front of you, in fact, right under your nose—look at the poverty, and so much of it; while the capitalist mode of production is the most productive in the history of mankind, there is so much poverty! It must because people are stationed at different levels in our society and access to wealth depends on where you are placed. Is there something called class? Is it because of this system that the inequalities are maintained so efficiently and legitimately? Is there no contradiction here? How is it that those who work the hardest in this system of production—(let's call it a mode of production, to be more precise, a capitalist mode of production), the workers and peasants to be precise, get the least?" These used to be remarkably serious questions then. They became issues of analysis later. Going through the intellectual demands made upon oneself, one began to rely as much upon oneself as on the other who had the ability to ask these question and transfer the required knowledge to understand them scientifically. This person was going to matter in one's intellectual life no matter where one went after passing out from the university. One's ambitions and desires were changed forever. Understanding the world correctly was the new desire and changing it, one's new passion now.

Randhir Singh would often scoff at the so-called academic scholars who would claim to know better than others but in practice produced anti-people politics and ideas. Yet they were the ones who were enjoying prestige in the academic world both in India and abroad as they acquired degrees to back themselves up. The point in his scoffing often arose from his disenchantment with the bourgeois knowledge system and its preconditions and its ideological content though he never forgot to assert the importance of understanding its theories. He often used this situation to talk amusingly about his own lack of so called scholarship. There would be sarcasm and contempt mixed in such statements, but also a brutal honesty about his lack of this kind of scholarship measured in academic terms. Even before he wrote his bio-note in which he has analysed this, he would repeat this lack of scholarly accomplishments as if it was his own unique possession in its obliqueness—a kind of qualification to be counted in real terms. It sounded quite radical in its being so presented or stated and this endeared him more to his students, and I think, he knew the effect it used to have on his young pupils. But the fact that as a Marxist teacher with no PhD, he used to face numerous mini-political battles in the university, that took his teaching and students very seriously. Whether this led to his reading of Marx as a critical thinker rather than a sacred deity, one can not say, but certainly it helped him to reflect on the dialectical positioning of his own existence in the given reality of India as an underdeveloped capitalist society with a dependent status in the global economy and him being a professor of political theory in one of its universities, Delhi university to be more precise.

It is in this historical setting in which Randhir Singh understood his own material being: a Marxist teacher, an active material element or cause which could effectively transform minds that came in his contact. His theoretical position that revolutionary politics ultimately takes priority when it comes to the transformation of existing reality was perpetually practised in the university setting. In this sense he was, indeed, transformative. Reflecting on his own material condition, and conflicts inherent in it, he finally wrote in his bio-note, "For me it has meant another continuous struggle from the day I started teaching. At the very outset, they asked for an undertaking 'not to teach subversion'. Later, they stopped you, again and again, from teaching a particular course. For long years, they would let me teach only Plato, not Marx—so that you learn to teach Marx via Plato, which is not only possible but is in some ways far more effective also, for obvious reasons. They can organise harassment and humiliation for you in diverse ways, with the lumpen elements in the academic community thrown in. One has struggled against all this and them along, and with a reasonable measure of success" (Singh, 2008: 17). And even though the university is not the conventional bourgeois field of politics—it is one of its parts, a 'university system' - and here, "There are problems and there are risks. And for better credibility here one must learn to say 'no' to at least to some of the innumerable benefits, the co-optive attraction the system has to offer even to a radical teacher. The most important thing is to be aware of the limitations, even ambiguities, inherent in the very nature of Robinhooding as an academic exercise. And for this reason one has to be modest about what one is doing or achieving here" (Singh, 2008: 17).

He joined the Communist Party of India at an early age just when he entered college. He went to Lahore to pursue his further studies and became deeply involved with the revolutionary politics of the Communist Party of India. But then the partition of India took place. The nature of politics changed. There was a veering away from the communist parties as they were themselves changing in terms of the demands of revolutionary politics in India. He writes in his Bio-data:

> I came to Delhi sometime after the partition, having lived with death the previous few months and on the way. Uprooted, a refugee, everything around me, including my politics in a shambles, I sought a new foothold in life- only temporally, I had then thought, mistakenly. I started teaching as what was then known as Camp College, an institution set up by Punjab University at Delhi for refugee students and teachers. Even as I began to enjoy my new vocation, the party, passing through a series of crises, both internal and external, finally opted for 'peaceful', 'parliamentary 'ways. And so it came to pass, with other tangible and not so tangible factors contributing that over a period in time –during which I still edited from Delhi its theoretical monthly in Punjabi, Sada Jug (till removed, charged with 'individualism' and 'intellectual arrogance' for refusing to publish a BTR criticism of Mao-Tse-tung), and translated Communist Manifesto and some more Marx into Punjabi-I just opted out of the Party. (Later, soon after its formation, I was to spend a few years in the Communist Party, Marxist). For me the comforting rationalization was that in our society, after revolution making', teaching perhaps holds the possibilities for a non-alienated life (Singh, 2008: 13).

But always alert to the demands of radical politics which he took upon himself, he made his teaching a perpetual reflective practice of Marxism. In his "In Lieu of Bio-data" he writes, "What is more, insofar as it is an exercise within the system, it is always in danger of itself becoming a form of cooption into it. In fact, the more you succeed in what you are doing, the more you are also, in an important sense, lending legitimacy to the system as a whole. Such is the dialectics implicit in this mode or style of teaching. That is why its quality is of decisive importance" (Singh, 2008: 17). And "Even so, how effective it is in its own modest manner, and how it contributes to any qualitative departures in the system, will be determined by other, larger social forces at work in the historical process in this country. We can only recognize and try to help these in whatever way we can" (Singh, 2008: 17). Randhir Singh carried on with his Marxist teaching and politics till the last day of his retirement and left a record of his own revolutionist praxis in his Bio-data, "I have, most of the time, done none of the things that scholars are normally supposed to do. I have been, most of the time, busy with what they normally supposed to keep away from. Which is as well, for life has been such fun this way I have functioned, in the profession and in the university, more as a militant on the Left—even when revising the syllabi in political science whenever and wherever I got the opportunity to do so, or putting in a rather noisy plea on behalf of Political Theory in general and Marxism in particular on the campuses of Indian universities" (Singh, 2008: 14). More than that, he helped build a teacher's movement aimed at fighting for democratic rights and reforms in the university. He carried on with the socialist education among workers, students and teachers, including school teachers. He continued to organise not only Marx Clubs to raise the consciousness of those willing to understand things, but write pamphlets and bulletins; editing, producing and distributing, circulating journals like *Enquiry, Socialist Digest, The Marxist Review, Monthly Review, Science and Society* and *New Left Review*. He campaigned on issues of Vietnam, Czechoslovakia; mobilising and marching for all sorts of popular causes, associated with almost any radical initiative on the campus and every revolutionary venture. He concludes this reflective story of the revolutionary self, "That is how it has been for the most part over nearly forty years" (Singh, 2008: 15).

But no less than these radical political practices, the fact remains that he taught us by the example of his life. He transformed our minds and set us on the path of creative thinking. This has fructified into a Marxist Social Theory which we have named Creative Political Theory which opened up the space for the feminist theory as well as for social movements, much as Jurgen Habermas did in Germany. The dialectical reading of Marx led Randhir Singh to critically look at Marxist Social Theory in India and accept the lack of openness of this social theory to new radical movements. In his *Of Marxism of Karl Marx* he writes, "Marx was, of course, very much—as much as anybody—a child of his time. This not only involves the implication of not looking for answers in his work which either do not exist or which are not at any rate to be found there, it also involves recognizing that Marx too like anybody else, carried his share of 'the mud of his times', including for example, a certain gender blindness and ecological short-sightedness" (Singh, 2008: 51). He banked on the openness of Marxist Social Theory as much as on his pupils who flocked to him to learn the nature of Marxist Social Theory and who were willing to take it up for its openness. He himself asserts, "It is important to recognize that Marxism of Karl Marx is a remarkably open body of thought, open in the best scientific sense of the word...It is, and needs to remain open to new ideas, to new data and experience, competing insights and bodies of learning, to newer fields of inquiry" (Singh, 2008: 58).

It is this sense that that one entertained the possibility of doing political theory as a feminist and also, ventured to write poetry with the same political understanding. Randhir Singh himself wrote poetry, that too, of the finest kind and his collection of poems, 'Rahan Di Dhoor', (1950) written in Punjabi was hailed as the 'best poetry of that period'. To recount the wholeness of his understanding of politics and literature, I remember asking him for a long reading list for understanding Marxism. He thought for a minute and said "Read everything Marx wrote including his poetry and letters he wrote to his friends and wife, Jenny (Von Westphalen) and her famous letters to Karl Marx himself. Read *Grundrisse* to understand the first volume of *Capital*, if it is too tough to begin with. Lukacs and Althusser much later. May be, read Gramsci before them. Leslie Kolakowski's *Main Currents of Marxism*, all three volumes, for understanding the history of Marxism. Read a bit about Jenny Eleanor, if you are still unhappy with how liberals including Rousseau treated women in their theory. In the new republic, women ought to have equal citizenship status. Read Engels' *The Origin of Family, Private Property and State* to understand the issues of women's oppression in a basic manner. Though you should also read liberal feminists ... but read literature as much as possible, novels, poetry in particular. Follow all the discussions that go on in art, aesthetics, architecture, theatre etc. See some good films as well. Prepare yourself for a critically reflective life. Just don't eschew dialectics."

What could one have done in one's life with this kind of help if not written some poetry, done creative political theory and worked upon oneself to remain committed to radical politics? On a personal note I may add that radicalism does not come by remaining committed to reading and following a set of writings by Marx, Engels and Lenin alone, but by reading them in the light of happenings in the contemporary historical setting. I went on to read much more around the core texts suggested by him and wanted to know what other texts he would suggest so that one could have a holistic view including that of transitions in ideas leading. One can have preferences, I had figured out from his own lectures, for a particular thinker from the same ideological stream of ideas and that, indeed, makes all the difference in terms of understanding. On some occasions I did mention this to him that I would like to read more books to make this transition within myself. Of all the thinkers he taught, Hobbes, Locke and Rousseau, he would get pretty soft on Rousseau. About Hobbes, he would be generous, but John Locke remained his intellectual rival. Locke's state of nature used to be more intriguing to him than the Hobbesian depiction of it as "solitary, brutish and nasty'. I used to be quite taken in by the way he would engage with these thinkers; especially the way he would read Marx backward and forward intervening and making sense of these bourgeois thinkers. One day, I asked him, if there was one book he would like to suggest which I must read to understand the transition period between liberal and Marxist social theory. He invited me home for a cup of tea one day. I had the opportunity to sit in his much envied red Maruti Car. He joked about it himself and told me that one must relate to a machine in a consciously unalienating manner for it is a commodity that is intended to alienate you. It is only by placing it in its context, that is, its production and commodification that one can free oneself from its power over oneself. The envy many people have towards others possessing it is a result of their own desire of possessing. It is an object of desire insofar as it serves the purpose of making a fetish out of. It is supposed to invoke the desire of possessing as something valuable and that is how it ensures its sale, profit etc. But it has a use value apart from exchange value, and to that extent it serves a need. "I need this car to travel to university and reach on time, teach comfortably; it saves time, enabling me to deliver the kind of lectures I give. It is not a very intelligent thing to pick up a primitive mode of communication if you can avoid it and if there is better option available". Every minute of his teaching resulted in transition in one's understanding. I had never thought that a machine could be understood in this complex manner. When we reached his house in East Patel Nagar, he brought out a book from his study and handed it over. He told me I had one week to go through it. That book was by Lucio Colletti *From Rousseau to Lenin*, published by Monthly Review Press, New York and London, 1972. Many more books he lent after this one and I returned them after a week or so. Rousseau's 'Discourses on the Origin and Basis of Inequality Among Men' has remained an important essay for me till today, but when I read Rousseau more thoroughly and came to know his views about women and his arguments as to why they should not be equal political citizens of his much applauded republic, Randhir Singh softly said, "limitations of his time presented themselves here. It is also his reality, this does not mean that he cannot be appreciated for the progressive ideas he held and also, that he cannot be criticized for holding regressive ideas. Nobody needs to be worshipped. They are there to help us to do better in our own times". When I read the same sentences written out in his *Of Marxism of Karl Marx* included in his *Marxism, Socialism and Indian Politics*, I realised that these were important theoretical formulations which made him the kind of Marxist he was and is. He was opposed to any kind of orthodoxy, bourgeois or Marxist. He sought openness as a theoretician as that requires critical engagement continuously, with no closure. No matter where one is located this is also the beaten yet unbeaten path of radicalism I find myself on, thanks to this unusual teacher.

REFERENCES

Singh, R. (1989). The tradition of Marxism. *Economic and Political Weekly, 24* (43), 2421-2422.

Singh, R. (1993). *Five lectures in Marxist mode*. Delhi: Ajanta.

Singh, R. (2008). *Marxism, socialism, Indian politics: A view from the left*. Delhi: Aakar Books.

6

Of Marxism and Creative Theory: Engaging with Randhir Singh

Manindra Nath Thakur

This chapter is an attempt to trace the legacy of Randhir Singh's reading of Karl Marx and its intellectual impact on the students who attended his classes. It is also about the nature of pedagogy that he used for teaching this radical philosophy to the students of social sciences in the university. As we know, he taught Marxism for more than four decades in the University of Delhi, in the Department of Political Science and he was one of the prominent public intellectuals in the post-colonial India, who despite the collapse of Soviet Union kept claiming himself as an orthodox Marxist without any apology and yet attracted huge audiences for public meetings. He was widely known as a legendary teacher and a great thinker. He was definitely one of the few intellectuals who influenced not only students in the university and even the academics of his own generation but also a large number of political activists of all kinds. What was so remarkable about him was his capacity to communicate most complicated ideas in the simplest possible language and he had the capacity to preempt the questions and queries of the audience and to tailor his lecture or speech accordingly. In this chapter, I would like to argue that through his lectures, speeches and informal or formal discussions with students and activists he could create a discourse on Marxism, which is a quite distinct interpretation of Marx. He himself used to call it 'Marxism of Karl Marx'. In this chapter, I wish to retrieve his version of

Marxism from the collective memory of his students, particularly of my generation, through an often repeated statement of Karl Marx that he used to make sense of this theory in his specific context. I would like to argue that methodologically, this exercise of retrieving a coherent theoretical framework of an intellectual from the collective memory of his students is not only a desirable but also a viable project. I am saying this in the light of the fact that there are several such intellectuals in the non-western world who despite being able to intellectually influence generations of activists and students through their direct interactive engagements have not produced many written texts. Nevertheless, they are considered to be creative thinkers and they have produced many new ideas widely appreciated by their students and fellow-travelers. In such cases, I would like to suggest, we should not miss out on their creative thinking just because they have not used the written medium for expressing their ideas. I think we need to develop some methodological tools for retrieving their ideas and making them part of the collective intellectual resources. Here I will try to do this in the case of Randhir Singh with whom I had the chance to interact as a student. I would like to tell the reader that though fortunately, he had a chance to produce a good amount of written text and someone may try to undertake a similar exercise by referring to them, his presence in the collective memory is largely due to his lectures and speeches. Though his written texts are much more organised and probably one can retrieve his Marxism through these texts better, I think it is a legitimate exercise to try this through a number of statements that he used for constructing his own reading of Marx, which has survived in the collective consciousness of generations of his students. The ideas of Randhir Singh, I will be presenting here, are mainly based on his lectures and discussions with my contemporaries. and less based on the readings of the texts he has produced. I hope the two would match but even if they do not, I would like to privilege the former as that is what is surviving as collectively shared ideas and it has been so powerful that many of us are continuously guided by that in our intellectual endeavours.

In a way, it is an attempt to answer the question that many of his contemporary teachers used to ask about his intellectual influence on the students' thought processes. I remember in one of the lectures in Delhi University, Bertell Ollman, a famous Marxist scholar made this comment about him that he was deeply impressed by his pedagogical experiments and eventually Ollman himself wrote on the method of teaching Marx. I also remember the farewell speech by the famous Marxist historian R.S. Sharma, who mentioned about Randhir's lectures on Marx, many of which he himself attended. He mentioned that once while walking through the corridor after his lecture, he heard the argument Randhir was making on Marx's theory of history and became curious enough to attend his classes for almost the whole semester. One can easily see the point I am making that if R.S. Sharma, who himself was a renowned professor and famous for his Marxian reading of ancient Indian history found Randhir's lectures interesting, there must have been some creativity involved in the way he interpreted Marx for the Indian context. The question is: 'Can we decipher the creative interpretation he proposed through the analysis of the series of quotations he used repeatedly to communicate his reading of Marx?'

Theoretical Importance of Autobiographical Anecdotes

In this section, let me reflect on the pedagogical experiment he conducted for teaching Marx in a specific milieu of the university where he assumed teaching an act of politics. This does not mean that he was acting as an ideological mouthpiece of any left party in the university. Instead, for him teaching was a political act in the sense of developing the capacity for linking between being, thinking and knowing. This, he thought would provide the students an agency to intervene in the politics on behalf of the weak. He used to say this in his very first class 'you cannot be politically neutral, either you are a part of the problem or that of a solution; if you claim to be neutral in a fight between weak and strong, you are actually with the strong'. In this section, I would like to argue that one of the pedagogical strategies he adopted in order to help the students in developing this highly vibrant political agency was the use of anecdotes. I would like to suggest that many of these anecdotes were autobiographical in nature but the purpose was pedagogical as they were used to bring home some theoretical points.

Let me inform the reader that as a teacher, Randhir Singh was famous for giving a lot of anecdotes during his teaching or in the public lectures. Many of my contemporary scholars who were not his direct students found this use of anecdotes quite uncalled for. However, a deeper understanding suggests that through these anecdotes, he used to ground his arguments in the real world and it was a wonderful pedagogical move as this used to give students the needed confidence to explore their real world through the concepts and categories of Marxism. There are several anecdotes that his students do remember and many of them are autobiographical too. For instance, the mentioning of his involvement in the Indian struggle for freedom provided the needed background for the kind of reading of Marxism he put forward for us. This is just to remind that Randhir Singh belonged that generation of Indians who participated in the Indian national movement. He did not write his autobiography, which probably would have been as revealing as that of Rousseau's Confessions as it would have informed us about a side of the freedom struggle which has scarcely been explored. We have some glimpses in the writings of his contemporary novelist Bhisham Sahani, who like him was a Marxist and participated in the Indian struggle for freedom. Both of them migrated to India after partition and provided intellectual leadership to the left movement in their own ways; Randhir Singh by organising Delhi University Teachers' Association and Bhisham Sahani by writing texts on the partition experiences. Randhir has written a small article titled as 'In Lieu of Bio-data' (Singh), which gives us some glimpse of the time of the Indian freedom movement from the point of view of the left activists. As we are informed that he read most of the Marxist literature in the prison which used to be smuggled inside by the comrades and obviously there were not many copies. So, these writings used to travel from prison to prison through the comrades being moved from one prison to the other. This tells us the story of the vantage point for reading Marxism as for these young men it was primarily a matter of commitment and not of mere intellectual engagement, the point I will discuss in the later part of this chapter. Let me make a pedagogical point here about the relation between anecdotes and communication in the classroom situation. I think it worked as a wonderful tool to communicate Marxism in a way that made the minds ready to engage in a thought experiment for creative reading. Thereafter, in a few lectures, he would deliver a complicated reading of Marx and without much effort, one would remember these statements through which a new framework started unfolding. The beauty of the framework was that it only provided a signpost leaving the students to think, reflect and connect with the concrete reality of their own time and space. Though he claimed himself as an orthodox Marxist, he redefined it as I mentioned earlier: 'Marxism and Karl Marx.'

There were many other anecdotes his students do remember even after so many years of their passing out from the university and I would keep referring to them as and when needed. Let me reemphasise the point that in an academic communication, passion for the argument one presents comes from the political commitment that one has. However, in the classroom situation the real challenge is to present it in a way that opinion and ideology are not used to replace the argument. It should be assumed that the students do have the capacity and they must have their autonomy to evaluate the strength and weakness of any argument and it should stand alone without any support from the political commitment. Probably in order to achieve this, Randhir introduced the element of anecdotes in his pedagogical experiment. This allowed him to provoke students for the reality check of the arguments he provided. And I would like to lay stress on the point that this space for reality check provided the scope for argumentative thinking and creative reading of Marx. Many of his students explored many fields of research from the Marxian perspective even without being formally part of any left political party and without being dogmatic about it.

That is the reason that a good number of his students even today consider themselves as Marxist and the collapse of Soviet Union did not affect their overall theoretical orientation, however, without losing the sense of creativity. I remember another anecdote he used to share with us. In a seminar, he happened to meet Prof. Manmohan Singh, the then Finance Minister of India and he asked Randhir if he was still a Marxist after the collapse of the Soviet Union. His witty answer was: 'What to do, Professor, if one is not a Marxist because of Soviet Union but because of the analysis of the capitalism and the dream to fight against the terrible system that it has to offer.' This is the idea he always emphasised as he argued that one should have the commitment to the knowledge and share the vantage point with Marx. It is not necessary to commit oneself to the ideology of the Marxist parties. This pedagogical technique provided the students from multiple class and cultural backgrounds some free space to engage with Marxism in their own way. As a consequence of this, many generations of his students do acknowledge his influence on their thinking. I must say that many of his students suffer from dissatisfaction with the way political theory is done in India and that has brought them together to think about an alternative which could be more critical but grounded in the concrete reality. The group has named itself as Creative Theory. I will demonstrate in the next section that through his numerous anecdotes and carefully selected quotations from Marx, he could carve out a perspective, which is definitely informed by the theoretical gains of this powerful philosophy but also has the capacity to continuously emerge on the basis of its confrontation with the contemporary reality. This framework and its creative capacity have made permanent inroads into the thought processes of many of his students. For him and as for his students "Marxism is, and needs to be, scientific in its philosophical foundations and commitment to criticism and continuing verification and development of its main principles, postulates, and conclusions. It is a living and creative theory that continuously interacts with the reality of the world around it and with the rest of contemporary thought, and grows with the growth of scientific and historical knowledge" (Singh, 2006: 47). This understanding of Marxism constitutes the core of the creative theory group, which aims at engaging with contemporary reality and its multiple understanding to develop a critical theory and philosophy for human liberation.

In Defence of a Commitment: Question of the Vantage Point

In the very first encounter with Randhir Singh, one got attracted to his persona carrying his radical past on his face and his hope to radicalise the new generation in his twinkling eyes. The more attractive thing was the way he introduced Marx by quoting him from his first written stuff. He informed us that Marx had a sense of commitment to the well-being of humanity from very childhood and with the growth of time he only chased this dream with more consistency. Consider this often quoted words from Marx's 'Reflections of a Young Man of on the Choice of a Profession':

> But the chief guide which must direct us in the choice of a profession is the welfare of mankind and our perfection. It should not be thought that these two interests could be in conflict, that one would have to destroy the other; on the contrary, man's nature is so constituted that he can attain his own perfection only by working for the perfection, for the good, of his fellow men.

If he works for himself, he may perhaps become a famous man of learning, a great sage, an excellent poet, but he can never be a perfect, truly great man.

History calls those men the greatest who have ennobled themselves by working for the common good; experience acclaims as the happiest the man who has made the greatest number of people happy; religion itself teaches us that the ideal being who all strive to copy sacrificed himself for the sake of mankind, and who would dare to set at nought such judgments?

> If we have chosen the position in life in which we can most of all work for mankind, no burden can bow us down, because they are sacrifices for the benefit of all; then we shall experience no petty, limited, selfish joy, but our happiness will belong to millions, our deeds will live on quietly but perpetually at work, and over our ashes will be shed the hot tears of noble people. (Marx, 1975: 8)

This was the quotation that he would read out from the text in his class and obviously this broke the ice in the sense that this was a student Marx very much like anyone present in the class, in fact, a few years younger to us. What a magic was performed in terms of establishing a link between the thinker and the reader? I must say that the young minds present in the class were exposed to the idea that as humans we were not there to study to earn bread and butter but to perform a duty towards the humanity by serving the common good. It raised the question of the purpose of life and I remember him mentioning that this was the vantage point of Marx which defined rest of his concerns throughout his life. Now if we accept this as the vantage point, we will have to accept that the rest of his work should also be evaluated on the basis of his central aim that is 'working for common good'. The aim of his theory was then not merely to understand or interpret the world but to change it in a direction that was necessary to make 'mankind' happy.

This commitment to common good and happiness of humankind makes Marx a philosopher of universal human liberation and the point that Randhir could communicate to us without mentioning it is that one can make sense of Marx better if one has some commitment to this project of Marx. In fact, this is a larger point that can be considered for understanding a political thinker who is not a philosopher in an ordinary sense of the term as the professional philosopher, but a revolutionary busy in struggling for human liberation. It is true for Gandhi, for Ambedkar, for Mao, for Che Guevara or anyone and anywhere in the world who owns the project of universal human liberation. So, the point is that we cannot understand them properly without sharing their dream of human liberation. No wonder in his first class, Randhir would mitigate the gap between being, thinking and knowing as for us it was no more as one of the papers from the syllabus to be opted for credit but an occasion to think creatively to formulate one's own philosophy.

By the time we were mustering the courage to think of ourselves as philosophers having some natural capacity to the reflect upon our reality in order to change it, he would throw another challenge: 'Everyone is a philosopher. It is your choice whether you are conscious about it or not'. So, you are not left with any choice except to think that you have to be conscious of your philosophy. But by the time you are contemplating on this point he would throw yet another challenge: "The head is your own but ideas of Girilal Jain". Now this is a sentence kept haunting haunting many of his students all the time and it definitely gave many of us sleepless nights. Let me explain this. Mr. Jain was the editor of The Times of India at that time, which was widely being read by the students of our generation. Randhir challenged us to find out if our opinions on several contemporary issues were actually opinions were received subconsciously from the newspaper. If we unpack this further, it would mean that we were challenged to examine whether we were the victims of common sense that we acquired from our surroundings and we falsely considered them as our own or they are products of our critical investigation And the final nail in the coffin was his declaration that 'common sense is no sense' and his direction that 'doubt everything'. I still remember how confused we were after the class. For several days, we could not reconcile with the idea and once we digested it, we experienced a new intellectual journey that helped us in establishing a relationship between thinking, being and knowing.

In short, Randhir Singh through his classes tried to generate a commitment not to the ideology but to the knowledge that Marx has to offer. This knowledge is important not because of his explanatory capacity but also its commitment to the well-being of the humanity. Can we consider the generation of this commitment as part of his pedagogical strategy to teach radical philosophy? Obviously the answer is yes. This strategy was less ideological and more humanitarian as it opened the space for a form of emergentist Marxism.

Unfinished Project of Marxism and Question of Emergentism

Let me remind that we are discussing Randhir's understanding of Marxism as it was delivered by him to his students through the classroom teaching. I have argued that he had developed a unique pedagogical method to undertake this project of making young minds aware of this philosophy which he thought was necessary for human liberation. I have already discussed two components of his strategy: a) use of anecdotes and key sentences carefully selected from Marx's writing, and b) linking the philosophy with the everyday experiences. The first component of the pedagogical strategy was helpful in installing the ideas in the consciousness and second was useful for opening the space for creative thinking.

In continuation with these, he argued that 'Marxism is an unfinished project'. By giving this statement, he further confirmed the need for a creative reading of Marx as if it is an unfinished project and designed to remain so. One of the implications of this takes us to another argument that the generations to come will have a capacity and duty to take it further. He would provide evidence for this from Engel's work Anti-Duhring:

> ...the generations which will put *us* right are likely to be far more numerous than those whose knowledge we ...have the opportunity to correct (Engels, 1987: 80).

But a man who applies the measure of genuine, immutable, final and ultimate truth to knowledge which, by its very nature, must either remain relative for many generations be completed only step by step, or which, as in cosmology, geology and the history of mankind, must always contain gaps and be incomplete because of the inadequacy of the historical material—such a man only proves thereby his own ignorance and perversity (Engels, 1987: 84).

This statement was an appeal to engage with Marxism not in any dogmatic fashion but in a more creative way. He always emphasised the point that reading Marx through text would mean Marxiology and not Marxism. Marxism of Karl Marx to him was not a rigid ideology but open knowledge acquired through revolutionary practice. One has to consider, he argued, the continuous growth and development in the thinking of Marx. One should not consider Marx as 'some sort of supra-historical genius who would be always fully consistent in what he said and wrote' as he was responding to the different issues in different periods and many responses were more polemical and less theoretical. It was almost a shock to us when he cited historical materialism as an example of this. Let me quote Randhir from his magnum opus to give the reader a clearer idea of this complex argument:

> One of the gravest of them, for example, could appeal to many statements in the thought of Karl Marx, particularly in popular or propagandist or polemical writings, which either articulated economist view or can be reasonably interpreted in an economist manners the most famous being Marx's frequently quoted formulation of the doctrine of historical materialism in the Preface to the Critique of Political Economy. Such statements came to be emphasized and exaggerated and thus misinterpreted, by the followers in the half-century after his death, as part of the justificatory ideology and political theory of the reformist working class movement which grew up in the industrial West (Singh, 2006: 42).

As students, we were unable to comprehend the transformation that was required to digest this idea. The kind of Marxism that came to us was having this as the basic tenet of the philosophy. He informed us that dialectics and materialism are two philosophical premises of Marxism quite distinguishable from 'dialectical materialism' of the official Marxism of the Soviet Union. He presented Marxism as a form of realism aiming at expelling the 'world existing independent of our knowledge', multilayered, constantly changing or evolving, full of contradictions and conflicts; however, yet it is knowable.

Consequently, he suggested, 'truth is a whole and constituted of interconnected parts' and 'more you know the interconnection more you know the truth'. He explained the whole and part relationship in terms of signature of the whole on the part and the signature of parts, on the whole, the relationship is almost undistinguishable. Now, if the truth is constantly emerging, the search for truth also has to be unending and that supports the point that no knowledge is final; we have to accept that knowledge is ever growing and generations to come will be more numerous who would correct our knowledge in the course of human history.

This makes Marxism an open project, unfinished, emerging, constantly rethinking and without any claim for finality. He would emphatically put it that we should not expect Marx to provide you answers to all the questions we have as he makes no such claims, promises and he has no such pretentious. Instead Randhir would argue: "On the contrary, as we have already noticed, Marxism has its 'silences' and 'empty spaces', its contradictions and any number of unresolved tensions: for example, between determinism and contingency, structure and agency, individuality and sociality, spontaneity and organization, and so on" (Singh, 2006: 41). He argues that there are intrinsic parts of our ever-changing real life. Instead of providing neat answers to these questions, Randhir argues, Marxism has provided a method to approach these questions, a superior mode of analysis of our social world. Therefore, he used to put forward Marx's appeal before the students to 'think as I am thinking'. This was not an ordinary appeal as it was full of confidence in the capacity of people to think about the ideas of social change. This made an ordinary student important in his or her own eyes. This was a pedagogical twist to Marx's statement and students got involved in thinking by becoming conscious of the method. Randhir emphasises that when the method is not final, one has to keep improving upon it in the light of new frontiers of knowledge.

In short, Randhir's reading of Marx was an opening for students in terms of thinking critically for enabling them to theorise the reality around them. It would be worth remembering that for him this theorisation was not to be merely an academic activity but it was aiming at supporting people in their struggle for freedom and dignity. On occasions of controversial social moments when the society was open to debate, he used to be invited for the public meetings in the universities and outside. In these meetings one would witness the skilful demonstration of the use of his Marxist method in explaining the issues at hand. For instance, his often repeated quote of the then Brazilian president's answer to the question about Brazil's economy—'Economy is doing fine, people are not', demonstrated the methodological distinction between economy and people while talking of a country. One of the often shared anecdotes was about his interpretation of the idea of 'mainstream'. He was invited by the Government of India to deliver a talk on national integration to the students from North-Eastern states of India. They were quite upset with the Central Government supporting as they did the insurgencies in these states. In a question about the central reason for their unhappiness, they replied that they would not like to be the part of the mainstream as the government was constantly making this plea. Randhir asked them a counter-question "Do, you have corruption?" His argument was that 'if you have it you are already in the mainstream as that is the mainstream of India.' The point I want to bring home is that with his kind of reading of Marx he could engage with contemporary issues in a much more creative way and this created space for emergentist Marxism.

Marxism, Science, and Positivism

One of the crucial points that Randhir Singh kept repeating in his classes was about the relation between Marxism and science. The mainstream Marxist parties through which most people of our generation were introduced to this philosophy were heavily dominated by the Soviet interpretation of Marx. Since, Plekhanov, one of the prominent Marxist thinkers of Soviet Union, was deeply influenced by positivist philosophy, his reading of Marx reflected this in many forms. Randhir presented a counter-perspective quite congruently and this prompted many students to undertake research in many fields, which did not conventionally attract the attention of the Marxist scholars. One thing is sure that as a teacher he could preempt the concerns of the students as for many of them Marxism was a science and a form of positivism. It was true for both who declared themselves as Marxist or as anti-Marxist. Both were convinced of the positivist reading of Marx. Having preempted this, Randhir took upon himself the task of addressing this issue in a very different way and exposed the students to the debates on science. In this section, I would like to demonstrate as to how Randhir could do it through his classroom teaching.

The first argument he put forward was about the language of Marx's time, which he argued was dominated by the scientific vocabulary as the world had recently witnessed the phenomenal emergence of the modern science. Randhir suggested that Marx was also a child of his time in the true sense; therefore, it should not surprise anyone if he spoke in the widely accepted language of the time. Moreover, Engels was more impressed by this language than Marx. I must mention that when he was making this point to the students his class, nothing of this kind was available to them in any form. Since we have an advantage of reading his written text, let me quote him from there:

> Marx was of course, very much—as much as anybody else—'a child of his time' (to borrow an expression from Hegel). This not only involves the implications of not looking for answers in his work with either do not exist or which are at any rate not to be found there, it also involves recognising that Marx too, like anybody else, carried his share of 'the mud of his time', including, for example, a certain gender blindness and ecological short-sightedness. He very much belonged to his age, even as he was, here and elsewhere, in his own magnificent manner, moving beyond it. Immediately important is to notice the fact that it was an age excessively confident of itself, drunk with the achievements of modern science. Marx was not immune to its intellectual or cultural ethos, its language or idiom. It had its impact on his work. And one important negative consequence was that Marx's thought

> did not always transcend the bourgeois-positivist model of the social science of his time, based on an arbitrary and unqualified extension to the social and historical sphere of the epistemological paradigm of the natural sciences, with its laws, its determinism, its purely objective predictions, linear development, and so on, all expressed in the strong, confident and even dogmatic language of the second half of the nineteenth century (Singh, 2006: 44).

This was quite a consent argument which was inviting for reflexive exercise while reading Marx. For him, even Marx was not beyond failings and scrutiny. This further opened Marxism and made the younger generation confident enough to undertake a project of engaging with different fields of inquiry that too without any apology for going beyond Marx. The scientism of orthodox Marxism was questioned without going into any detail of the textual evidence, by providing a simpler and absorbable yet convincing argument. One remembers his forceful argument against the claims concerning the necessities of history or infallibility of leadership understood on the basis of so-called 'science of Marxism' and its discovery of laws of society or economy. Randhir would stand with Gramsci in his call for rejection of pronouncement of 'funeral eulogy', which was made basis for supporting 'scientific-deterministic' reading of Marx.

Having said all this, Randhir, would then creatively engage with his idea of science and its relation with Marxism. For him, the scientific resilience is the strength of Marxism and not its weakness. To be scientific, to him, was to be ready for accepting new explorations, confidence in the idea of 'growth of knowledge' and 'the endless human quest to acquire a better, truer, understanding of the world'. This approach to science and its relation with Marxism has successfully initiated a process of creative thinking being carried forward by many of his students. Let me quote him once again to demonstrate the ignition that he could set for his students:

> To question scientism in Marxism, the scientific emasculation or mangling of Marxism, by both its supporters and detractors, is not to deny the scientific credentials of Marxism but assert them

> by focusing them on how precisely it claims to be scientific, what indeed it has to offer as a critical science of society, with careful attention to certain long-standing misuses of the word 'science', Marxism is, and needs to be, scientific in its philosophical foundations and commitment to criticism and continuing verification and development of its own principles, postulates and conclusions. *It is a living and creative theory that continuously interacts with the reality of the world around it and with the rest of complementary thought, and grows with the growth of scientific and historical knowledge* (Singh, 2006: 47). (Italics mine)

It is in this sense Randhir considered Marxism as scientific. Since, Marxism is a science in the sense of being committed to the growth of knowledge, critical self-reflection, continuous interaction with the reality and critical thinking, it is a form of creative theory. This idea of Marxism as a creative theory helped his students to get rid of dogmatism and legitimately opened it up as knowledge instead of being merely ideology. This is what has invited the intellectual movement called Creative Theory, which engages with Marxism without being dogmatic and consciously reflects at three different levels: empirical, theoretical and philosophical. A good number of scholars are working on different themes and undertaking empirical research and simultaneously contributing to the theoretical debates and expanding the philosophical horizons as well.

I remember asking him almost toward the end of his intellectual journey about his opinion on the Indian philosophy. I was surprised by his reply that if he were to get another few decades at his disposal he would have read Indian philosophy. This was the kind of Marxism he adhered to. This goes well with what he has argued in the following paragraph:

> Marxism was open in its origins: it arose, as is well known, acknowledging its debts—a 'critical settling of accounts' Marx called it—to English political economy, German philosophy and French socialism. It is, and needs to remain, open to new ideas, to new data and experience, competing for insights and bodies of learning, to newer fields of inquiry. Marxism must continue to learn from other intellectual traditions, confront them not merely for the sake of critique and dismissal but drawing out elements to

> enrich itself, just as it does so through corrections, rectifications, and criticism inspired by its own experience and social practice. *To be able to grow and develop as a living creative theory, Marxism has to recognize that it 'cannot generate all its intellectual capital out of its own resources'...it must be receptive to what may possibly be secured from competing theories* (Singh, 2006: 48). (Italics mine)

I think this openness has to be understood by anyone who claims to be a Marxist as without this it would be difficult for this philosophy to survive in the twenty-first century. This openness also demands, as he acknowledged in a personal discussion with me, critical engagement with the Indian intellectual traditions too, which has generally been ignored by the Marxists scholars and activists. His notion of science was not positivist but being a knowledge capable of constantly evolving by absorbing whatever was innovated. It was not science in terms of the Newtonian model but in terms of the Creative Realist model. The difference between them is that former considered regularity as a necessary and sufficient condition for being science and therefore, ignoring the complexity of social reality; whereas, the latter argues that regularity is neither a necessary nor sufficient condition for being a science (Bhaskar, 2C08).

Marxism and Religion

I have been arguing till now that Randhir was a Marxist of a new kind as he has provided a new interpretation based on his experience as a political activist and political observer in India. More importantly, I have tried to suggest that he used his classroom teaching as a site for articulation and expression of his take on Marxism and he innovated a new pedagogy to teach Marxism to the students of a Third World country. A large number of his students were deeply impressed by this kind of Marxism and got engaged in a varietty of research work culminating in an intellectual movement what they call as Creative Theory. His pedagogical innovation had two major elements: a) encouraging the students to doubt everything and consequently to think creatively and b) constantly linking his theoretical or philosophical point to the real live experiences so that they could get into the habit of a reality check for any theory including Marxism. In this section, I would like to take a particular example to show the way some of his students, including me, got inspired to work on religion and Marxism.

I remember the days when some of us became his students in the mid-eighties, after the 'operation blue star', which was a military action against the occupation of Golden Temple by the Sikh militant movement run by Bhindranwale. It was a difficult time for a Marxist who happened to be a Sikh also. He also had a personal story of trauma to share as Delhi witnessed a major anti-Sikh riot. However, his personal agony did not deter him from reflecting on the crisis in Panjab as a Marxist scholar. He was the first one to tell the world that the crisis was a fallout of the failures of Green Revolution, which converted the State into a 'chicken and whisky land'. He explained the political economy of the crisis but without being an economic reductionist. He explained it in terms of the relative autonomy of culture. He continued meeting the revolutionary groups of Punjab peasantry and kept evolving his understanding based on his observations on the changing scenario.

As the semester was coming to an end, we were anxious to hear his explanation on religion. Many of us who were not ready to accept standard Marxian theoretical formulation popularly known as 'opium thesis', i.e. 'religion is the opium of masses', were waiting for him to come to this chapter as we thought it would raise a sustained difference. He surprised us by suggesting that this sentence was a part of a larger quote: 'Religion is the sigh of the oppressed creature, the heart of a healthess world, and the soul of soulless conditions. It is the opium of the people.' His argument was that this opium thesis was not Marx's theory but it belonged to mechanical materialists. His explanation for Marx using this statement was interesting and convincing. He argued that Marx had a typical style of combining two extreme opinions. Consider, for instance, his in answer to the question 'Who makes history?'. One extreme answer used to be 'man makes history' and the other was 'circumstances make history'. Marx combined the two and answered 'man makes history but not as he pleases'; he makes history but within the limits of the circumstances. Similarly, Randhir argued, Marx has combined the two extreme ideas on religion to demonstrate the complexities of this phenomenon. We can see as to how even great Soviet thinkers missed this point. Randhir in his own favour would quote Engels from Anti-Dühring as it is here they (Marx and Engels) have made their perspective on religion clear. They have rejected Herr Dühring's approach to religion which suggested that "In the free society there can be no religious worship; *for* every member of it has got beyond the primitive childish superstition that there are beings, behind nature or above it, who can be influenced by sacrifices or prayers" (Engels, 1987: 300). Against this, they argued for a more complex understanding of religion and the possibility of it survival till every form of alienation gets over. We can find this rejection in the following paragraph from Anti Dühring:

> All religion, however, is nothing but the fantastic reflection in men's minds of those external forces which control their daily life, a reflection in which the terrestrial forces assume the form of supernatural forces. In the beginnings of history, it was the forces of nature which were first so reflected, and which in the course of further evolution underwent the most manifold and varied personifications among the various peoples. This early process has been traced back by comparative mythology, at least in the case of the Indo-European peoples, to its origin in the Indian Vedas, and in its further evolution it has been demonstrated in detail among the Indians, Persians, Greeks, Romans, Germans and, so far as material is available, also among the Celts, Lithuanians, and Slavs (Engels, 1987: 300-301).

Engels continues:

> But it is not long before, side by side with the forces of nature, social forces begin to be active—forces which confront man as equally alien and at first equally inexplicable, dominating him with the same apparent natural necessity as the forces of nature themselves. The fantastic figures, which at first only reflected the mysterious forces of nature, at this point acquire social attributes,

> become representatives of the forces of history. At a still further stage of evolution, all the natural and social attributes of the numerous gods are transferred to one almighty god, who is but a reflection of the abstract man. Such was the origin of monotheism, which was historically the last product of the vulgarized philosophy of the later Greeks and found its incarnation in the exclusively national god of the Jews, Jehovah (Engels, 1987: 301).

Therefore, natural religion gets transformed into social religion and in the process of transformation, it takes different shapes. It adapts to the needs of power relationship. Randhir would argue with Engels that any effort to forcefully kill religion similar to that of Herr Dühring would create a serious problem. This explains what happened in the Soviet Union. In the bourgeois society alienation of capitalist and workers would sustain religion. Randhir Singh's supported Engels prescription to minimise the social and political role of religion, suggesting that instead of forbidding religion's control one must focus on the alien forces that control the life of people. So, he would support their argument that 'only then will the last alien force which is still reflected in religion vanish; and with it will also vanish the religious reflection itself, for the simple reason that then there will be nothing left to reflect' (Engels, 1987: 301).

I remember, on many occasions, our friends from left political parties and the self-proclaimed orthodox Marxist groups did not agree with Randhir's formulations. However, both in the era of post 'Operation Blue Star' and 'Babri Mosque demolition', Randhir asserted that they should read Marx more carefully and creatively. With the contemporary resurgence of religion, we can see easily that Randhir was right. With his reading of Marx on religion we can not only explain the contemporary resurgence but also think of the new form of Left politics in today's world. At least one can argue that his approach to Marx's ideas on religion opens new possibilities of engaging with it. I would not go into another domain widely discussed in this context called secularism. However, I would like to leave the reader guessing his approach to this concept by quoting his one of the pet sentences: 'fight for secularism has to be fight for socialism'. This sentence summarises his reading of Marx on religion, secularism, capitalism, socialism and their inter-relations.

Conclusion

This chapter attempts to argue that in the intellectual history of the post-colonial societies, there are many people who combined their profession as teachers with the preoccupation as social thinkers. Many of them have made their classroom teaching as the site for articulation and expression of their creative thinking. Their commitment to critical social theory helped them in experimenting with a pedagogy of radical philosophy. Randhir Singh belongs to this category of intellectuals. A more serious engagement with his ideas is yet to be done. I am sure with the kind of crisis we are facing in the contemporary times, we have to access his thinking again and again for insights to understand the reality for the purpose of transforming it. It should not be difficult to see that in this new context, his idea of Marxism being a form of creative theory would gain more ground.

REFERENCES

Bhaskar, R. (2008). *A realist theory of science*. London: Verso.

Engels, F. (1987). Anti-Duhring. In *Karl Marx—Frederick Engels, Collected Works, Volume 25*. New York: International Publishers

Marx, K. (1975). Reflections of a young men of on the choice of a profession. In *Karl Marx—Frederick Engels, Collected Works Volume I*. New York: International Publishers .

Singh, R. (2006). *Crisis of Socialism: In defence of a commitment*. Delhi: Ajanta Publications.

7

Randhir Singh—A Tribute to a Maverick Academic

Veena Ravikumar

Prof. Randhir Singh came into the Department of Political Science like a breath of fresh air or like a welcome rain after a drought. The syllabus till then was structured. While the study of constitutions and political thought was necessary, Prof. Randhir Singh's teaching took an unconventional approach. Taught with great savoir faire, the students enjoyed his lectures which included instances that they identified with.

My first encounter with him was at teaching theory sessions which I felt I had to attend to broaden my intellectual understanding of Marxism. After which, one tried to attend everything he wanted to impart to his students. The innate fascination for him and his lectures came from students of different disciplines—history, sociology, literature, and political science. And in his own words, only those from Commerce and Business Management probably did not attend his lectures. He was highly regarded and appropriated by all. There was an award instituted in his name in the Department of Political Science at Lady Shri Ram College when I really began to get to know him. This award was so akin to what he believed in. Even if the student did not score very high marks in the university system but was engaged, interested and good with political theory, she could aspire for the award.

It brought out the talent, freshness and research capability in the students. They were to choose their topic and present it before Prof. Randhir Singh, the faculty and their peer group. It was to bring out critical thinking and reasoning amongst students. It did not necessarily have to do with Marxist thought but sound political theoretical constructs.

He made an impressive speaker, dressed in a smart shirt with a turban to match. Almost up to his last year, he would totally forget the refreshments offered and immersed himself with students' queries and faculty interjections. It was as if he presented a different insight into problems of Marxism. He was presented as a simple intellectual most of the time. If ever there was an oxymoron, it was this.

While some of us take a year to teach the basics of Marxism, it seemed as if Prof. Randhir Singh could explain it effectively in an hour. The text was simple, with personal examples sewn in and Gramsci became personal and easy.The papers by the Randhir Singh awardees were of high quality, and printed in the Political Science journal published by the Department.

Many were awarded the Randhir Singh Prize. Nila Mohanan who wrote: United States' Hegemony in the World Order—A Gramscian Interpretation, became an IAS officer and one hopes, keeps Prof. Randhir Singh's teachings in mind. The essay surely did.

Radhika Kumar who is in academics now, wrote: Democratic Development and the Civil Society Approach—A Comparative Study of the States of Madhya Pradesh and Andhra Pradesh in the Post-Liberalisation Period. Lakshmi Radhakrishnan's essay was on Amartya Sen and Gender Development. She has joined the IRS. Sunalini Kumar's essay: Environmental Discourse, Civil Society and the Public Sphere, has joined our department as a faculty member. Sidhya Balakrishnan, a later awardee had a 'capitalist' mindset as she called it and yet began reading Marx and Prof. Randhir Singh's essays. Many more awardees form the band who went on to other professions, always felt privileged to have been chosen for this award.

Prof. Randhir Singh was born and brought up in Lahore by his father, a doctor, but he did not want to follow his father's profession. Instead, at a young age he became a revolutionary, and was known as one of the first to start a students' movement in the country in the 1930s. He was jailed as a freedom fighter in 1940s and if one recollects correctly, he finished his undergraduate studies from the prison. Maybe it was following in Regis Debray and Gramscian steps that he acquired a certain amount of charisma and was beheld the same way by the students he later taught. Whatever the reasons, he himself looked at his days in the terrorist ward of the prison as some of his happiest days. One can see why, he was in touch with comrades and the philosophy he believed in, in a visceral manner.

He was not just a lecturer, but an activist, organising workers in factories and peasants in the villages. The language of exploitation of the masses was not just an epistemological reference; he lived it. So much so that Balvant Gargi, the famous Punjabi writer wrote that Randhir Singh was one of the brightest young intellectuals and was considered the Marx of the group as he is profiled in one of the bio-notes. After his jail-term, he worked on the Communist Party's Punjabi weekly *Jang-i-Azadi*. He also wrote a biography of the legendary Ghadar hero Baba Gurmukh Singh and a book of Punjabi poems. *Rahan Di Dhoor* (Stormy Dust of the Paths), which added the poetic nom de plume *Josh* to his name.

It was teaching that became his first love. Teaching made him feel least alienated in his Marxist scheme of being. But, he had his grounding in aesthetics, which he felt gave him true perspective—in art, literature, poetry, a truly 'Marxist Man', not just a limited or boundaried Renaissance Man.

Along with Prof. Bipin Chandra, Randhir Singh brought out a Marxist research journal 'Enquiry'. Some of the famous scholars of eminence contributed to it, like Prof. Irfan Habib. Prof. Randhir Singh published some of his critiquing articles of the political thinker Michael Oakshott. This was later developed in his book entitled *Reason, Revolution and Political Theory* (1967) which received widespread appreciation.

A very strange, but creative way of teaching Marx was

through Plato, as Prof. Randhir Singh did. His lectures on Hobbes, Locke and Marx were to say in the least, brilliant. This was a profile he went with through his teaching career, becoming legendary and having a massive student fan following. Coupled with a different strand of humor, his jokes never lost their sheen. "The economy is doing good, the people are not" would get a good laugh after which he explained the nuances of Marxist economics. Yet he claimed not to know true economics.

When he taught, he taught with a passion and it was after retirement that he wrote much more. A paper on why Communism still exists at the time of the Soviet decay explained as long as there was inequity, Marxist principles would prevail, and communism would never fade away. His words proved right when after the crisis in the United States of America, and the fall of the Lehman Brothers, even hedge fund bankers and joint investment experts were trying to buy Das Kapital to see how the alternative works.

Other books written by him were *Crisis of Socialism: Notes in Defence of Commitment*, *Of Marxism and Politics* and *Five Lectures in Marxism Mode*.

When asked for his bio-data, in true Randhir Singh style, he wrote an 'autobiographical note' in lieu of a bio-data (Published in *Mainstream*, March 12, 1988). He writes about having no credentials to scholarship. He takes us through his life, and the fact that his poetry was celebrated. But he goes on to say that he might only have been a "might have been." He had a winsome way of putting it that a bio-data had been a perennial embarrassment since he had no fellowships, research projects, no 'seminaring', national or international, and not even a visit abroad. (He was very proud of this, carrying it almost as if a badge of honour). He called his contemporary work Marxist orthodoxy. The innocence and integrity of thought is perceivable in Prof. Randhir Singh, a rare quality. And further, the need not to be co-opted into the system.

Prof. Randhir Singh in 2010 brought out some of his thoughts as a monograph, *A Note on the Current Political Situation:*

Some Issues and a Conclusion. The original was published in *Mainstream*, August 14, 2010. This piece underlined his thoughts of the time, the path India was taking and some issues which were interlinked presenting a gamut of serious questions. He was, in essence, questioning the path India was taking, the neoliberal capitalist path of development for the country which the Indian ruling classes have now openly opted for. According to him this forms a threat to the Adivasis and the marginalised people, propelling the Maoists to the centrestage. According to him Operation Green Hunt has only added to the sympathy for the Maoists and Adivasis. Further, he feels that only the revolutionary Left can offer alternatives as both the Government and the media use negative factors to delegitimise Maoist politics and Naxalite or any other revolutionary politics as well. Government focuses on violence, invoking support for 'democracy', 'nationalism', helping mobilise people for support of official policies of the capitalist path of development.

Further, the revolutionary Left, needs to shift the focus of debate and struggle from violence to politics, to policies and programmes, to the issue of the country's path of development, which to be pro-people has to be a socialism-oriented path of development. He emphasises this almost as the only model of survival and alternative and a path to a revolutionary transformation of society. According to Prof. Randhir Singh, the mainstream Left has to link itself to the revolutionary Left to restore honour to the word 'Communist'. Marxism critically needs to examine itself and parties too, are in dire need of this.

A radical revolution of the Left is necessary, according to him.

History has been cruel and it would be cruel to the Left, Prof. Randhir Singh said, paraphrasing Engels. He rues the turn to 'globalisation' as a strategic option for India by both the Congress and the BJP (after the failure of a 'socialist pattern of society' and the collapse of the Soviet Union). The higher the rate of economic growth along this pattern becomes, the greater would be underdevelopment of India. The so-called 'trickle down', if and when it occurs is no better than 'feeding the horses with oats so that some of it passes down to the road for sparrows', as Galbraith once said, quotes Prof. Randhir Singh.

According to him, whatever have been the benefits of economic reforms, they have polarised Indian society, playing havoc with lives of common people and pushed them to the edge of the peripheralised existence with the global capitalist system. He ascribes this to Special Economic Zones (SEZs). Amit Bhaduri, too called the Special Economic Zones of which Randhir Singh had spoken of as 'developmental terrorism'. He backs it up with Klaus Schwab even writing, "We are living in an increasingly schizophrenic world, where economies are booming and global signs are promising, but underneath are political and social risks, as well as imbalances and inconsistencies".

According to Prof. Randhir Singh, a market-oriented growth simply cannot deliver 'inclusive growth'. It is by its very nature exclusionary. He traces the economic path and comes to the conclusion that the way it was structured had to lead to 'market economy'. From the feel good factor in economy in India, to creating two nations in India, equity and justice do not seem to exist for the common man and 'economic reforms' and democracy do not go together. In fact, it gives rise to an utterly reactionary ideology. Also the shift to globalisation or 'economic' reforms was unaccompanied by any debate or discussion, serious opposition or questioning. A perception of Prof. Randhir Singh's is that what has led to BJP to follow the same path of so called earlier economic development also may have led to its aggressive nationalist posture which could be an advantage in the harsh competitive world of global economy and politics, an astute price of thought.

According to Prof. Randhir Singh, to truly explore the alternative, the present mode would have to be given up. He also talks of diversification and development of internal markets to achieve goals to alleviate poverty. He makes a strong case for a socialism-oriented pro-people autonomous development process, which will draw upon people's strengths, domestic resources and capacities, including those of the hardworking poor who yet remain the most creative and productive force in our society. It will give a further fillip to both socialism and democracy which seem to be interlinked. He admits that socialism in the former Soviet Union did not really work because of abuse of power, lack of rights and the like. But the takeaway from this is that it is feasible; it can be done. What kind of society would we, as human beings want to have would be the important question. Moving towards building a humane, democratically functioning socialist society that fosters equality, cooperation, solidarity and respect for universal ethical values would be the crucial answer. Revolution is best understood as a complete process of structural transformation of society - with special complexities of its own in regimes of bourgeois democracy.

The world over any effort to seek revolutionary change through democratic processes has been seen by the ruling class as a challenge to capitalism and not allowed to proceed. He does emphasise the need for extra parliamentary class and mass politics for any renewed struggle for socialism, to bring about changes in society. He does not imply any kind of lawlessness nor an aprioristic rejection of electoral or parliamentary politics.

In the cause of true socialism, he still remains loyal to Marx as his guide: 'peaceful if possible, with arms if necessary'. The above note on the current political situation was to lay out and extrapolate Prof. Randhir Singh's ideas, the personal and the political and theory constructed in the present global scenario. He very much had the pulse on the politics and thought deeply and politically. In essence, he was a humanist and a true marxist.

8

Commitments Never Die

Hilal Ahmed

Speaking in the stereotyped tongue of industrialists of Old Delhi, Randhir Singh was my *dada ustad* (master). In other words, he was the teacher of teachers and in his seminary, I learned the skills to gain knowledge (or tried to learn them). When I became a student of politics in the University of Delhi, Randhir Singh had retired. By that time his classroom, his reading—teaching pedagogy, dreams of changing the world, and the belief that a better society was possible and desirable- had taken the form of discourse and Randhir Singh had acquired the status of a legend.

As happens with every legend, along with the people who liked him, perhaps there were equal numbers who disliked him desperately. Those who loved him presented their and Randhir Singh's narrative exaggeratedly that post-Karl Marx, the truth of social exploitation was understood only by Randhir Singh. Randhir Singh's fashionable fans had learned this truth directly in the classroom and therefore they were going to change the world after teaching Marxism and probably had changed themselves substantially. Interestingly, the world of Randhir Singh's fans was confined to campus boundaries and their revolutionary conversation usually took place in English. Thus far, Randhir Singh's haters controlled their tongue. Perhaps, it was due to the domination of the Indian academic circles by Marxism and challenging it in the late eighties was almost impossible. Despite the national debate on Babri Masjid-Ram

Temple movement, the politics of Hindutva was on the margin in the university campuses. Post-Mandal, caste was taking shape as a political category. However, Ambedkar's name was not relevant. Yes, the feminist discourse had started with the insistence that the women's question should be considered along with the question of the primacy of class. Amidst these, opponents of Randhir Singh were left with the depoliticization of education. It was stated that people like Randhir Singh were turning the pious sphere of education at the universitty level into a political arena which was a very immoral act.

It becomes important to mention an interesting point here. In the world of Randhir Singh's fans, there was a villain who was known by the name of Harnam Singh. Harnam Singh was the former head of the Department of Political Science, University of Delhi. Harnam Singh was chairing the post-election meeting celebrating the victory of Randhir Singh in the Delhi University Teachers' Association polls. As was expected of him, he gave the maximum opportunity to opponents of Randhir Singh to speak. The defeated candidates were also amongst the speakers. After these speakers, Randhir Singh's chance came. Harnam Singh said that he had just one minute to make his points. Singh said that he needed just thirty seconds. He said: "Today, I have understood that losing an election after contesting is academic work and winning an election after contesting is political work".

For me, as a Hindi medium student who hailed from the common lower-middle class, judgement about Randhir Singh amidst these images was no easy task. Arguments of Randhir Singh's opponent did not affect me much. It was equivalent to the tactics of the rich for whom the meaning of depoliticization was the cool life of college which included studies and sports. However, there was no room for bitter experiences which had to encountered often in everydayness. On the other hand, Marxism, resembled what was called liberation.

Even before joining college, I was familiar with Marxism due to the availability of books in Hindi from Soviet Russia (used to get them for free). But then I was not puffed up with conceit to call myself a Marxist. Contrary to this, among Randhir Singh's fashionable fans who were promoting a kind of Marxism, I did not see any feeling of pain. Despite this dilemma, I was inching closer to the fans of Randhir Singh and finally, I met Randhir Singh one day.

In the meeting two things happened which helped immensely in shaping the image of Randhir Singh for me. Nehru Place was home to that encounter. When we reached, he was not at home. He came and welcomed us warmly. First, he asked for our names. Then, without further ado, he started the conversation by calling us by our proper names. Till then, I had not seen any teacher (who was also a legend) being so frank in the very first meeting. I was the shy student of the group and remained mostly silent. My inability to speak English was the primary cause. Randhir Singh perhaps understood this. So after that he just spoke in Hindustani. I felt, for him, English, Hindi, Urdu were mere languages whose job was just to communicate ideas, and not to make any ostentatious impression.

Meanwhile, he picked up a glass of water in the middle of the conversation and told me to look at the glass; it could be described as half-empty or half-full. It indicated certain similarities in politics. Finding a readymade method for it was foolishness. It was important to know the context from whose womb the popular meaning of politics was taking shape. Therefore, the arena of possibilities could be called politics. I realized that this understanding of the politics was not merely bookish. This included a combination of his experiences, struggles and intellectualism. I also felt that through this understanding of politics, Randhir Singh was appealing to us to explore the meaning of politics.

After the meeting, I began to read, the most popular book of Randhir Singh, *Reason, Revolution and Political Theory*. The book was in difficult English but my excitement had gone up. I read each sentence many times. The most interesting thing was that till then Randhir Singh was heard from the mouths of fans; there was nothing like that in this book. Marxism was not merely the apotheosis of the book; rather the detailed rendering of the argument was the result of systematic study. Randhir Singh was telling us through the book why we needed to think beyond Marx and how Marx's theory could be helpful in maintaining 'context-suitable' distance. The introduction to this book of Randhir Singh for me established him as a political theorist and the most systematic teacher.

By the mid-1990s, the end of Randhir Singh's fashionable club happened with the same enthusiasm as it was formed. After the collapse of Soviet Union, those who were 'worshipping' Marx came under the scanner (however, some declared and audacious Marxists continued to hold on to their belifs). It was a time of dilemma for Randhir Singh's fashionable fans. Therefore, for them the messianic image of Randhir Singh was becoming an untenable position. That perhaps explains why Randhir Singh was conferred titles such as the 'Grand Old Man of Marxism'.

I think that Randhir Singh also felt the change. Probably, he had also decided that he would necessarily respond to the fashionable, anglicized, and meanest intellectualism. At that moment, his political activism was over. But he was conscious intellectually. His commitment to work on argument/ logic was probably continued to grow strongly. After meeting with him, Randhir Singh revealed that he was working on a book on Socialism. Later on, the book was published as *Crisis of Socialism: Notes in Defence of a Commitment*. The core argument of this book was not the worship of Marx but a historical analysis of the thinking which had challenged western capitalism ideologically. As feared, the book was ignored. Randhir Singh's old fashionable fans (now the new leaders of Political Science) were neither interested in the logic of Randhir Singh nor the theoretical evaluation of historical political phenomena such as the collapse of the Soviet Union. But this book was discovered by another class of readers. It was the readership of social activists. These activists found their mirror of politics, which was different from the soft tickle debate of Delhi's air-conditioned Marxism, in Randhir Singh.

I also understood Randhir Singh's grassroots popularity in

a different way. I would not say that I was his fan, but this is also true that I never let go any chance to meet him. Whenever I met him, the first question he would ask me was if I had got a job or not? He had realized the significance of a job for a low-middle class student like me. They cannot survive only through political struggle and ideals of learning, and perhaps that was why he used to say that the beginning of the change of the world should start first with the family.

Randhir Singh knew of my research interest to analyse India with particular reference to Islam as a political movement. He was very excited about this topic. In a conversation, he told me that in his view religion before modernity was a movement by itself. At that time, there was no political vocabulary of the modern secularism; therefore movements expressed themselves through the religious language. Randhir Singh was convinced that a Marxist interpretation of Indian religions was possible and even desirable. This fact became clear to him in his youth when he was part of the communist movement and started political mobilization in the villages of Punjab. Another example of his ideological openness was exhibited through his perspective on Gandhi. Once he asked us as to who should be considered the most loved Indian political person by the people? For us, the question was odd. In the parlance of politics today, there is no such thing as love. Besides, Randhir Singh was a Marxist too. He looked at us and spoke, "Gandhi". Randhir Singh said that he had read a number of original documents of Gandhi when the work on Gandhi's collected works was going on. He had copious notes on Gandhi which were never published.

The last meeting with Randhir Singh was on the occasion of his ninetieth birthday. As I have already explained, the era of his fashionable fans was over. Only his old friends, some students and political activists were meeting him. During the birthday celebrations, he mostly remained silent, and was possibly unable to speak. However, his presence rekindled those arguments which were generated by him through his writings and study.

The news reached us on January 31, 2016 that Randhir Singh was no more. The news was not shocking. His age was ninety-four and we knew his health had been steadily declining. But even then it seemed that Randhir Singh could not die. His enthusiasm, his belief in the victory of life and his towering stature reminded us again and again that he was not dead. This end of the dilemma ended or rather got over at the cremation ground. His facial complexion turned into yellow; his light purple turban slid diagonally; and after seeing the inanimate body, anybody would say that he was dead. However, in my eyes, there was warmth in his face. It was the warmth of political commitment. Of course my master, Randhir Singh is not dead, because political commitments never die.

PART III

Advancing the Domain

9

Dialectical Method and Creative Theory: Insights Offered by Randhir Singh

Manoranjan Mohanty

Modern education has made many divides in the name of promoting specialisations and has described it as a hall-mark of modernity. Separating arts from sciences, social sciences from natural sciences, scientific knowledge from folk knowledge and other such divisions have given rise to narrow expertise all around. In that process some disciplines such as commerce, business management, economics and information technology are much sought after as they have market value at present. A subject like philosophy has little attraction. 'Concrete', 'behavioural', 'practical', 'empirical', 'useful' subjects, we are told, are needed by the contemporary world rather than abstract, speculative subjects. In this environment, the fact that every branch of study and every aspect of human life has a philosophical dimension was stressed by Randhir Singh who sharply questioned the modderernistic trends throughout his life.

Uniting Science and Philosophy

Thinking deeply about something and finding interconnections and seeking systematic meanings of phenomena may at one level involve training one's mind for abstract interrogation as the discipline of philosophy does. But such an exercise in abstraction must not remain far from human practice. Behind our actions in everyday life there is philosophy. And every philosophical statement can be stated in day-to-day parlance using actual practice or possible practice. Philosophy is no mystery, even when aspects of a problem may not have been fully explained yet. In fact, philosophy, while enlightening you about deeper forces at work, should make you circumspect, self-critical and humble; acknowledging limits to one's knowledge about a problem. Randhir Singh always emphasised the need for an element of 'healthy scepticism' in pursuing the scientific method as well as the philosophical enquiry. Randhir Singh and the group associated with the journal *Enquiry* had an integrated view of science and philosophy. This was evident in his treatment of dialectical materialism.

Dialectical Method

Many people find dialectical method abstract and incomprehensible, and therefore difficult to put into practice. Randhir Singh showed how in day-to-day life one confronted conflicting situations which continued to evolve. Some of the situations did not easily change while others experienced dramatic changes and even the former went through big changes when conditions made that happen. Dialectics is about change, about the laws of motion, and about movement of things.

Once you grasp that dialectics is about change you can distinguish between Hegelian dialectics and Marx's dialectical materialism as also its further articulations by later Marxists. 'Unity of opposites', or a contradiction, as a definition of dialectics, means a dynamic relationship between conflicting forces that characterise a system. This understanding would enable an analyst to comprehend the nature of a historical situation in terms of contradictions which are in motion. The direction of change and possibilities of intervention can be ascertained once the dialectical materialist method is applied.

Dialectical materialism is different from mechanical materialism on the one hand and idealism on the other, as Randhir Singh emphasised. This was a critical issue in all Marxist analyses during the past century, the century since the Bolshevik Revolution. It was debated within the communist movements in Russia during Lenin's time and thereafter. This was the central point of ideological battles in China at various points of time before 1949, during the Great Leap Forward and the Cultural Revolution, and the post-Mao reforms. The many streams of the Indian communist movement were also divided on these issues which led to diverse strategic lines.

Were the material conditions in Russia matured enough to justify the workers' armed insurrection led by Lenin in 1917? Those who take the view that the material base of capitalist political economy had not developed adequately for the proletariat to seize political power can be called mechanical materialists. On the other hand, the critics of Mao Zedong during 1927-1931 (Jiangxi Soviet period) onwards described him as an idealist, prematurely leading a workers-peasants' army against a nationalist government. His political line formulated during the Yan'an period addressed this question by innovating the theory of the people's democratic revolution. It sought to avoid economic determinism by asserting that the revolutionaries must not wait until the material conditions of capitalist development were sufficiently grown. As Randhir Singh pointed out, this is where the role of politics was important. Far from being an idealistic assertion not rooted in reality, people's democratic revolution responded to the contradictions generated by feudalism and imperialism. Much of the international communist movement sees this as a successful illustration of practising dialectical materialism. Even in the post-Mao China where critics of Mao have strongly denounced his economic policies as idealist have acknowledged this.

The radical economic policies of the Great Leap and the cultural and political mobilisation during the Cultural Revolution to establish an egalitarian society were seen by many as idealist initiatives for which objective material conditions were not ripe. It has been a big debate within China and across the globe whether economic growth along the lines of the European Industrial Revolution was necessary for developing the productive forces in the modern era before promoting and before embarking on a path of equality.

Deng Xiaoping has strongly argued that a preliminary stage of socialism was necessary for a long period of time to promote the growth of the economy before full-fledged socialist policies were adopted. China's reforms were launched on that theoretical proposition. Answering charges that it might lead to capitalism, Deng said that the Communist Party of China would ensure that it did not happen. After four decades of reforms and tremendous economic success in China, it became one of world's most unequal societies with much social alienation and environmental destruction. So it may be said that if Mao's Great Leap policies reflected idealism, the 'reforms and open door' policy practised mechanical materialism.

Randhir Singh warned that it was not easy to formulate dialectical materialist policies. With hindsight, historians and political ideologues may pass judgements. But the consciousness of the nature of dialectical materialism provides some check against wrong strategies and policies. While the method of dialectical materialism was laid out by Randhir Singh in his powerful philosophical treatise, *Reason, Revolution and Political Theory*, its practice or violations are explained in great detail in his magnum opus on the Soviet collapse, *Crisis of Socialism: Notes in Defence of Commitment*.

Applying dialectical materialism to the Indian conditions presented some major insights into theory and practice.

Explaining the Indian Reality

Applying dialectical materialist method to the Indian conditions, Randhir Singh pointed out the need to see the nature of social contradictions in their totality and in depth. A mechanical understanding of class relations and formulating political strategy based on that failed the Indian communist parties in gathering adequate strength. Caste as a social contradiction had to be comprehended. Here his grip over the dialectical method became evident. Was caste merely a phenomenon in the superstructure? Was it a product only of Brahmanical ideology that can be combated by counter-ideological campaigns? He contested that. Caste had an economic basis as well. A stratified evaluation of labour, a related property structure and a system of power relations sustained this unequal socio-political system for centuries. Those who missed the class dimensions of caste relations and their economic base were as mistaken as those who missed the caste linkages of class. The reservation debate in India had become mostly one-dimensional missing the dialectical relations of class and caste. As he pointed out, reservation was needed and its premature abolition must be questioned. But without structural changes in the economy, and a comprehensive programme of transformation in economic, cultural and political spheres, caste domination and discrimination would not end.

This insight was not limited to the caste question. It also applied to other social and cultural issues including gender, nationality and ethnic communities. Randhir Singh was one of the earliest analysts of the commodification of women in the capitalist society. In his role as a teacher and an academic leader, the commitment to gender equality and women's dignity was always evident. His women students and colleagues always valued this quality of Randhir Singh and cited this as an example to emulate. When we launched the Women's Studies programme in Delhi University, first as a research group in Political Science and then as the Women's Studies and Development Centre he was one of its most inspiring supporters. He laid out a framework of feminist studies that still resounds as a powerful reference point. He applied the dialectical materialist method and interpreted the Marxist discourse on the gender question in the same way as in the case of the caste question. Women's movement in the West, the dominant liberal stream had been disconnected from the class question in a major way. On the other hand, many socialist feminists had put so much stress on class that the autonomous significance of the gender dimension was missed. He noted the failures in the Indian communist movement to theorise and practise gender equality. More importantly, he pointed out how on this question, among others, we should learn from the negative experience of the Soviet Union. The assumption that class politics through the socialisation of means of production and exercise of political power by the communist party would automatically establish conditions of equality among men and women was proved wrong. Patriarchal relations in the party, state organs and economic management persisted to a large extent in the Soviet Union. At the same time, Randhir Singh stressed, in his in-depth study of the socialist experiment in the Soviet Union that the economic measures did produce much employment opportunity for women and especially equality of educational and health opportunities for the girl child. But as Aleksandra Kollontai pointed out in her debates with Lenin, unless special measures were undertaken at every level, in every sector, including the top political leadership, women would remain oppressed.

Besides the dialectical relationship between class and gender, both needed to be connected with caste in the Indian context, race in the US context and nationality and ethnic community wherever these situations had elements of oppressive relations. In the Indian context, therefore, interconnection of class, caste, gender was the basic framework to understand the complex reality of social contradictions and act upon them to change that reality. Thus, Randhir Singh led us to grasp the complexity of social contradictions in a framework of intersectionality much before this became a familiar concept in the West and in India. What was specific to Randhir Singh's formulation was his insistence on intersectional class analysis and not intersectionality replacing class analysis.

This dialectical perspective applied to the question of nationality, ethnic community and religion as well. Randhir Singh's writings on Kashmir, Northeast, Punjab and some theoretical pieces and more importantly, his lectures on these issues in those areas and in various parts of the country gave us valuable insights into political theory and political action. The framework was one of intersection of class and nationality. How the autonomy movements faced the repression of the state machinery—the Army and the paramilitary forces on the one hand and external pressures, imperialist or otherwise which had their eyes on getting access to natural resources on the other were at the centre of his analysis. A much-quoted line from Randhir Singh from a lecture in the Northeast was an answer to a question from the floor as to why the Northeast had still not been fully integrated with the rest of India. His counter-question was "Do you have corruption here?" When the chorus from floor was a loud 'Yes' he said that the region was very much integrated through trade and commerce by the Indian capitalists who extracted minerals from the region and sold their goods in the market in this region. So, the question was, he pointed out, to understand the nature of the linkages in various spheres. That many nationality movements were led by the regional bourgeoisie and that the formation of Jharkhand, Chhattisgarh and Uttarakhand did not alter the exploitative power structure was evident. The perspective on handling demands for autonomy and self-determination therefore had to be based on a political understanding of the nature of exploitation in the region.

His writings on the Punjab question were most significant in that its theoretical and practical implications would be relevant for a long time. His understanding of the Sikh militancy was different from those who looked at it from the lens of the Indian nationalism that was under threat from it. Many of his dear friends were on the side of the Indira Gandhi Government on this issue and he was a frank and open critic of that position. He stressed the point that the Indian nation was in the making and various social forces, especially the rising Indian bourgeoisie was trying hard to shape it in its favour using State power. It neglected the interests of the Punjab peasantry, and the unemployed youth who were alienated from the existing political processes. To treat the upheaval of the alienated youth merely as terrorism was wrong. He also strongly differed with the militant Khalistan movement as they resorted to violence without a political and economic programme and hence would lose mass support sooner or later and would be suppressed by the Indian State eventually. He was a critique of the Akali Dal politics too which failed to present an alternative socio-economic platform to meet the economic and social needs of the people of Punjab. He pointed out how the Akali movement which originated as an anti-colonial, anti-feudal and anti-caste force using the egalitarian Sikh ideology as its distinct form had degenerated into a corrupt, opportunist political organisation focused on coming to power through electoral alliances. Historical events vindicated the prognosis presented by Randhir Singh. He also firmly condemned the repressive measures by the State through the Army and paramilitary operations that violated the democratic rights of the struggling people in Kashmir, Northeast and central Indian Adivasi areas. Building Indian democracy using even the limited promises given in the Indian Constitution by responding to people's demands was important.

Randhir Singh's reflections on Punjab illustrated his approach to religion. He was happy about his Sikh identity being evident from his turban. He was a proud Punjabi, speaking and writing in Punjabi language and produced that amazing little book of poems, *Rahan Di Dhoor*. He charged fellow Marxists with not studying religion from the dialectical and materialist viewpoint seriously. We as his students and colleagues were privileged to look at this important question differently from many others, reading Marx closely and following the debates in the communist movement, practices in socialist countries and above all, observing the heated controversies on secularism and communalism in India. That the oft-quoted statement, 'religion is opium of the masses' did not represent the fuller understanding of religion according to Marx was stressed by Randhir Singh again and again. 'The religious world is but the reflex of the real world' was more accurate. Even more relevant was the following statement of Marx in his critique of Hegel's *Philosophy of Law*: "Religious distress is at the same time the expression of real distress and the protest against the real distress. Religion is the sigh of the oppressed creature, the heart of a heartless world, just as it is the spirit of a spiritless situation. It is the opium of the people… . The abolition of religion as the abolition of the illusory happiness of people is required for their real happiness. The demand to give up the illusion about its condition is the demand to give up a condition which needs illusions" (Marx, 1970: 56). This was a far more complex formulation that had a great deal of implications for believers, atheists as well as agnostics.

Such theoretical positions in the tradition of Marxism embodied what we call the creative theory. Randhir Singh took Marxism as the most persuasive of the existing philosophical systems and applied the dialectical materialist method to analyse and understand the entire body of knowledge and each of its core theoretical formulations to respond to contemporary and future problems. His recalling of Rosa Luxemburg's critique of capitalism as barbarism for it destroyed nature was a powerful premise for the emerging environmental movement. He applied the theories creatively with full respect to the classic and earlier formulations. He focused on civilisational goals of the human kind and pointed out that Marxism aimed at eliminating sources of alienation of men and women from each other, from nature and from the production process. That presented Marxism as a philosophy of transformation whose central values were freedom, peace and beauty. Interpreting and changing the world through struggles by the oppressed people aimed at achieving structures, cultures and processes to realise the creative potentiality of all humans. Thus, creative theory is the creative application of the existing body of knowledge to new situations without losing the strength of previously available knowledge and at the same time critiquing it and going ahead beyond it. This is the dialectics of dialectical materialism. It never ceased to develop in the course of practice. Theory-practice-theory or praxis continuously evolved in creative theory. Randhir Singh's political philosophy opened up great many new possibilities of future thinking and action on the path of continuous pursuit of freedom of all individuals, groups and regions.

REFERENCE

Marx, K. (1970). *Critique of Hegel's "Philosophy of Right"*, translated by A. Jolin and J. O'Malley, and edited by H. O'Malley. Cambridge: Cambridge University Press.

10

Furthering the Legacy of Randhir Singh

Anand Teltumbde

I have never met Professor Randhir Singh but thought I always knew him as it happened with many of his ilk. Randhir Singh was a Marxist by conviction and not by affiliation to some mainstream party that flaunts its label but acts in questionable ways. He never hesitated to speak out what he thought was right and never chose to play to the gallery. There are few such people who evoked that kind of respect in me. The first of course was D.D.Kosambi, whom I considered my intellectual role model but failed to follow in the vortex of activism. He was the one who without associating with any of the communist parties remained a Marxist and had the guts to dismiss them as 'official' communists. Today, nearly three decades after the fall of the Soviet regime and the capitalist reversal in China, the two exhibits of the Marxist revolutions, and neoliberalism gaining firm hegemony over the globe, we would have wanted many Randhir Singhs around; but sadly they are passing away one by one, leaving behind a bigger and bigger void.

*

Marxism emerged as the assurance to the mankind that history is not just a game of chess being played by the powerful but has its own momentum that would lead human destiny to its eventual fulfilment. This assurance was constructed not as a wishful thinking but was based on the method of physical science to the extent it could be applied to the human world. Marx, making use of the philosophical method, discovered dialectical materialism to be underneath all the processes of change in the universe and tried to comprehend the flow of history through it. The phenomena in the inanimate physical world well confirmed this principle of dialectical materialism. Hegel's example in his *Science of Logic* of water being converted into steam or ice (phase change) by heating or cooling respectively illustrates the dialectical process of change of quantity into quality. When water was heated (transferring heat energy to water), its temperature increased gradually until it reached 100^0 but after that even if the heating continued, the temperature did not show any rise. Only after absorption of sufficient heat, does water begin to boil and if the heat is continued, it would evaporate into steam. The reverse process would transform it into ice exactly in the same way: gradually decreasing its temperature to a zero degree and thereafter, with extraction of the 'latent heat', it would convert it into ice, by the phase change.

Dialectical materialism is confirmed beyond doubt in the inanimate world. However, its application to human society and history needs to be handled carefully. Because while we can look at the physical phenomena objectively, the human society is extremely difficult to be so examined, basically because the observer itself is a part of the observed and the dialectic processes could turn complex in manifold ways because of the human agency. Each human being has a brain that controls the integrity of the human body and in the process reacts to its environment comprising natural forces as well as organisms around (humans as well as non-human species). Therefore, it makes it an extremely complex system to comprehend. The only solace is that the entire system is basically a manifestation of matter. But when one thinks of the human destiny, this solace is not enough because one necessarily deals with processes that may cohere eventually but have infinite interactions with indeterminate outcomes. The process is made more complex because of the memories the organisms possess, both individual and collective, which exert positive and negative influence on its present dealings. What it means is that although the broad nodes of human history may be discernibly marking progress towards human destiny, when humans assume the agency to accelerate it, it necessarily has to take into account these indeterminate outcomes.

Marx and Engels, viewing history through the prism of dialectical materialism found classes in society in contention with each other. In the earlier phases, these contentions were in the form of eddies, diffused, but in the higher phases they progressively became sharper. It may, however, be recognised that social classes through which Marx conceptualised the dialectics of history manifesting are themselves not an objective reality but just convenient categories to see the process of progress. In pre-modern societies, as Marx admits, the classes as well as their struggle were fluid and only could be broadly seen manifesting at the point of inflexion (transition). The myriad struggles among these classes pushed societies to achieve quantitative strides, reaching a point where no further progress would accrue. At that point, the classes in antagonistic relations with each other, one trying to preserve the status quo and the other wanting to transcend it, have a decisive fight that ushers in a qualitative change, pushing the society to next higher 'mode of production'. This battle represented the concentrated force that was necessitated to transform quantitative change into qualitative change.

Marx and Engels conceptualised this force to be an upsurge of the classes that craved for change and the change itself as a revolution. Having fathomed the explanatory prowess of dialectical materialism in the human world, Marx and Engels applied it to analyse the current phase of 'capitalist' mode of production so as to change it to the socialistic/communist phase. They saw that unlike in the previous modes, the capitalist mode was characterised by two predominant classes of proletariat and bourgeois in perpetual contention. While it was largely true, more so important to neatly imagine driving the force of future transition, the existence of other classes and their dynamic interaction with these processes could not be ignored.

Marx and Engels found that the dominant classes of people

were the analogue of positive and negative found in the natural sciences and history was itself a product of their contention. This contention propelled the progress of mankind in quantitative terms within a particular mode of production but when it reached its extreme point, it craved for resolution with a large chunk of energy into a qualitative change which represented the next higher mode of production. Marx postulated progression of these successive modes of production in his historical materialism and extrapolated the transition of the current mode of capitalism to communism through a proletarian revolution. He devoted his major efforts in dissecting capitalism in order to develop his theory of revolution.

As per this theory, the advanced industrial economies like Germany and England were the first candidates for socialist revolution. However, these revolutions occurred in majorly peasant economies like Russia and China and soon engulfed half of the globe under its fold. Although these revolutions in the first half of the last century inspired the oppressed people of the world to emancipate themselves, there was no addition save for the lone exception of Cuba. While they presented to the world glimpses of what is possible through socialist revolution, they soon degenerated into what may be called their antitheses. There are many reasons, indigenous as well as exogenous for these unfortunate developments; nonetheless they should impel Marxists to examine what has gone wrong with scientific attitude and commitment. Paradoxically, most of them defensively refuse to undertake this exercise as though it were a blasphemous act. The Marxists have developed a curious vocabulary that proscribes even doubting the inadequacy in their ideology. This overzealous attempt of the Marxists has reduced Marxism to a quasi-religious dogma not open to scientific scrutiny except for its hagiographers. Whence such an attitude overtook the scientific tenor of Marxists is a puzzle.

The biggest strength of Marxism was its theoretical integrity. Many well-meaning people imagined a socialist future for mankind after seeing the exploitative and morally repugnant capitalist system. Marx for the first time systematically fathomed the internal contradictions of capitalism and predicted the inevitability of such a socialistic future. This scientific foundation of Marxism has posed a big challenge to the capitalist camp which made spirited attempts to refute or at least dispute its theoretical claims. But none really succeeded. Dialectical materialism had unwavering support from the natural science. When the Heisenberg's principle of uncertainly was introduced in particle physics in the late 1920s, it was used to the hilt to disprove dialectical materialism. But the latter survived these attempts. As such, the foundational core of Marxism is held by the physical world as the underlying truth. However, the same cannot be said with any certainty about its applications to the human world. Its structure comprising economic, social and political theories continued being variously criticised as they related to the messy world of humans. While much of it is a canard of the resurgent capitalism, some warrant serious consideration by the Marxists.

The Marxists need to fundamentally recognise that Marxism is a science of history and needs continual validation in the wake of any change or challenge. Defensive posturing betrays their weakness and not strength. Nobody needs to defend Newton's or Einstein's theories. They hold true as long as they are not disproved by some contrary scientific evidence. Marxism as a scientific theory therefore should be ready to embrace the truth even if it is contrary to postulations of its progenitors and still stays as Marxism. Marxism represented a great theoretical feat to give a scientific foundation to the progression of history to the ultimate human destiny, its species being as Marx defined. But one needs to bear in mind, this scientific foundation needs to withstand the changes in the soil as well as in the superstructure and needs continual monitoring. If it needs to stay scientific with its explanatory prowess intact, it has to continually validate itself with the new data set being produced by the contemporary world. I may offer a few points within this perspective that need the attention of the fellow Marxists. They are: conceptualisation of classes relative to abstract modes of production whereas what obtain in reality are the hybrid modes of production: the conception of the binary of reform and revolution and its associated baggage; the obsessive clinging by the Marxists to a metaphor of base and superstructure as though it was a basic tenet of Marxism; huge theoretical rework prompted by the paradigmatic changes in technologies; question of violence in revolution and construction of a model of post-revolution society. These are by no means the only problems that Marxists have to grapple with but are certainly the dominant ones at least in the Indian context.

*

Although class composition of a society and the struggle between these classes as the motor of history is not disputed, the precise conception of classes in a given instance and the definition of principle contradiction between them, may not be as indisputable. It is important because the revolutionary forces should orient the struggle between them towards revolution. Marx and Engels left classes undefined perhaps because they did not want them to be constrained by particularities of any instance. Classes were abstract categories and had to be conceived of in relation to their situation specific to a mode of production. While Marx spoke of the proletariat and the bourgeois as the two predominant classes in capitalism unlike in the earlier modes of production wherein the contradiction between the classes was diffused, in clear contradiction with each other, it did not mean that classes other than them did not simply exist. The very existence of these indicates the survival of the earlier modes of productions. If it was a case of the most industrialised countries like Germany and England in Western Europe, the condition of the rest of the world still mired in feudal mode could well be imagined. The modes of production in the Marxian conception are also an abstraction insofar as a particular mode only reflects the dominant characteristics associated with that mode and not necessarily all of them. At any time in practice, there may not be a pure mode of production but only a hybrid of it with the previous one and with the traces of the next one. It implies that the classes also may have to be conceived of in a hybrid manner keeping in view their contradictions with each other. When one speaks in terms of the working class, one should not be deluded that it will have homogeneity of interests. It will never be. Casual labourers, contract workers, and workers of the companies in the modern supply chain that extends over the globe necessarily has contradictions with the permanent workers of the factory and the class struggle is expected to incorporate their concerns so as to forge them into a force against their enemy, the bourgeois, again not a concrete entity but an abstraction of the global bourgeoisie. In the absence of such a composite class conception and more importantly incorporating their internal struggles amongst themselves into the struggle against the global bourgeoisie, they would engage in an internecine struggle and jeopardise their struggle against the enemy.

India presents a good case of such classes of the proletariat divided into several castes, giving rise to the class and caste syndrome. Many leading communists in the Communist Party of India, who came from the middle class and upper caste background rooted in urban centres, imagined that India was a capitalist country and excluded castes from their conceptual class analysis of the Indian society. The victims of the age old oppression that constituted the majorly of its proletariat however preferred to organise on the basis of their caste identity that addressed their concrete problems than associate with an abstraction of class that rather tended to gloss over the caste contradiction between them and the others. It led not only to the emergence of a separate Dalit movement but also its antagonistic development vis-à-vis the communist movement. The case of castes was stark: they being a life-world of people for millennia that ordained all aspects of life could not be excluded from the class analysis. But even other social categories like race, gender and ethnicity, etc., should also be incorporated into class conception, making thereby the obliteration of contradictions due to them as part of the class struggle. It is essential for the mass of people to primarily develop into a class in itself. While the revolutionary class struggle is expected to be complex, the criticism of the major two revolutions, Bolshevik and Chinese, that they were more of the products of exogenous factors like nationalism and war than endogenous class struggle cannot be reasonably dismissed.

The second binary in the Marxian circles is reform and revolution. Without a clear definition of these terms, reforms are axiomatically denigrated and revolution is praised. It degenerates to the practice that anyone speaking of arms or violence is taken as a revolutionary and in corollary, ones using peaceful means, as reformists. It smacks of romanticism than any theoretical support. The basic theory of dialectics of quantity and quality referred to above should resolve this issue. In the example of heating of water towards the phase change, there is no way that water could be transformed into steam than raising its temperature. No amount of the big bang heating could transform water into steam. There are myriad activities that need to be completed before the last act of defeating the current state, and all of them may not be obvious to their linkage. If these activities, tactical in nature cohere well with the strategy, the strategy for revolution, they ought to be taken as part of revolution. Reforms are only the activities carried out with the belief that the existing state can be improved without replacing them with something new. Revolution thus becomes a line concept; it happens over a time period, and not a point concept as usually it is understood. The insurrectionary capture of state power that happened until the previous century created that impression but in the future such revolutions may be scarce.

In the Indian context, the anti-caste struggles of Dalits were summarily termed as reformist and denigrated by the communists. This is the root cause for their alienation from the communists. It is a different matter to aim at just certain kinds of reforms, say by mending traditions and customs or demanding temple entry or promoting intermarriages but quite another to aim at the annihilation of castes. If the struggle has no perspective to create a class consciousness for a structural change, it may be appropriately called reformist but if it aims at altering the power structure, it will certainly qualify to be revolutionary. When Ambedkar mobilised people against castes and spoke of their annihilation to create a society based on liberty, equality and fraternity, it did not remain just reformist. The very fact that his plan for state socialism being ordained in the Constitution so that a simple majority in the Parliament could not alter it, did not come through, bespeaks of its radical character. It should not matter that he did not speak the language of Marxists or rather expressed disagreement with certain Marxist postulations. Many a communist party mouths revolutionary slogans but in their conduct would reinforce the status quo cannot be taken as revolutionary. The misconception of this binary has constricted the mobilisation of people for the revolutionary cause.

The third issue is created by a Marxian metaphor—base and superstructure—which has done more harm than good. This metaphor is as such nothing but the corollary of materialism, that in the ultimate instance the material base would determine the outcome. The humans are not inert beings and have their accumulated baggage to carry in terms of culture, traditions and institutional structures to manage their collective and conflictual affairs. All these constitute the so-called superstructure, which certainly is determined by the economic base, i.e. the mode and the relations of production, but in the 'ultimate' instance. When is this ultimate instance to be conceived? Practically, there is no ultimate instance in the flow of history in which the base as well as the superstructure interacts on each other. During the lifetimes of Marx and Engels itself, the enthusiastic Marxists had come up with a mechanical interpretation of this metaphor to disregard all superstructural issues. Engels had to extraneously intervene with the explaination that it was not what he and Marx had meant by it. He did explain that the base and superstructure both interact on each other and that the superstructure itself could impact the base. However, it did not have much impact on the practices of the Marxists. As a result, many a non-economic mechanism of oppression of majority of people was simply ignored by the Marxists as non-issues thereby alienating a large section of the downtrodden masses from Marxism.

There have been many changes in the structure as well as the processes of capitalism since Marx's times. The competitive capital got transformed into monopoly capital. While some of these changes have been incorporated into the Marxist theory, changes due to new technologies are barely captured. These technologies have already altered the profile of the working class with significant changes in the relations between them and capital. With Information and Communication Technologies (ICT) and nano-technologies potentially eliminating human labour in the production process, what happens to labour and the labour theory of value? How does Marxism cope with these changes? What happens to the basic schema of Marx of capitalist production and reproduction? As I see, its implication is the progressive genocide of people. It necessarily impinges upon the basic schemata of the capitalist system and has huge implications for the theory of revolution. Unfortunately, the Marxists refuse to see the change and keep seeing everything explained in *Capital*, quite like some Indian communists saw communism in Vedas or the present-day Hindutva acolytes find everything given in them.

As stated before, Marxism is not a creed to be zealously protected. It demands continual review and validation in the face of slightest contra-evidence. To doubt does not mean renouncing. Rather *De omnibus dubitandum* was the famous motto of Marx. It depicts scientific tenor. It is futile to see that Marx had anticipated the modern technologies and had incorporated their implications or to argue that there is nothing qualitatively new in modern technologies. These technologies have paved the ways of surveillance and manipulation of human nature. With big data and analytics technologies, the control of the ruling classes over the masses could be near complete. The neoliberal offensive over the last three decades has already pulverised societies into discrete individuals. The new technologies have aided it further closeting them into their own selves. The entire young generation vents off its anger on the social media without having anything to do with reality. How does one in such a world conceive of class consciousness germinating?

One of the issues is the place of violence in revolution. There is a plethora of explanations about how Marx and Engel's' 'force' got transformed into 'violence' at the hands of their enthusiastic followers. The dialectics demanded an input of latent energy to bring about a qualitative change when it is quantitatively ripe. Without that it could return to its natural state. Marx explained that force does the role of a midwife in revolution. The metaphors are clear enough to explain that a midwife is not an essential factor in human birth. This being the theory, the insurrectionary model of revolution has become almost synonymous with the Marxist revolution. The uprising of people for change is certainly a precursor of revolution but their taking up arms may not be. The necessity of arms cannot however be wished away because the ruling classes, through their state, would certainly try crushing this uprising with repressive violence. The revolutionary forces imperatively have to defend themselves with arms. What remains of the defensive armed strategy of a revolutionary group can be easily projected as blood-thirsty offensives by the rogue state to unleash its might as it has done in the case of Naxalite/Maoist forces, but that could only be countered by the masses. The existence of mass organisations is the only guaranteed defence for the revolutionary forces.

The question of violence or alternatively an insurrectionary method of revolution becomes important in the context of the might of the modern state. The modern state has come to assume monstrous power with technologies and its ideological apparatus, (the latter, largely due to the weakness of the revolutionary ideologies). No revolutionary group can imagine directly confronting this monster except by the ideological uprising of the masses against it. The Marxists have to theorise and strategise to build the mass organisations.

One of the lacunae of Marxism has been in terms of its failure in creating a convincing prototype. Revolutions inspired by it during the last century have not been without bright patches but they were overwhelmed by the negativities they eventually produced. While The Soviet socialist system eventually collapsed, socialist China remains just in name having been transformed into its perfect antithesis. We could console ourselves taking them as experiments that failed but for the people, it represents great betrayals. The human cost of these experiments was too high to justify its gains. One has to add to it the consequential costs of this reversal. The resurgence of neoliberalism and devastation it caused should be directly attributable to this reversal. It has taken the movement decades back. It is therefore imperative to theorise the post-revolution model of the society. How shall be its institutional structure that would provide the superior version of democracy? How will it facilitate multitudes of people realise their human potential? How will such a paradigm be sustained? If we fail to provide a convincing alternative to people, they may not come out of the trap of neoliberalism that promises them prizes at the roulette of life.

*

One needs to mind, besides the above points, the fact that the world is changing at an accelerated pace. The use of isms, the ideologies was premised on the relatively static world. The isms were the postulates constructed after analysing the past data and were expected to explain the future world. In the past, with the pace of change being modest (world was never static but changed at an extremely slow pace), they could work to a large extent. But this is no more the case with the contemporary or the future world. It is only the inertia of our minds that we still cling to isms which are really anachronistic. Marxism being the latest may not fall in that category is not out of it either. If we wish to extend its utility, it will have to be continually renewed to keep approximate pace with the changing world. This, according to me, shall be the true way of furthering the legacy of Professor Randhir Singh and many more people of his ilk, from the past and in the coming future!

11

The Radical Pedagogue Who Demolished the Meaningless Borderlines of Academia

Ravi Kumar

These are strange and difficult times when meanings of even liberal bourgeois freedom and democracy are being revisited. It ought not be a surprise as the bourgeois politics had to develop strategies of politics and invent new meanings of the existing concepts because the time demands it. It is also a question of their survival. The authoritarianism of bourgeoisie is on rise and more visible as they arrive in seats of power through popular support. It is this popular support which is significant. On the other hand, surprisingly the radicalisation of anti-systemic offensive has also been on the decline and the Left slips more and more into social democratic politics. When the crisis is deepening, when authoritarianism is on the rise and when the need for transformation grows sharper, we do not see the sharpening of contradictions on the ground. We again seem to be relapsing into the post-world war argument of frontal politics through an excuse for survival. The biggest casualty of such politics has been the working class politics, which has been looking forward to a concentrated expression on the ground as the industrial zones have been consistently throwing up extreme cases of conflict between the workers and the industrial bourgeoisie. The rural countryside has been witness to this unparalleled crisises. It is in these difficult times that one would like to recall a thinker and a person of praxis such as Randhir Singh who remained committed to the project of socialism.

This brief reflection is about how he demolished the meaningless boundaries of academia and the everyday social-political realities and through his writings, lectures and continuous engagements with the everyday politics on the ground showed the intellectuals that there can be a version of intellectualism which needs to go beyond the narrow confines of something called a specific form of politics meant for the intellectuals. He embodied resistance to so many things that we imbibe because we think them to be compulsions or because we think it is not our task to resist them. His was an internal critic of the way forces within the Left were looking at the working class politics. When there was/is a misdirected revolutionism in course formulation or pedagogical endeavours in general, he stated in different ways how there is a continuous need to engage with Marxism. It is through these endeavours that this paper tries to look at how can one conceptualise the idea of radical pedagogy in Randhir Singh.

What Should the Teacher Do?

What should a teacher do? What are the duties of a teacher? These questions cannot be answered unless one understands the significance of how we understand education itself. If education (even formal) is understood in disjunction with the processes that pave way for emergence of particular educational regimes (which includes the formal as well informal realms) then one would be compelled to have a narrow vision about education. It has to be seen not only as part of the ideological state apparatus but must also be seen as an instrument of resistance, a place which has the potential to subvert the system in interesting ways. One way of understanding it can be through defining what critical education is as Paulo Freire puts it:

> ...the teaching of content, deposited in the learner, will sooner or later bring about a critical perception of reality does not convince me. In the progressive perspective, the process of teaching—where the teaching challenges learners to *apprehend* the object, to then

> learn it in their relations with the world—implies the exercise of critical perception, perception of the object's reason for being. It implies the sharpening of the learner's *epistemological curiosity,* which cannot be satisfied with mere description of the object's concept. I must not *leave* for a random tomorrow something that is part of my task as a progressive educator right now: a critical reading of the world, alongside a critical reading of the word (Freire, 2007: 75).

Freire's insistence on critical education is trying to critically reading the world rather than falling into the trap of the hegemonic idea that uses education for the purposes of reproducing the labour power and the imagination of the world which suits them. Glenn Rikowski brings the connection between education and society closer when he says:

> On the other hand, teachers and trainers are implicated in socially producing the single commodity - labour-power - on which the whole capitalist system rests. This gives them a special sort of social power. They work at the chalkface of capital's weakest link, labour-power. Hence, they have the capacity to work with Red Chalk...: to open up visions of alternatives to capitalism in the classroom, or at least provide vital critiques of its violent class relation and market inequalities. Teachers are in a special position regarding their capacity to disrupt and to call into question the capitalist class relation. Furthermore, teachers can also insert principles of social justice into their pedagogy, principles that are antithetical to the generation of the class divide and also market and social inequalities... (Rikowski, 2001).

The questions around the role of a teacher then have to be seen in conjunction with the nature of production relations that characterise a society and it has to be understood as if she (the teacher) is a warrior in a battlefield where the conflicts in society have found place within the intellectual realm (schools, universities and other intellectual forums). Now, how does this warrior fight the battle becomes an interesting ethnography and Randhir Singh was also, in this a sense, a warrior who stood his own ground in the battle.

The Academic and the Social World

Since the times when Randhir Singh taught his students, the world has changed drastically. The emergence of the API (Academic Point Index) regime and the further strengthening of the idea of teacher as a non-worker has strengthened the idea that a teacher should play minimal role in, what Freire would have said, the conscientisation process of the students. After the death of Randhir Singh, many obituaries were written in his memory and not many of them pointed towards the idea of pedagogy that he had. His popularity and eloquent ability to transmit the ideas had the intrinsic characteristic of a radical pedagogue who was intervening in the crisis that the academic had already started to experience. For him, the crisis was multifold - the academia was talking against 'biases' and in a way arguing for value neutrality; he also resists the idea/trap of 'academic' that we all have fallen into - the quantifiable intellectualism of the most obscene kind; and he is simultaneously engaging with the crisis within the Left.

He writes in 'In lieu of a Bio-Data':

> ... 'bio-data' has been a perennial embarrassment—for I never managed to acquire one as a scholar. I have no research degrees, no string of scholars working 'under' me, no fellow-ships, no research projects, no study or other academic leaves, no 'seminaring', national or international, nothing—not even a visit abroad, that has come to certify any sort of achievement or standing as a scholar these days! (Singh, 1988).

What he is arguing against is the idea wherein an intellectual is trapped in a race to have as many conferences or research supervision or paper publications listed in his bio-data. In other words, the idea of quantification opens up avenues for an oppressive 'academic' regime to come into existence which starts recognising, a in a better sense, that the intellectual in an university has to meet targets like the worker in the factory. This similarity between the factory and the university may be contestable insofar as the question of surplus value production is concerned specially in the context of state-run education and it does not constitute the matter of debate here. However, it needs to be noted that there is an increasing tendency towards state withdrawal from such responsibilities by either giving away of the space to private capital or towards an increasing cost of state-run education itself and that cost having been transferred to the individuals. In both senses there is a capitalisation of higher education in this context the intellectual ceases to be one who would think, contemplate and only teach. The choice has been taken away from the individual as globally the idea of 'publish or perish' dominates the academic regimes. Randhir Singh becomes a standing symbol within this situation where there is cut-throat competition to have external funding or to ensure that more publications inevitably mean better intellectualism. For him, the greatness, perhaps, lay in the nature of communication and knowledge transfer between the teacher and the taught. In this sense, he represented a counter-position to this world of academia. He explained his position on how he viewed an intellectual in a meeting at Delhi University:

> I responded that given the 'functional rationality' governing the organised structures of teaching and research, so that scholarly writing is increasingly addressed not to problems of publics but to peers and to prestige and preferment in the highly bureaucratised academic professions, and given the growing, and often mindless, specialisation in the social sciences (including Political Science) which is resulting in a situation where fewer and fewer people were hearing more and more about less and less—given all this, a certain lack of conventional academic scholarship may even be an advantage; it may be of some help not only towards recognising and addressing ourselves to the real problems of our society but also in not missing the wood for the trees and seeing the social reality as it essentially is, 'a structured interdependence of parts', a whole—complex and differentiated and rich with the dialectics of its mediations, but a whole nevertheless (Singh, 1988).

The further extension of this twisted sense of being an academic is that it makes the academic as non/un-social. The knowledge becomes more and more hegemonic let alone useless because the idea of knowledge as experiential gets substituted with the knowledge being generated in a social lab with the respondents.

The people with whom we interact, engage and meet are no longer respondents but rather the respondents may be either one of the above categories. When Randhir Singh says that he was doing some research with ICSSR which was "political" and "not scholarly" because he sought to understand "Indian politics which may, it is hoped, help towards 'a more effective people's intervention in what is happening in our country' ". Along with this tendency to be critically engaged with Political Science as a discipline he critiques the "fashions in the world of Marxian scholarship, where "orthodoxy" is almost a dirty word", "post-Marxism" is comfortable and comforting and say that his "work [is] an exercise in Marxist orthodoxy!" (Singh, 1988).

In fact, for Singh, academia cannot exist as a separate world and it recurs time and again when he talks about the relation of the world of teaching with the world of writing and teaching. These worlds as stated above were very much located in the battlefield where the hegemonic political and intellectual force consistently tells us how important it is to be neutral and objective. It delegitimises, by such an argument, the fact that the knowledge production is a political process and any knowledge cannot be outside of this process. Hence, Singh (1976) talks at length about the nature of 'bias'. He says:

> One cannot, even if one wanted it, be entirely free from 'bias', from one's philosophical preferences or preconceptions. Or, to put it more comprehensively, one cannot be ever without one's philosophy. It has been said that there is none so poor as not to have a philosophy of his own. One may add that there is none so rich either as to be able to do without one. We are all, in a sense philosophers, whether we know it or not; we all have our more or less open, more or less clearly or consciously formulated assumptions, opinions, beliefs, principles, and attitudes towards life, on which we habitually act, by which we indeed live. These together constitute our philosophy, to which also belong our more or less general ways of looking at things and ideas, our philosophical preferences and preconceptions, The very language we use reflects and bear witness to the philosophy we have (Singh, 1976: xiii).

Randhir Singh in a certain sense argues that there cannot be an intellectual without any linkages with the social formations. This comes out once again when he brings out the relationship of the philosopher/academic and the society"

If I have, nevertheless, drawn attention to the close and dialectical relationship that exists between the philosopher and his society, it is only to suggest, at the moment, two things. Firstly, there is no philosophy, including the sceptic's anti-philosophy, which is without social origins and therefore without social and political significance, Secondly, it should not be considered odd or 'inappropriate' to find that contemporary political theory or philosophy, including the most abstract and esoteric, is indicative not only, positively or negatively, of the intellectual achievement of the age, but also immediately or remotely of the great social and political conflicts of our times. The rise and decline of particular political doctrines, the supplanting of one theory, mood, or habit by another, significant shifts in the view taken of the nature and purpose, and indeed the very possibility or otherwise of political theory, changes in the methods of study and in the very tone and temper of political speculation, all *ultimately* reflect the fluctuating fortunes of political struggle, the ever changing conditions of our social and political life (Singh, 1976: 2).

This connection between the intellectual engagements and the social-political concerns could be centrally located in his works when he says that,

> If I have, most of the time, done none of the things that scholars are normally supposed to do, I have been, most of the time, busy with what they are normally supposed to keep away from, which is as well, for life has been such fun this way. I have thus functioned, in the profession and the university, more as a militant on the Left—even when revising the syllabi in Political Science whenever or wherever I got the opportunity to do so, or in putting in a rather noisy plea on behalf of Political Theory in general and Marxism in particular on the campuses of the Indian universities (Singh, 1988).

The Political Being

He was part of teachers' movements, fought militantly against the University administration, carried on "socialist education among workers, students and teachers, including school-teachers, running Marx Clubs and putting together socialist groups... writing and publishing pamphlets and bulletins, editing or producing or distributing journals like Enquiry, Socialist Digest, The Marxist Review, etc., campaigning on issues like Vietnam and Czechoslovakia, collecting signatures for Iranian students and others, mobilising and marching for all sorts of popular causes, associating with almost any radical initiative on the campus and every revolutionary venture off it..." (Singh, 1988).

The pedagogy that Randhir Singh seemed to have evolved indicates that (1) knowledge is not merely about mindless productions that are counted in one's bio-data; (2) the teaching-learning has to evolve through an engagement with the social-political realities of time; (3) a good teacher cannot be one who produces subservient labour-power in classrooms; it has to be an *effort* to produce subversive labour-power; (4) the teacher cannot be one who gets immersed into an instrumentalist, administrative idiom and kills the creative potential of academia; and (4) more importantly, it has to build a body of knowledge which demonstrates that the university and classrooms are places of immense conflict and one cannot remain unaware of these conflicts.

Randhir Singh was neither one of those typical teacher-politicians that you find today in university campuses nor a dry, unpopular teacher in the classroom. As one of his students reminisces:

> Singh's weekly classes were an event on our calendars. A healthy student crowd, even lazy 'hostellers' like me, would start milling around the gigantic Arts Faculty lecture hall at which he was due. A hush would descend as he approached the gothic corridors. You could recognise him from a mile. Erect and imposing without being intimidating, he had a free-flowing white beard that was not tied in the conventional Sikh fashion, always dressed in a white

> or blue bush-shirt, his trademark sky-blue turban worn loose. That Singh emanated the inner calm of a ragi—who chants verses from the Granth Sahib, the holy book of the Sikhs—was in sharp contrast to the impassioned way in which he delivered lectures. For most of the time, he spoke extempore, but every now and then, he would clip the ends of his spectacles into the folds of his turban near his ears, their bridge balancing on the tip of his nose so that he could simultaneously consult his notes and address the class. The point, once made—gently, with a twinkle of the eye and a smile—would be accompanied by a twitch of the shoulder. The spectacles would then disappear into his pocket.

So compelling were his lectures that it was only after it ended that one realised that the gigantic lecture hall was packed, with students spilling out on to the corridor (Bhushan, 2016).

It was this popularity, which led Bertell Ollman to remark that "If I wasn't already over 50, I would probably say something like when I grow up I want to be a professor like Randhir Singh." For Randhir Singh, the intellectual is not somebody outside of the society and by this he meant not being outside the social and political struggles as well. He would identify himself with it and, hence, he defined in an unsaid manner the contours of pedagogy and a pedagogue.

When he describes the idea of an intellectual as somebody who traverses with ease and great comfort, the unnecessary borders between everyday struggles and every type of knowledge he is not merely challenging and mocking at the idea of knowledge that capitalism seeks to develop within the laboratories with human clones but he is also defining the historical moments/roles in the lives of intellectuals. The role of an intellectual, as Rikowski would say, is to strike at the weakest link of capitalism—where the commodity of labour-power is produced. That site is the university in this case. Singh would not say it directly but would strongly hint at his vision of how a university should be and what should the teachers be doing. It is a sight where knowledge is not seen in mere abstraction but political philosophy, for instance must be an "activity' that shall not divorce "the idea or words from the things they represent, the concepts from the reality they are the concepts of, the explanation from what is explained and the language from what it expresses and from its purpose of communicating useful information about the world" (Singh, 1976: 29) He critiques Oakeshott by saying that his idea "tends, in fact, to dissolve the relationship between the thinking mind and the objective world, leaving reason to work upon itself, thought to feed upon thought" (Singh, 1976: 29). He further critiques Oakeshott for purging "'the study of politics' at a university of all moral and political purpose, of all taint of truth and knowledge" (Singh, 1976: 28). He sees, in other words, a purpose of university education and that is not vocational. That is much more than that. That is to generate critical knowledge, to create a certain hope about possible alternatives, to defy the propaganda that there is no alternative to the existing order of things.

Randhir Singh had his own conception of academia. For him academia is not about getting drenched in the discourses ushered by capitalism. It is in fact to go against the grain of things, a practice which is defined through a commitment to an ideology. He was perturbed by how these commitments were dwindling and how the rat race to be the 'top' academic was becoming the dominant way of life in academia. He writes:

> At the very least, one must recognise that Marxism is of central importance to any viable social science today. I know that in this age the desire to 'go beyond' is very strong in different fields of social and political inquiry. And it is a very legitimate and necessary desire too, *when it is not merely an itch born of entirely unacademic and non-scholarly considerations like the search for easy academic prestige and success* [emphasis mine], or the desire to appear more than up-to-date and, perhaps, catch the eye of Ford Foundation directors, by copying the very latest academic *mode* [italics original] in the west, or the need to keep up in the rat race which is now on, in the universities as much as elsewhere in our society (Singh, 1976: xi-xi).

The best way to pay tribute to such a mind is to remember what he stood for and the way he led his life and defined what an intellectual should be.

REFERENCES

Bhushan, S. (February 6, 2016). The last of a kind: A student's reminiscences of the professor Randhir Singh, *The Caravan*. Retrieved September 12, 2016, from http://www.caravanmagazine.in/vantage/student-reminiscence-marxist-scholar-professor-randhir-singh

Freire, P. (2007). *Pedagogy of the heart*. New York and London: Continuum.

Rikowski, G. (2001). After the manuscript broke off: Thoughts on Marx, social class and education'. Retrieved March 7, 2016, from http://www.leeds.ac.uk/educol/documents/00001931.htm.

Singh, R. (1976). *Reason, revolution and political theory*. New Delhi: People's Publishing House.

Singh, R. (March 12, 1988). In lieu of bio-data. *Mainstream*. Retrieved October 10, 2016, from http://www.mainstreamweekly.net/article6207.html.

12

Environment, Green and Red

Abdul Rahman

> *There is widespread consciousness about the environmental degradation around us, of the disastrous consequences if it continues. But there is very little understanding that this is the natural, a necessary, result of capitalism* (Singh, 2009: 70).

Introduction

Randhir Singh (1922-2016), a teacher, intellectual and an activist has written substantially on several issues including environment. The present book is an effort to acknowledge his contributions in all these different fields. This chapter is primarily focused on his take on the ecological crisis the world and humanity are facing. His presentation of the crisis reflects his rigorous training in Marxism and his undying faith in socialism. The book, *Contemporary Ecological Crisis: A Marxist View* published in 2006 was written at the age of eighty-four. His unmatchable commitment to Marxism even at a time when it was on the receiving end due to the circumstances created after the fall of the Soviet Union and growing strength of globalized capitalism is reflected in this work as well.

The book establishes capitalism's undying thirst for profit as the central cause of the destruction of nature. Prof. Randhir Singh is critical of the present ecological movements, both in the form of its NGOs' avatar and its more political expressions such as Green Parties. For him, both streams have failed to identify the structural reasons of the ongoing environmental crisis. He establishes that any solution of the ecological crisis is impossible within capitalism and hence socialism, with its structural change, is required. He acknowledges the fact that environment issues, as they are today, were yet to emerge on significant levels when Marx and Engels were writing. Despite their limited exposure they were able to see the tendencies within capitalism which has led us to the brink of destruction. Randhir Singh sees 'socialism' as the only possible and viable remedy to the ecological crisis created by capitalism. However, he argues that socialism needs to get rid of its past mistakes and theoretical shortcomings identified as 'productionist bias' to present itself as a credible alternative.

Prof. Randhir Singh has written along with several other intellectuals such as John Bellamy Foster and Paul Burkett to present a Marxist view on the contemporary issues. Their writings are a collective effort to put across the point that the dominant understanding of Marxism as an anthropocentric discipline indifferent to ecological concerns is not correct. They argue that capitalism has successfully adapted itself to the changing times giving an impression of its capacity to improve as per changing circumstances. This coincided with the writings of the likes of Ted Benton and James O'Connor who criticised Marx "for allegedly failing to address questions of sustainability" (Bellamy, 2015). Both these suppositions were wrong. Nonetheless they were able to hold back distracted Left intellectuals and movements from declaring a 'post-Marxist' world where 'old methods' are not enough to fight capitalism. Randhir Singh with this short intervention tries to counter both these suppositions and the pessimism of the Left. Through this book he has been able to strongly state the need to revisit Marx and Engels to find a true alternative to capitalism to save the earth from the ecological crisis.

The Crisis

An environmental or ecological crisis is multidimensional. The earth is fast becoming uninhabitable for all kinds of species including the human beings due to the rising surface temperature, rising sea levels, changing climate at regional and global levels, pollution of air, water and all other natural resources. This crisis is not natural; rather it is a result of human activities. The encroachment of humans in the environment is so overwhelming that it is destroying all kinds of natural habitats of different kinds of species including the living conditions of humans. The extinction of almost fifty species every day is the latest data input which underlines the severity of the situation. The forests, including the rain forests are getting reduced in size, rivers are dying and the ozone layer is being destroyed. Any conception of life on earth is impossible if air, water, soil etc are polluted and temperature rises beyond a level. The rapid development of economy and the rapid growth in population have created massive demands which have led to the intensification of the hostility between the human and the nature. Though as Randhir Singh points out, this relationship is as old as human existence, it was only in the last few centuries and particularly in the last century that it has become a relationship of mutual destruction. The increase in the frequency of natural calamities which includes failures of rain or excess of it etc are reflections of over exploitation of the "free gift of nature" as pointed out by Marx in the nineteenth century itself (Brett and Foster, 2010: 142-156). Randhir Singh points this out very succinctly. According to him, "it is enough to indicate the general nature of the crisis as a radical, and growing, disjunction between on the one hand the demands placed on the environment by the modern global economy, and on the other, the capacity of the natural forces embedded in the environment to meet these demands. There is the 'brutal fact', that the normal course of social production inexorably destroys the natural basis of society" (Singh, 2009: 33).

Earlier, there were regional ecological problems such as desertification here and floods there or extinction of life saving species. The twentieth century has seen and recognised the global effects of ecological crisis. The hole in the Ozone layer or the destruction of rain forests in Brazil, the pollution of the seabed and the melting of the glaciers are no more regional issues. This realisation in the second half of the last century has given birth to various kinds of intellectual and political movements to save the earth. The immediacy of the problem has forced a number of states to take these movements seriously and try to achieve a consensus through conferences and legal regimes. However, there is a lack of seriousness in all the efforts taken due to the inability to see the structural reasons of the crisis among all the stakeholders. Agreeing with Randhir Singh, Brett Clark and John Bellamy Foster too argue that there is a tendency to see ecological problems as economic problems even among the so-called eco-Marxists such as Ted Benton and James O'Connor (2010: 143) leave aside the liberal ecological movements.

Who is suffering due to the destruction of natural environment the most? Though in the long term, entire humanity is in danger it is the poor who are suffering the most due to the ecological crises. According to Randhir Singh "it is well established that it is the working classes, oppressed minorities, women and the rural and urban poor worldwide who suffer the most from both economic and ecological exploitation" (p. 60). The rains are erratic, the soil is becoming infertile, pure water is fast becoming a commodity which only the rich can buy, the air is polluted and the forests, a source of livelihood for millions of human beings are shrinking. All these are making the living standards of the poor worse. As we will see below, Randhir Singh is very clear that in the process of so called globalisation, the North is shifting its hazardous and harmful industries to the South. This is in addition to direct transfer of hazardous waste to the South in many forms. However, it is not only the poor regions of the South which are used to pass on the burden of ecological crisis. The rich use the poor neighbourhoods even in the North, such as the black populated regions in the USA to establish heavily polluting industries. There are both classist and racist elements in such acts. Randhir Singh calls it "Environmental Racism". The rich in the west are suffering from the syndrome of 'Not in My Backyard' in which ecologically unsustainable economic activities and development projects are shifting out of the advanced countries to the underdeveloped South. All these are short term measures. Even the managers of capitalism in the North know this. Hence, they have started talking about the solutions. They seem to be unaware of the fact that ecological crises cannot be solved under the present social and economic structures.

In the last few decades there have been 'attempts' such as moves to make the development process more sustainable and ensure direct reduction in the emissions of the green house gases among many others. All these are symptoms of desperation among the capitalists. They need to understand that until capitalism is there the ecological crisis remains. This is because it is capitalism and its 'productionism' and 'consumerism' which are the causes of the crisis.

Structural Logic of Capitalism

According to Randhir Singh, one of the most problematic aspects of the current discourse on environmental crisis is its inability or rather reluctance to point out the culpability of capitalism. Everyone is worried about the fate of ecology, but when it comes to diagnosing the causes most of them are clueless. It is "their single-minded pursuit of profit, in which none can refuse to join on the pain of elimination, capitalists are continuously driven to produce and sell and make more profit, to accumulate even more capital, and this becomes both their subjective goal and the motor force of the entire system" (Singh, 2009: 51). Profit is central to any definition of capitalism. The development of productive forces, innovation of new technology and exploration of new areas are all motivated to earn more, accumulate more. As Marx said, "Accumulate, accumulate! That is Moses and the prophets!" Randhir Singh argues that "capitalism is not some neutral process of technological progress for the satisfaction of human needs. It is the production of goods and services for the profit of those who own the means by which they are produced. The realisation of profits for the few and the satisfaction of the needs of the majority rarely coincide" (Singh, 2009: 50).

The greed to increase the levels of profit propels the capitalist to search for cheaper means of production and higher rate of consumption to create demands. Similar to Marx's analysis of 'Metabolic Rift' where capitalists in order to increase their spatial reach with increase in the profit as the ultimate objective destroy the conditions of metabolic reproduction of nature (Paul, 2006: 41) Randhir Singh argues that the twofold objectives of cheaper means of production and higher rates of consumption are achieved through manipulation of the environment. Unlike the neutrality of earlier technological progress and simplicity of earlier systems of production with the limited objective of satisfying human needs, capitalism creates new needs and technologies for accumulation. Randhir Singh identifies this as the main reason of the destruction of the environment in the last three centuries.

Since capitalism can never stand still, it is trapped in the unending and uncontrollable cycle of expansion without ever giving a second thought to the finite natural resources. In their greed they forget what Marx said in *Capital Vol. 1* that nature and labour together constitute the dual source of all wealth. Capitalists suffer a curse of "grow or die" which makes them tied to an automatic system where they are not free to not grow. This makes capitalism dynamic. As Marx said, "bourgeois cannot exist without constantly revolutionising the instruments of production." In its constant search of profit capitalism does not only create poverty and unemployment but also a crisis for environment too. It clears jungles to establish new industries; it pollutes rivers and seas to cut the cost of production and creates machines which emit a lot of greenhouse gases. All through this, capitalism destroys the natural conditions of production in the long run. Randhir Singh rightly points out the irony of capitalism is that all these acts of self-destruction are supposed to be of "free" choice and of great vision. In reality, he argues, in capitalism no one is free, not even the capitalists themselves who control and exploit others. It is obvious that in such a situation where acts of destruction are inherent parts of the system of capitalist production, no solution of environmental crisis is possible. It is so because in capitalism no 'free act' is possible.

Under capitalism, nature is something which needs to be mastered and controlled for unhindered use and for human satisfaction. The relationship between the nature and the human becomes a relationship of a master and a slave where the master takes the slave's potentials as inexhaustible and thinks nothing about its needs of rest and refreshments. As Marx argues, nature needs time to refresh itself. It can only refresh and replenish if the "metabolic interaction" between human and nature is maintained (Brett and Foster, 2010: 144). However, capitalism first creates needs through consumerism and then to fulfil those needs exploits the nature further.

Consumerism or the insatiable lifestyle, according to Randhir Singh the so called "American way" of life has become ideal for most of the people in the world. This is not an innocent development. It is created through media and other sources of communication as the process of development. Every society wants to be like the West, and wants to consume like them. No one is bothered about the fact that living like the West is impossible. It is impossible because nature has limits and it will crumble faster if the level of consumption in the rest of the world follows the example of the West. Randhir Singh points out, "give or take a few per cents, the first world or the industrialised North, with 25 per cent of the world's population and owning 86 per cent of the world's industry, consumes 80 per cent of world energy" (Singh, 2009: 58). This living standard of the North is unsustainable in two ways; in its exploitation of the finite natural resources and its creation of different kinds of harmful wastes. Despite all the expansion of industries in the South and exploitation of their natural resources it is the North which contributes the maximum in the global emissions and waste production. Most of the societies want to imitate the same style. This is defined as 'development'. The so-called developing societies such as China and India are fast catching up with the North in the absolute amount of emissions and destruction of the harmony between the nature and the human. It is but natural that the condition would be unimaginable if the rest of the 75 per cent comes even closer to that of the 25 per cent.

Human population has increased fivefold within less than five centuries since the beginning of the industrial era. It is a result of human ability to control the natural conditions of life through technological innovations. Capitalism in its search for profit has facilitated the ruthless exploitation of the "free gift of nature". The unsustainable demands generated due to the lust of growth have damaged the ecology. The big cities, intensive and industrial agriculture, massive industries and huge consumption of energy resources are giving no breathing space to nature to get replenished. This process, a result of colonial and imperial expansion during the nineteenth and twentieth centuries has globalised the environmental crisis along with creating unlivable conditions for the world's poor.

Colonialism provided the capitalists in the West the opportunities to go to unexplored regions and establish there similar systems of exploitation of nature. Clearing of forests in the Americas and exploration of minerals through thoughtless destruction of ecology in colonies have created numerous environmental problems. Today, though direct colonialism is over, capitalists in the North have devised newer ways of colonising. Randhir Singh uses the terms, popular among the ecological Marxism (Foster and Clark, 2004: 230-246), 'environmental imperialism' or 'ecological imperialism' and 'garbage imperialism' to describe neo-imperialist forms of capitalist exploitation of the natural habitat in the South. The process of globalisation is actually a process of finding access to more and more unexplored and unexploited resources. In the age of Washington Consensus the access to ecologically sensitive regions is placed open by the weak state leadership sometimes under the pressure from the external forces, but also sometimes due to pressures from the local or national bourgeoisie. Randhir Singh rightly argues that, "to its worldwide scramble for resources and markets and outlets for profitable investment, which has already taken the form of technological anomalies, unregulated chemical hazards and environmental degradation, sporadic war and chronic hunger in the Third World, global capitalism has recently added a specific new objective: a search for the most regulation-free sites for environmental destruction, whether in the form of deforestation, pesticide poisoning, dangerous industrial processes, or toxic waste dumps" (Singh, 2009: 64).

Randhir Singh also identifies the fact that how capitalism has created war industries. The industry is directly related to environmental crisis at many places. It is not only the nuclear armament which threatens the existence of life on the earth. There are numerous other armaments both chemical and conventional which have the potential of damaging the ecology beyond repair. The bombing in Vietnam, movements of submarines under the sea and aircraft carriers on the surface of the sea etc are producing as much pollution as any other industrial and commercial movements. The wars related to energy resources and industrial accidents including nuclear accidents are creating permanent damage to the environment. All this is happening in the name of development and democracy. The slogans come handy in getting legitimacy for the acts of destruction of both human and natural lives.

Randhir Singh puts the blame on the peripheral capitalist's obsession with the neoliberal 'developmentalism' for unhindered destruction of nature in the southern countries. The desire to grow at the level of the North is making the State in the South to comply with wishes of international as well as local capitalists. The growth fetishism is compromising the future of the human existence.

Though the governments in the South concede the gravity of the situation from time to time, they "insist that pollution is a global problem that the main responsibility for cleaning it up should fall on the developed countries". According to Randhir Singh the argument "that if the developed countries wanted the developing countries to adopt clean technologies, they should provide financial assistance for technology transfer" is a "reasonable and justifiable position to take" (P-69). However, what needs to "be explicitly stated is that with the environmental crisis nature has even less regard for national borders than does capitalism" and hence capitalists from neither the North nor the South can have a free hand or guilt-free existence.

Green Movements

Environmental movements emerged on the horizon around the beginning of the second half of the twentieth century. According to Randhir Singh, it is not surprising that environmental concerns became explicit at the same time when capitalism was at its peak. He argues that "environmental awareness is typically a product of the period of capitalist development. In the pre-capitalist society, an explicit notion of environmental limits was generally lacking." This is because the limit was not yet reached. In simple words "environmental consciousness has grown with the growth of the environmental crisis" (p. 45). The past human civilisations' interaction with the environment did change it. Sometimes it destroyed it too. But all those destructions were local or regional in nature. "The advent of capitalism meant a radical change in the situation. On the one hand, there was not only a shift from natural resources-based agriculture to industry on a large scale, both agricultural and industrial revolutions of the seventeenth and eighteenth centuries-came to be geared to the market. On the other hand, methods of production yielding maximum profits for the capitalist took precedence over any concern for the environment" (Singh, 2009: 46).

The problem of ecology has started getting attention from the world and that is reflected in the global conferences such as the one at Rio which was held in 1990 after three decades of preliminary talks regarding the various aspects of it. The method of rectification was identified as "sustainable development". There was a growing consensus about sharing the burden to clean the environment among all the stakeholders. The success of environmental movements and global initiatives has been limited to the wider acceptance of the notion of collective responsibility. However, in the last three decades the world is divided among the countries of the North and the South on the basis of who should share the greater burden. It is a debate which is approached from developmentalist logic as to tackle the environmental crisis one needs to sacrifice its unhindered pace of growth.

The failure of the states to devise a common mechanism of the sustainable development has given way to the emergence of different national and international NGOs. These NGOs try to create awareness among the people and lobby with the governments to make laws related to environment protection. Some of the NGOs have led local movements against 'harmful' projects initiated by big corporate houses with the explicit approval of the State. According to Randhir Singh, some of these movements have done tremendous work and socialist movements should engage with them and participate in the ongoing movements. However, most of these movements are limited in their objectives due to the uncritical attitude towards the structural reasons of environmental disasters. The 'successes' of these movements have been limited. They have slowed down the pace of destruction through the closure by force of one plant here and closure of another there. According to Randhir Singh, "popular movements confined to the community, municipality, or village cannot by themselves deal effectively with most of both the economic and ecological aspects of the general destructiveness of global capitalism, not to speak of the destructive dialectic between economic and ecological crises. Such movements or struggles have remained mostly 'populist' and 'localist' and have thus been incapable of countering capitalism's increasingly broad and deep, and destructive, exploitation of natural and social wealth" (Singh, 2009: 81).

Corporate responsibility or individual responsibility in protecting environment is also not going to help in the long run as the kind of consumerism prevalent in capitalism makes individuals break their personal vows to not to pollute the environment. A corporate entity does or would not want to lose an opportunity to its competitor while adopting a "sustainable" method of production for the simple logic that it increases its production costs or makes its products unattractive in the market. In fact, by not questioning the structural reasons of the ecological crisis and focusing on local and individual events the present environment movements have 'deodorised' its stench and hence has made ecological disaster more tolerable "at the expense of the common people, their jobs and livelihood" (Singh, 2009: 78). Randhir Singh hints at the lack of free choice in capitalism here. As Marx says, no one is free to do what is best for oneself in capitalism because of the structural constraints.

Randhir Singh is critical of the supposedly left environmentalist movements such as Green Parties too. He finds them too bereft of a proper theory. Their lack of a structural criticism and a proper alternative is the cause of their marginalisation in the politics of their respective countries. His criticisms of the mainstream leftist intellectuals are similar to the criticisms put forward by Brett Clark and John Bellamy Foster (2010: 142-156) as we will see below. One specific point needs to be highlighted here though. According to James O'Conner, the crisis in ecology is a crisis of capitalism. He sees it as an economic crisis. According to Randhir Singh, Brett Clark and Foster this is a wrong application of Marx's understanding of the capitalist crisis. This example proves what is wrong with the mainstream leftist movements of environment today.

Randhir Singh appreciates the 'biocentric' vision of ecology among leftist environmental movements; however; he questions the so called Deep Ecology movements' exclusive concerns relating to nature. Their exclusive focus on the 'rights' of the animals and ecology and putting them against humans, according to Randhir Singh is self-defeating. He questions their understanding of anthropocentricism as the root of the environmental disaster and their alternative 'biocentric' approach. He argues that "the major ecological problems facing the world today, for example, worldwide consumerism of the rich or growing militarisation with its regional wars, arms race and the prospect of nuclear annihilation, have no tangible connection to the anthropocentric-biocentric distinction. Their causes cannot be reduced to any anthropocentric attitude towards nature, and the ecological degradation they cause does not even serve the best interests of human beings. To see or understand such threats to environment in terms of anthropocentricism is at best irrelevant and at worst a dangerous obfuscation" (Singh, 2009: 86). He argues that, "it evades and obscures the fact that the most destructive assaults upon nature come not from humanity as a whole, but from the priorities, the artefacts, and the actions of particular sets of human agents, whose interests are as detrimental to the majority of the humankind as they are to the natural environment" (Singh, 2009: 82). He reproaches their failure to understand the simple fact that the so-called duality between nature and human being is created by capitalism. He denies the argument that this dualism is "essential". It's unreal because human beings cannot live without nature and the existence of both nature and human beings is mutual and essentially based on harmony. As P.T. Saroja Sundararajan quotes Marx "for all its universality and freedom, still the human species has only one home—the Earth" (1996: 377-378). The humans cannot live without ecology and the ecology without human beings is meaningless consideration.

Randhir Singh is amused that some of the Deep Ecologists are more critical of modernity and blame it for the ecological crisis romanticising the pre-modern period. He points out their confusion. According to him it is not modernity which has caused destruction of ecology; it is capitalism and it seems Deep Ecologists are either unable to see the simple difference between the two or they want to exonerate capitalism shifting the blame to modernity.

Despite all the concerns shown, the resolution of environmental crisis is not possible under capitalism. The enthusiasts are hopeful that global conferences and adoption of sustainable development methods would be able to stop the degradation. However, capitalism's search for newer ways of profit making never ceases to surprise. It is not the capacity of the capitalism to adapt which will help it resolve the ecological problem. It is rather its capacity to make profit even from the same crisis created by it. As Burkett and Foster remind us about Marx's use of Lauderdale Paradox where all kinds of fall in the

Public Wealth creates Private Riches in the sense that if one is able to create scarcity in basic requirements of life, i.e. air, food, water etc., it enhances the richness of the some individuals or even the country at the expense of the Public Wealth (2010: 149-50).

Capitalism resists most of the regulations attempted by states under pressures from both local and global movements. They are observed through violations. Capitalism sometimes uses its power to control the State from interfering in its profit making endeavours. It moves out, shifts its base causing immediate concerns of livelihood and revenues if pushed beyond a point. All these are well known. However, Randhir Singh points our attention to another aspect of capitalism adapting itself and even using environmental crisis for generating new sources of profit. He quotes Marcuse to this effect. According to him, "Marcuse had drawn our attention to capitalism's capability of absorbing, repackaging, and commodifying dissent in capitalist societies" (Singh, 2009: 89). If the water is polluted, create a new industry of bottled water, if there is an oil spill it needs to be cleaned using latest technologies which costs millions of dollars paid for by the public exchequer. The government projects to "clean" rivers, create alternative sources of energy such as solar etc., is a multi-billion (according to some estimates a $300 billion) profit generating industry (Singh, 2009: 91). Randhir Singh quotes American Council of Environmental Quality which has recorded that "at least a million dollars is pocketed in the course of the elimination of three million dollars worth of damage to the environment" (Singh, 2009: 91). Randhir Singh sites how Joshua Karliner and Brian Tokar in their books have detailed the growth of "Corporate Greenwash" in which corporate funded environmental NGOs try to shift the blame for environmental disasters to the poorer sections and countries of the world. Randhir Singh is firm in his belief that capitalism cannot address the environment issues. He says it is not a management problem but a design problem; the design of the social and economic production (Singh, 2009: 94) and therefore its resolution is beyond the logic of capitalism.

In the context mentioned above, it is very clear that the slogan of sustainable development coined by Rio summit in 1991 has but rhetorical value. Its meaning, at best, is elusive and it is different things to different people (Singh, 2009: 42). According to Randhir Singh, in "its meaningful sense, sustainable development assumes not only that development is essential to the elimination of poverty and provision of decent living for all human beings, but that it has to be a development which meets human needs without destroying the natural systems; which can continue indefinitely into the human future without generating such constraints as resource depletion, environmental injury, burgeoning human population or economic and political repression; which would address the urgent problems of present generations without penalising future generations" (Singh, 2009: 42-43). He further argues, "Yet the conventional debate on sustainable development is marked by a remarkable lack of interest in understanding the existing pattern or an equally remarkable inability to understand it. Even when it is realised that 'the market is ill-adapted to deal with long-term effects, inter-generational responsibilities and common property resources', the government is expected and urged to discipline and control it, ignoring the fact that under the existing (capitalist) pattern of development, it is the market which controls the government and not the other way around, that the solution thus preferred is itself a problem" (Singh, 2009: 43).

Randhir Singh warns that "if humanity constructs a kind of society that systematically destroys the natural ground of its own existence then it is heading for a disaster. Or, to put it more specifically, if our society continues to be dominated by capitalism, then it is only a matter of time—be it a few decades or a few centuries, neither of which amounts to much in the long stretch of history—before it expires from the lack of essential life supports. It is not apocalyptic to warn about the disastrous dimensions that capitalism's threat to environment has now acquired" (Singh, 2009: 146). In fact it is a wake-up call to come together and fight against capitalism because "winning against capitalism means winning socialism that is, winning conscious rational control of humanity's metabolism with nature. It is to win our freedom 'in the realm of necessity' as Marx called it, which capitalism by its very nature denies us, and which, to repeat Marx again, 'can only consist in this that the socialised man, the associated producers, govern the human metabolism with nature in a rational way, bring it under their collective control instead of being dominated by it as a blind power, accomplishing it with the least expenditure of energy and in conditions most favourable to, and worthy of, their human nature" (Singh, 2009: 150).

"Not Their Problem"

According to Randhir Singh the common understanding propagated by the critiques of Marx and Marxism is that Marx and Engels have failed to grasp the intensity of the environment problem in their writings and instead have been followers of the dominant liberal discourse of the time of "prometheanism" in which man should control the nature and use it for its own purposes, and enslave it instead of being tied to its conditions. The critiques quote *Communist Manifesto* and Engels' *Anti-Duhring* where defining socialism Engels hopes that "....the objective, external forces which have hitherto dominated history, will then pass under the control of men themselves.." to argue that Marx and Engels were advocating "control over nature" and an antagonism between human purposes and nature. Some of the critiques such as Ted Burton argue that Marx has exaggerated the potential of productive labour processes in transforming the limits put by nature. In the eyes of the critiques of Marxism it is an ideology which propagates the hostility between human and natural environment and hence has no real alternative to capitalist exploitation of the ecology. Randhir Singh counters this reading of Marx and Engels. According to him all these readings are based on superficial understanding of Marxism. He points out the fact that when Marx and Engels were writing there was not much clarity about the effects on nature of the capitalist enterprise.

Destruction of nature in capitalism was obvious but in Marx and Engels there was a hope rather a belief that capitalism won't last for long because of its internal contradictions and revolt of the proletariat would soon establish socialism. In brief, ecological crisis as it is today was "not *their* problem" (Singh, 2009: 111).

Randhir Singh quotes Marx and Engels extensively to establish that ecology and environment and man's harmonious relationship with it was one of their major concerns nonetheless. According to him, "Marx had, well ahead of most contemporary environmental thought, already in the nineteenth century posed many of the essential ecological questions that are our concern today: questions regarding the overall relation between nature and human society, the inter-dependent 'metabolic' character of the exploitation of the earth and other forms of exploitation, and above all the question of sustainability" (Singh, 2009: 113). He points out Marx's *Economic and Philosophical Manuscript of 1844* in which Marx refers to "nature as 'man's inorganic body' and to man as 'a part of nature'". Marx says, "Man lives from nature, i.e. nature is his body, and he must maintain a continuing dialogue with it if he is not to die". According to Randhir Singh, "for Marx all human production is socially mediated production and occurs within a co-evolutionary context. The notion of co-evolution of nature and humanity is central to Marx's understanding of the relation between the two".

Randhir Singh argues that in Marx's understanding of capitalist production has alienated man from its natural environment too. He points out that "Genuine wealth consists of use of values which are produced only with the help of nature. Nature is one of the sources in the creation of wealth, along with labour power. Marx wrote that 'labour is the natural condition of the human, the condition of material exchange between human and nature, independent of all social forms', but 'the labourer can create nothing without nature, without the sensuous external world" (Singh, 2009: 114). Marx in *Grundrisse*, though accepts the revolutionising impact of capitalism on the prevalent superstitions about nature, he is very critical of the fact that it "robs" or "degrades" the "free gift" of nature. Capitalism does not take into account the need of reproduction of nature and violates the natural limits through its exploitative practices. In his *Capital Vol I* Marx writes that "...all progress in capitalistic agriculture is a progress in the art, not only of robbing the labourer, but of robbing the soil; all progress in increasing the fertility of the soil for a given time, is progress towards ruining the lasting sources of that fertility. The more a country starts its development on the foundation of modern industry, like the United States, for example, the more rapid is this process of destruction" (quoted in Singh, 2009: 119). Marx argues that "even an entire society, a nation, or all simultaneously existing societies taken together, are not owners of the earth. They are simply its possessors, its beneficiaries, and have to bequeath it in an improved state to succeeding generations, as *boni patres familias* (good heads of the household)" (Singh, 2009: 121).

According to Randhir Singh, Marx and Engels were also aware about the problem of pollution caused by capitalist development and urbanisation. Engels in his *Anti-Duhring* says that "the present poising of the air, water and land can only be put an end to by the fusion of town and country. The division between the city and countryside creates serious ecological crises. "Communism for Marx included restoration to the human species the lost dimensions of their relationship to their non-human natural environment" (Singh, 2009: 124). Friedrich Engels' other book, *Conditions of Working Class of England* published in 1887 narrates the effect of gradual destruction of the harmony between the nature and human being incited by capitalism and urbanisation.

On the issue of Marx and Engels' treatment of the ecological question Paul Burkett, John Bellamy Foster and Clark *et al* have done tremendous amount of work recently. Marx's detailed study of the concept of 'waste' generated due to urban-rural divide, his elaboration of soil being robbed of its fertility due to intensive farming and import of guana from colonies in the Latin America and his engagements with Malthus and other leading liberal economists about the nature as free gifts etc., are some of the works highlighted by the above mentioned writers in order to establish that there is enough ecological concerns in Marxism and one need not look beyond Marxism for developing environmental disaster and its links with capitalism. These authors have also tried to counter the perceptions of Marx's insensitivity towards nature. Randhir Singh however, is not that keen to argue that Marx had diagnosed all the ecological problems. He is ready to give Marx and Engels a historical reading while arguing that ecology was not their problem. They could have a limited understanding of the ecology crisis given their lack of any experience of massive destruction caused by capitalism after their death.

Socialism and Ecology: In Order to be 'Green' It's Necessary to be 'Red'

Randhir Singh sees the attempts to address the environmental crisis by the present movements under the existing social and economic system as at best attempts to slow down instead stop destruction of environment. He argues that, "the sustainability of both human civilisation and global life processes depends not on the mere slowing down of these dire trends, but on their reversal" (Singh, 2009: 95). This is only possible under socialism. He is sure that "under socialism, profit can and may serve as a criterion of viability and accounting but does not have to be maximised. What are to be maximised are social good and accumulation of public capital production and distribution of goods and services to respond to the needs of the population. Based on collective ownership of the means of production (whose forms can be varied) and planning, it can allocate resources for achieving the desired results, and one, right at the top, can be the protection and preservation of the environment, or it ought to be" (Singh, 2009: 96).

Randir Singh criticises the existing and past socialist experiments for their failing in protecting the environment. He argues that the failure of these societies, Soviet Union and Eastern European Countries along with China, was not due to some structural reasons as in capitalism though. He attributes two causes for their failure; one, due to the historical and political contexts the departure of these societies from the principles of socialism, the historical context in which they were trying to survive against imperialist attacks. The second reason is the theoretical bias among classic Marxism towards what he calls 'economistic productionism'. According to Randhir Singh, the underlying the departures from socialism in Soviet Union "are the historical conditions governing the construction of socialism...and a specific theoretical *deficit*—the minor economistic tendency or 'productionist bias' within classical Marxism which thanks to these conditions, acquired a new lease of life to become, as 'economism', a dangerously effective deforming influence on what ultimately got constructed there" (Singh, 2009: 98). He argues that in order to "catch up" with the western industrial development in the shortest possible time" and also in order to put off the pressure of economic backwardness of the society, Soviet Union "competed with capitalism not in terms of socialist principles or values, but on the latter's own terrain-the terrain of economic growth. As a result, the socialist project in the Soviet Union was never able to distance itself from the capitalist criteria of success or its structures and methods" (Singh, 2009: 99). Because of this "the planning process lost its vision of socialism-which is primarily about changing social relations of production to create a fraternal and egalitarian society and not just developing the forces of production-and its implementers their ability to recognise discrepancies between what they were doing and what they ought to or might have done" (Singh, 2009: 102). The result was massive exploitation of natural environment. The eventual death of Lake Baikal and massive poisoning of Caspian Sea etc., are some of the examples of the effects of the capitalist system.

About the productionist bias, Randhir Singh is clear that it was a minor tendency within classical Marxism. Nevertheless, "Marxism in its own way, shared in the prevalent ideology of progress, the hopeful ethos and scientific-technological optimism of the nineteenth century, which saw the development of the productive forces as the very basis of all material progress and therefore by its nature something positive. This productivist orientation got reinforced by Marxism's understanding of capitalism and its future and the origins and purposes of socialism as a mode of production which transcends it. Even as capitalism was subjected to a remarkably perceptive empirical and ethnic critique and its transitory nature underlined, capitalism was seen as playing a progressive historical role in that it creates the objective, material basis for socialism by its development of the forces of production" (Singh, 2009: 103). It was partially influenced by the aim of creating an egalitarian society where no one's needs should be sacrificed on the pretext of "natural limits" put by the environment. Randhir Singh argues that this productionism is not an integral part of Marxism as Marx and Engels have been critical of any obsession with the development of forces of production without considering the costs on ecology. According to him, the natural limit is important and one needs to learn to live with it. According to Randhir Singh, for Marx, "the goal of social life would not be work and production, in the narrow forms in which they have been understood, in possessive-individualist society of capitalism, but the all around development of human creative potential, for which, he further argued, 'the shortening of the working-day is a basic prerequisite'. This would set the stage for what Marx spoke of as 'the realm of freedom...beyond the sphere of actual material production (where) begins that development of human power which is an end in itself" (Singh, 2009: 106).

Randhir Singh argues that what happened in the Soviet Union and other experiments with socialism in terms of environment was not inevitable, or natural to socialism. "Marxism can and must do without productivist bias and socialism does not have to necessarily yield to it and lose it 'utopian' vision" (Singh, 2009: 106-107). He warns however that, "argument here is *not* that socialism will automatically go on to deal successfully with the threat of ecological disaster that has been inherited from centuries of capitalism, or that it guarantees that none of its other immediate or long term goals will obstruct ecological wisdom. But in practically eliminating the market-based vested economic interest which perpetuates ecologically harmful practices, it does acquire the potential of making significant advances towards ecologically rational production" (Singh, 2009: 107). He gives examples from Cuba and Sandinistas in Nicaragua where some change after experiments with plastic-free and eco-friendly development have been successfully implemented.

According to Randhir Singh "socialism is not simply an extension or an improvement upon capitalism, a society that eliminates the most objectionable features of capitalism such as gross inequality of income, mass unemployment, cyclical depressions, financial panics, and so on. Expropriation of capitalists certainly makes possible a planed use of the social surplus available, but socialism is not to be understood merely as a transfer of ownership or planning leading to a more just distribution of wealth while other relationships remain alienated and reified as before. Marx and Engels always conceived socialism as the quintessential *negation* of capitalism" (Singh, 2009: 140). He proposes the concept of alienation which is primarily a product of capitalist production as central concept to understand the relationship between the nature and human beings. Socialism is a systemic remedy of any such alienation.

Technology

Technology is one of the most important aspects of human existence. New technologies have improved the living conditions of human beings. It has helped humans to take control of their material existence and become free from natural conditions. However, there is no doubt that technological advancement has been one of the tools of ruthless exploitation of nature too under capitalism. However, the thinking that many environmentalists have about technology itself being the cause of ecological disaster, according to Randhir Singh is as wrong as seeing it as the solution.

Marx was criticised for having too much faith in technology

and termed as "a votary of technologism" (Singh, 2009: 135). Many critiques have identified some Marxist Technological Optimisms in the writings of Marx and Engels (P T Saroja Sundarajan 1996: 364) including Hannah Arendt blaming them for glorifying it as providing solutions to every problem. Randhir Singh calls such critiques as ignorant of "the social embeddedness of technology". He says, "Technology, once it has come up does come to acquire a certain dynamic of its own, but at a deeper level it is oriented by economic and socio-cultural systems of a society. In other words, it is always socially embedded" (Singh, 2009: 136). Though he agrees that technology can be used to address some of the problems, he quotes Istvan Meszaros, having blind faith in it is like believing in witchcraft. We can use technology for our purposes only after reorienting it from its current use as a tool of profit maximising.

Randhir Singh reminds us of Marx's linking of alienation with technology under capitalist system in which "the workers' activity, reduced to a mere abstraction of activity, is determined and regulated on all sides by the movement of machinery and not the opposite" (Marx, quoted in Singh, 2009: 138). If we want the technology to help us control our problems, we need to control it and it can only be done under socialism. He concludes with reiterating the point that "what has to be done to resolve the environmental crisis, hence also to ensure that humanity has a future, is to replace capitalism with a social order based on an economy devoted not to maximising private profit and accumulating ever more capital but rather to meeting real human needs and restoring the environment to a sustainably healthy condition" (Singh, 2009: 39).

Conclusion

The ideas elaborated by Prof. Randhir Singh in his book give us enough food of thought. One can have several questions on some of the issues raised in the book, for example, his ideas of "productionist bias" in classical Marxist theory being one of the reasons of the environmental crisis in existing socialist societies and the nature of methods used in a socialist society to fulfil the human needs without breaking the harmony with nature. The way he criticises Soviet Communism's faith in this productionist bias leaves us with the question whether he is arguing for a more romantic version of Marxism where production concerned with providing better living standards will be suspended. In a socialist society what would be the mechanism to deal with population pressure? His argument that Marx and Engels' understanding of ecological crisis in the future capitalist societies was limited due to their faith in socialist revolution defies and raises questions on the works of Foster and other Marxist ecologists. The broader point that capitalism is the cause of ecologists destruction and there is no real solution of the problem under it is beyond any doubt. It is also beyond any doubt that socialism is the alternative where a real harmony between nature and the human being is possible. However, there is the lack of any elaborate scheme of socialism and how it will deal with ecological problems in the short term immediately after the transition from capitalism. Will ecological destruction and mass deprivations it creates be able to create disenchantment with capitalism or do we need a vanguard to do so?

REFERENCES

Burkett, P. (2006). Two stages of ecosocialism? implications of some neglected analyses of ecological conflict and crisis. *International Journal of Political Economy, 35* (3), 23-45

Clark, B. and Foster, J.B. (2010). Marx's ecology in the 21st century. *World Review of Political Economy, 1* (1), 142-156.

Foster, J.B. (2015). Marxism and ecology: Common fronts of a great transition. *Monthly Review, 67* (7) .

Foster, J.B. and Clark, B. (2004). Ecological imperialism. in Leo Panitch and C. Leys (eds.), *Socialist register 2004: New imperial challenges* (pp. 230-246). New York: Monthly Review Press.

Singh, R. (2009). *Contemporary ecological crisis: A Marxist view*, Delhi: Aakar Books.

Sundararajan, P.T.S. (1996). From Marxian ecology to ecological Marxism. *Science & Society, 60* (3), 360-379.

13

Communalism, Secularism and Socialism

Rityusha Mani Tiwary

The Debate

Of the many divisive, regressive and complex problems of Indian politics, communalism is one and as such, has been discussed, decoded and theorised in order to, prima facie, *deal* with it. Occasionally, while confronting communalism, the ideological spectrum in Indian politics has intervened critically in emergent normative and methodological structures. In normative discourses, the idea of communalism has elicited primarily two kinds of arguments. One, that communalism is a manifestation of the social-cultural-psychological divide sourced into diversity and plurality of religions that India has. The central argument here is that religious communities perceive their interests in different ways often at odds with each other and this in turn gives rise to antagonistic behaviour reflected in violent conflicts (Ahuja, 1992: 104). Here it is argued that particular religious identities give rise to common political (Dumont, 1964: 48) and economic interests (Chandra, 1984: 1); these identities are ascribed by birth and channelled by personal sentiments (Saberwal, 1971: 57). To these analyses the individual's relationship with society invariably has a psychological/sociological vantage point with emphasis on identity formation along religious communities and the superimposition of religion—primarily a private affair—on the larger public canvas. As a methodology, this argument does not wish away the social conflict of communalism with the aid of just economic development because doing so would mean that it is about a rational individual, without any irrational prejudices and obscurantism (Bhardwaj, 1990: 68). The second argument regarding communalism is primarily about political power struggle which is an agenda of the elites from competing religious communities (Chaudhuri cited in Zakaria, 2002: XVIII; Dixit, 1974). Here communalism is a phenomenon with secular struggle for political power as its root cause, and religion is merely a mobilising force behind communalism (Engineer, 1995: 52). A third argument about communalism emphasises on the interconnection between the ideological apparatus of religion and the social structure (Panikkar, 1990: 95) and presets caution against viewing the question of communalism through the prism of nationalism (Pandey, 1987: 983; Singh, 1988: 1545). Indeed, Randhir Singh in his two essays *Theorising Communalism: A Fragmentary Note in the Marxist Mode* (1988) and *Communalism and the Struggle against Communalism: A Marxist View* (1990) brings out the dissonance in these normative frameworks against the social, cultural, political and economic reality of communalism. For Randhir Singh "It is wrong to argue that 'the basic cause of communalism is cultural and psychological', or that 'communalism is above all a communal ideology... a false view, ... a wrong understanding of reality'. Such arguments reduce the struggle against communalism to an educative, ideological-cultural exercise in which, while 'falsity' or evils of communalism are exposed and appeals continue to be made in the name of 'true religion'" (Singh, 1990: 14). Randhir Singh rejects the obscurantist nationalist perspective that holds imperialism squarely responsible for all problems in the Indian society by ignoring the primary causes of many problems, communalism included. "The nationalist perspective thus obscures the all important distinction between the essentially indigenous creation of most of these problems and imperialism's contribution to and taking advantage of these for its own ends." (Singh, 1988: 1542)

Randhir Singh points out that nationalism cannot be the explanatory principle of social-historical processes in India as it is not a 'supra-historical force' in itself (Singh, 1988: 1542). Randhir Singh did not credit a simplistic, overarching economic development narrative as a solution to communalism. The deeply unequal and uneven exploitation and oppression of the people cannot adequately be addressed with overall economic development as it fails to take a nuanced note of the question of opportunism, co-option, status-quoism, group or identity-based elites' politics. The dialectical process of nation-in-making post-1947 in which the contradiction of imperialism was resolved without economic or social structural change continues to work in favour of the few (Singh, 1988: 1542). Randhir Singh makes a crucial intervention by pointing out methodological errors that run in abundance in most of the theorisation in this field: empiricist and ahistorical reading of contemporary communalism (Singh, 1990: 4). This addition to the lacunae in normative frameworks of social-cultural or psychoanalytic or nationalist or economic explanations. Randhir Singh suggests that as a method to combat communalism, the rhetorical normative of 'a vision of socialism' cannot replace a people's movement for socialism (Singh, 1988: 1543).

In post-independence India, communal conflicts, riots and killings have been recurrent, showing a steady increase in the intensity of the communal problem. It is ever in sharpening conflict with organised politics behind it. It also exposes a severely compromised model of Indian secularism in the tedious processes of inquiry and tardy dispensing of justice, to name the major instances: large scale organised violence against Sikhs in Delhi and rest of India in 1984[1]; the demolition of Babri Masjid followed by large scale riots in 1992; riots in Mumbai in December 1992 and January 1993[2]; pogrom in Gujarat in 2000[3]; violence and killings of Christians in Orissa by the Hindu extremist organisations in 2007-08; and more recently Muzzaffarnagar riots in 2013. The empirical evidence of continuous organised communal violence problematises the nature of Indian secularism and points towards its normative as well as methodological failings in the establishment of a secular state.

Communalism through Secular Ambivalence

In India, secularism was accorded a place in the Constitution with the 42nd Amendment enacted in 1976, where the Preamble to the Constitution asserts that India is a secular nation. Yet, the Indian Constitution does not define secularism that it espouses. It is understood and interpreted through provisos embedded in the Constitution[4]: citizenship (Article 9); non-discrimination on grounds of religion, race, caste, etc. (Article 15), generally and specifically in public employment (Article 16); the fundamental rights to freedom of religion individually (Article 25) and collectively (Article 26); ban on discrimination in state-aided educational institutions (Article 29(2)), taxes for the promotion of religion (Article 27); religious instruction in them (Article 28) and exclusion from the general electoral roll on any such ground as well (Article 325).

Even though the State cannot direct citizens with regard to choice of religion and there can be no State religion, there are diverse ways in which secularism has been interpreted in India. The amorphous boundaries of secularism in praxis have led to the rise of various issues in the Indian polity. In Indian Government's practice, secularism is understood as treating all religions equally or equal respect for all religions. By another interpretation, the relationship between individual, society and the State is based on the legal framework which keeps equidistance from all religions. The Supreme Court categorically declared in *S.R. Bommai v. Union of India* ((1994) 3 SCC 1[5] that secularism is a part of the basic structure of the Constitution and the Parliament has no powers to dilute it in any way. It declared that there must be complete separation between the State and the religion, and a political party must not be linked to any religion, as otherwise, the religion of such a party is perceived as a State religion (Godbole, 2016). The inclusion of the word 'secularism' in the Preamble and later the interpretation of this part of the Constitution as the 'basic structure' by the Supreme Court is part of political-constitutional strategy to combat the menace of communalism.

In spite of the ideal of separating the State and religion, the Indian State in several cases has intervened in the affairs of religion (Sand, 2006: 3). This reading of the Indian praxis of secularism finds much currency in definitions of secularism as: "Secularism... is not anti-God, it is not atheism, it is not anti-religion or anti-religious, it is not Godlessness; it is not irreligious" (Estevis, 1996: 82). Similar sentiments are reflected in the liberal-socialist political class in the post-independence India. Jawaharlal Nehru spoke in this connection of: "A secular state does not mean an irreligious state. It only means that we respect and honour all religions, giving them freedom to function" (Nehru, 1968: 48). In tune with these sentiments, the constitutional framework as it has evolved, did not adopt indifference to religions, and instead has been attempting to treat every religion with equal distance. Randhir Singh suggests that "the Indian ruling classes have always found religion, religiosity or *dharmikta*," most instrumental in establishing their "hegemony and social control" to justify "an unjust and iniquitous social order" (Singh, 1988: 1543). In the light of Randhir Singh's argument, a scrutiny of the Indian State's attempts at equality or equidistance with all religions, reveals its ambivalence on issues such as the rights of minorities (specifically conversions), uniform civil code and the recent incident of banning of beef.

In the next section, the glaring issues that highlight the ambivalence of Indian secularism are briefly explored.

The Rights of Minorities

The concept of secularism is linked with recognition and protection of minorities. Since the term minorities is undefined in the Constitution till date, the Supreme Court has adopted the criterion of numerical strength. According to Census 2011, religious minorities constitute about 20 per cent of India's population, with Muslims accounting for 14.2 per cent; Christians make up 2.3 per cent and Sikhs 1.72 per cent of the population[6] (*The Hindu*, 2015). Given these figures, it is evident that all religious minorities have a vital interest in the maintenance of the secular State; discrimination by the State on the basis of religion can only mean difficulties for the entire societal fabric. The secular democratic tradition of modern Indian State is however challenged by many factors.

D.E. Smith suggests two broad approaches vis-a-vis the protection of minorities by the states: "integration of the individual, by assuring his equality; and protection of the group by providing some sort of a *cordon sanitaire*[7] around it — in effect by insulating it from other socio-religious groups" (Smith, 1963: 405). While the second method operates along communal lines (for example as in Lebanon, or followed for some time in British India[8]), it is the first individual, citizenship-based method that is espoused in the Indian Constitution and enacted by the State (Nambiar, 1964: 949).

The socio-economic indicators of Muslims brought out by Justice Sachar Committee[9] show how this segment of the population has remained at the margin all these years. Taking cognisance of these arguments, the major recommendations of the National Commission for Religious and Linguistic Minorities Report[10] included 10% quotas for Muslims and 5% for other minorities in government jobs and reserved seats in educational institutions of 8.4% out of the existing OBC quota of 27% for minorities and SC reservation to Dalit converts. Similarly Articles 25 to 29 of the Constitution are the defining features of Indian secularism. Article 30 (1) which gives the right to minorities to establish and administer educational institutions was inserted, particularly at the instance of the Christians and Anglo-Indians who had a number of educational institutions. This article did not find consensus in the Constituent Assembly with severe dispute over long-term implications of perpetuating separate identities and undermining the spread of secular education (Godbole, 2016). It is frequently seen that in India, as in the western countries, citizens have been seeking exemptions from the laws of a secular liberal state on the grounds of culture and religion (Bilgrami, 2007: 316). As a counter-current to this tendency, Neera Chandoke warns that India's political culture is increasingly being dominated by majoritarianism. "The defence of secularism against these trends," she points out, "may well require a shift in our perceptions of how people of different religious persuasions can live together." She attempts to supplement secularism with "other definite political norms" that is equality, to regulate inter-group relations (Chandhoke, 1999). Adding to this perspective, Zoya Hasan points out that official discourse in India revolved essentially around issues of caste-based discrimination, "by implication leaving unaddressed many other critical areas of deprivation and discrimination" (Hasan, 2009). The constitutional promise of an egalitarian society has been fulfilled through affirmative actions based on caste-based reservation. But "there are indications of a perceptible shift in....reflected in the recognition of the multiple axes of disadvantage that characterize our society" (Hasan, 2009). The recent debates on equality in the wake of the Sachar Committee Report are indicative of this shift beyond the caste paradigm of inclusion and bring in the rights of minorities within the ambit of inclusion.

Uniform Civil Code

A secular democratic state has no religion of its own. By that virtue, the citizen of a state cannot be bound by any religious laws. A uniform civil law is in many ways at the heart of the secular political system (Nambiar, 1964: 948). "Religion impinges on every human right in the civil law—whether its birth, death, marriage, divorce, —the religions have laws on all of these," and so making India secular necessarily means demarcating religion out of our social institutions. A uniform civil code is needed in a democratic polity to ameliorate all the socio-legal inequalities that every religion embodies (Thapar, 2015b).

As early as during Macaulay's time, some of the difficulties were evident when he argued for the need for *uniform lex loci* in India. While the Law Commissions, initiated by Macaulay, were able to unify Criminal Law, hopes of the regulation of Civil

Law were not readily realised (Nambiar, 1964: 948). The realisation of uniform civil code becomes problematic if perspectives from multiple religions in India are to be taken cognisance of. For instance, in matters of various rituals pertaining to ashramas (life cycle of an individual) in Hindu religion, a range of religious civic laws exist. Among India's three largest minorities, only the Christians (and only Protestant Christians) have a real tradition of church-state separation behind them. Both the Muslims and the Sikhs have strongly theocratic elements in their traditions, and secularism does not have much inherent appeal, apart from their minority status (Smith, 1963: 438).

Killings by the extra-constitutional bodies like Khap Panchayats, and perpetuation of socio-religious-cultural oppressions and inequalities in marriages remain some of the problems of the Hindu majority which highlight the importance of a uniform civil code. However, in India the debate on the Uniform Civil Code has arisen most intensely with the Shah Bano controversy[11]. What should have been a women's rights issue grew into the focal point of religious antagonism between Hindu and Muslim extremists. Muslim religious leaders issued a proclamation against the judgment as a violation of Islamic Law. Chief Justice Chandrachud expressed his belief that "Interpretation of law, personal or otherwise, is not only the function but the obligation of the Court" (Supreme Court, Criminal Appeal No. 103, 23). Secular nations cannot allow religion to distort their commitment to egalitarianism, and yet the Shah Bano controversy threatened India's tradition of religious tolerance, and raised the question of how a secular nation should treat a religious minority that threatens national sovereignty (Oglesbee, 2015). In this regard, the biggest concern remains 'How to introduce a uniform law in a society that has been regulated for ages by parallel systems of 'personal' law?' The consciousness of being citizens that have rights is needed to tackle this issue (Thapar, 2015b). The people need to decide what kinds of civil laws they would like to see removed. This brings in a lot of difficult but not insurmountable problems in decision making. The courts have sought to make a transition through secular laws and dynamic judicial interpretations. For instance, adoption was made possible for Muslims and Christians only through an expansive interpretation of the Juvenile Justice Act[12]. This is the role that the judiciary must play—of identifying and ironing out internal and external inconsistencies—but developing a comprehensive code is a legislative function, and not for judicial resolution. In December 2015, the Supreme Court said that "it is not for the Court to direct Parliament to frame a specific law and that lawmakers only can take a call on a common code that may bring all religious personal laws under one umbrella" (Indian Express, 2015).

A three-judge bench led by Chief Justice T.S. Thakur said the apex court's observations for enacting a common code can only be in the "realm of hope and expectations" but a mandamus (directive) cannot be issued to the Government. At the end of the day, a Uniform Civil Code can only emerge through an evolutionary process, which preserves India's rich legal heritage, of which all the personal laws are equal constituents (Shah, 2016).

Ashutosh Varshney (2003) traces the issue of communalism to the British rule. He notes that the myth of primordial antagonism between Hindus and Muslims was spread by the British in their pursuit of the 'Divide and Rule Policy' even when it was evident that the two communities had peacefully coexisted for long. He highlights that the pre-existing local networks of civic engagement[13] between the two communities —trade unions, professional associations—that go beyond communal divide, have been the single most important and proximate cause for peace. Another important aspect is that ethnic violence on the whole, tends to be highly localised and is not spread across the length and breadth of the country (Varshney, 2003). More importantly, Varshney refers to the statistical fact that till date, almost 96% of all deaths in communal riots in India took place in cities. A very important point worth noting, according to Varshney is the steady rise of Hindu

Nationalism[14], especially after the year 1989. Four specific political factors were responsible for the rise of BJP and Hindu Nationalism in the 1980s, specifically, the rise of separatist movements in the 1980s, institutional decay of the Congress party, an absence of other centrist alternatives and lastly, opportunistic twisting of secular principles in Indian politics.

Many times, in the modern Indian politics, the differances between ideologies of secularism and communalism have been cited as a cause of various core concerns. Some scholars like Paul Brass focus on Hindu nationalism as a violent force feeding into the growth of communalism.[15] Political thinkers like Gandhi, Jawaharlal Nehru and scholars like Romila Thapar, K.N. Panikkar, and Christophe Jaffrelot[16] however, do not neglect the role of Muslim communalism in various places in India.

Ashutosh Varshney (2003, 2016), Asghar Ali Engineer (1991) and others look at socio-economic aspects of communalism. Taking the debate further, Shabnam Tejani, questions the simple dichotomy between secularism and communalism that has been used in scholarly study and political discourse on Indian secularism (Tejani, 2008). Tejani starts with the constitutional ideal that religion be excluded from "public presence", then draws our attention to recent events in India, such as the destruction of the Babri Mosque in 1992[17], to note that this has not happened (Tejani, 2008: 2). K.N. Panikkar adds a new factor to the definition of communalism, namely communitarian and communal identities. A communal identity is an identity of belonging to a community. A communal identity does not necessarily need to be against another religion or community. Yet it is important to recognise that such an identity could be transformed into a communal one by posing as an antagonistic relationship. Therefore, religious and communitarian identities form necessary pre-requisites for communalism (Panikkar, 1991: 10). Romila Thapar remarks that what happened to Babri Masjid should be seen in the context of religion fomenting hostility, placing it within the larger historical context. She points out that in the past there were several instances of violent acts against sacred sites[18] (Thapar, 2015a). Owing to communal cases like these, observers point out the absurdity of secularist aspirations in a society as committed to the *vita religiosa* as India (Raychaudhury, 2000: 262). Zoya Khaliq Hasan (1982) and Engineer (1991) point out to the uneven and fragmented process of uneven capitalist development that created pockets of backwardness which in turn facilitated communalism.

The Question of Religious Conversions

Religious Conversions has always been a major source of communal tension. Article 25 of the Constitution gives the freedom of propagation of religion. There are a number of decisions of the High Courts and the Supreme Court according to which *the right to propagation is not a right to conversion.* The recommendations of the Niyogi Committee[19] focus on the seriousness of the problem of conversion, particularly in the tribal areas. The *Ghar-Wapasi* movement undertaken by the Hindu organisations has also led to communal tensions and agitations in various places. The present-day emphasis on Ghar-Wapasi has roots in V.D. Savarkar's address to the Hindu Mahasabha wherein he advised Hindus to resist conversion on the ground that "a change of religion amounted to a change of nationality" (*The Times of India*, 1954 cited in Smith, 1963). There is another possible interpretation of conversions: especially of non-Western people to Christianity. It is envisioned as a type of conquest, the implicit moral psychology being that conversion is a "colonization of consciousness" (Roberts, 2012). Drawing on examples from Pentecostal conversion in Indian slums, and in the national context where violent anti-conversion activism is prevalent, Nathaniel Roberts argues that "while both conversion and opposition to it entail power, this power is not well understood through the model of mental colonization, or 'resistance' by uncolonized subjectivities" (Roberts, 2012).

In recent years, more and more states in India have enacted laws to restrict religious conversion, particularly targeting conversions via 'force' or 'allurement'. Current laws stem back to various colonial laws (including anti-conversion, apostasy, and public-safety acts) in British India and several princely states. Implementing such laws seems to require judging the state of mind of the converts by assessing their motives and volition or, in other words, determining whether converts were "lured" or legitimate (Jenkins, 2008: 110). In contemporary India, government assessments of the legitimacy of conversions tend to rely on two assumptions: first, that people who convert in groups may not have freely chosen conversion, and second, that certain groups are particularly vulnerable to being lured into changing their religion (Jenkins, 2008: 110). These assumptions, which pervade the anti-conversion laws as well as related court decisions and Government committee reports, reinforce social constructions of women and lower castes as inherently naive and susceptible to manipulation (Jenkins, 2008: 110). Such views (whether in the legal realm or popular) restrict freedom in highly personal, individual choices and thus must be carefully scrutinized.

The Issue of Banning of Beef

The public discourse on Article 48[20] which is a part of the Directive Principles of the Indian Constitution is a holly debated as an issue of hurt religious sentiments. The basic question is whether such a total ban on slaughter of cows and their progeny is justified on any grounds at all except that of the religious sentiments of the Hindus. There is no universal demand for a total ban by all Hindus (Godbole, 2016). Most importantly, such a ban is not in keeping with secularism (Godbole, 2016). Particularly in the drought-hit areas in a number of states such as Maharashtra, it is causing large-scale distress to farmers. The mobilising of the sadhus in November 1966 set a precedent which has been followed since by both the BJP and the Congress; and its propaganda, by helping to further embed the image of the 'sacred' cow in popular consciousness, was one of the several factors responsible for the sharp rise in Hindu-Muslim communal violence that occurred over the latter part of the decade[21] (Copland, 2014: 437). Cow-killing was the second most common trigger during this period for communal friction[22]

(Krishna, 2005). The question has to be asked whether banning cow slaughter is in keeping with the concept of secularism. The Supreme Court upholding the constitutional validity of these enactments by a majority decision of 6:1 on 26 October 2005 ((2005) 8 SCC 534) has closed such options since then (Godbole, 2008: 69). After the BJP Government came to power at the Centre in 2014, the demand for banning cow slaughter has gained strength to the extent that communal killings and violence[23] have shaken the core of secular India.

These empirical observations and debates regarding the issue of religious intolerance, uniform civil code, conversions, beef ban and communal violence have concrete philosophical moorings for Randhir Singh who offers a tentative definition of communalism in 1990 that is all the more relevant today: "Communalism in contemporary India, as ideology and practice, is above all an aspect of the politics of the ruling classes in a society with a massive feudal-colonial inheritance, deep religious divisions, and undergoing its own, historically specific form of capitalist development. Communalism is an aspect, open to the impact or influence of the ebb and flow of country's politics in general as well as the inevitable shifts in bourgeois politics itself" (Singh, 1990: 19). Secular ambivalence, in short, is no match.

Secularism with Socialism

The ambivalence of Indian secularism is incapable of dealing with divisive trends of intolerance, extremism and communal violence without structural transformation. The limits to secularism are manifest in its propagation as a doctrine of equidistance from all religions as a necessary condition for 'ideal religion' to thrive. It is not an adequate answer to the challenge of contemporary communalism (Singh, 1990: 14) which is politically organised. It is immensely significant that "a secular state was set up in India *despite* the massacre and displacement of millions of people on ethno-religious grounds, and it has survived in a continuing context in which ethnic nationalism remains dominant throughout the world" (Bhargava, 2010: 20).

But this survival is shaken to core as the Indian State's ambivalent secularism is forever caught in perpetual indecisiveness regarding the exclusivist tendencies such as issues of uniform civil code, rights of minorities, conversions, beef banning, intolerance, communal violence and riots. No society can hope for reconciliation, conflict resolution and peace if one-fourth of its population feels not merely marginalised but threatened. India's multi-religious, multi-lingual, multi-racial, multi-cultural society would thrive in a secular polity that can be rid of its ambivalence by infusing transformative methods of combating communalism.

Randhir Singh makes a significant attempt to elaborate this transformative method. He begins with the premise of understanding religion. According to him, Indian secularism thrives on *Sarva dharma sambhav* [all religions can co-exist] which is a celebration of all kinds of religion and religiosity (Singh, 1990: 14). The classic liberal view that treats religion as 'a private affair', evades all the real or difficult issues of structural oppression and exploitation. Another version of liberalism that espouses secularism as 'scientific temper', is a better yet inadequate challenge to communalism. Very significantly, Singh reiterates Marx's position that religion is not merely a set of false, erroneous ideas, just waiting to yield to a rational, scientific understanding. There is a need to understand its essential socio-psychological nature and the complex and powerful historical presence in human affairs, in India as elsewhere (Singh, 1990: 14). Singh quotes Marx: "Man is the world of man, state, society. This state and this society produce religion, which is *inverted consciousness* of the world, because they are an inverted world. Religion is the general theory of this world." (Marx cited in Singh, 1990: 15). Further: "the abolition of religion as the *illusory* happiness of the people is the demand for their *real* happiness. To call on them to give up their illusions about their condition is to *call on them to give up a condition that requires illusions*" (Marx cited in Singh, 1990: 15).

Why Socialism?

Randhir Singh points out that a nuanced Marxist understanding of communalism taking account of its basic structural interconnections of economic base with personal life, politics, ideology, culture will inevitably point towards the need for transformation. Through revolutionary struggles, inclusive of the liberals and the radicals, this transformation is towards socialism (Marx cited in Singh, 1990: 18). It is not a question of 'against communalism' versus 'for socialism'. Indeed these must not be seen as two separate struggles with binaries of either/ or, before and after, now and later. The struggle against communalism and for secularism in India can only the rid of this ambivalence with struggle for socialism in India.

A note of caution on the part of Randhir Singh is of profound significance to understand the contemporary dimensions of communalism in India: "As a product of the crisis in Indian polity and ruling class politics, fascism in India, whenever it comes and whatever the ideological mask, will be another, explicitly authoritarian, form of the rule of the dominant, exploiting classes, just as, in another setting, 'democratic-secular' is the preferred form" (Marx cited in Singh, 1990: 20). Categories of Hindu fascism or Muslim extremism are immensely harmful as with their "implicit treatment of communities as one undifferentiated mass, they make entire communities succumb to the communal politics of the ruling classes" (Marx cited in Singh, 1990: 21)...Not 'Hindu communalism' but Hinduised nationalism is going to be part of its ideological mask" (Marx cited in Singh, 1990: 21).

In the past three decades of politics in India, Randhir Singh's observations retain their significance: "... the ruling class politics, while preserving the organised structures of exploitation and oppression in India, has been producing only tragedies for the Indian people. Today they are fully self-reliant; they can produce all the tragedies they need for the Indian people, by themselves. They don't have to depend upon imperialism..." (Singh, 1990: 21). Secularism that upholds a normative framework of dignity, rights, freedoms of individuals, communities and groups in a state requires structural transformation against this ruling class which is possible only through socialism.

END NOTES

1. The Justice G.T. Nanavati Commission was a one-man commission headed by Justice G.T. Nanavati, a retired judge of the Supreme Court of India, appointed by the National Democratic Alliance (NDA) government in May 2000, to investigate the killing of Sikhs during the 1984 anti-Sikh riots. The Commission was mandated to submit its report within six months, but it took five years. The report in two volumes was completed in February 2005. The report is available at: http://www.mha.nic.in/hindi/sites/upload_files/mhahindi/files/pdf/Nanavati-I_eng.pdf.
2. Justice B.N. Srikrishna Commission of Inquiry was constituted by the Government of Maharashtra under Justice Srikrishna for investigating the causes of the Bombay Riots. For five years until 1998, he examined victims, witnesses and alleged perpetrators. The report of the Commission stated that the tolerant and secular foundations of the city were holding even if a little shakily. Justice Srikrishna indicted those he alleged as largely responsible for the second phase of the bloodshed and to some extent the first, the Shiv Sena. Justice Srikrishna Commission Report is available at: http://pib.nic.in/archieve/others/2011/jan/d2011010502.pdf.
3. The Nanavati-Mehta Commission was the commission of inquiry appointed by the Government of Gujarat to probe the Godhra train burning incident of 27 February 2002. Its mandate was later enlarged to include the investigation of the subsequent violence in Gujarat. It was appointed on 6 March 2002, with K. G. Shah, a retired Gujarat High Court judge as the only member. It was later re-constituted to include G.T. Nanavati, a retired judge of the Supreme Court of India, after protests from human rights organisations over Shah's closeness to the Gujarat Government. The credibility of the Commission's report was called into question when the investigative magazine Tehelka released a video recording showing Arvind Pandya, counsel for the Gujarat Government, discussing the Commission. The Report can be accessed on http://home.gujarat.gov.in/homedepartment/downloads/godharaincident.pdf.

Also, the following sources may be referred: Jaffrelot, Christophe (July 2003). "Communal Riots in Gujarat: The State at Risk?". *Heidelberg Papers in South Asian and Comparative Politics*: 16; Jaffrelot, C. (2011). *Religion, caste, and politics in India*. C Hurst & Co; Metcalf, B.D. (2012). *A concise history of modern India*. Cambridge: Cambridge University Press.

4. Pantham (1997) enlists the main articles of the Constitution providing for a "secular state" as:
(1) All persons have equal freedom of conscience and religion; (2) No discrimination by the state against any citizen on grounds of religion; (3) No communal electorates; (4) The state has the power to regulate through law any "economic, financial or other secular activity" which may be associated with religious practice; (5) The state has the power to provide for "social welfare and reform or the throwing open of Hindu religious institutions of a public character to all classes and sections of Hindus"; (6) Untouchability stands outlawed by Article 17; (7) Subject to public order, morality and health, every religious denomination has the right to establish and operate institutions for religious and charitable purposes; (8) All religious minorities have the right to establish and administer educational institutions of their choice and they cannot be discriminated against by the state in its granting of aid to educational institutions.
5. The understanding of secularism in *Bommai* is perhaps best expressed in the judgment of Justices Sawant and Kuldip Singh. "Religion", they asserted, "cannot be mixed with any secular activity of the State. In fact, the encroachment of religion into secular activities is strictly prohibited. The state's tolerance of religion or religions does not make it either a religious or a theocratic state. When the state allows citizens to practise or profess their religions, it does not either explicitly or implicitly allow them to introduce religion into non-religious or secular activities of the state". (Swamy, 1997) What constitutes a violation of secularism under the Constitution is spelt out in the judgment of Justices Jeevan Reddy and Agarwal: "Under our Constitution, no party or organisation can simultaneously be a political *and* a religious party (original emphasis). It has to be either. Same would be the position *if a party or organisation acts and/or behaves by word of mouth, print or in any other manner to bring about the said effect, it would equally be guilty of an act of unconstitutionality. It would have no right to function as a political party*" (emphasis added)

(Swamy, 1997). More critical perspectives on S.R. Bommai Case include Praveen Swamy (1997) "Protecting secularism and federal fair play" *Frontline*, Vol. 14, No. 22, Nov. 1-14; Soli J. Sorabjee (1994) "Decision of the Supreme Court in S.R. Bommai v. Union Of India: A Critique" Available on: http://www.supremecourtcases.com/index2.php?Option=com_content&itemid=1&do_pdf=1&id=223.

6. According to the Census, 2011, the distribution of data is of the total population by six major religious communities—Hindu, Muslim, Christian, Sikh, Buddhist and Jain—besides "Other religions and persuasions" and "Religion not stated". As has been the case since Independence, the rate of increase of the Muslim population is higher than that of the Hindu population as a result of higher Muslim fertility, higher child mortality among Hindus and a greater life expectancy among Muslims, demographers say. However, Muslim fertility rates in India are falling faster than among Hindus, Pew Research's Future of World Religions report showed recently, and the Muslim community is expected to reach replacement levels of fertility by 2050.
7. A measure designed to prevent communication or the spread of undesirable influences.
8. It was suggested originally in British India that separate communal electorates should be provided. This idea was eventually given up.
9. The Rajinder Sachar Committee was commissioned in 2005 by Indian Prime Minister Manmohan Singh to prepare a report on the latest social, economic, and educational conditions of the Muslim community of India. The committee was headed by former Chief Justice of the Delhi High Court Rajinder Sachar, and had six other members. The Committee prepared a 403 page report and presented it to the Lok Sabha, the Lower House of the Indian Parliament, on 30 November 2006, 20 months after obtaining the terms of reference from the Prime Minister's Office. This report highlighted issues facing the Muslim community and their representation in Indian public life, but it has faced criticism for some of its recommendations and methodology. Sachar Committee Report is available at: http://mhrd.gov.in/sites/upload_files/mhrd/files/sachar_comm.pdf.
10. National Commission for Religious and Linguistic Minorities, also called as Ranganath Misra Commission was constituted by

Government of India on 29 October 2004 to look into various issues related to Linguistic and Religious minorities in India. It was chaired by former Chief Justice of India Justice Ranganath Misra. The Commission submitted the report to the Government on 21 May 2007 which is available at ncm.nic.in/pdf/compilation.pdf.

11. In 1978, Shah Bano petitioned for and was awarded maintenance under India's CrPC by the Judicial Magistrate of Indore. Despite the paltry amount awarded to her, of 25 Rs per month by the Lower Court, and later 179.2 Rs per month by the High Court, her husband Khan took the case to the Supreme Court, demanding that the relatives of Shah Bano take the responsibility for her care. Mr. Khan then divorced Shah Bano through the triple-talaq method of unilateral divorce, the least approved method of divorce under Islamic law. He proceeded to take the case to the Indian Supreme Court, arguing that the lower court rulings violated his rights as a Muslim by inhibiting his adherence to the Shariat. Lawyers who have seen the Act in operation say that there is good reason to take another look at the Act. It contains provisions which have left it open to liberal interpretation. Flavia Agnes, a Mumbai-based lawyer, says that liberal interpretation has not been wanting. Clause A in Section 3 (1) of the Act says that a divorced woman shall be entitled to "a reasonable and fair provision and maintenance to be made and paid to her within the *iddat* period by her former husband." The injunction that 'a reasonable and fair provision is made' and 'maintenance paid' leaves enough scope for gender-sensitive judgments. The following sources may be referred to: Shahida Lateef, *Muslim Women in India* (London: Zed Books, Ltd.), 192; Ali Asghar Engineer, *The Shah Bano Controversy*, (ed.) Ali Asghar Engineer (Hyderabad: Orient Longman, 1987), 7.
12. Geetha Hariharan's (1999) case recognised the mother as a guardian irrespective of the age of her child. After Shah Bano (2010) and Danial Latifi (2001), a Muslim divorced woman became entitled to just and fair maintenance even beyond the iddat period (Shah, 2016).
13. Varshney (2003) makes a distinction between 'associational' forms of engagement and the 'everyday' forms of engagement. Business associations, professional organizations, reading clubs, film clubs, sports clubs, NGOs, trade unions, and cadre-based political parties are examples of the former. Everyday forms of

engagement consist of simple, routine interactions of life, such as whether families from different communities visit each other, eat together regularly, jointly participate in festivals, and allow their children to play together in the neighbourhood. Both forms of engagement, if robust, promote peace: contrariwise, their absence or weakness opens up space for ethnic violence. Of the two, according to Varshney, the 'associational form is sturdier than everyday engagement'.

14. Hindutva, or "Hinduness", a term coined by Vinayak Damodar Savarkar in 1923, is the predominant form of Hindu nationalism in India. The Bharatiya Janata Party (BJP) adopted it as its official ideology in 1989. While in 1952, the Bharatiya Janta Party's (BJP) share of national votes had been 3.1% with only 3 seats in the Lok Sabha. However, the figures in 1999 rose to 23.8% of the voting share and 182 seats in Lok Sabha. In 2014 Lok Sabha elections, the vote share of the BJP was 31% of all votes cast.
15. Hindu Nationalism is taken as an example of cultural nationalism where the central idea is the belief that a community consists of one common culture and it recognises one nation as the nucleus of the nation (Panikkar 2001: 534). Blom Hansen sees Hindu nationalism both as an expression of the politicisation of Indian public culture, and a reaction against it (1994: 83).
16. Bipin Chandra (1991: 134) and Christophe Jaffrelot (1993: 165) make a distinction between opportunism and communalism of political parties. 'The secularism displayed by opportunistic parties has not been totally unbiased. Some expressions of communalism by the minorities were tolerated, especially when the party might benefit from them.
17. The Babri Masjid, in Ayodhya (Uttar Pradesh), was destroyed in 1992 when a political rally developed into a riot involving 150,000 people, despite a commitment to the Indian Supreme Court by the rally organisers that the mosque would not be harmed. More than 2,000 people were killed in ensuing riots in many major Indian cities including Mumbai, and Delhi. The Liberhan Commission (Liberhan Ayodhya Commission of Inquiry) was a long-running inquiry commissioned by the Government of India to investigate the destruction of the disputed structure Babri Masjid in Ayodhya in 1992. Led by retired High Court Judge M.S. Liberhan, it was formed on 16 December 1992 by an order of the Indian Home Union Ministry after the demolition of the Babri Masjid in Ayodhya on 6

December and the subsequent riots there.

Read more on: "Ayodhya attack report submitted" BBC News, 30 June 2009 Available at: http://news.bbc.co.uk/2/hi/south_asia/8125927.stm; "Tearing down the Babri Masjid", (Mark Tully) BBC, 5 December 2002, Available at: http://news.bbc.co.uk/2/hi/south_asia/2528025.stm; "Babri Masjid demolition was planned 10 months in advance" Outlook/PTI, 30 January 2005 http://www.outlookindia.com/newswire/story/babri-masjid-demolition-was-planned-10-months-in-advance-book/276473; A.G. Noorani (2013), "How a mosque became a temple", *Frontline*, March 8; A.G. Noorani (2014) *Destruction of Babri Masjid; A National Dishonour*, New Delhi: Tulika.

18. For instance, Romila Thapar points out, there are pieces evidence of Buddhist sites being attacked and destroyed, and monks killed, by Shaivites. The *Râjtarangani* and similar literary sources are, she said, replete with examples of hostile acts carried out in the name of religion. Such hostile acts, she said, are also seen during the early Turkish invasions which witnessed destruction of religious sites. Prof. Thapar pointed out that Hindu and Muslim rulers at times desecrated their own temples and mosques respectively. In this context she again cited *Râjtarangani* in which one comes across several references of such instances (Thapar, 2015 Available at: http://peoplesdemocracy.in/2015/0104_pd/compilation-babari-masjid-documents).
19. The Niyogi Committee Report on Christian Missionary Activities is a report published by the Government of Madhya Pradesh in 1956. It is divided into two volumes and three parts. It is a controversial report on missionary activities in India. The Committee which was chaired by M. Bhawani Shankar Niyogi, a retired Chief Justice of the Nagpur High Court included five other members. The report recommended the "legal prohibition" of religious conversion not "completely voluntary", which was not implemented as it would have been "difficult to formulate and indeed to apply without violating the precepts of religious liberty enshrined in the Indian Constitution", and therefore the recommendations have been considered controversial and unconstitutional. It demanded Indianisation of Church and called upon the churches to severe all relations with all ecclesiastical bodies abroad. This demand was repeated by K. Sudarshan, the Sar Sangh Chalak after Kandhamal violence in

2007 and 2008. More critical reviews on the findings of this Committee include: Thomas, Abraham Vazhayil (1974). *Christians in secular India*. Madison, NJ: Fairleigh Dickinson University Press; Parvathi Menon, (1999) "An old debate in a new context" *Frontline*, Vol. 16, Issue 8, April 10–23.

20. In the interest of 'organisation of agriculture and animal husbandry' the Constitution recommends prohibition of the slaughter of cows and calves and other milch and draught cattle.
21. The riots at Bagodar (Bihar) in 1968 and at Ahmedabad and Baroda in 1969 are cases in point, though Ornit Shani's careful analysis makes it clear that the presence of cows at the Ahmedabad flashpoint was incidental rather than integral to the violence: BJS Central Office, 'Recent Communal Riots – a Report', dated 15 October 1968, in Political Pamphlets from the Indian Subcontinent, Part I, No. 633; *New York Times*, (22 September 1969); and Shani, *Communalism, Caste and Hindu Nationalism: The Violence in Gujarat* (Cambridge 2007), 161–2.
22. For the seven years 1964–70, the average number of communal incidents per year was 1025, as against 81.5 for the previous 14 years (Krishna, 2005: 154).
23. In Uttar Pradesh, a Muslim man was lynched in Dadri for allegedly consuming beef on 28 September 2015. In UP, slaughter of cow, bullock, and ox is banned. The law prohibits one to store or eat beef. It carries a punishment of seven years' jail and/or Rs. 10,000 fine. In July 2016, the flogging of seven members belonging to a Dalit family by Gau Rakshaks in Gujarat led to widespread protests in the State, with many activists attempting to commit suicide. The Dalit family was attacked by cow vigilantes for allegedly slaughtering a cow. For more information, related to the banning of beef in various parts of India, read: http://indianexpress.com/article/india/india-news-india/beef-madhya-pradesh-video-cow-vigilantes-gau-rakshaks-2938751/.

REFERENCES

Ahuja, R. (1992). *Social problem in India*. Jaipur: Rawat Publications.

Bhambhri, C. (1990). State and communalism in India. *Social Scientist*, *18*(8/9), 22-26.

Bharadwaj, K. (1990). Economic development and communalism: a note. *Social Scientist*, *18*(8/9), 66-70.

Bhargava, R. (2010). States, religious diversity, and the crisis of secularism. *The Hedgehog Review*, Fall, 8-22.

Bilgrami, A. (2007). Secularism and the very concept of law. In A.D. Needham, R.S. Rajan (Eds.), *The crisis of secularism in India*, Ranikhet: Permanent Black, 317-330.

Chandhoke, N. (1999). *Beyond secularism: The rights of religious minorities*. Delhi: Oxford University Press.

Chandra, B. (1984). *Communalism in modern India*. New Delhi: Vikas Publishing House Private Ltd.

Copland, I. (2014). History in flux: Indira Gandhi and the 'great all-party campaign' for the protection of the cow, 1966–68. *Journal of Contemporary History, 49*(2), 410-439.

Dixit, P. (1974). *Communalism: a struggle for power*. New Delhi: Orient Longman.

Dumont, L. (1964). Nationalism and communalism in India. *Contributions to Indian Sociology*, 7 (3), 30-70.

Engineer, A.A. (1991). *Communal riots in post-independence India*. Delhi: Sangam Books Ltd.

Engineer, A.A. (1995). *Communalism in India—a historical and empirical study*. New Delhi: Vikas Publishing House.

Estevis, S. (1996) *Nationalism, secularism and communalism*. New Delhi: South Asia Publications.

Godbole, M. (2016). Is India a secular nation?. *Economic and Political Weekly, 51* (15). Retrieved 23 September, 2016 from http://www.epw.in/journal/2016/15/web-exclusives/india-secular-nation.html.

Hasan, Z. (2009). *Politics of inclusion: castes, minorities and affirmative action*. New Delhi: Oxford University Press.

Hasan, Z.K. (1982). Communalism and communal violence in India. *Social Scientist, 10*(2), 25-39.

Jaffrelott, C. (1993). *The Hindu nationalist movements and the Indian politics*. London: Hurst and Company.

Jenkins, L.D. (2008). Legal limits on religious conversion in India. Retrieved October 19, 2016 from http://www.law.duke.edu/journals/lcp.

Krishna, G. (2005). Communal violence in India. In S.I. Wilkinson (Ed.), *Religious politics and communal violence*. New Delhi: Oxford University Press.

Nambiar, V. (1964). India: How secular?. *The Economic Weekly*, 16 (23), 948-950.

Nehru, J. (1968). *Jawaharlal Nehru's speeches, Volume V, 1963-1964*. New

Delhi: Publications Division, Government of India.

Oglesbee, J. (2015). The Shah Bano controversy: case study of individual rights, religious tolerance, and the role of the secular state. *Inquiries Journal*. 7(*08*). Retrieved 16 October, 2016 from http://www.inquiriesjournal.com/articles/1061/3/the-shah-bano-controversy-a-case-study-of-individual-rights-religious-tolerance-and-the-role-of-the-secular-state.

Pandey, G. (1987). Questions of nationalism and communalism. *Economic and Political Weekly, 22* (25), 983-984.

Panikkar, K. (1990). Wrong equations. *Social Scientist*, 18(8/9), 94–97.

Raychaudhuri, T. (2000). Shadows of the swastika: Historical perspectives on the politics of hindu communalism. *Modern Asian Studies, 34* (2), 259-279.

Roberts, N. (2012). Is conversion a 'colonization of consciousness'?. *Anthropological Theory*, September (12), 271-294.

Saberwal, S. (1971). Secularism: a threat to religion?. *Religion and Society XVIII* (3), 46-57.

Sand, E.R. (2006). State and religion in India: The Indian secular model. *Nordic Journal of Religion and Society, 19* (2), 3-15.

Shah, A. P. (2016). Towards a modern code. *The Indian Express*. October 28. Retrieved 8 October, 2016 from : http://indianexpress.com/article/opinion/columns/uniform-civil-code-towards-a-modern-code/.

Singh, R. (1988). Theorising communalism: a fragmentary note in the Marxist mode. *Economic and Political Weekly, 23* (30), 1541-1548.

Singh, R. (1990). Communalism and the struggle against communalism: A Marxist view. *Social Scientist, 18* (8/9), 4-21.

Smith, D.E. (1963). *India as a secular state*. Bombay: Oxford University Press.

Tejani, S. (2008). *Indian secularism: A social and intellectual history, 1890-1950*. Bloomington: Indiana University Press.

Thapar, R. (2015a). What secularism is and where it needs to be headed. *The Wire*, October 18. Retrieved 26 September, 2016 from: http://thewire.in/12539/what-secularism-is-and-where-it-needs-to-be-headed/.

Thapar, R. (2015b). Secularism begins with uniform civil code. *The Hindu*. October 27. Retrieved 11 September, 2016 from: http://www.thehindu.com/news/national/secularism-begins-with-uniform-civil-code-romila-thapar/article7806714.ece.

The Hindu. (2015). Muslim population growth slows. Retrieved 27 August, 2016 from http://www.thehindu.com/news/national/

census-2011-data-on-population-by-religious-communities/article7579161.ece.

The Indian Express. (2015). Uniform Civil Code: SC refuses to interfere, won't issue directive to Centre. December 8. Retrieved on 8 January, 2016 from: http://indianexpress.com/article/india/india-news-india/uniform-civil-code-sc-refuses-to-interfere-wont-issue-directive-to-centre/.

Varshney, A. (2003). *Ethnic conflict and civic life: Hindus and Muslims in India.* New Haven, Connecticut, United States: Yale University Press

Zakaria, R. (2002). *Communal rage in secular India.* Bombay: Popular Prakashan.

14

Reading '1917' as an Event: Randhir Singh avec Badiou

Pavel Tomar

> Inside the museums, infinity goes upon trial
> Voices echo this is what salvation must be like after a while...
> **Bob Dylan** *Visions of Johanna*

The insignia of a truly great thinker are fully present in Randhir Singh. Beneath the apparent lucidity of style lurks the most dangerous terrain of political theory. There are no easy explanations, no ultimate references which can always be summoned for comfort. The illusion of lucidity, to put it in Marx's own terms, is a necessary and objective illusion, the prehistory of whose working out would reveal the most arduous labour of creation and presentation, and of thinking as such. His choice of a teaching career was not meant to fill the void created by the absence of revolution, but to help think through the tragedy of its non-realisation. That is exactly what his autobiographical 'biodata' reveals: the inner world of a Marxist radical is nothing more private than an eternal thinking of the communist hypothesis (Badiou, 2010). When he was mischievously asked to teach Plato and not Marx by his department of political science, he must have smiled knowing how Plato could be a better way of arriving at Marx than Marx himself. If his choice and shaping of a teaching career reminds us of a similar elevation of teaching to a form of political praxis in Adorno (Jameson, 1990), intervening in academics in moments of political or even subjective despair, and his awareness of the pitfalls of such a position cannot but affirm his 'extimate'[1] (what he calls as 'Robinhooding') relationship to his profession.

Today, when everyone from the Donald Trumps to the Hindutva brigade, from the big capitalist enterprises to technocrats, financiers, demigods in cricket and mass culture are all so rapidly changing the world so as to produce a 'future shock', it is perhaps a better option to withdraw from action and elucidate a modest interpretation of the world, which is what Randhir Singh opted for. What remains central in this enterprise is a fidelity to the Event (in this case, the October Revolution) and an eternal quest for the communist hypothesis. We thus get a Marxist understanding which remains at the cutting edge of today's radical politics, which is orthodox and innovative at the same time.

If in India, the tragedy was that the revolution did not happen; the tragedy in USSR was that it did. Further, if the existence of Soviet Union was problematic, its vaporisation was even more problematic. It meant the disappearance of space from where to imagine not only an alternative to capitalism but also to its regrettable negation in the Soviet Union. Randhir Singh's book *What was Built and What Failed in Soviet Russia* (Singh, 2011) is an effort in reinventing Marxism not through prescriptions or ideological pills but through rigorous dissection of what happened and how. In a sense, even the title of the work is misleading: it is an invitation to an easy answer—that there is no harm to Marxist theory because there was no communism in Russia - which is later debunked for being convincing only for those who are already convinced, inverting Pascal's dictum that magic is visible only to those who believe in it to that believers hope all the time that their belief will never be realised (the Hegelian beautiful souls). The true question to ask vis-à-vis twentieth-century communism is not whether it lived up to its promise of liberation (of course, it was a disaster), but how did it become possible for a liberation movement to turn into its opposite? This can be done only when one abandons today's hegemonic questioning of the history of Soviet Union: from a liberal-democratic framework.

An interest in the history of revolution in Russia is not simply a historical interest, nor a matter of Russophilia. It is central to a self-understanding of Marxist history, and thereby, Marxist theory. There are multiple diagnoses today to the dilemma posed by the Soviet Union, all based upon *a priori* 'solutions' of their advocates. The neoliberals claim that the market system is the most natural system of not only distribution but also of production; hence, the demise of the Soviet Union can only point out to its violent nature and unsustainable career. In other words, all alternatives to the present system are totalitarian. One need not point out how much of daily effort does it take for the state institutions worldwide to sustain the 'natural order' of the neoliberal model, and the massive production of waste and misery that this system entails world over. Especially after liberal utopia's second demise[2], it is hard to believe that such a system can even work with democracy as its political superstructure. And if one has to look for a perfect market utopia today, it is not the advanced western countries but China, which combines the neoliberal model with the ruthless authoritarianism of the official communist party - a model which is now spilling to the liberal-democracies too. This is today's proper 'dialectic of post-enlightenment'. From the point of view of Marxist theory, therefore, the arguments of the enemy camp only end up exposing their brutality.

But there are those too who derive the symmetrically inverted conclusion: as an economic system the USSR was successful but what it lacked was democracy. A further radicalisation of this idea is brought upon by Chantal Mouffe (2010: 83-88) who proposes that communism as an end itself is problematic. Beginning with the question whether the communist hypothesis is actually necessary for an emancipatory project, Mouffe comes to reject the Marxist politics *tout court*, for its limitation of the struggle against hegemony to the narrow social stratum called the working class (Mouffe (2010: 85). In this exchange of communism for democracy, Mouffe forgets how hegemony itself is just one part of domination. In fact, as Zizek reminds, hegemony and domination can even form a "disjunctive synthesis", wherein hegemony facilitates domination precisely by articulating its opposite (Zizek, 2000). Hence, it becomes crucial to hold on to the old notion of 'dictatorship' which should not be read as a direct opposite to democracy. Randhir Singh comes with the same argument, how democracy itself is the mode of functioning of bourgeois dictatorship, through a reading of Marxist classics alone. Even in the freest of elections, one cannot discount the role of the state which organises them, with all its threat of violence if things go awry. Badiou calls this as the state's excess over what it represents.

Democracy being a superior political system, if we could somehow combine the two we can get the best of the two worlds. This argument has the perfect structure of a fantasy: it imagines, much like Marx himself, the undialectical disunity of forces of production and relations of production, hoping one day to join the forces (rather than separate, as in Marx's case). Randhir Singh rejects this second option too (Singh, 2011: 371). He rather calls for an examination of the theory that underlines the transition from capitalism to socialism in the former USSR, i.e. the subjective experience of its history. Here, Badiou reminds us that in Lenin, we have two answers to the accusations that his actions were undemocratic. The first involved the well-known distinction between bourgeois democracy (with its focus on representation) and socialist democracy (privileging radicalisation of the conditions of existence of the former variety). The second, however, is more 'interesting': democracy is also a form of state, bound to dissolve with the withering away of the State (this immediately raises the question about Mao's idea of class struggle pervading even under socialism) (Badiou, 2005). If both the State and democracy wither away, then how does the field of political find its expression? To demand a solution to this question is to believe, like Marx, that history poses only those questions which can be solved. What if, however, the task of revolution is precisely to provide us a new ground from where to rethink the fundamental political questions? This idea, I think, takes us closer to Badiou's notion of the Event, which rests upon a negation of history precisely by locating itself into the past (Jameson, 2016: 99-117).

Continuing with this critical insight (the idea of putting democracy into the Soviet economic system being a fantasy), Singh developed his basic and crucial insight when he applied historical materialism to the history of communism. He thus argues that the Soviet system had contradictions from the very beginning which shaped its later history. There is no room here to blame particular individuals (i.e. Stalin) like bourgeois historians do, tracing their pseudo-psychoanalytic histories and looking for pathos in their beginnings. Thus, when Foucault says that to trace the genealogy of Gulag, one should begin not with Stalin but with Marx himself (Foucault 1980: 135), Singh would totally agree with him, but with a twist: the same texts which resulted into Gulags also provide us with a frame from where to question them. The phenomenal presence and harassment of so many Marxist dissidents in Soviet Union is a direct proof of this. If only Gulags became a possibility, it was not simply due to those texts alone, but also thanks to the totality (the old Marxist notion) of social relations and international politics in which those theories operated. One study pointing out such an outcome is a recent one, by Stephen Kotkin (2014) which argues how the worst of Stalinism became possible not simply because of the internal churning of Bolshevism, but because of the context of the World War, wherein it became possible for modern regimes to use violence against their populations almost on a daily basis.

What were the contradictions in Bolshevik theory and practice which determined the course of history as it happened? According to Randhir Singh, they related to the unique situation of the revolution happening in a backward country than an advanced one, where capitalism survived mainly through the formal subsumption of pre-capitalist relations of production. Lenin's first innovation was to argue that capitalism had already developed in Russia to an extent where only a socialist revolution could be on the agenda, and not a bourgeois-democratic revolution (as the Mensheviks argued). Further, the peasantry was an ally for the working class, because it would gain from the completion of a democratic revolution. This worker-peasant alliance was broken by Stalin when he purportedly moved for industrialisation.

Secondly, Lenin, while developing his theory of weak link in the chain, also hoped for a simultaneous outbreak of revolution in advanced capitalist countries too, which unfortunately did not happen. It fundamentally constrained the Russian Revolution and virtually identified the interest of the world revolution with that of the Russian Revolution. This demanded that the Bolsheviks under Lenin temporarily suspended their more democratic and theory-oriented politics in favour of terror. While Lenin was aware of the temporary nature of those necessities, Stalin elevated them into a principle and a general feature of political practice.

Third, the temporary features reified by Stalin into the permanent meant, on the one hand, continuation and strengthening of the repressive apparatus of the post-Revolutionary State, and on the other, the nomenklatura that finally overtook social and political power after Stalin worked through bureaucracy (Singh, 2011: 343-346). Here, the argument runs into problems. Several times it is highlighted how the progressive role of Stalin should be judged from his fight against fascism, by his leadership in building a modern superpower out of a backward economy. What if, on the contrary, the huge number of casualties from the side of Soviet Union (approx. 27 million) is an indicator not of the might of Hitler's blitzkrieg but that of the weakness of Soviet Army, which is said to have lacked even basic amenities? Ultimately, the Second World War was decided not by technological or militaristic advantages but by how much human sacrifice could a country afford to make - a war in which the Holocaust appears not as one aspect of the 'dialectic of Enlightenment' but sheer irrationality. And what if, contrary to the misperceptions of a juggernaut bureaucracy, what the Stalinist State lacked was indeed a bureaucracy, so that it did not have to mark everyone as an enemy of socialism and eliminate them using repressive force? In fact, the much maligned bureaucracy has indeed played a progressive role in most historical situations (Jameson, 2016).

There are various interpretations today trying to prove how the Russian Revolution was not a 'revolution' but a small, regrettable Bolshevik *coup d'état*: Lenin and his party simply appropriated the genuine people's revolution which had happened earlier that year.[3] What emerges through them is the denial of the Event proper: by saying that the Russian Revolution was not a revolution, its dignity of an authentically liberating event is denied. A similar exercise is done vis-à-vis the French Revolution by François Furet, who denies its status of a Revolution. Chomsky says that Lenin was essentially an opportunist who covered his greed for power in anarchist vocabulary (*State and Revolution*, *April Theses*, etc.), abandoning it no later than when it was not needed. What if, the theoretical status of those writings far exceeds than what Chomsky attributes to them? What if Lenin is arguing, contrary to the Menshevik apprehension of the revolution arriving too soon (before the conditions were "ripe") to make a "pre-emptive strike", and also against the voluntaristic strand which always discards the "concrete analysis of a concrete situation"?

Randhir Singh makes it clear how even the previous "genuine" revolution was a product of two decades of Bolshevik efforts. If the Russian Revolution was not a revolution, then what accounts for the enthusiasm it generated across its borders and far, where even in India most anti-colonial leaders not only welcomed it but also drew inspiration from it? Singh's argument here runs close to that of Kant's who, apropos the French Revolution, said how the importance of it should not be judged by the blood in the streets but by the enthusiasm it has generated across borders. No wonder that the French Revolution generated its further subversive supplement: the Haitian Revolution. Similarly, the Russian Revolution cannot simply be judged from its empirical output, which is ambiguous, but by the historical dynamic that it unleashed. Indeed, the gulags were a result of a theory. What if, there were alternative possibilities arising out of the same theories, which could have produced an entirely different outcome? This is what should fidelity to the Event mean, and not any nostalgic celebration or re-enactment.

ENDNOTES

1. To borrow a neologism from Lacan, by which he meant how something that could be outside could well be inside.
2. The reference here is not only to the Great Depression of 1929 and 2008, but also between 2001 September attacks and 2008 crumbling of the world market system. See (Zizek, 2009).
3. This includes also Noam Chomsky, who writes that Lenin was not a theoretician but an opportunist.. See https://chomsky.info/20130312/.

REFERENCES

Badiou, A. (2005). A speculative disquisition on the concept of democracy", in *Metapolitics*. London: Verso.

Badiou, A. (2010). *The Communist hypothesis*. London: Verso.

Foucault, M. (1980). *Power/knowledge, selected interviews and other writings 1972-1977*. New York: Pantheon Books.

Jameson, F. (1990). *Late Marxism*. London: Verso.

Jameson, F. (2016). Badiou and the French tradition. *New Left Review*, 102, 99-117.

Jameson, F. (2016). *The American utopia*. London: Verso.

Kotkin, S. (2014) *Stalin: Volume I: paradoxes of power, 1878-1928*. New York: Penguin.

Mouffe,C (2010). Communisme ou démocratie radicale ?. *Actuel Marx*, 2 (n° 48), 83-88.

Singh, R. (2011). *What was built and what failed in the Soviet Union*. New Delhi: Aakar Books.

Zizek, S. (2000). *The ticklish subject*. London: Verso..

Zizek, S. (2009). *First as tragedy then as Farce*. London: Verso.

PART IV

Highlighting the Concern

15

Sad Rural Stories

Yoginder K. Alagh

Introduction

Prof. Randhir Singh was a Marxist political scientist intensely concerned on issues of inequality and poverty. Amongst economists it is fashionable to begin papers on rural poverty with poverty numbers and controversies on them. Being the grand daddy of what is called the Official Poverty Line set down by a Task Force I chaired in the seventies I know how futile that is by now. But one gets bored of repeating all the arguments again and anyway since I was the fellow who said a decade ago that Gujarat and other States had indicator-based poverty surveys as now required by the Planning Commission for implementing food security; and that who said that there should be only one line for all entitlements (Alagh, 2010), it is déjà vu to repeat all that. The Food Security Bill and MNREGA were passed and it seems better to get back to the village and see how we can have sustained agricultural and rural development growth as the basis of food security and avoiding distress[1]. Many years ago, I had modelled in the plans that redistribution always needs to be intertwined with growth (Alagh, 1995, 2006). I am not an Ashok Gulati fan, who says "Don't have an employment and food security scheme because hundred percent desi ghee agricultural growth takes care of all that." I know that in high growth areas poverty remains and correlations of growth with reduced poverty (and there Gulati is right) do not help the women and men and their children left out. But any food security scheme will only work best in the larger context of widespread and diversified agricultural and rural growth and in that sense Gulati is again right. So back to the village with some stories to anticipate what will happen and what to do about it. And then some macro analytics.

Village Stories

The typical image of agriculture in the eastern region is hard working poor farmers producing paddy in the monsoon, getting hit by floods and then again gambling in the winter rains, which when they fail lead to drought. Yields were traditionally high in this fertile soil, but did not rise. All that is changing, as we see the Second Green revolution in the Eastern Region. We need more and better versions of that for growth is in spasmodic spurts, rather than a continuous oiled machine and also not everywhere. When I last went there, the district was Midnapur; it was not as fertile as Hooghly or the 24 Parganas. As you drive out of Howrah, it is all factories, but surprise, surprise there are now dairies and nurseries. After a few hours of driving we stopped by for a meal and the fish curry, rice and channa dal and topping off with a sandesh and mishti dohi, brought back my childhood in Calcutta. The waiter was happy that an obvious Pathan like character could eat fish and *bhat* in the Bengali style without first taking out the bones even when the fish was the delectable but not so easy to eat, *Rohu*. The Midnapur I landed up in was red laterite soil and the slope of the land did not retain water. It drained back into the rivers, an agricultural extension man's nightmare.

The village was Kaspal in the Borkollah Gram Panchayat area. There were urban demand centres around (the famous Census Towns I discovered as 'Large Villages' in 2007) and now Kolkatta is not perceived as the only centre. It is lucky for it is near the bed of a small river—the Kasai. If it does not rain they can virtually take out the water in buckets, but again not surprise, surprise any more, they almost all have tubewells. The first area I have gone to in quite a while, where a public sector bank actually gave credit on a more or less universal scale for water development. Here it was the State Bank of India. I could not touch base with the local banker and so we do not know if it was the land holding rights under operation Barga or some enthusiastic banker. I talk with Hari Prasad Samantha, Chitto Maiti and Jhath Lenka. Nobody farms more than two acres. This is a densely farmed territory and the reverse tenancy of land to middle peasants has not taken place, as in my Gujarat or in North Western India. The prosperous peasants do not lease in more land. They diversify. The technology is fairly good. The original seeds came from the university although there is little replacement in paddy. But they make more money from cash crops and it is vegetables all the way. Potatoes are a craze. The seeds come from commercial companies, are expensive, but they make money even when the market is down. BT seeds from unknown unregulated(?) producers are common, although some famous brand name 'approved' seeds are also there. A great thing that happened on the way was dairying. Almost all of them have between three to five cows. The women folk look after them. This is now spreading.

There is a feeling of unease and it is not WTO. It has all happened and they do not see where to go. This growth game. You have to run to keep where you are. They are not quite clear where to run. But they are organised and after we talk of a number of possibilities it is their turn to ask questions. They are full of what is going on in the North and West. They know the best pulse seeds come from Maharashtra and M.P. and oilseeds also from there and that Gujarat has castor. Their mustard is good and now NDDB has it spread. The landless say hunger is less and some girls go to school but it is there, Gulati Saheb.

The land slopes up from the river. About two to three hundred metres up and a distance away I check out another village. Not much has happened here. Around half of the population is poor. It is a monocrop region with the second crop, if, any depending on the rains. Yields are low. Many answers are possible, but with the plan and public investment a non-starter, it would be a cruel joke to talk about them. We are doing nothing to integrate these villages with markets and prosperity. The largely tribal and scheduled caste population carries along, as it has been doing through the centuries.

Yes, as he would say, "We need a public food security packet until the growth millennia arrives" and I am all for it coming. But that old man who made us fight for freedom and had a *chela* who dreamt when the world slept and India awoke to life and freedom, made us keep our head in the stars, but feet on the ground.

Now I come to my Gujarat. When I took over as Chairman IRMA, I knew I didn't have my hero Kurien's personality, but I would institutionalise. Everybody has a term there now, but the Chairman's terms were decided first; two terms of three years each and I handed over smooth as silk. But when I would go there I would walk the tracks in the area between Anand, Petlad and Khambat and Wataman Chowky. It is a fascinating area, good soil in the main until you enter the problem area we call the Bahl. I did not succeed in getting more land around IRMA and I was always looking for a location where we could expand and hope my successor would look at this larger area I am talking of. With my friend in Agricultural Economics, Prof. Mahesh Pathak I went to the village of Khanpur in the Bahl a few kilometres away from Tarapur. This is an area where after the monsoon water collects from both Saurashtra and North Guarat since it is a low lying area, it gradually drains out. In the Rabi, we grow the famous Durhams the 'Bhalia Wheat', the Daudkhani and others. Since irrigation, particularly drainage was always a problem we could never irrigate and so yields are low as compared to say the Wheat Durham Ludhiana. It is a poor region, perhaps not advanced much more than at the time when close by Lothal was prospering 5000 years ago. In Khanpur progress was obvious. They were not growing Bhalia Wheat but they were growingthe MP 'Tukdi' which is a high yielder. Irrigation came in a strange way. The Sardar Sarovar Project has a drinking water scheme and it fills up the village pond in Khanpur. The official provision of water for drinking purposes was enough to leave water for crop irrigation. I have always wondered at the difference between what our project planners consider our requirement and what our poor people can manage with. In a similar case when the IPCL built an effluent disposal canal from Vadodara to the sea, the polluted water was used for irrigation. I asked Maheshbhai, the farmer, I met as to why he was not growing Bhalya wheat, which always gave a good price. He said since farmers around the area were irrigating, if he sows the Bhaliya seeds, with the accumulated water, the pods get the pest Gheru and therefore there would be no yield. Irrigation had led to the cropping pattern changing from a quality product to a standard product and we call this growth. My worry is a little greater since the drainage capability of the area is bad and even with the limited irrigation that it gets we may move to salinity of which there is a lot in this region. That can be a terrible curse when it hits an area suddenly when the salt rises to the surface. But I pray for my Bhaliya friends. Also for a not very far away area called the Chuvahl (the land of forty-four villages which I walked as we laid out the SSP canals) and where Narmada waters came but we at Delhi and Gandhinagar decided to industrialise them. A thousand tractors came out from there in protest and not only brought out their ladies in large numbers but also made me go along with them in peaceful protest, quite an experience for a dyed in the wool 'central planner'.

Himmatnagar is on the central castern border of Gujarat with Rajasthan. The Chelleahs settled in urban areas after the 2002 riots and there are very uplifting stories of the indomitable human spirit in their rehabilitation, including in setting up franchises. But my story goes north east when you cross Radhanpur and get into Rajasthan. This is jungle territory and the Meena Adivasis sheltered Rana Pratap here. Off the main road, is the village of Bhajpur and is largely inhabited by the Meenas (names changed to maintain confidentiality). Dinesh Rajghoda, a Meena, is one such man. He has worked with us since he was a grown up boy. They have plenty of land (around 8 acres) but no water and when it does not rain they starve since the yield of one crop does not go very far. You can not keep chicken because the snakes eat them. You rear a lot of cattle but it is risky and in the years of rainfall failure, fodder is not there and so the survival rate is low.

But things are changing in Bhajpur as in many other such areas. There are the employment works and under MNREGA they get almost a hundred rupees even after some leakage. The leakage is not much since the Sarpanch is also of the same tribe and caste. He takes his dakshina but is really an 'Uncle' as it were. So you really do not have to go to either Udaipur or Ahmedabad and can also do some supplementary activity in the village, now, inspite of all the leakages.

In the village and so in many such places, in spite of all the skeptics and knowalls on channel TV where nothing works apart from the curled lip of the compere, they keep two pieces of paper under lock and key for they are essential support systems. The first is the ID for the employment work. The second is the ration card. The UDAI hasn't been seen as yet. You can get work only when your chance comes and so it is like a queue. Your purchee (clip of paper) is important. The second is the ration card for you get your wheat at three rupees a kilo. You don't get it all the time and not enough when you do, but it is there. For the first time since millennia, since history began you fill up your tummy and become a human being. As the late P.N. Haksar said it is only when the grain goes down the gullet the body juices start flowing. Those two pieces of paper are very precious for the poor rural Indian.

What about other possibilities? Non-farm employment is a buzz word. This economy is much too primitive. Going to the city has a cost. A recession there makes things worse. They like Gehlot, who they remember since they believe that he got them the purchee and the wheat at three rupees a kilo and pray that the Rani who defeated him keeps it up. But they are apprehensive for they voted for Gehlot and know that everybody knows that.

Now all this should not happen for as Gulati Saheb tells us the answer is broad-based agricultural growth and of course he is right. But broad-based agricultural growth here will take a long time. Maybe some day the aquifer will be mapped and deep tubewells will be possible. Maybe not, for at present we do not even know. Maybe some day, the local agricultural university at Udaipur or in Gujarat will develop a dryland drought resistant corn seed, but the problem is until then what. Minimal government and the market is not an answer for there is nothing to sell and no purchasing power to buy. You have to give work in a way if necessary doing nothing, digging up and filling ditches as Keynes said. And you have to give subsidised grain. In fact, I do not see a school coming up there and if it is far away they do not have the calorie reserves to go there. We precisely do not know how many Bhajpurs there are in India. The poverty debate is caught in a cul de sac of the Lakdawala-Tendulkar-Alagh Poverty Lines and Panagariya says he will do it for the NDA Government and they will have other ideas and their own experts. Some of the protagonists have in fact already removed poverty. In a perverse way that makes me happy for I do want the tiresome totally irrelevant Alagh Poverty Line to move into history rather than be caricatured by Tendulkar as a fact.

My last story is in a tribal region. In the Panchmahals, a somewhat different babu, A. Tiwari decided to introduce a Sunshine Project. The Adivasi eats maize as staple. He farms the land with one and a half quintals per hectare and always remains hungry. Tiwari introduced biotech maize seeds. They came from Monsanto with around sixteen quintals plus per hectare but our own agricultural universities in fact did better as a field survey by Sadguru, one of our best land and water NGOs showed. Now here hunger had really gone. Tiwari was transferred and an NGO stopped all that. Sadguru and Vivekananda, again a famous NGO working out of Kutch, was left high and dry.

I was elected the first Fellow of The Indian Society of Agricultural Economics, an honour I value more than the ministership I was invited to. In my acceptance speech printed in the March 2011 issue of the Society's Journal, I spoke on the work needed on agriculture beyond the approach paper to the

Twelfth Plan. I spoke on water, the lack of markets in the rural urban continuum in which farmers come with their produce, technology and perverse policies hindering diversification and the need to recognise and remedy them. I talked of a focused approach to MNREGA and food security. If you do not diversify, incomes do not rise. For that you need infrastructure and technology. Seeds are important. You need MNREGA and food security because a lesson of world history is that rise in wages triggers technical change in agriculture. Its not the other way around as Burrah Saheb advisers of UPA say. Read any good book on the economic history of England and Europe. All these problems are there in Kaspal in the Borkollah gram panchayat, Khanpur near the Wataman Chowky and in the tribal villages in Dahod. For those who are left behind until you catch up we need MNREGA and food security.

We Can Turn Things Around

But does it always have to be so? The answer is a resounding "No!" I have written a book on The Future of Indian Agriculture which has met the market test in the sense that the first edition is sold out. A small model in that book shows that Indian agriculture can meet the requirements of food security and rapidly diversify itself. It can function in a rural urban continuum, with rapid developments of markets and shifting of working populations from villages to linked small towns and also from crop production to value added activities. Employment growth will be high in these activities chasing a high rate of economic growth. All this will happen if the institutional structure gives the appropriate signals in terms of technology and organisational support and the necessary economic support in terms of pricing and infrastructure support.

There is a type of growth in the agricultural context in which rural employment and wage levels can be visualised. As always, many of agriculture's problems lie outside agriculture. A benign process will be in the following larger framework:

	India 2020
Total Population (million)	1273
Rural Population (million)	738
Labour participation rate %	46
Labour Force (million)	340
GDP growth (% annual)	8.5
GDP agricultural growth (% annual)	4%
Employment elasticity w.r..t.. Agricultural growth (Low)	-0.3%
Employment elasticity w.r.t. Agricultural growth (High)	-0.1%
Land augmentation through Increase in cropping intensity (High)	0.5%
Increase in cropping intensity	0.0 to 0.2%

Source: Alagh, 20013/14.

In a benign framework of development, agriculture will grow at 4% annually. Technologically change and diversification will be high so the shift away from agricultural on this account will be 20% over the decade 2010-2020. (Elasticity of -0.3%). This will mean a corresponding increase in real wages of the agricultural labor force.

If the shift does not take place on account of poor agricultural productivity increase, with an employment elasticity of minus 0.1, and a growth rate of three per cent annual, the shift will be 4% and an insignificant increase in real wages of the agricultural sector. The need for a programme like MGNREGA will be intense with the present trends of marginalisation of small farmers increasing. This will be a very cruel process of economic transformation.

The only other factor which will affect outcomes in this logical framework is the augmentation of the land base of Indian agriculture. If land augmentation emerges again with success of the interrelated issues of land and water management, cropping intensity increases by 0.5% annually and in the decade

2010/2020, real wages would rise by 7% additional or 27% in the total and rural-urban inequality would go down.

An increase of more than a quarter in the living standards of farmworkers is worth aiming at.

This model shows that Indian agriculture can meet the requirements of food security and rapidly diversify itself. It can function in a rural urban continuum, with rapid development of markets and shifting of working populations from villages to linked small towns and also from crop production to value-added activities. Employment growth will be high in these activities chasing a high rate of economic growth. All this will happen if the institutional structure gives the appropriate signals in terms of technology and organisational support and the necessary economic support in terms of pricing and infrastructure support. Otherwise there will be rising food prices chasing too few goods and immiseration.

The prospects for Indian agriculture are good. Demand will grow fast and if we create the correct incentive and organisation systems, the Indian farmer will not fail us as he has responded well in the past when our policies were supportive. In fact, four crore farmers moved from villages to Large Villages which according to the Census 2011 are Census Towns. The farmer has made them towns but our Babus still call them villages. More important, they are deprived of agricultural markets and agro-processing infrastructure.At this level small farmers are also labourers and they remain in distress inspite of a globalising seven percent growth economy. As the last para shows they need infrastructure and marketing support. Research and support systems will have to concentrate on a much larger cafeteria of crops and support to non-crop agriculture, including animal husbandry, pisciculture and forestry.This will need newer organisational systems for technology, financing and price and tariff support systems

The real dangers apart from anti-agricultural policies, having devastating effects as we saw above are in running into real resource constraints. Again here the strategies for land and water management are known and agricultural research can fill in the gaps. Unfortunately, the Eleventh Plan of the Manmohan Singh Government was the first plan without a chapter on the Perspective of the Economy. Now the Planning Commission has been abolished. We have to rely on the efforts of people concerned on India's future outside the Government. We may hope for a more serious effort in the future as these policies are reversed. As a member of the Planning Commission it was my good fortune to develop Manmohan Singh's vision of a detailed agro-climatic strategy for India. The prospects are better and it is more urgent now.

NOTE

1. For alternative future scenarios, see chapter 4 in Alagh, 2012/14.

REFERENCES

Alagh, Y.K. (1995). Development models: The next phase. *Indian Journal of Pure and Applied Mathematics*, 26 (6), 617-142. [also reprinted in B.L.S. Rao (ed.) (1995). *Statistics and its Applications, Essays in Honour of P.C.Mahalanobis*. New Delhi: Indian National Science Academy].

Alagh, Y.K. (2006). India 2020. *Journal of Quantitative Economics*, 4 (1), 1-14.

Alagh, Y.K. (2010). The poverty debate in perspective; moving forward with the Tendulkar committee. *Indian Journal of Human Development*, 4(1), 33-44.

Alagh, Y.K. (2013/14). *The future of Indian agriculture*. New Delhi: National Book Trust, India.

16

Democracy in Deep Crisis: Mass Mobilisation for Reforms Needed

K.B. Saxena

While talking of democracy, even the more mature and perceptive people in India are prone to talk in self-congratulatory terms and take the high moral ground when comparing our situation with that of the neighbouring countries which are dubbed as failed or failing states. Democracy in India is commended for its stability, functioning character, high rate of participation and vibrancy, precisely the characteristics which in their view democratic politics in some of these neighbouring countries lack. But in doing so, the increasing hollowness of democratic institutions and practices and the loss of trust and confidence of people in them in India are ignored. The ethos of democracy represented by respect for rule of law, guaranteeing dignity, equality, justice and protection to all citizens, accountability to people, transparent governance and a level of participation which generates confidence in its utility and offers hope for change is getting severely eroded. The authoritarian forms of behaviour are increasingly surfacing in social imagination, behaviour and political culture. It is ironic that while at the global level there is greater acceptance of the idea of democracy among people in their vision of polity and society, there is a progressive decline of democratic spirit in India both in State action and social intercourse. This can be witnessed in the growing intolerance of and disregard for contrary views, increasing resort to extralegal action, widespread violation of human rights and deepening frustration of the ordinary citizens, particularly of the marginalised groups against injustice of the social and State institutions. The battle of democracy is being lost speedily in respect of tolerance of dissent, readiness to have dialogue with and effort at accommodation of the citizens' point of view, lack of reaction and absence of anger and moral hurt against the wrong and rationalisation of expediency over ethical conduct. Exasperation is building up in the functioning of democracy as it is getting unfolded requiring urgent serious introspection and intervention from citizens. This crisis of democracy has many dimensions—Political, economic social, cultural and ideological and those relating to governance. There is the need to understand their interrelatedness for developing a coherent response to it.

Political Dimensions of the Crisis

Polarized Vision of the Polity

The crisis of democracy is most evident in the unfolding of a conflictive and divisive vision of polity. The divide on class lines is getting crystallised with the upwardly middle class, political and bureaucratic elite, and those in business and industry and professionals on the one side and the large sections of the poor, socially marginalised groups and insecure religious minorities on the other. The former represents the dominant class even though it is numerically smaller while the latter constitutes the subdued strata, larger in number but weak in everything else. The vision is sharply polarised on class lines and can be seen in their views on economy, polity and social evolution. On the economy, the members of the elite section advocate a fast-paced, capital intensive, hi-tech, market driven economic growth which creates opportunities for their advancement—jobs, accelerated incomes, higher mobility, value for individual talent and incentive for entrepreneurship. The members of this class yearn for world class infrastructure which provides amenities comparable to the best in the developed countries and are in favour of privatised social services-education, health etc. which furnish consumer satisfaction. They put a premium on efficiency of use as a determining factor in access to productive resources and flexibility in labour force utilisation so that optimum output can be generated with least cost and the product acquires a competitive edge. The focal point of this model revolves around high wealth creation and its consumption. The vision of society of this social segment is rooted in the essentiality of social differentiation in which merit, talent, and achievement determine distribution of rewards and benefits. This societal view contemptuously rejects the pursuit of social and economic equality or even equitable distribution as a goal of development but stresses equality of opportunity and open competition which permit the process of selection and elimination on the basis of merit and unrestricted high degree of mobility. The harshest criticism of persons in this group is reserved for affirmative policies particularly reservations in jobs and entry into educational institutions which, in their view, encourage inefficiency and punish the meritorious and should, therefore, be replaced by stress on individual discipline and effort to pursue the desired goal. The members of this class are totally opposed to State subsidisation of services and state regulation of economic activities whether of the media or the industry. Self-regulation is considered by them to be the preferred mode for protecting social interests. On the vision of polity, this class is highly critical of the representative democracy and contemptuous of politics which is evident in their scorn of politicians and disdain for political institutions. The Parliament is regarded as a waste of public money and a useless talking shop. The politician is criticised for populist profligacy, corruption and incapability to take hard decisions. The democratic system is attacked for permitting illiterate people with no knowledge and responsibility to elect rulers who can be easily manipulated. This set of persons is unabashedly in favour of an authoritarian form of polity with centralisation of power which can take unpopular decisions and enforce discipline in the country to insulate it from structures of democratic scrutiny and interrogation (Raina, 2015). They view the Government as a bloated organisation of lazy, slothful, obstructionist and corrupt babus. Their vision of good governance is one of least government and where decisions are taken by technocrats based on the merits of the issue. The external vision of this group for the country is to become a superpower with defence and economic capability to aggressively pursue its interests.

The vision of the 'other' class is the totally opposite of it. The members of this class would like to have an economy which protects their existing access to productive resources and further enhances this access by redistribution. They favour a model of economy where economic growth, even if slow-paced, values labour and absorbs it to the optimum and promotes a pattern of production which increases domestic demand progressively and enhances the purchasing power of the people (Bhaduri, 2008). Its focus should be to meet the essential needs of the people and raise their standard of living as well as to create human resources to enhance their capability to participate in opportunities for improving their income and status on equal terms. They strongly advocate effective regulation of working conditions so as to assure decent wages, prescribe ceilings on hours of work, comprehensive social security and opportunity for skill development and upward mobility. The people belonging to these social groups constituting this class favour State-provided and subsidised social services—education, health, drinking water, sanitation, housing and would, therefore, like progressively high levels of taxation of those with high incomes so as to generate sufficient resources to finance these activities. They are totally opposed to access to resources, opportunities, services to be determined by market forces and would like it to be regulated by the State to ensure equitable outcomes. This social segment is extremely critical of the wide and growing inequalities in income and consumption and desire State intervention to reduce the disparties by redistribution of income and checking wasteful consumption of the affluent sections. The vision of society of this group emerging from these premises is a progressively less differentiated society in which benefits of growth and development are equitably distributed.

In view of the unequal levels of income and wealth, social status and cultural resources, their members would like the State to pursue vigorous affirmative action to enable persons from the disadvantaged and excluded communities to access opportunities for advancement. As for their view of the polity, they are also critical of the existing politics not on account of its irrelevance or wasteful nature but due to elite dominance and its tilt in favour of elite interests . They censure politicians for their failure to take up issues concerning the masses. But they still favour democracy despite its capture by elites, authoritarian tendencies, widespread human rights violations and unequal treatment by law enforcement agencies because it is the only space where a level of equality, however notional, exists. For this reason, they consider politics as the only legitimate means of their collective assertion and influencing vital decisions. They, therefore, value their right to vote the most and participate in the elections in large numbers. They would, however, like politics to reflect diversity—social, economic, cultural so that an inclusive polity can emerge which would promote an inclusive economy and society. The constituents of this social combine still repose faith in government institutions notwithstanding their disappointment and even frustration with its operations and would like an effective mechanism of social accountability of governance agencies to be established. They would like the country to improve the human development and economy of its people as a route to earning respect and commanding attention in the international arena rather than to strive for a superpower status on the strength of a fast growing economy and burgeoning defence capability with impoverished people.

It is evident that the divide in the paradigm of nation building is wide and growing. The democratic institutions and processes have failed to bridge this divide, forge an inclusive vision of societal goals which harmonise the contending concerns and interests and design a political arrangement where the two social segments work together to realise it. The State has decisively opted for the vision subscribed to by the dominant class and continues to pursue the divisive agenda notwithstanding the few concessions made to the other section under electoral compulsion. This polarisation is creating enormous tensions and, at places, serious conflicts are emerging from actions of the dominant class to push the agenda enshrined in its vision. This is meeting with increasing resistance from the other social formation. Our democracy thus faces a grave threat because the people on the other side of the social divide, who are its mainstay, are getting disillusioned with it and looking for alternatives.

Federalism Under Strain

The Indian Constitution has institutionalised the democratic polity for the country in many ways. Besides protecting the fundamental rights of the citizens, it created a representative legislature, accountable governance institutions and the mechanism of judicial superintendence. Taking into account the geography and the history of the country, it established a federal system which dispersed powers and responsibilities between the Union and the states and thus pre-empted any concentration of authority or encroachment by one government into the domain of the other. The federal arrangement is also the most concrete recognition of diversity in the country and its accommodation. But from inception, the Central Government has been subverting this arrangement by expanding its area of activities into the domain earmarked for the state governments. This makes the polity progressively more central (CSDS, 2008) and tends to concentrate authority in the Central Government which makes it less responsive to the local needs and, therefore, less amenable to democratic accountability.

Encroachment into State List

The expansion of the central sphere has been pursued in many ways, the most important of which is by transferring subjects from the State List to the Concurrent List. One of the significant examples of this mode is the inclusion of 'forest' in the Central List. This enabled the Central Government to enact the Forest

Conservation Act, 1980 which introduced sweeping restrictions in the use of the forest land and, therefore, deeply hurt the interests of the tribals living in and around forests. Such a law could not have been enacted, if the subject had continued to be in the State List. This Central Act created a chain of events leading to the eviction of millions of tribals from their land and habitat in the forest which led to a countrywide mobilisation against the Government culminating in the enactment of the Scheduled Tribes and Other Forest Dwellers (Recognition of Rights) Act, 2006.

Planning Process

After independence, the trend towards centralisation was most extensively firmed up through the planning process and the steering role given to the Planning Commission which neither has a statutory nor constitutional backing. Yet, it virtually decided the crucial issue of transfer of central resources to states and the pattern of plan expenditure. The states had little autonomy in this regard because of the leverage exercised by the Commission in the release of funds. Planning Commission has recently been replaced by the Niti Ayog with a modified mandate, But the directional role in development matters continues. Yet another mode of enlarging central jurisdiction has been through numerous central sector and centrally sponsored schemes most of which operate in respect of subjects which fall in the State List. The states have no decisive say in their designs or delivery arrangements which are settled at the Central level. Some of these schemes have lately been transferred to the states but with a view to reducing the Central share of funding and putting a greater burden on states to finance them. This is justified on the ground of higher devolution of resources to states. This is the only policy manifestation of the 'Cooperative Federalism' of the current NDA Government at the Centre that can be observed. But new ones are added in virtually every annual budget. The externally aided projects whose number has increased manifold since the economic reforms were initiated have added to this route of Central encroachment into the state domain. These projects have created vertical structures of management for implementation designed by the Central Government at the behest of funding donor agencies.

Deployment of Central Police Forces

The third major device of Central expansion and potentially more debilitating for democratic accountability is the deployment of Central security forces for maintenance of law and order in the states. These forces are accountable only to the Central Government and state governments where they are deployed cannot exercise any control over such personnel. This deployment has increased manifold with insurgency movements engulfing large areas in many states where state police forces are considered ill-equipped and ill-prepared to deal with the situations arising. The latest in this security architecture is the constitution of National Investigation Agency to deal with investigation of terror cases. At the political level, the Central manipulation of the federal system is effected through the imposition of President's rule to overthrow democratic Governments the instances of which are many. There are also other examples of centralising tendencies in the polity. The states do feel resentful about this encroachment into their sphere but are unable to effectively resist it. This creates tensions in the political system.

Disinclination Towards Decentralisation

Lately, the federal arrangement has been extended to self-governance at the level of the district and below by setting up Panchayati Raj Institutions as the third tier. This tier of government has been assigned separate jurisdiction for which subjects to be dealt with by these institutions have been specified. Admittedly, this tier of government is not as autonomous as the other two tiers. Still it does enjoy a constitutional status. But this addition to 'federalism' is being defeated by the state governments due to their reluctance to transfer resources, powers and functionaries to these institutions which enable them to function as per the Constitutional vision.

The institutions at this level are even more crucial for democracy than those at the higher levels. This is because people at the level of the Panchayati Raj Institutions (PRIs) can effectively participate in their deliberations. These developments send out a disturbing signal for the health of federalism. The politics at the Central level is subverting autonomy at the state level and the politics at the state level is doing the same thing to the empowerment of the people for self-governance at the PRI level. There has been no resistance to political intervention from democratic institutions to correct these undemocratic directions of the polity.

Creeping Authoritarianism

Independent India inherited the colonial legacy of governance embedded in the ideology of supremacy of power underwritten by a legal structure and system of justice administration. This enabled concentration of huge power in the administrative machinery through repressive laws to prevent any disturbance, and suppress dissent or protest with the sole objective to maintain 'order'/stability. Indian people were treated merely as subjects with no civil rights (Kannabiran, 2014).

Colonial Legacy

With the ushering in of a democratic polity after independence and coming into force of the Constitution, civil and political rights were granted to citizens and the State was exhorted to provide social and economic justice. This transformed the people from being the mere subjects of a colony to citizens of an independent country. This change was not carried out in the structures of governance, legal system and ideological ethos of their operations. As a result, the colonial legacy continued and colonial repressive laws retained which subordinated the rights of the people to the power of the State. The courts have also not promoted any radical break in this legacy and have upheld ever more repressive laws and accretion to State power in their enforcement (Kannabiran, 2014). This power is now being exercised not only for maintenance of law and order and control of violence but, ironically, even for preservation of democracy. But a democratic political system with enforceable rights has raised the consciousness of people. They now resort to collective assertion to demand social and economic justice against structural violence, failure to deliver socio-economic entitlements, deprivation of their assets and livelihood, and diminishing access to public goods. This assertion is perceived by the State agencies as a threat to order and stability. The increasing assertion by people leads to more repressive laws and grant of greater freedom of operation and enhanced power to security agencies resulting in larger incidence of violations of rights with no accountability (Kannabiran, 2004). This criticism of rights violations is severely condemned and the demand for a credible enquiry ignored. There is neither any initiative from democratic institutions to democratise and humanise law and order governance nor has a larger social movement emerged to dismantle this legacy.

Legitimisation of Oppressive Laws

The merit of a democratic polity with its recognition of basic rights of the people along with a credible mechanism for its enforcement lies in its ability to thwart authoritarian forces to emerge. The failure of democracy to achieve this objective in India exposes its fragility. This is most glaringly evident in its denial/curtailment of constitutionally recognised rights on grounds of 'security' by not only retaining the colonial period oppressive laws but, far worse, enacting even more draconian laws which make fundamental rights inoperative in areas of their application and grant impunity to security forces from any legal action for violation of human rights. Certain parts of the country affected by insurgency and terrorism have remained under these oppressive legal arrangements for decades where people have been denied any justice against numerous human rights violations. The democratic institutions have failed to bring pressure on the Government to restore the basic rights of the people by changing its security-centric policy to political movements and to address the situation through political dialogue with those involved in them. The Government has stubbornly refused to abrogate these laws or even to humanise them despite sustained protests from the people of the affected areas and recommendations of commissions of enquiry set up by the Government itself due to resistance of the security establishment. Democratic Institutions expose their hollowness when political decision making is subordinated to the veto of security forces and courts validate such draconian laws and their continuation endlessly.

Unequal Treatment

Democracy is distinguished from other forms of polity in that it is firmly rooted in the rule of law. This rule of law is enshrined in the Constitution of India and operated through the structures of governance. But there is widespread violation of this norm in the interface of the common citizens with the Government which belies the claim that the rule of law operates in the country equally for all sections of the population. Justice administration is the most significant arena to test it because arbitrary action of the law enforcement agencies can cost the affected persons physical harm and loss of reputation. The highhanded action of police against the poor and the socially marginalised groups and those protesting against injustice and state repression is a very common occurrence because these powerless and resourceless persons have no capacity to challenge it. The same agency is more circumspect when persons in powerful positions are involved. It is common knowledge that persons with status, money and muscle power are able to manipulate levers of justice to get away with crime or escape its harsh consequences while the poor often languish in jail even for a minor offence (in quite a few cases, falsely implicated by powerful adversaries) and can even lose life as a result of torture by police. The politicians, film stars, gangsters and businessmen accused of heinous offences manage to avoid prosecution and when convicted, obtain bail. While in jail, they have no problem in getting good treatment. Others are even denied the facilities a prisoner is entitled to in terms of the Jail Manual. The harshest treatment of police and justice administration system is reserved for human rights activists because they attempt to expose the violations of law and the conduct of the security agencies.

Violation of Human Rights

A democratic polity is distinguished from other forms of government by the comprehensive range of human rights which the citizens enjoy and an effective mechanism by which these rights can be enforced. These rights are the best bulwark against authoritarian actions of the State which have the effect of denying or abridging such rights through its ever expanding and quirky activities. A constitutionally guaranteed framework of protection is the best conceivable guarantee that a citizen would be able to checkmate the State against the arbitrary use of its power. But this entire edifice of rights collapses when the disadvantaged and disillusioned people are in conflict with the State. The dissent with the governments and resistance to their policies is viewed as 'sedition' and curbing it at all costs becomes the top priority. In this manner, social movements against displacement, corporate land grab, denial of access to entitlements, inaction of police against atrocities, unresponsiveness of local officials to injustice etc. are considered threats to the security of the State. Worse, the leaders of and participants in these movements are branded as 'terrorists' to justify strong repressive action against them. The executive, thus, acquires freedom of action unrestrained by normal law. This task is executed by enacting/applying/extending draconian laws, facilitating preventive detention even on mere suspicion without the provision of bail and even killing of a person under certain circumstances. The growing recourse to this instrument has already delegitimised democracy. This is because draconian laws such as Unlawful Activities Prevention Act (1967) as amended in 2004, the erstwhile Prevention of Terrorist Activities Act, 2002, Terrorist Activities Detention Act, Chhattisgarh's Special Public Security Act, 2005, and J&K's Public Security Act grant de-facto impunity to the security forces for their actions requiring prior permission before starting legal proceedings against members of the Armed Forces in the areas to which they apply. Not to speak of denial of civil rights, even the right to life does not exist since security forces can enter into any house, arrest any individual, torture and even kill him/her without being accountable to any local institution of law or governance. The victims of the security forces in these areas are denied access to the constitutionally available mechanism of redressal against violation of their human rights as a matter of public policy. For the affected people in such areas, the idea of democracy ceases to hold any attraction as a superior and accountable mode of governance. Democratic institutions and processes, therefore, face severe erosion of legitimacy and credibility. This is precisely the case in certain parts of the country, such as the North East and the Jammu & Kashmir, and lately in Central India which have witnessed continuing militarisation of large areas. Democratic institutions have been mute spectators to such arbitrary forms of governance continuously for years. The war on terror has provided additional justifications for such operations which have resulted in fake and 'staged' encounters, custodial torture and killing, enforced disappearance after arrest etc. The Bhopal encounter in which SIMI undertrials were gunned down as they were trying to escape from the prison is only the most recent one in such episodes. "An entire network of trespassing and transgression has been generated and peoples' lives have been trampled on. In order to secure the nation's territory, several other territories have been violated. Slowly and with conscious design, the citizen has been dispossessed of rights that should be guaranteed in a free country (Bhattacharya, 2016). Barring intervention by Supreme Court in a very small number of cases and routine reports sought by the National Human Rights Commission from the state governments, democratic institutions in the states or the country have failed to question the culture of impunity that pervades the operation of security forces.

Unresponsiveness to Moral Indignation

Democracy is shamed when peaceful moral protests by people

against the excesses of the security apparatus in such a dispensation fail to stir its institutions and the consciousness of the people to respond. Even such powerful expressions of anguish and disgust as were observed in the naked Manipuri women inviting security forces deployed in the area to rape them as the ultimate moral option to highlight in this telling manner the custodial rape of women of the house during search and seizure operations or the sixteen long years of fast unto death by Irom Sharmila, a Manipuri woman, for withdrawal of the Armed Forces Special Powers Act from Manipur or mass protects of Kashmiri people against the excesses of Army and other security forces including the recent blinding of youth resulting from pellet injuries have failed to move the Central Government to relax the iron grip of the Armed Forces over these areas or even to punish security personal found guilty of fake encounters murders and other excesses. Still worse, even the recommendations made by a Committee headed by a retired justice of the Supreme Court constituted by the Central Government itself failed to persuade it to withdraw such laws or at least to substantially change their provisions so as to make them more humane in application and to remove the immunity provided to the security forces against legal action for violation of human rights. The response of the Government to the demand to get transparent enquiries conducted and punish those officials found guilty is that such an action would cause demoralisation among them and adversely affect their resolve to carry out their duties effectively. Can such a humiliating response to victims ever create any value for democracy for them? Even Supreme Court in a recent case of 'Extrajudicial Killings' in Manipur was forced to argue that living under the shadow of a gun that can be wielded with impunity and outright acceptance of this proposition is equally unsettling and demoralising and questioned the prolonged use of the military to curb continuing unrest in certain areas of the country. (Writ Petition No. 129 of 2012). (cited in *Liberation* magazine August, 16, 2016). It is ironic that the draconian laws and excessive powers given to the security forces against Naxalities are justified on the ground that they are necessary to protect democracy. Can such a prolonged denial of rule of law and human rights ever be a condition for preserving democracy? That the suffering population in the affected areas which happens to be the politically marginalised ethnic/cultural and religious minorities, evokes no emotional support for their cause from the larger population called the 'mainstream' is proof enough that the idea of democracy does not create any bonding between people with diverse cultures even on such a basic political issue and poses therefore, a greater threat to the survival of democracy.

New Instruments of Surveillance and Tracking

Data collection including by fingerprinting has emerged as one such instrument of infringement of individual freedom. National Population Register is collecting huge data live with their biometric identification. This data would feed into UID data based National Intelligence Grid (NatGrid) and the proposed DNA bank. It is being carried out under Citizenship Act 1955 and Citizenship Rules 2003 which have no provision of confidentiality. The vast information with the holder poses serious threats to privacy and gives enormous power for exercising control over the lives of people (Ramanathan. 2010). The threat becomes graver when the Government even denies the right to privacy as a fundamental right. The poor would be most threatened by being branded as criminals and anti-socials and social activists can be harassed into silence or submission. 'The interim orders of the Supreme Court that attempted to rein in the project... have been flouted with impunity' (Gupta, Kashyap and Khera, 2016). Similarly, DNA Profiling Bill raises huge risks of misuse .... (Henry and Devulpathi, 2015). The proposed National E-Health Authority which will oversee digitisation of information is yet another such instrument. There is little awareness even among educated citizens about the potential threat this exercise poses to personal liberty and even less about the need for building safeguards against its misuse.

Narrow Base of Political Participation

The strong point in favour of democracy is that it affords wider opportunities for political participation to citizens and social groups in decision making at different levels and enables them to exercise some control over the Government in order that governance emerges as a balanced exercise of harmonising conflicting interests. It provides a better mechanism to assess people's needs and incorporate them in policy (Beetham, 2003). This participation also ensures that grievances, if any, emerging from the decision making can be addressed through dialogues with diverse interest groups and accommodation of their interests so that all participants have a continuing stake in its institutions and processes. Having taken into account the entrenched inequalities in society which would constrain participation of some communities, the Constitution mandated the reservation of seats in legislative bodies and appointments to public services based on their numerical strength in society. This ensures political representation of the Scheduled Castes and the Scheduled Tribes (OBCs have been provided reservation in public services but not in legislature) so as to neutralise exclusionary factors to their participation. The requisite number of representatives from these communities, therefore, do get elected to the representative bodies. But this does not translate into sharing of power and influencencing decision making. The representative bodies and institutions of governance wielding political power have disproportionately high representation from the dominant communities than is warranted by their numerical strength. The minority religious groups and women are considerably underrepresented in relation to their numerical strength (CSDS, 2008) as there is no prescribed norm for their representation either in law or political practice. The political parties themselves have taken no steps to ensure that, even without reservation, these communities are adequately represented in their activities. With regard to the marginalised sections, such as the Scheduled Castes and Scheduled Tribes, while the numerical representation exists, this does not translate into substantive political participation, which may give them a share in political power (Makkad, 2009). These groups neither get proportionate representation in positions of political governance nor in other political formations. There is little attempt in any political party to mobilise the underrepresented and disempowered groups to widen the existing base of its activities. The involvement of the Scheduled Castes, Scheduled Tribes, religious minorities and women in the processes of decision making becomes an exercise in tokenism rather than a genuine attempt to share power. The result is that the highly skewed distribution of political power remains entrenched. The democratic institutions and decision making positions continue to be captured by the dominant social groups which block opportunities for the socially marginalised groups to raise their political status (CSDS, 2008). Without a requisite share in political power which enables them to influence decision making on issues of vital concern to them, there is no way by which the Dalits, Tribes, minorities and women can get their problems addressed and improve their prospects of advancement particularly where their interests are in conflict with those of the dominant groups. These groups then look for alternative platforms of political assertion. Some rally behind regional parties which espouse their cause strongly or form political associations which predominantly represent their interests. This option too disappoints when these political formations seek alliances with dominant social groups to gain political strength sufficient enough to occupy powerful positions. In such an arrangement, their interests again lose the focus and priority. In some cases, the acute dissatisfaction from existing level of participation and the frustration resulting from failure of the alternative modes to compensate it turn these groups against democracy itself which is then exploited by radical groups to restructure distribution of power through non-democratic ways. This stage has already reached in some parts of the country. The appropriation of major avenues of political power by the dominant social groups, therefore, gravely jeopardises democracy.

Universal Adult Franchis under Threat

But, now even this formal democracy in the form of universal adult franchise which in the words of Granville Austin is "the single note whose reverberations might awaken—or at least stir – sleeping India" (Cited in Rao, 2016) faces its gravest threat. Rajasthan Government enacted a law last year restricting people's rights to contest local body's elections if they did not have prescribed educational qualifications. Haryana Government has gone further and added further disabilities such as outstanding debt to agricultural cooperatives and electricity bills due. The Act has unfortunately been validated even by the Supreme Court. This would hurt the marginalised sections the most and would deprive them of the only barometer of equality which they possessed. Yet, the political parties have failed to use their clout to prevent or reverse it.

Elite Capture of Institutions

The other dimension of the narrow base of political participation results from elite capture of democratic institutions (CSDS, 2008) which leaves the remaining sections powerless. It also implies that the elite use the democratic support base to advance their interests which often are in conflict with the interests of the poorer sections. This leads to loss of trust in the institutions among the larger sections of population in their ability to represent their interests and consequently weakens the desire to have a stake in these institutions. The elite capture of democracy is evident in all political parties, a classical example of which is the manner in which political domination based on family, caste and class interests is perpetuated and avenues of political mobility for the poorer sections and weaker groups within the social formations are effectively blocked. The elite capture has a natural tendency to get entrenched because the elites are privileged by the skewed access to education, experience, financial and cultural resources which gives them a head-start in managing political processes. The disillusionment and frustration this generates among the masses within their social groups turn them against democracy and politics. In such a situation, they are naturally drawn towards non-political formations which take up their causes, seek their active participation and give them leadership position. There are numerous social movements espousing interests of the poor and the marginalised on diverse issues such as land, forest, water, environment, food security, relief, displacement, employment, transparency in governance, human rights which political parties fail to take up. But these movements do not get any legitimacy from democratic institutions as platforms for wider political participation and, therefore, extension of democracy but are rather considered a threat to them. Here lies the irrelevance of 'formal' democracy for those who participate in these movements.

Hollowing out of Institutions

The idea of democracy acquires its concrete shape in the form of institutions which embody its enduring principles in the processes which operationalise them in order that the people develop a stake in their legitimacy for pursuit of the goals of the polity. These institutions consist of elective legislative bodies, collective decision-making executive institutions, independent judiciary, free and fair elections, unrestrained and fearless media, neutral and accountable civil service, political parties wedded to the vision of polity and a vibrant civil society. Democracy is vibrant when these institutions are strong and show vitality and effectiveness in their functioning as per their norms and operate without fear and pressure. The barometer of this vitality lies in the trust people repose in them. Sadly, what we witness is a hollowing out of these institutions rather than their maturing over a period of time. Each institution has slid down in reputation and lost the confidence of the people.

Parliament

The erosion of the Parliament is observed in the increasingly lower number of days of its sittings and deliberations, virtual absence of debates on crucial matters, low attendance and absence of quorum even when important subjects are under discussion, frequent obstructions in the passage of business by the aggrieved sections, unruly behaviour of some members and the poor quality of debates if ever they take place. The increasingly witnessed corrupt practices of the members in the parliamentary transactions, failure to transact business even when the Parliament is in session, neglect of larger national interest for pursuit of narrow political gains, virtual absence of accountability etc., are discrediting the institution and generating disillusionment among the people who expect their elected representatives to raise their concerns. Democracy also gets subverted by encouraging defections, toppling governments, disruption and imposition of President's Rule (CSDS, 2008). The Cabinet system is getting devalued due to the poor quality of decision making, little collective deliberations, ill preparedness of ministers in facing the Parliament, unresponsiveness to accommodate views and concerns expressed by members, particularly from the opposition on vital matters, manipulated action to get certain agenda transacted without discussion, lack of synergy between different wings of the government, increasing avoidance of the Parliament in taking important political decisions, corruption in matters involving corporate interests etc. "The bargains and concessions in the political economy have become deals, sold, bought and paid for rather than being a morally defensible exchange" (Khare, 2009).

Judiciary

The institution of judiciary has assumed extraordinary power of mediation between federal and state governments, President and PM, Government and the Opposition and legitimisation of government formation (CSDS, 2008). Some of its recent judgments lack sensitivity to deeply conflictive social issues which adversely affect the poorer sections and convey its class bias (Bhushan, 2009). Leaving aside a few cases in which it has intervened at the behest of civil society activists, the judiciary has also failed to check the proliferation of draconian laws, excesses of security forces and protect the human rights of the people particularly when they are locked in conflict with the State. It has encroached into the area of executive and legislative domain. This 'judicial overreach' has even extended to prescribing a code of behaviour for displaying patriotism (Sorabji, 2016; Palshekar, 2016). Even complaints of corruption among judges of higher courts have now begun to be mentioned. There has also been reluctance by the higher judiciary to submit to any process of social and political accountability on the ground that it would compromise their independence. Judiciary has also assumed total autonomy in selection of judges with virtually no role of the executive and struck down the law establishing the National Judicial Appointment Commission. This has enlarged the area of tension in its relationship with the Executive.

Elections

Elections are the soul of representative government. The process of election stands hugely manipulated by widespread use of muscle power and capturing booths, astute and clever management of vote banks through appeal to caste and religion to the neglect of ideological issues, sponsoring of candidates charge-sheeted in heinous crimes and also possessing doubtful integrity and discredited pasts, (34% of the winners in 2014 Lok Sabha had criminal cases against them as compared to 30% in 2009 Election; 21% of the winners had serious criminal cases. Party wise, 35% of winners were in BJP, 18% in Congress 16% in AIDMK (National Election Watch [NEW], 2014) increasing 'monetisation of political space' (Khare, 2009) through distribution of tickets, high level of expenditure, doling out unfair concessions to businessmen/industrialists, domination of caste-based power structures, unabashed attempts to bribe voters, calculated use of hate campaigns to polarise voters for garnering support and disregard for decency, morality and propriety in political rhetoric. Going by the data provided by the NEW, a coalition of 1,200 civil society organisations, persons with criminal records are increasingly seeking political positions and politics has become one of the most profitable professions.

The economic assets of those included in the cabinet of the second UPA were close to Rs. 5 billion and 47 of 64 Ministers were crorepatis. Though data is not available, the position in respect of NDA may not be very different. The average worth of MP in Lok Sabha in 2009 was 51 million (Sainath, 2009[a]). Among the candidates contesting recent elections, in 2014, out of winners, 82% are crorepatis as compared 58% in 2009. This consisted of 84% winners in BJP, 80% in Congress, 78% in AIDMK and 62% in Trinamul Congress. 77% of the winners occupy the top three highest asset positions in their respective constituency. 30% of the winners have the highest declared assets in their constituency and 29% of the candidates with assets more than Rs. 10 crore won the election in 2014 Lok Sabha. The average individual assets per winner for Lok Sabha 2014 elections was Rs. 14.70 cr while it was Rs. 5.35 cr. in Lok Sabha Election 2009. The percentage increase in value of assets of 165 winners re-elected MPs is 137% (NEW, 2009 and 2014). The chances of winning an election goes up for those with high assets and is particularly low for non-millionaires (Sainath, 2009[b]). A recent study informs that parties like BJP and Congress spent 30-40 crore per seat, while small parties like CPM around 8-10 crore. Candidates have no chance of winning unless they have this kind of money (Bhaduri, 2015). This is the reason which pushes many politicians to develop business activities once elected. Between 2007 and 2012, among 95 reelected MLAs in UP, 41 had shifted from a non-business-related professions (agriculture, teaching, medicine) to business related occupation/ (Verniers, 2016). Election Commission is attacked for the lack of transparency and is even accused of the lack of neutrality in its decisions. Political parties are captured by the elites and have long lost any interest in reaching out to the masses, mobilising them for membership, educating and training them and developing mechanisms for creating in them a stake for participation in the political processes. They represent authoritarian and leader-centric structures with little internal democracy and transparency in their decision making and financial transactions.

Executive

The executive has displayed the lack of will and capacity to govern perhaps guided by political considerations. It fails to discharge its responsibility to ameliorate the corrosive disregard for the rule of law exhibited by fascist vigilante groups enforcing moral policing and inflicting violence on those perceived guilty of hurting religious sentiments and resorting to private violence substituting for legal action in the case of grievances. It has also shown reluctance to respond to numerous issues of social concern highlighted in the media and elsewhere in discourse. The nexus between the decision makers and the entrepreneurs in the economy is an open secret (Khare, 2009). The Army is opaque and totally closed to any scrutiny and social accountability. The bureaucracy is viewed as insensitive, rent-seeking and citizen-unfriendly. This collapse of institutions is being cemented and reinforced by the increased political role of the corporates, upwardly mobile middle class, film actors, and media (CSDS, 2008). This class castigates politics, denigrates democratic institutions, discredits electoral processes and unabashedly advocates rule of technocrats. Democratic debate thus gets hugely constrained and restricted. These powerful sections consider casting vote as a wasteful exercise but seek to capture political power through other ways to increase their hold over decision making so as to project and protect their interests and sideline the burning issues which affect the common people. It is ironic that the hugely disempowered poor still exercise the right to vote albeit without much choice but find that this does not translate into a say in the decision making even on matters which are of vital concern to them.

Justice Administration System

The classic case of institutional collapse lies in the total breakdown of the justice administration system. The mounting arrears of cases, some of which have not been disposed of for decades, lack of deterrence for criminals and elites due to their enormous power to manipulate the system are noteworthy. In addition, the poor rate of convictions, disinterestedness to punish perpetrators of organised riots and other cases of mob violence, caste/class biased custodial excesses of police, resort to extra-legal action out by security forces with impunity, a judicial system that is expensive, dilatory, distant and user-unfriendly and which induces people to seek settlement of disputes outside the law are some of its features. SCs/STs, minorities in particular and the poor in general feel that the system is not meant for them. They get entrapped in the system as the accuseds rather than as seekers of justice (Daghamvar, 2006). In sheer despondency, they suffer atrocities, intimidation and subjugation by their tormentors and the hostility of the police. It is not surprising that the Naxalite system of dispensing instant justice, however abhorrent, attracts the poor and the marginalised in the areas of their operations. This happens in other areas too when people seek services of criminals to get their property and other disputes settled. Builders often use this route as the quickest way to dispossess the poor occupants of land. Even banks have resorted to engaging local toughs to get repayment of their outstanding loans. Democracy cannot survive for long if people cannot settle their disputes in an orderly way and through the rule of law.

Civil Services

Civil Services are an integral part of the Government. Civil servants carry out the orders and the decisions of the political masters. They have in this sense no autonomy of their own. Their role has generally been regressive notwithstanding some exceptions. Not only their supposed neutrality has long been exploded, but also they are quick to go along with the ruling dispensation for their advancement. In doing so, they even fail to discharge their duty to place facts before the decision makers and offer honest advice to them. Lately, they have shown ideological inclinations towards political parties. They, therefore, provide no strength to democracy. But their most undemocratic role lies in the failing to sincerely implement laws and programmes for the poor and the marginalised and display sensitivity and concern for them in the discharge of their duties.

Watchdog Institutions

The decline of institutions extends to watchdog agencies as well which were set up to protect the rights of the people against the actions of the governments violating them. These institutions include the constitutionally created—the National Scheduled Caste Commission, National Scheduled Tribes Commission, and the Statutory Commissions—National Human Rights Commission, National Minority Commission, National Backward Classes Commission, National Safai Karamchari Commission, National Commission for Women, National Commission for Protection of Child Rights etc. State governments have also set up their own commissions covering all or some of these interest groups. These commissions are ineffective and virtually toothless in delivering justice to their target groups. The National Human Rights Commission despite its high powered composition has failed to take action against police officials in matters involving serious violations of human rights even when evidence has been presented (Committee of Concerned Citizens, 2002). It has routinely relied on reports of state governments defending police action and satisfied itself by awarding token compensation to the victims in such cases. As a result, it focuses on softer issues of development and governance which do not bring it in conflict with State agencies. The national commissions dealing with SCs/STs/Safai Karmcharis have themselves confessed that they are powerless and their reports are not even discussed in the Parliament let alone acted upon. These institutions have been reduced to parking lots to provide berths to the politicians defeated in elections or those who have to be accommodated for political reasons. They, no doubt, lack sufficient powers and resources. But even with their existing capacity and resources, they have failed to act boldly and decisively to inspire confidence among the aggrieved persons . These commissions routinely present their reports to the Parliament which are not even discussed. The concerned groups which constitute the focal point of their attention have no faith in them to protect their interests. For how long this fragile attachment to democracy will last is not difficult to guess. Already the signs of disenchantment with democracy are evident, ironically among the rich as well as the poor. The rich have no hesitation in articulating their preference for an authoritarian regime which can quickly and ruthlessly deliver their agenda. The poor and the marginalised find democracy increasingly irrelevant for them since it subordinates their interests to those of the rich.

Cultural Dimension

Attack on Plurality

The democratic sprit is embedded in the acclamation of diversity which upraises a society and reforms its values (CSDS, 2008). The demographic spirit not only protects and preserves the social fabric but also builds on its positive elements so as to forge a composite culture for the well-being of the people. The democratic institutions and processes are intended to reflect this ethos and facilitate furtherance of this synthesis. This conceptual frame of democracy collapses when social and cultural diversity is viewed by sections of dominant community as an existential threat and the people constituting this plurality are subjected to vicious attack—physical, cultural psychological, political and economic by them. This hegemonic agenda gets expanded and consolidated when the State fails to curb it and those opposed to this evil design are reluctant to aggressively counteract it politically. This is precisely the situation which exists today. This hegemonic agenda is manipulated by religious fundamentalists and social fascists for aggressive communal mobilisation by demonising religious minorities (specially Muslims and lately and to a lesser extent, Christians), portraying them as enemies of the country. and creating a frenzy of hate which motivates organised violence against the targeted group. The rhetoric has been fine-tuned into well crafted instrument of political consolidation for capturing political power. Minority bashing is also systematically used to exclude its members from access to productive resources, jobs, education, opportunities for advancement and higher mobility thereby forcing their ghettoisation and consequent alienation not only from their immediate neighbourhood but also from the mainstream society and the nation. The other dimension of this campaign is observed in raising the bogey of forced conversion with the help of foreign funds against minority religious groups (specifically Christians) with a view to frightening the converted groups into acceptance of the dominant religion and dissuading the religious organisations from carrying on with their function of preaching and propagating their religion and providing social services as per the rights granted by the Constitution. The failure of the institutions of governance to provide protection to the victim communities against violence, counteract the vicious rhetoric against them and proactively neutralise attempts at denial of human rights and exclusion from development. This results in their alienation and becomes fodder for their counter mobilisation by the 'radical' groups which not only creates instability in society but also threatens democracy. Neither democratic institutions nor civil society have strongly come forward to check these forces, democratise governance structures and inform the society of the divisive agenda behind these forces and mobilise people to resist them.

Ideological Assault

This assault on plurality is not merely political but ideological as well. It is embedded in the conceptualisation of 'nation' and 'culture'. The 'nation', in terms of this ideological attack, is not a political but a cultural construct (Panikkar, 2009). This implies that culture becomes central to its definition. The culture itself is defined in terms of its identity with religion. Thus, the nation as a cultural construct becomes an integral part of religion. On this ideological premise, the nation is defined in terms of the 'ethno-majoritarian' cultural construct (CSDS, 2008). While its construction of the 'nation' is used to enforce a version of polity and the agenda of governance, development and future where ethnic/ religious minorities are denied any special consideration for their marginalisation or accommodation of their interests, the construction of 'culture' is put into service to push aggressive social assimilation of ethnic minorities (Panikkar, 2009). The latter is carried out by deprecating the cultural practices of these groups, denying them autonomy for pursuing their own way of life, castigating them as 'backward' accusing them of blocking the progressive transformation of society and coercing them in various ways to change their lifestyle and values on the lines of the majority community. This is manifested in the Hindusation of animistic tribal communities and reforming Muslim Personal Law, deprecating beef eating etc. This 'communal' construction of 'nation' and 'culture' has become central to the political discourse of mainstream political forces which currently are in power. This ideological assault is vigorously pursued through the reinterpretation of Indian history as seen in the writings of the Hindu ideologues during the colonial period. The allegiance to a common culture is considered to be a necessary component for forging emotional bonds among the people to consolidate nationhood. This construction of 'nation' and 'culture' completely ignores the secular cultural processes occurring in the Indian society historically which brought together divergent cultural groups without disturbing the social togetherness and were expressed in various kinds of synthesis in the social practices of the people (Panikkar, 2009). These cultural groups are deeply hurt at the bankruptcy of democratic institutions and the silence of its adherents for the lack of efforts to vigorously counter this ideological assault which is increasingly turning fascist. The alienation resulting from this loss of hope is the clearest indication, if any is needed, that the future of democracy as a pluralist and diversity celebrating enterprise in India is no longer assured.

Social Dimension

Social Order in Conflict with Law

There is a mutuality in the relationship of the State with the society. The State is the creation of society and represents its collective will to function as its instrument for peaceful evolution and realisation of its vision. Society depends upon the State to create conditions for pursuit of its goals and for its members to carry on with their lives with dignity security and freedom

(CSDS, 2008). A major conflict between the State and the society would hugely threaten this delicate relationship. The idea of democracy sustains in the belief that a democratic State can exist if only the society is democratic. If the society is essentially undemocratic, a democratic state cannot survive unless it transforms it and if the state turns authoritarian, a democratic society is expected to resist and change it.

In India, a sharp conflict is discernible between an apparently democratic state (in terms of structures, institutions and their processes) and an inherently undemocratic social order which has its historical roots. The democratic State is manifested in the constitutional scheme, (a number of) progressive laws and governance institutions with earmarked responsibilities and specified systems of accountability. The undemocratic society is reflected in the remnants of feudal, hierarchical and oppressive caste-based social order which thrives in the highly skewed distribution of status, power, control over productive resources, access to advancement opportunities and an institutionalised arrangement of subjugation of some groups sanctified by religious beliefs and enforced by physical force. The Indian Constitution established a liberal democratic polity, eliminated all forms of inequality and established mechanisms for protecting the interests of the social groups subordinated and oppressed for centuries by the caste-based ideology. The State did translate this broad vision of the Constitution into various instruments for its realisation such as the laws for ensuring physical security, protection of human rights, redistribution of productive assets, elimination of labour exploitation and socially degrading practices. The State has, through affirmative action, extended development benefits to these marginalised groups by earmarking a specified share for them. But the bulk of the society in India has refused to accept this political order and persisted in perpetuating the old social practices in defiance of the Constitution, law and governance structures by skilfully using its power, resources-material, intellectual, cultural, and social capital. This happens because the power in society is disproportionately wielded by a small section due to its overwhelming control over land, labour and access to financial capital, near monopoly in political positions and structures of governance, enormous advancement opportunities and the higher social status enjoyed on this basis. Thus, a democratic State exists in an undemocratic society. It was expected of the State to democratise the undemocratic features of society by rigorous enforcement of the provisions of the Constitution's progressive laws and other democratic policy instruments. But the State has not shown the requisite political will to eliminate institutionalised inequality by effectively curbing the power of the dominant sections and ensuring that the weaker sections are enabled to enjoy genuine equality (CSDS, 2008). It has even failed to protect the victims against physical violence inflicted by the dominant castes and their private armies. It has also shown no enthusiasm for enlarging participation of these sections so as to give them the requisite share of power. The State has, thus, failed to democratise society. This failure is due to the dualistic character of the State which creates doubts about its commitment to the democratic goal. This duality lies in projecting a democratic face of the State by putting in place liberal and progressive policy instruments but at the same time displaying a lukewarm attitude to eliminate the undemocratic features of society which tend to defeat them. This calculated strategy serves its purpose. It seeks to assure the marginalised sections that it stands by them and is committed to secure social justice against the higher caste groups but fails to act ruthlessly against the latter when denial of justice takes place. It enacts progressive laws, puts in place policies and programmes but shows no enthusiasm for implementing them vigorously. This is done due to its propensity to rely on higher class elites for 'managing' democratic institutions and operating the levers of power.

Vulnerable Social Groups

Democracy is considered to be the only form of polity which has the potential of managing social diversity and promoting inclusive politics, equitable development and harmonious social relations. If a democratic polity fails on this count, its democratic character is under severe strain. This is the situation democracy in India faces for various reasons already outlined. It is precisely in managing social diversity that the faultlines in democracy are most evident. This diversity consists of primarily religious minorities, lower caste groups and ethnically distinct tribes. Marginalisation of women pervades all social groups. The culturally diverse groups within the dominant religion do not face such discrimination or exclusion as they constitute an integral part of the majority as perceived by its adherents. These social groups which constitute the most marginalised sections of the society are also the most disaffected. This disaffection in the perception of these groups is on account of the failure of democratic institutions to protect their rights as citizens, create enabling conditions for enjoyment of their entitlements under the Constitution, laws and State policies against all pervasive discrimination and exclusion and provide opportunities for participation comparable to those enjoyed by the dominant sections. All three groups are deeply alienated from institutional democracy which has betrayed them. They experience similar social reality in diverse ways. These groups feel physically insecure because of violence inflicted on them by the members of the dominant sections of society. In the case of religious minorities, this physical insecurity is the most severe because they are victims of organised violence and 'communal riots' by members of the majority community against which they fail to get protection from the State and justice under the law. Their frustration mounts when the police and other security forces display communal bias against them in maintaining public order and further victimise them in the subsequent processes of action under the law. Scheduled Castes are not only victims of violence on individual basis unleashed by the dominant castes as a routinised phenomenon in their daily lives but also face organised violence by members of the locally dominant communities and their private armies when they resist injustices meted out to them. They too fail to get protection from the State agencies (the police in particular) despite special laws and institutional arrangements made for this purpose. Scheduled Tribes broadly suffer the same experience as the Scheduled Castes do except that in their case, the violence on them is inflicted by the non-tribals. Besides the above, all three communities face another form of violence. This violence is inflicted by the State in retaliation of their resistance against the failure of government to protect them and punish the guilty. The resulting frustration and helplessness over a period of time takes the form of insurgency as can be seen in the North-Eastern states, Jammu and Kashmir and the Naxalite movement in central India and individual acts of terrorism among Muslims. This resistance is perceived as a 'grave threat' to the internal security of the State and met by counter-insurgency/terrorism operations during the course of which a great deal of excesses are committed against the whole community and human rights of their members are violated. There is no protection against these excesses of the State agencies and little relief from the courts.

All three communities face a variety of discriminatory and exclusionary practices by the State agencies and, in addition, by members of the dominant majority community in the case of the minorities, and the dominant social groups in the case of the SCs/STs. This exclusion relates to the access to productive resources, distribution of benefits of development, opportunities for upward mobility, entry into institutions of learning and jobs in the Government and the private sector. The discrimination also extends to accessing credit, market, housing, health, education, and skill development facilities. All three groups experience deep-seated prejudices against them in social intercourse. The officials of the institutions charged with the responsibility of delivering public services also carry biases against them. Laws and policy instruments to combat this discrimination and protect them against violence are poorly implemented. Within this broad picture, there are minor variations with regard to the particular forms of discrimination and exclusion in respect of each group.

Civil Society No Pillar of Strength

The contemporary discourse on democracy places great trust in the power of the civil society to exert pressure with a view to correcting the wrongs of the State, giving voice to the voiceless, taking up issues not usually raised by political parties, mobilising public opinion on matters of concern which get ignored or obliterated in State policy and acting as a bulwark for upholding the human rights of citizens against the arbitrary actions and excesses of the State and organised interests. In this manner, it bridges the gaps in the functioning of democracy and is complementary to its processes. The civil society is conceptualised as a loose formation of diverse groups/interests such as the media, NGOs, academics, professionals, social activists etc., which, by virtue of their enlightened thinking, autonomy from State control and organisational strength are credited with requisite capacity and courage to discharge this role.

Media

This ideal role of civil society, if it ever existed or exists anywhere is, not observed in India. The media which is a powerful institution of the civil society, for example, far from being neutral and objective in its activities, mirrors the interests of the dominant sections of society. Its workforce overwhelmingly comes from the upper castes and upwardly urban middle class. The coverage of news, stories and programmes reflects this bias starkly. The vast sections of rural and urban poor and socially marginalised groups receive very little attention. The control exercised over the media by business interests ensures that the selection, coverage of news editorials and presentation of views reflect their ideological position on important matters and agenda of policy and governance. Its undemocratic character is not merely evident from its irrelevance to the large majority of population whose concerns, suffering and struggles, fail to find space in its action but also from its politician bashing and concealed contempt for representative institutions. While it is hugely applauded by the interested class for taking up their causes and exerting pressure on the Government, it rarely gives voice to the victims of State policies and actions of State agencies such as displacement from land, human rights violations by security forces, poverty, hunger, exploitation, denial of justice and all round neglect of and the bias against the marginalised groups. Media even fails to assert its autonomy and buckles down under pressure from Government agencies. It suppresses news, fails to broadcast stories/interviews under this pressure, projects the narrative of the Government and explicitly supports the establishment and applauds the work of security forces and ignores their excesses, and human rights violatious in areas where people are in conflict with the State. It has failed to inspire confidence in its role as an objective observer of the situation and an unbiased reporter of the truth. The huge damage it can cause to the democracy is on account of the power it exercises in moulding public opinion and shaping the direction of the policies.

NGOs

NGOs too provide no sustenance to democracy. These organisations, largely manned by persons from the middle class, have neither a representative character nor a democratic structure. They are also reluctant to submit to any social accountability. They are skewedly spread with presence largely in the urban and the more easily accessible rural locations and do not evolve from grassroot level mobilisation. Their proliferation in the recent past is on account of the liberal funding provided by the national and international donors and the government. Their activities are, therefore, confined to the agenda of their financiers and continue as long as the funding is available. They choose to focus on the delivery of programmes of the Government or the execution of donor-funded projects and avoid issues which may bring them in conflict with the State. For these reasons, NGOs are reluctant to raise their voice against the State or the donors even when their policies and actions are responsible for the plight of the people they claim to serve for fear of losing their 'funds'. In many areas, where people have mobilised themselves or with external help against the State policies/actions which hurt them, the role of NGOs has usually been negative and counterproductive. While there are some exceptions which defy this description, overall, the NGOs neither deepen democracy nor provide correctives to the neglect of people by the State nor support to the people in their own efforts to seek social justice. The best among them can be credited with highlighting of the problems faced by the people, articulating their interests and advocacy of the viewpoint of struggling people in the limited area in which they work.

Academia

Likewise, academia is no pillar of strength of democracy. The academic research is virtually captured by funding agencies—the international donors, private funding organisations or the governments. This research, therefore, caters to the agenda and interests of the donor agencies and the governments. With little untied funding available, the bulk of research on social issues fails to provide substantial information and findings necessary to unravel the impact of State policies and actions, hold the Government accountable and lend intellectual support to those raising their voice against them so as to strengthen democracy. The academics/professionals are also too easily co-opted by the Government/donors with assignments and other favours to take a stand which may be unpalatable to them notwithstanding the few exceptions who refuse to be attracted to such enticements and do voice their views whether against the Government or international funding agencies.

Intelligentsia

The role of intelligentsia in raising issues of social justice, equity, human rights communalism, authoritarian tendencies etc., is far from inspiring . This is evident from the lack of sensitivity and commitment to speak up on such issues or lend their moral support to them. Even in the capital city, it is difficult to get sufficient numbers for a peaceful demonstration or a protest march or meeting to express solidarity with people struggling for their rights, dignity equity and justice. They are too busy with their daily lives to find time to share the agony and anguish of a large number of their countrymen who are victims of oppression, neglect, violence and injustice.

Social Movements

The brightest aspect of the civil society is observed in the movements emanating from grassroot level mobilisation of poor people by social activists on issues which concern them most and which political parties do not take up. These issues revolve around displacement, land and forest rights, food security, education, health, information, transparency in development, exploitation of labour, degradation of environment, water scarcity, electoral reforms, human rights violations, atrocities etc. Some of these public campaigns have achieved substantial success. These movements have provided a platform for participation to the marginalised strata of society which the political institutions with all their legitimacy fail to do and, therefore, further the cause of democracy. But social activism is plagued by fragmentation, lack of solid organisational strength and the individual-centric nature of operations and lacks the potential to build a composite countrywide mass movement which can energise and deepen democracy. The civil society, therefore, fails to live up to its contemplated role of bridging the wide gaps in our democracy. This, by no means, underestimates the achievements registered by its institutions in respect of some important social issues.

Governance Dimension

Flawed Strategy to Deal with Social Tensions

Tensions can arise in any polity for a variety of reasons. The most common cause is the resentment in some social groups about the perceived injustice or feeling of discriminatory treatment meted out to them and the failure of the existing institutions to address it. This is particularly true of those who are marginalised on account of their numerical strength, cultural, ethnic, religious or historical factors. These tensions are more likely to occur in a society where there are diverse social groups with unequal status, power and access to productive resources, benefits of development and advancement opportunities. The tensions also result from State policies which have differential impact on people. Those who experience the adverse impact of such policies may feel aggrieved and agitated. These tensions can develop into conflicts, if not resolved in time. The conflicts often turn violent, if the aggrieved persons lose hope of getting the conflicts settled or if the agencies concerned do not handle them with empathy and consideration. This is precisely what has happened and has resulted in a million mutinies' to use Naipaul's characterisation. There are several typologies of tensions in India emerging from a wide variety of factors which include political neglect, inequitable policies, social exclusion, economic exploitation, physical insecurity, cultural assault, denial of human rights, poor performance in implementing progressive laws/declared policies and programmes, failure to deliver justice and unresponsiveness of the institutions to redress grievances. These causes are not mutually exclusive and a number of them may exist in a given case. The aforesaid tensions have been permitted to simmer for too long and have, therefore, progressed into full scale conflicts involving the concerned groups with the State. The aggrieved groups have launched movements of varying intensity to draw attention to their grievances. The protests have usually been curbed with strong police action. If no remedial measures are taken by the State agencies to address the root causes of protests and they are suppressed with massive use of force and leaders implicated in multiple serious cases, such groups may take to violence. This violence then becomes the ground for repression and counter-violence by the State, resulting in the formation of conflict-ridden zones which invites even harsher measures from the State such as the extension of draconian laws, combing operations, closure of an area/areas to outside agencies, relocation of population etc.

This progression of tension into violence typically reflects the failure of the State to constructively deal with the perceived injustice or feeling of discrimination experienced by some social groups. Its initial response is to ignore the early stages of social tensions and, when it assumes a violent expression, the attempt is to concentrate on curbing violence rather than addressing the cause/causes which gave rise to them. It is precisely this nature of response that jeopardises democracy because violence and counterviolence then become endemic rendering normal institutional functioning unviable. Politics takes a back seat and security forces take over the area. This is what may be termed as 'security oriented response' to social protest movements and political conflicts with violent overtones. This response has characteristic features which have grave implications for democracy. These features are:

a) State targets violence in such movements and not the causes of it since violence disrupts normal life and functioning of the Government. Dealing with violence, therefore, becomes its sole preoccupation. This view is justified on the ground that unless violence is curbed, no alternative mode of conflict resolution is possible.
b) The 'violent' expression of these movements is viewed as a problem of maintenance of public order to be handled by security agencies. In the more serious type of cases, such as the insurgencies, the response of the Government is to elevate the level of disorder to that of 'grave threat' to internal security and curb it through military operations. The approach conveniently fails to contextualise the movements in the perceived injustices and long standing grievances which have remained unaddressed. This view provides no space for addressing violence through delivery of justice, participatory development and responsive governance and involvement of the aggrieved in decision making. Government often does talk of speeding up development of affected areas in such cases in its official discourse but only as a minor adjunct to its security-

centric strategy to deal with the situation. In practice, however, this development part gets ignored or deprioritised and security-centric governance predominates. Further, the little development that is undertaken in such areas is oriented towards infrastructure creation facilitating security operations rather than meeting the acute needs of the affected people. This strategy forecloses political options to engage in negotiation and accommodation of grievances and further erodes the relevance of political institutions and processes to their lives.

c) Security forces in such situations are freely granted enormous powers to curb violence backed by draconian laws which deny the civil rights guaranteed by the Constitution. The sidelining of civil administration forecloses even the limited space of registering complaints against the highhandedness of security forces and seeking their intervention. In states affected by such situations, usually a retired army or police officer is appointed as the Governor to ensure that the elected government does not interfere in the work of the security forces and the latter get a free hand to restore order.

d) The preoccupation to curb violence results in condonation by the Government of excesses of security forces, violations of rule of law and disregard for human rights such as fake encounters, enforced disappearance of persons detained by security forces, torture of those in custody, sexual abuse of women etc. The draconian laws virtually provide impunity to these forces from any external accountability—social, political and legal.

e) The excessive use of force is further reinforced by keeping a lid on information. This is done by disallowing civil society groups, political workers, academics, activists to enter the area and looking into the ground reality by talking to the affected people. The victims or their relatives are threatened not to speak.

Anyone who questions the action of security forces is treated as a terrorist/Maoist or its sympathiser. Recently one highly acclaimed academic and two others who accompanied her who had visited the area to look into the situation were implicated in a murder case allegedly to punish her for her critique of the security establishment (Gupta, 2016). Journalists are arrested, intimidated and cases foisted on them. Physical attacks on them by vigilance groups are covertly encouraged by the State and or powerful politicians (Gupta, 2016) Human rights activists are dealt with scorn and are specifically targeted for action under draconian laws so as to dissuade others from 'daring' to probe the police action. They are charged with abetment of terrorism.

f) The failure in curbing violence of the movement by counterviolence of the State and the desire to reduce risk to the lives of their own men (security personnel) induces the security forces to encourage non-state actors to resist and appropriately respond to the violence of the insurgents for which they are given arms, political support and protection against legal accountability. This virtually amounts to outsourcing the core function of the State. 'Salwa Judum' in Chhattisgarh was a typical example of this strategy which was being adopted elsewhere also. As a part of security-centric strategy, the victimised people in some areas are often shifted from their land and homes and huddled together in makeshift camps ostensibly to 'protect them from violence' of insurgents where they live in abysmal conditions under the vigil of security forces. The non-state actors then become the unofficial arm of the security forces and target those whom they suspect to be sympathisers of insurgents for violent elimination. This violent action which involves loss of life and physical injury and destruction of material, abuse of women etc., neither attracts legal nor police action. This strategy is given the cover of a spontaneous movement of self-defence. In this fratricidal war, the aggrieved people face the brunt of mortality and injury. The bulk of the people in the affected areas who are neither on the side of insurgents nor the Government become victims of violence from all agencies—Government, insurgents and the non-State actors of the self-defence movement. The strategy 'continues' to be practised in covert ways (though officially discontinued) despite the observation of the Supreme Court that "lawless violence in response to violence by Maoist/Naxalitie insurgency, has not solved the problem, and instead it will only perpetuate the cycles of more violence" (cited in Guha, 2016).

g) The scale, intensity and approach of security operations lead to considerable collateral damage. The restrictions on outsiders moving into the area is precisely aimed at preventing the flow of truthful information from the area and the registration of an investigation into the complaints of the victims against excesses of the security forces and the violence of the 'self-defence' movement. The area becomes a 'war zone' and there is total loss of democratic space.

Notwithstanding the fact, elections are regularly conducted on time in the areas under security cover, can such an approach ever sustain faith in democracy of the people who are victims of violence from multiple sources and condemned to live in camps? Can they even get over the perceptual fear and feeling of deprivation in villages or retreat into the forests or migrate to other areas? Democracy has rendered itself irrelevant because it endorses this approach to deal with a movement which delegitimises politics, dehumanises people, degenerates those engaged in their 'security', insulates the affected area and people from civil society groups, media and political organisations and penalises those who seek to establish contact with affected people to gather information about violations of the rule of law and human rights. This strategy abandons the alternative of mobilising people democratically to evolve a humane, constructive and socially acceptable mode of managing conflict and its violent fall out. It cannot bridge the wide gap between its declared policies and performance, engage in dialogue with the aggrieved groups, or address their grievances and accommodate their legitimate interests and aspirations (CSDS, 2008). That all major mainstream political parties have failed to resist this 'security oriented response' shows that even they have no confidence in the ability of democratic processes to deal with such conflicts.

Economic Dimension

Paradigm of Development

Democracy and development are interrelated. Democracy is assumed to promote equitable development which, in turn, strengthens the foundations of polity and society. If, however, the nature of development fails to ensure equitable outcomes, it tends to weaken the urge for democracy and people become inclined to look for alternative forms of polity where this could be achieved. The development paradigm pursued since independence has served the interests of the dominant sections of society which are placed higher in the hierarchy of caste, class and the distribution of power. The large sections of the poor and socially marginalised groups have, in fact, been victims of 'development'. They have neither achieved higher incomes nor improved access to productive resources. They have also not got opportunities for advancement, or human development and better quality of life. The development model has, in fact, by and large, worsened their condition. It continues to deprive them of whatever little access they had to productive assets and livelihood opportunities and life supporting environmental resources. It displaces them from land and living space without any provision for alternative arrangement. The technology used by development activities undervalues their labour. Overall, the development has caused a spiral of impoverishment, social disruption and an uncertain future for them. It has tended to exacerbate inequalities and promoted the flow of benefits from the poor to the wealthier sections.

Globalisation

The vision of democracy is now facing severe strains from the forces outside the state as well. The most powerful of such forces are the global economic interests with which the country has progressively integrated. The subservience of the nation state to the imperatives of neoliberal globalisation has led to the severe erosion of its autonomy in making decisions which are in the interests of its people. The nation state is now increasingly required to submit to the agenda of global institutions, multinational corporations and other forces. The agenda of globalisation only responds to the interests of the international capital and the developed countries which have deeply adversarial implications for large sections of the poor in the country. The nation state is in no position to disregard this agenda and to accommodate the aspirations of the people and, therefore, increasingly translates this agenda into national policies and programmes. This policy process makes democratic institutions totally irrelevant. They end up by becoming mere rubber stamping authorities for these policies. The democratic processes turn out to be rituals to endorse the decisions taken under this pressure increasingly, the policies that are being pursued tend to divert control over productive resources from the people to the corporate agencies, rob people of their livelihood and expose them to the destitute labour market. Similarly, the development sectors like education and health have to be opened up for the international capital. This results in increased costs and graded provision of services and quality based on the paying capacity. Simultaneously, the State provision of services shrinks. This hugely restricts the access of the poor to these services on account of their unaffordability. The infrastructural and industrial development is ruining the environment irreparably and thus causing immense misery to the people dependent upon it for their survival. The State when faced with this evidence is reluctant to rigorously implement its environmental laws, however weak, to protect the people adversely affected by the deteriorating environment and inter-generational interests. It looks the other way to the fast deteriorating water resources, quality of air and degradation of land and biodiversity to placate the capital. Regrettably, the democratic institutions—legislature, executive and even judiciary endorse this model of fast track economic development leaving the people with no constitutional channel redressal. Lately, higher judiciary has taken up a few cases such as addressing the problem of severe air pollution in Delhi.

Increasing Inequalities

This paradigm of growth and development has enormously increased inequality. This inequality has many facets—economic, social, regional, spatial etc. Every dimension of inequality has grown rapidly. While the country has boasted a high rate of growth (7-8%) during the past few years, enhancing incomes and opportunities of advancement for a small class the growth process has adversely affected the economic and social conditions of the overwhelming majority (Bhaduri, 2008).

- As regards inequality in income, wealth and assets, around three-fourths of the population (836 million) are poor and vulnerable with DPCI levels of less than $2 per day. Of this, 392 million live with an average per capita consumption of Rs. 20 a day (NCEUS, 2006).
- On the basis of $ 2 a day as purchasing power parity 80% of rural and nearly 70% of the urban inhabitants would be poor (Mander, 2015).
- In the 2016 Global Hunger Index, India has almost the lowest score of the 36.9 in the list of 132 nations with only three African States (Central African Republic), Chad and Zambia below it and has a very low position of 130 in the UN Human Development Index. On the other hand as per the Credit Suisse's Global Wealth Data Book 2014, the top percentile of population owns upto 49% of India's wealth.
- The net worth of billionaires in India increased twelve times in 15 years (Mander, 2015). From two resident billionaires with an income of $ 3.2 billion in mid-

nineties, the number grew to 46 and their share in GDP from 1 to 10% in 2012. This number has now risen to 97. India has the third largest number of billionaires, third longest middle class and single largest concentration of poor in the world (Mander, 2015).

- The richest 10% hold more than half of country's assets. The poorest 10% own only 0.4% of the share (Jaydev et al, 2007). Income of the richest 0.01% of the population was 150-200 times larger than that of the poorest (NCEUS, 2006). Its regional dimension is that the ratio of urban income to rural income has increased from 1.6 (1951) to 4.5 in recent years (Kurien, 2007).
- As per 68th Round (2011-12) the MPCs of Rs. 1,281.45 for rural areas is half of Rs. 2,401.68 for urban areas. Underlying this economic inequality is the entrenched social inequality driven by the hierarchical social structure of society. This social inequality also overwhelms regional inequality and exercises dominance over gender inequality (Kannan, 2008). The SCs and STs are at the bottom of this layer with Muslims just above them.
- The educational and health status, consumption level and informal nature of work are associated with social inequality, poverty and vulnerability. Another dimension of inequality is sectoral, revealing the vulnerability of the farm sector.
- Due to distress, nearly three lakh farmers have committed suicide in recent years. Though at a macro-level as per NSSO 59th Round almost 50% of farming are indebted, households, around 82% of the farm households are in perennial debt in Maharashtra and AP (Reddy & Mishra, 2009). In a Maharashtra Government survey of over 17 lakh households, i.e. all farmers households in the six 'crisis districts', close to seven million persons were in distress (Sainath, 2008, Kamath, 2008).
- The disparity is also reflected in inter-sectoral and intra-

> sectoral growth. From a social point of view, the disparity between different classes creates resentment when people compare their position with other groups. This undemocratic nature of economy, therefore, carries the risk of derailing political democracy unless there is a radical reversal of the course.

An economy driven by flows from foreign capital and oriented to external demand or demand for luxury goods from the richer sections of its own society at the cost of employment for the masses, access to land and rural assets for peasants and social needs of the people (health, education, social security, etc.) cannot sustain political democracy. Already the process has begun to limit access to political democracy as evident in the laws enacted by Rajasthan and Haryana Governments to restrict the right to contest only to those who fulfil certain qualifications in Panchayat elections.

Changing Character of Elite

With the shift to the neoliberal economy and its alignment to global economic order, the social character of the elite domineering over the State has undergone some change. Earlier, the landed class was the most powerful among the organised groups in the Indian society followed by the industrial and urban elite. The State apparatus was effectively used by this class to serve its interests. In the current dispensation, while industrial and urban elites continue to be part of the power structure, landed elite has lost its pre-eminence. The corporates have emerged as the most organised group in the country exercising their clout in economic decision making. This capturing of the State apparatus is facilitated by international financial institutions—IMF, WB, WTO. These corporates have penetrated the State apparatus effectively and use it to further their interests despite the intense opposition and even hostility of the people. Never before the State in India has so heavily tilted in favour of the capital and its economic and political institutions have so completely embraced this tilt. While there are many areas where this tilt can be observed, its most pronounced manifestation lies in the transfer of productive resources—land, water, forests, minerals to the corporates from the people who draw their livelihood and sustenance from them. Trade unions have been decimated through so-called labour reforms. The existing legal protections have been diluted and the remaining ones have been rendered virtually unenforceable and violations by employers are ignored Corporates have consequently extracted huge financial benefits. The corporates have co-opted the legislators to support such decisions. They have effectively infiltrated the electoral process through a number of ways. These include funding of political parties, procuring tickets for their candidates, contesting elections in 'crucial constituencies' directly, financing the election expenses of many candidates, providing 'various facilities' to some elected members for supporting their interests and even by managing seats in the Rajya Sabha. In this manner, they succeed in getting laws enacted and policies enunciated to further their interests. This has serious implications for democracy as the multinational corporations are outside the ambit of social and political accountability of the nation states.

Governance Dimension

Unresponsive, Insensitive and Partisan

The strong point of democracy is its ability to assess the needs of the people and to provide them space for influencing decision making to secure them. In short, it lies in the feeling that they matter in deciding how the State relates to their lives and translates their needs and aspirations into deliverables. The quality of governance is crucial to the sustenance of that feeling. It concretises the collective will of the people into tangible policy instruments, design of institutional arrangements and processes to deliver them and ensures through monitoring and political control that the benefits reach the target groups. Good governance sustains faith in democracy and the lack of it alienates people from it. Democracy in India is getting discredited, besides other factors listed above, due to insensitive, unresponsive and partisan governance. This insensitivity is reflected in the lack of performance in respect of precisely those areas where the interests of the poor and the socially marginalised sections are concerned whereas the interests of the elite are pursued with vigour and effectiveness. For example, there is a wide gap between the policy instruments of affirmative action such as the right-based entitlements and protection from violence which target the vulnerable groups and the performance with regard to their implementation. The poor performance in this regard is on account of the indifference as well as caste/class bias of the implementing agencies which is compounded by resistance of the dominant sections who perpetuate the existing iniquitous order. The Governance failed to reorient the implementing agencies and eliminate resistance from the society. In this manner, the democratic will to transform society gets defeated as the governance fails to deliver what it has decided. On the other land, the clearance of projects relaxing the existing provisions of law/laws is pursued with alacrity in order that the delay does not increase the transaction cost to the corporates.

The insensitivity of governance is also markedly reflected in the push towards the neoliberal economy and globalisation replacing the welfare economy. The governance reforms have facilitated this policy change which serves the interests of a small class—corporate groups, political rulers, bureaucracy, technocracy, larger farmers and upwardly mobile sections. A large section of people are its victims. They lose land, living space, livelihood, fail to get subsidised social services and get pushed into casual, insecure work at low wages, suffer hazardous working conditions and poor quality of life and face displacement, impoverishment, and social disruption. The governance is insensitive to this adverse impact. The political leaders ignore the will of the vast majority of people who want changes in economic policies. The democratic institutions fail to mould governance in terms of decision making in a manner that benefits different sections of society.

Governance is not merely insensitive but also unresponsive. This is the commonest refrain when ordinary people talk about their interface with officials and the working of institutions in their daily lives. The unresponsiveness of governance is also evident from the widespread dissatisfaction which people in general and poor people in particular have with persons in authority. The refusal to meet people and give them a hearing, failure to register their complaints, indifference to attend to complaints when registered, lack of transparency in dealings, and rude behaviour are only some of its manifestations. Common people have to move from pillar to post to get their ordinary problems settled. The frustration on this account frequently leads to protests and sometimes to violence. The interface of police and civil administrators with people is replete with such instances. This unresponsiveness also displays a class bias. The behaviour of people in authority is extremely solicitous when people with status, position and money are involved. This differentiated response irks ordinary people even more. There is pervasive cynicism that nothing can get done without the recommendation or '*sifarish*' from a VIP. It also lowers their trust in democracy.

The governance has also lost its credibility on account of its partisan attitude in contentious matters. This is so commonly observed when rules and regulations are bent or ignored in the case of those with influence and power while they are minutely and rigorously observed in the case of others. This inequality of treatment generates resentment in people and cynicism about democratic credentials of the polity. Not merely the common people, but political workers also experience this partisanship in governance when institutions fail to act in a politically neutral manner and brazenly tilt their discretion and decisions to favour the ruling party. Even autonomous institutions like the CBI, CEC have been accused of overt or covert political pressure not to speak of the personnel in the bureaucratic apparatus.

Pervasive Corruption

Governance also derails democracy on account of pervasive corruption. This has reached such a state that appointments in public services can be purchased (Sen, 2009). Economic decisions carry their price tag, seats in elective bodies can be managed with financial contribution. Some have argued that in some cases, judicial decisions at lower levels can also be influenced with a variety of favours. The corruption in dealing with the police is too well known to be mentioned. Even in insurgency-affected areas, decisions on detentions, release and the level of treatment meted out to the detainees in many cases are reported to be driven by the readiness of the kin of the affected persons to pay the amount sought. The beneficiaries of Government programmes are routinely asked to pay in order to get the requisite entitlements. When corruption rules the roost, the common people, particularly the poor, get most alienated from the system because of their incapacity to meet this 'cost'. When they do not get what is due to them, their faith in the system gets shattered.

Weak Accountability Mechanisms

Democracy in India could have redeemed some of its credibility if governance was transparent, subjected to intense public scrutiny and was amenable to effective political accountability. None of these features exists, notwithstanding the recently enacted RTI, constitutional arrangement of parliamentary accountability of the executive, intra-organisational structures of vigilance and judicial review of Government decisions. The political and bureaucratic corruption rarely gets punished. Even if trapped and prosecuted, the corrupt manage to get away without any damage. The pervasive denial of justice to the poor and the marginalised does not even become a cause for disciplinary action against officials found guilty let alone result in their prosecution. The action against officials in such cases may at best involve transfer from their existing assignments but nothing more. On the other hand, there are huge rewards when officials use their position for partisan action whether to please the ruling political class or serve the interests of the corporates. The complaints of caste/ethnic/communal bias against the members of the SCs/STs/Muslims by officials even when loudly voiced through protests and agitations are simply ignored rather than lead to investigation and action. The ritual of internal enquiries is all that is resorted to in the case of encounters, custodial deaths and torture etc., when a complaint gets wide publicity. But such enquiries invariably support the official version with no penal action against those involved. Rather, some officials known for their propensity to use such methods of policing get rewards and medals.

Flawed Direction of Reforms

Ironically, there has been a huge discourse on governance in the recent past. The Tenth Five Year Plan, for the first time, carried a chapter on the subject. The Second Administrative Reforms Commission produced volumes on it. The Central Government has drawn up a huge agenda of good governance and promoted it with vigour. But this agenda has a narrow checklist of institutional and procedural reforms which do not call into question policies loaded against the poor, the social biases of the institutions and personnel and the abysmal failure to implement affirmative policies, and pervasive denial of justice to the poor. There is no reference to the interface of governance with SCs/STs and minorities. It does not even mention the nexus between corporate interests and officials which is destroying even the neutrality and objectivity of bureaucracy. The 'governance' in official parlance is conceptualised ignoring the political social and cultural context and, therefore, fails to identify those aspects which need reform from this viewpoint. The agenda of governance reform, like the governance itself, is geared to address issues which affect the elite sections. The interests of the poor and marginalised are not on its radar. With this picture of governance, there is little to enthuse these sections, sustain their interest and inspire their trust in democracy.

The Positive Side: Institutional Stability

The optimists amidst this gloom cite the following positive features to sustain their faith in democracy and argue that everything is not lost yet (CSDS, 2008). One, democracy has survived despite challenges faced from time to time except for a brief interruption of the Emergency. The fact that the mass mobilisation of people forced the Government to restore democracy is itself an assurance about the strength of people's power to check such drifts even though this mobilisation was done outside the structures of the representative democracy. But similar efforts are not forthcoming in respect of the prolonged 'emergency' conditions in some parts of the country and numerous other serious erosions of democracy.

Second, the institutions of democracy—the federal structure, representative legislature and an executive formally accountable to it, independent judiciary, numerous watchdog institutions looking after the interests of special groups, a 'free' media and a reasonably active segment of the civil society are intact. These institutions may have been captured by the elite or become moribund, dysfunctional or disoriented, but their continued existence is a sign that the democratic foundations have not broken down and institutions can be rejuvenated, reformed, reoriented and subjected to greater public scrutiny and accountability. The proceeding analysis however, brings out that this assumption lies shattered as all these institution have been hollowed out though the formal structures remain.

Third, the elections are held on time without much obstruction though with considerably more degenerated politics and increasing input of financial resources. The level of electoral participation at an average of 50%, while not vigorous is definitely an indication that the people in general are still attracted to it and wish to use it for seeking redressal of their problems. But the penetration of money and muscle power in managing electoral system the low level of rhetoric and open use of caste and religion for consolidation of vote banks are eating into the vitals of democracy. Besides, political leaders use the electoral system, to come to power by making tall promises to the people but ignore their concerns thereafter. Despite the awareness in the civil society of falling political standards and the floating of several ideas to check it, no correctives have emerged in politics on this issue.

Fourth, the Constitutional structure has functioned without

being unduly mutilated, certain aberrations notwithstanding. But the proliferation of draconian laws and their extension to certain areas continuously for long periods leading to the denial of fundamental rights and the massive human rights violations by security forces without any punitive action against them are causes for serious concern. This is particularly so when even the judiciary has failed to check this impunity much to the suffering of the affected persons. No wider political platform has emerged to support the 'local people's movements' against the withdrawal of these laws. We have not put in place effective checks to prevent their misuse nor initiated punitive measures against their misuse in future. Worse, despite political control over the Army, the latter has persistently and strongly opposed any dilution of AFSPA not to speak of replacing or withdrawing it. Such is the fragility of democracy that the Home Minster in the last UPA government confessed that he was unable to push through the reform of AFSPA and humanise it, because the Defence Minister/representing Armed Forces strongly opposed it/and the PM was unable to overrule him. This situation is much worse in the existing NDA government as it demonises any attempt to question the actions of security forces.

Fifth, the federal structure survives with occasional tensions but with expanding central jurisdiction. The resistance of states to this trend is, regrettably, low. One of the reasons is that when the same party is in power in the Centre and states, the states then toe the line of the central leadership even if they have a different view. In such a situation, it becomes difficult to build a strong political front to reverse this trend. Similarly, political decentralisation by devolution of powers and resources to the Panchayati Raj bodies is not moving forward due to the resistance of political leaders and bureaucracy at the state level. Kerala has been an exception in this regard. No pressure from elected representatives of the PRIs and the people's movements has been forthcoming to break this resistance. No political party has ever raised it as an election issue as they all share the same antipathy to devolution of power.

Sixth, the emergence of a large number of regional parties

has widened the area of political participation reversing the trend of single party domination. The smaller groups now find some space to share power. Though regional parties are castigated by the large all India parties, for their narrow political base, their positive feature lies in a certain amount of accommodation of the diversities. But this power sharing is restricted to the dominant castes/caste which form/forms the political base of the party. Minorities and women fail to get adequate representation in any major all India party while the representation of SCs/STs in ministerial positions is tokenistic. Other small groups just get left out. This reduces any hope of achieving inclusiveness in politics.

Seventh, social groups which feel alienated and disillusioned and resort to a variety of protest movements with or without violence are making a political statement that the existing institutional mechanisms have failed to deliver justice to them. They are exerting pressure on the Government to act. This is a serious challenge to which the Government has failed to respond positively. Such a response would have given primacy to dialogue and negotiations to resolve conflicts and to address their grievances, rather than to decimating such movements. Despite achieving some degree of success in pursuing this strategy in the case of Mizoram, Bodoland, Gorkhaland and partially in Nagaland, this has not been attempted in J&K and in Naxalite areas and other states of the North East. The valiant efforts of the civil society to facilitate such a dialogue in the case of the Naxalite movement in Andhra Pradesh (CCC, 2002) however collapsed due to the faltering commitment of the State Government and the trust deficit on either side.

Eighth, a peasants' spontaneous movement, later backed by a local political party and some groups in civil society against acquisition of their land and state violence unleashed on them in response to their peaceful protest culminated in the closure of the car project in Singur and the scrapping of land acquisition in the Nandigram area of West Bengal. The State Government later decided not to acquire land against the wishes of the peasants. A wider political mobilisation later resulted in the loss of power at the state level and seats in the Parliament. The wider mobilisation on this issue at the national level forced the Government at the Centre to change the colonial Land Acquisition Act which conceded some of the demands of the movement. The NDA Government at the centre, has however, reversed most of the concessions through an ordinance. This was hugely resisted by peasants' movements across the country. The matter is currently held up in the Parliament. But some states have already enacted laws to reverse those changes so as not to hamper the economic growth. This shows, the nexus between the corporates, the political class and the bureaucracy and undermines even minimal faith in democracy to get justice against the powerful forces.

Ninth, some groups in the civil society have shown the 'capacity to mobilise the political opinion for exerting pressure on the Government to make interventions to protect the interests of the poor and the marginalised groups which were not taken up by any political party. The success in this endeavour was observed in the enactment of the Right to Information Act, 2004, the Scheduled Tribes and Traditional Forest Dwellers (Recognition of Rights) Act, 2006, the National Rural Employment Guarantee Act, 2007, and Right to Food Security Act, 2013 and Right to Fair Compensation and Transparency in Land Acquisition Rehabilitation and Resettlement Act, 2013. The Social Security for Unorganized Workers Act, 2009, though not the outcome of civil society efforts, still responds in some measure to the demand of the trade unions for long ignored by the neoliberal economy. But this success means little as the implementation is tardy and there is little political will to activate it.

Tenth, a small number of social activists, backed by certain sections of the media and radical sections of intelligentsia also have succeeded in keeping alive the issue of justice to the victims of Gujarat pogrom. They were responsible for bringing out citizens' reports on Gujarat communal riots against concerted move by the then State Government and the Government at the Centre to put a lid on this episode and cover up their role in it. When the judiciary at the state level failed to inspire confidence in dealing with the alleged process of manipulation of investigation and trial of riots cases, the same pressure was also responsible for urging the Supreme Court to reopen the closed cases, get them investigated afresh under the direct supervision of the Court and to transfer their trial to another state. Regrettably, no political party took up this matter. With the change of Government at the Centre, even this little success is eroding and the prosecuting and investigating agencies are buckling under pressure to dilute these cases so as to benefit the accused persons. Besides, even this little success was not registered in respect of the 1984 anti-Sikh riots and the post-Babri Maharashtra communal riots. This underlines the subservience of criminal investigation and prosecution agencies to political influence and control.

Eleventh, the pressure by media has been responsible for the expeditious hearing of the criminal cases against some celebrity accused persons who manipulate the investigative and judicial processes to their advantage. This again exposes the fault-lines of the political institutions which were not willing to take up the issue of denial of justice. But this campaign by the media is confined to a few cases involving persons from the middle class. The same media is not persuaded to take up the same type of cases relating to the numerous poor persons who have suffered the same fate if not worse. The media exposure to hate speeches, communalisation of politics, assets and criminal records of contestants in elections etc., are matters which democratic institutions should have raised but did not.

Despite the global financial meltdown and the resultant recession in global economy and the jobless growth in the country there is no diminution in enthusiasm for a corporate-financed faster economic growth model for its ability to trickle down benefits to the poor in terms of jobs and prosperity. The never ending march of the predatory nature of extractive capitalism therefore endures. This unfounded trust runs across political parties. There is little hope that the institutional democracy would force a direction change in political economy to alleviate the suffering of the masses.

Emerging Fascistic Trends

But the more disturbing development is the emerging fascistic trends in Indian polity with the ascendency of the ultra-Right forces riding piggyback on democracy, 'grasping astutely the political potency of resentment in the left behinds of globalization' and rampant corruption in the establishment and promising jobs and prosperity to millions of frustrated aspirants. Foreign political observers have found this triumph of 'Alternative Right' a global phenomenon attributed to the 'incendiary appeal of demagoguery' (Mishra, 2016) demonisation religious and ethnic minorities, immigrants and projection of the leader as an efficient executive who could shake up the ossified set-up (Ayers and Twinning, 2016) to provide jobs and restore power, wealth and glory to the nation (Mishra, 2016). This fascistic shift in governance and politics is seen in the deification of the nation, unquestioned acceptance of authority and support to the Armed Forces, pursuit of a muscular foreign policy, expansion of the power of the State over the lives of citizens, building personality cult of the leader (Guha, 2016). It also covers filling institutions with loyalists sharing ideological inclinations of the ruling party, intimidation of NGOs, human rights activists, writers, artists, journalists with dissenting views, control of universities to sanitise their social ambience by preventing free debate, criminalising contrarian views and influencing the content of the academic curricula and monitoring every word put out in the media (Phillipose, 2016). There is a pronounced push towards changing the public discourse with the aggressive pursuit of thought and behaviour change of people in conformity with the ruling dispensation's idea of culture, nationalism and moral propriety. Its cruelest expressions were manifested in the violence perpetrated on Muslims and Dalits under the garb of checking cow slaughter. These forces draw strength from the current political regime and have expanded their activities enormously. The reaction from the civil society is subdued while the political parties, as in other matters, have, failed to stand up to these challenges. This underlines as never before that not only the democracy but even the fundamental Constitutional values and entitlements are in peril as the nations institutions and processes are unable to guarantee them.

Salvaging Democracy: A Challenge

The above narrative points towards the need for shaking up democracy in radical ways so as to salvage it from its existing slide to the bottom. There is a huge deficit of political mobilisation for this purpose. The pressure for this radical transformation has to come from outside the institutional politics for which the consciousness generated by the people's movements including those of workers and peasants has to be sustained, widened and deepened so as to convert it into a force strong enough to compel the political class to take note of it. Such a mass movement has to necessarily take on board various insurgency groups to accommodate their transformative agenda as also wean them away from violent methods to achieve their goal. Efforts are also called for to present a blueprint of the political economy indicating institutional and societal change, and the widening and deepening of participation which puts masses and particularly the marginalised and their interests centre stage. The task is daunting and virtually looks impossible considering the experience in the preceding more than fifty years. But if the requisite forces do not emerge to use the route of mass democratic movements for restructuring and reforming institutional democracy and its processes, the prospects of lapsing into an authoritarian regime and worse stare at us. It is our common task as citizens to push for the this agenda of change.

REFERENCES

Anand, S. (2009). Caste and the world. *The Hindu*, May 24.

Ayes, A. and Twining, D. (2016). Trump's win similar to Modi's in 2014. *Hindustan Times*, December 4.

Beetham, D. (2003). Democracy and human rights: Civil, political economic, social and cultural. In Janusz Symondes (ed.), *New dimensions and challenges for human rights*. New Delhi: Rawat.

Bhaduri, A. (2008). Predatory growth. *Economic and Political Weekly, 43* (16), 10-14.

Bhaduri, A. (2015). Development by dispossession. SR SC Public Lecture Series No. 1. Hyderabad: National Institute of Rural Development and Panchayati Raj.

Bhattacharya, K. (2016). The semantics of lawlessness. Bhopal's 'encounter' mirrors a wider culture of impunity. *India Express*, November 8.

Bhushan, P. (2009). Misplaced priorities and class bias of judiciary. *Economic and Political Weekly, 44* (14), 32-37.

Centre for Study of Developing Societies (2008). *State of democracy in South Asia: A report*. New Delhi: Oxford.

Committee of Concerned Citizens (2002). *Third Report (1997-2002)*. Hyderabad.

Daghamvar, V. (2006). *Role and image of law in India: The tribal experience*. New Delhi: Sage.

Global Hunger Index (2016). Trends in hunger. Retrieved September 12, 2016 from http://ghi.ifpri.org/.

Guha, R. (2016a). Republic of unfreedom. *Indian Express*, November, 14.

Guha, R. (2016b). Hero worship hurts democracy. *Hindustan Times*, December 4.

Gupta, A., Kashyap, P. and Khera, R. (2016). India's Aadhaar project: An assault on welfare, privacy and democracy; need for urgent debate. *Countercurrent*, November 2, 2016.

Hasan, Z. (2009). *Politics of inclusion: Castes, minorities and affirmative action*. New Delhi: Oxford.

Henry, N. and Devulapalli, R. (2015). DNA profiling bill triggers debate. *The Hindu*, July 28.

Jacob, K.S. (2009). A human rights checklist. *The Hindu*, May 20.

Jaydev, A., Motiram, S. and Vakulabharham, V. (2007). Patterns of wealth disparities in India during liberalization era. *Economic and Political Weekly*, 42(38), 3853-63.

Kamath, P. (2008). Address entrenched structural inequalities, says Sainath. *The Hindu*, February 6.

Kannabiran, K.G. (2004). *The wages of Impunity: Power, justice and human rights*. New Delhi: Orient Longman.

Kannan, K.P. (2008). Dualism, informality and social inequality. *Indian*

Society for Labour Economics, Annual Conference, December 13-15.

Khare, H. (2009). Monetization of political space. *The Hindu*, April 25.

Kurien, N.J. (2007). Widening economic and social disparities: Implications for India. *Indian Journal of Medical Research, 126* (4), 374-380.

Liberation (Central organ of CPI(ML)). Supreme Court questions the indefinite reign of AFSPA.

Makkad, S. (2009). Dalits gets posts but not power. *Hindustan Times*, May 12, 2009.

Mander, H. (2015). *Looking away: Inequality, prejudice and indifference in* New India. New Delhi: Speaking Tiger.

Mishra, P. (2016). The Incendiary appeal of demagoguery in our time. *The New York Times*. Retrieved November 13, 2016 from http://nyti.ms/2evt5DB.

Mitra, A. (2008). 85 percent of the people left out of growth process. *The Hindu*, April 2.

National Commission for Enterprises in the Unorganized Sector (2006). *Report on Social Security for Unorganized Workers*. New Delhi: Government of India.

National Election Watch (2009 and 2014). Association of democratic reforms. Retrieved June 10, 2009 and May 22, 2014 from http://national election watch.org/pages/34.

Palshikar, S. (2016). Citizens into subjects. *Indian Express*, December 2.

Panikkar, K.N. (2009). Culture as a site of struggle. *Economic and Political Weekly*, 44 (7), 34-41.

Philipose, P. (2016). No questions please; you are the media. *Indian Express*, December 12.

Planning Commission (2008). *Development challenges in extremist affected areas*. New Delhi: Planning Commission.

Raina, B. (2016). Do we need a Parliament. *Indian Express*, December 6.

Ramanathan, U. (2010). Implications of registering tracking, profiling. *The Hindu*, April 5.

Rao, Sachin (2016). People like them. *Indian Express*, February 25.

Reddy, D.N. and Mishra, S. (2009). *Agrarian crisis in India*. New Delhi: Oxford.

Sainath, P. (2009a). Price of rice, price of power. *The Hindu*, June 10.

Sainath, P. (2009b). The age of aam crorepati. *The Hindu*, June 20.

Sainath, P. (2008). Of loan waivers and tax waivers. *The Hindu*, May 19.

Sen, S. (2009). The roots of corruption. *The Indian Express*, June 25.

Sengupta, A., Kannan, K.P and Ravindran, G. (2008). India's common people: Who are they, how many are they and how do they live. *Economic and Political Weekly*, *43* (11), 49-63.

Sorabji, S. (2016). Judicial overreach. *The Indian Express*, December 1.

Sridhar, V. (2009). Corporate India has no reason to sulk. *The Hindu*, March 3.

UNDP (2015). Human development and its components. Retrieved November 22, 2016 from http://hdr.undp.org/sites/default/files/2015_human_development_report.pdf.

Verniers, G. (2016). Neta cum businessman. *Indian Express*, November, 28.

17

Labour Under Stress in Gujarat?

Atulan Guha

Section 1. Introduction

That Gujarat is one of India's fastest-growing states is widely accepted today. The statistics proclaim the fact with panache. Witness this: its per capita income is much higher compared to the All India average. The per capita income of Gujarat was 1.38 times that of All India average in 2004-05. By 2011-12 this ratio became 1.51. The unemployment rate too in Gujarat is also much lower than the All India average.[1]

One should expect, a high growth coupled with low unemployment should translate to higher wage earnings compared to the rest of India, leading to a higher standard of living for the workers. But is that really the case? Not really, as this study reveals.

Broadly speaking, three factors may be responsible for this—lack of bargaining power on the part of workers, the State's labour department's ineptitude at safeguarding workers' interests, and perpetuation of the power structure prevalent within the various village communities in the factories. These factors, or possibly their combination, have conspired to shortchange the state's labour force—both rural and urban—with respect to wage earnings. A higher output growth in farm and non-farm sectors (with the manufacturing sector contributing substantially to the non-farm output share) has not, regrettably, translated to higher wage earnings in Gujarat relative to the rest of India.

This chapter looks at both the state and All India macro-level data, case study of a GIDC (Gujarat Industrial Development Corporation) area, named Vithal Udyognagar, at Vallav-Vidyanagar (Anand District), which was conducted by the author in conjunction with relevant studies conducted by other academicians.

The structure of the chapter is as follows: Section 2 discusses the state of urban workers' earnings; Section 3 discusses the case study in Anand, and Section 4 the state of rural workers' earnings; plus there is a concluding Section.

Section 2: State of Urban Workers' Earnings

The large sample survey conducted by NSSO in 2011-12 found that the wage rates of regular salaried and casual urban workers in Gujarat were lower compared to the All India average (Table 1). In the context of casual workers this average was 1.18 times higher and for regular salaried urban workers it was 1.41 times higher than Gujarat.

What is more, both male and female urban workers continue to garner lower wages than their counterparts in daily regular urban jobs. The gap is wider for males engaged in regular employment and for females working in casual jobs. In any case, the wage gap for urban regular workers is more marked than for urban casual workers.

Table 1: Average wage (in Rs.) per day for Regular and Casual Urban workers of age 15-59 years, 2011-12

S. No.	*Casual*			*Regular*			*Gender Gap (male/female wage)*	
	Male	*female*	*person*	*male*	*female*	*person*	*Casual*	*Regular*
1. Gujarat	160.64	88.84	144.52	326.34	271.86	319.71	1.81	1.20
2. Gujarat at All India CPI-IW Price	167.07	92.39	150.30	339.39	282.73	332.50		
3. All-India	182.04	110.62	170.1	469.87	366.15	449.65	1.65	1.28
4. The Gap (S.No. 1/3)	1.13	1.25	1.18	1.44	1.35	1.41		

Source: NSSO 2011-12

Table 2: Average Wage (Rs.) per day for Regular and Casual Urban Workers of age 15-59 years, 2007-08

S. No.	*Casual*		*Regular*		*Gender Gap (male/female wage)*	
	male	*female*	*male*	*female*	*Casual*	*Regular*
1. Gujarat	108.76	55.75	215.02	181.95	1.41	1.18
2. Gujarat at All India CPI-IW Price	112.02	57.42	221.47	187.41		
3. All-India	104.63	59.57	276.04	212.86	1.62	1.30
4. The Gap (S. No. 1/3)	0.96	1.07	1.28	1.17		

Source: NSSO 2007-08

It may be observed from the above tables (Tables 1 and 2) that the gap between urban workers' daily wages in Gujarat and All-India has been growing over the years. For casual urban male workers, the All-India average daily wage was lower than Gujarat's in 2007-08. By 2011-12 this All India daily wage multiplied to 1.13 times that of Gujarat. The All India casual urban female average daily wage was 1.07 times that of Gujarat which, rose by 1.25 times by 2011-12. Similarly, the gap involving regular urban daily wages for both males and females broadened in 2011-12 from 2007-08. The gender gap narrowed down, on the other hand, for regular urban workers, while widening marginally for casual urban workers.

One may argue that this gap between All India and Gujarat wages exists due to the different sets of prices exposed to the workers. The broad trends observed in the wage-gap between Gujarat and the All India average do not change much as the All India consumer price index number for industrial workers is only 3.56[2] per cent higher than that of the consumer price index number for industrial workers in Gujarat in 2011-12. In 2007-08, this figure was 3.04 per cent.

Table 3: Contribution of Gujarat in the Sectoral GDP of India (in per cent share)

	2007-08	*2008-09*	*2009-10*	*2010-11*	*2011-12*
Agriculture & Allied	6.6	6.2	6.1	6.8	7.0
Organized Manuf.	14.7	14.6	16.6	15.7	15.9
Unorganized Manuf.	8.0	7.9	8.4	8.3	8.4
Manufacturing	12.4	12.4	14.0	13.5	13.7
Industry	11.0	11.2	12.4	12.1	12.3
Services	5.9	6.0	5.7	5.8	6.0

Source: CSO, 2013

The situation is an interesting one since Gujarat has been hailed as an industrialised state with an entrepreneurial and industry-friendly policy framework in place. The industry (including mining, manufacturing, electricity, gas and water and construction) contributed 37% GSDP to the state in 2011-12 where industries all over the country contributed 27% to India's GDP. Compared to all the Indian states, Gujarat's contribution in total manufacturing GSDP increased from about 11% in 1993-94 to 14% in 2011-12. Notably, registered manufacturing witnessed a steeper rise- from about 11% to 16%. As a matter of fact, Gujarat's contribution to India's GDP in the three sectors – agriculture and allied, industry and services has risen, if anything. Gujarat's contribution to India's agriculture and allied went up from 6.6 per cent in 2007-08 to 7 per cent in 2011-12, in industry from 11 per cent to 12.3 per cent, and in services from 5.9 per cent to 6 per cent in the corresponding periods. The State's maximum industrial contribution—also the highest—comes from organised manufacturing.

Contrary to expectations, this high growth in industries and services (coupled with low unemployment), has not translated to augmented wages relative to the rest of urban India. We can have two kinds of explanations for it.

First, the incremental manufacturing output (as pointed out by Nagaraj, 2013) of Gujarat is mostly attributable to a single industry—petroleum refining—with its share in gross value added in the state's registered manufacturing having risen from

4% in 2000-01 to nearly 25% a decade later. This is because of the output from only two refineries—the shore-based refineries of Reliance and Essar in Jamnagar. In other words, excluding petroleum refining, contributions from the other manufacturing industries has actually declined in the State. Besides the direct employment generation capacity of the refinery industry not being very high, the lowered GSDP contribution on the part of other manufacturing industries means lowered labour demand in organised manufacturing. This directly should translates to lowered urban regular wages and rising urban unemployment: the manufacturing employment rate did register a decline (with a growth rate of -2.4%) between 2004-05 and 2009-10[3]. This factual detail, however, poses a conundrum, which is that urban employment went up at the rate of 4.9 per cent in the same period. One explanation could be the increase in casual employment in the service sector. And yet, even for male urban casual workers, the wages measured at 2007-08 prices declined marginally by 2011-12.

The second line of explanation could easily have to do with the fact that the benefits of output growth are not percolating down to the workers who are not well organised to begin with and have, thus, very little bargaining power.

We did not manage to acquire data on the number of workers who are members of trade unions in Gujarat. We looked at the website of the Bhartiya Mazdoor Sangha (BMS), the trade union of the RSS and hence, a sister organization of BJP, which has been the ruling party of the state for last 15 years. The BMS website does provide a detailed membership profile: it shows that only 2.54% of its members come from Gujarat. Of India's largest states, Gujarat's membership strength ranks 13th, which reveals how the workers of Gujarat are so little organised. Organisational paucity hampers the workers' ability to fight for a greater share in the output growth or value addition.

In this situation, the State Government through its various departments including the labour department can play an important role to ensure the reasonable well being of workers by enforcing various existing laws applicable to the workers.

The dearth or scantiness of labour unions cannot be considered independent of the State's political canvas. It has to be said that workers' issues are barely heard in the State's dominant political discourse. This could be the reason for the major political parties' paltry efforts towards organising workers. If there is apathy to look into workers' interests by the major political parties of the state, naturally the State Government department too is expected to be remain inactive to protect the workers' rights.

Indira Hirway (2011) discovered in her study, *Labour and Employment under Globalisation: The Case of Gujarat*, that the labour department's capability in Gujarat regarding enforcing labour laws is far from adequate and has declined considerably over the past two decades. . The Directorate of Industrial Safety and Occupational Health, which is responsible for the enforcement of labour laws in both the organised and unorganised sectors, is highly understaffed. This is due to an unsatisfactory number of positions that are not duly filled. Add to that an ever-spiraling number of factories, the Directorate's purview expanding over unorganised units and its mandate to pay special attention to chemical factories in the state; the existing staff is spread out thin accounting for the inadequacy. This happens to hold true for all the major divisions of the state including Bhavnagar, Junagadh, and Surat. The labour commissioners' offices at the Surat division (a major industrial belt comprising a range of power looms and textile, diamond jewelry and food processing units) as well as the Vapi, Navsari and Valsad divisions are understaffed. The labour department is neither in a position to conduct inspections nor entertain complaints, let alone enforce labour laws for which a de-motivated and frustrated staff has little enthusiasm to begin with. Besides, it also has to contend with political pressure from time to time. The working environment is, thus, perfectly conducive to corruption.

A combination of all the factors mentioned above is responsible for the wage rates in Gujarat to go up at a much lower rate than the rest of India whereas, the profit rates are going up at a much faster rate than the rest of the country. The

State's high growth and high per capita income get accompanied by the higher rate of inequality in comparison with the rest of the country. As a matter of fact, urban inequality[4] (measured via the Gini Co-efficient calculated on the basis of consumption expenditure) has grown by 14.29% between 1993-94 and 2009-10. Compare this figure to the all India growth rate of 12.35% in the same period.

The unorganised urban workers are no better off. That Gujarat's urban casual workers earn lower wages than their counterparts in the rest of India has been already mentioned in Tables 1 and 2. We also discovered, during our case study (discussed in the next section) at the Vallav Vidyanagar GIDC, that the organised factory sector is faced with large scale casualisation of its workers. These workers are neither organised, nor do they have employment security. The two major labour laws primarily dealing with workers of the informal sector include the implementation of Minimum Wages Act 1948 and the Contract Labour (Regulation and Abolition) Act 1972. It stands to reason, then, that these workers who lack employment security and have a paltry trade union are unlikely to complain about the non-payment of minimum wages or violation of labour laws. This open violation can easily be arrested with regular inspections on the part of labour officers. The Hirway study (2011) indicates high inadequacy in the number of inspections conducted by the labour department under the aforementioned Acts. The number of inspections under the Minimum Wages Act covers roughly around 3-5% of the requirement while only roughly around 20-25 per cent inspections get converted into prosecutions. The number of inspections carried out under the Contract Workers' Act (5,629 in 2008) too is inadequate with a very low proportion of inspections (6-7%) converting into prosecutions. A similar plight afflicts the Child Labour Act, Inter-state Migrant Workers' Act and Equal Remuneration Act in the State of Gujarat.

In sum, both regular and casual urban workers in Gujarat earn substantially lower than their counterparts in the rest of India. And this gap in the workers' wages of urban Gujarat and urban India is increasing over time. This is despite Gujarat's higher per capita income relative to the All India average. Even as Gujarat's per capita income races ahead, its workers earn proportionately less. In other words, a rising share in profit has only fostered growing urban inequality; although just to set the record straight, urban inequality is on the rise at the all India level too albeit at a slower pace. The inadequacy of bargaining power owing to poor organisation and the labour department's inability to protect workers' interests notwithstanding, the laws of the country, have both compounded the problem.

Section 3: Case Study of Vithal Udyognagar (Vallav-Vidyanagar) GIDC in Anand

[This case study is based upon the narratives provided by the workers of this GIDC who were interviewed by the author.]

Vallav-Vidyanagar GIDC comprises four to five large companies. A large number of factories among the rest in GIDC primarily supply parts to these big companies. Apart from these companies there are other smaller companies. Most of the workers come from villages that are around the Anand-Vidyanagar city. Factory owners hail from the Patel community primarily, who also own large tracts of land on the Charotar belt. Our visit to Anand's Vallav-Vidyanagar GIDC and interaction with the workers (through semi-structured interviews) in February 2014 served to confirm the macroeconomic picture of the urban workers' earnings mentioned in the previous section.

We discovered that most employees were hired on a contractual basis, even in the big companies. There was not one factory worker who was not contract-based. Permanent employees were to be found only in the higher echelons (highly skilled professionals) of the big companies. The workers in these big companies are employed with contractors who hires them out to the big companies. While the contractors would change every 2 to 3 years, the workers continued with their same jobs in the same companies. Temporary workers, thus, work permanently in the same factories. In other words, behind the façade of 'outsourcing' jobs of a permanent nature are given to temporary workers who work more or less permanently in the same factory. Regular workers are, thus, used for permanent jobs but under the terms and conditions governing temporary workers. Thus, the labour market inflexibilities applicable to the industrial labour market through the Industrial Disputes Act are non-existent. Factories employing over 100 workers are not, employing workers under a permanent contract [In this GIDC, the smaller factories that employ less than 100 workers too do not employ workers under permanent contract.].

These contractual workers often obtain marginally less than the minimum wages applicable to skilled labour—between Rs. 210 to 230 per day. There is enough reason to believe that these big companies pay contractors at the minimum wage scale. However, the shortfall in receipt could be due to the cut taken by the contractors. Workers' wages outside the big factories within the GIDC have been generally found to be lower than the prescribed minimum wage with a high degree of variation. For skilled workers it ranges between Rs. 80 and Rs. 200 per day. Workers who have graduated from ITIs receive higher wages with a minimum of Rs. 150 per day. It needs to be borne in mind that the current minimum wages in Gujarat, even for unskilled workers outside the municipal corporation and in towns of more than 1 lakh population, amount to more than Rs. 200[5] per day. The latest figure pertaining to the minimum wages for skilled workers in the State varies between Rs. 210 and Rs. 253 (linked to sector, geographical location, and inflation). Overtime work does not merit compensation in the form of double wages. Generally speaking, single wages are paid for the overtime period. To be sure, overtime has become something of a rarity with a slowdown in industrial growth. We came across workers who, having worked on higher wages in factories closed down due to recession, now work at almost half the wages of the earlier jobs.

Our findings in the Vallav-Vidhyanagar GIDC indicate the market clearing wage rate for industrial workers as being much lower than the minimum wages. There is a substantial degree of labour market flexibility with the Minimum Wages Act not offering much resistance against wages sinking below the prescribed minimum wages. The Industrial Disputes Act too has not been coming in the way of hire and fire with most workers on temporary contracts.

The question then is: why do big companies pay higher wages (around the same as minimum wages) than the market clearing wages, which are far lower? This finding violates the neoclassical framework of the labour market according to which, if all workers and jobs are homogenous and information, search costs, and the issues concerning worker motivation and risk shifting are absent, the equilibrium wage is determined at the point where demand and supply of labour match and the labour market clears. The long run equilibrium wage would simply be equal to the value of the last worker's marginal product across all firms. Any transitory wage differentials indicate differences in labour productivity (perhaps) due to fluctuations in labour demand at the firm or sectoral level. This results in the movement of labour between segments leading to equalisation of productivity and restoration of wage equality across sectors. The question of why big companies pay higher wages may be answered via the efficiency wage hypothesis kind of argument[6]. Paying at the prescribed minimum wage rate helps the big companies retain the individual workers at the same jobs for long periods enhancing, thereby, the efficiency in the production process.

The big companies provide group medical insurance wherein the premium is partly contributed by the main employer and partly paid by workers. We did not come across contractual workers in the big companies who said they had provident fund benefits or ESI. Workers in smaller factories have no group medical insurance but in case of health problems during work all medical expenses are borne by the employers.

We did not come across any trade unions in this GIDC. The workers informed us that factory owners disallowed the formation of workers' unions and any attempt in this direction was thwarted by terminating the job contract. Another aspect of this owner-worker relationship may be linked with the socio-economic relationship among families within the villages that are around Charotar region where this Vallav-Vidyanagar GIDC is located. In these villages, the socio-economic relations are primarily dominated by the various Patel families. Some among them own the factories of the GIDC too. And it is likely that the power relations within these factories are highly influenced by the power relations within these village communities.

It needs to be emphasised that firms are legally bound to pay minimum wages, which is denied to a large number of workers as this case study indicates. In fact, the wages of many of these industrial workers do not touch the minimum wages on average. Given this situation it would be unrealistic to expect the firms to pass on the benefits of output growth to workers. And it is highly unlikely that the wages would be linked with productivity as predicted by the neoclassical theorisation of the labour market. Yet, the minimum wage scale does have a role in fixing wages as it influences the minimum reservation wages of workers, below which they are not going to work. Inflation has pushed up the workers' nominal wages since the minimum wages are inflation-linked while reservation wages reflect the workers' standard of living, which is expected to be close to subsistence level. So, the real wages are likely to be stagnant.

The macro-data of wage rate for the Gujarat State is also indicative of this fact (Table 3). Comparing the urban wages of 2011-12 measured at 2007-08 prices (the deflator used here is the ratio of end of the year consumer prices for industrial workers for 2007-08 to 2011-12) with the urban wages of 2007-08 measured at current prices we find that the wages for casual male and regular female workers have declined marginally while the wages of casual female and regular male workers have concomitantly increased. It means that the urban wages, measured at 2007-08 consumer prices, have remained more or less stagnant for urban workers, a large chunk of whom are industrial workers.

Table 4: Average Wage (Rs.) per day for Regular and Casual Urban Workers of age 15-59 years in Gujarat at 2007-08 prices (CPI-IW)

	Casual		*Regular*	
	male	*female*	*male*	*female*
2007-08 (at current price, reported by NSSO)	108.76	55.75	215.02	181.95
2011-12 (at 2007-08, end of the year price)	106.60	58.95	216.56	180.41
The Gap (S. No. 2/1)	0.98	1.06	1.01	0.99

Source: Calculated by the Author

In a nutshell, this section argues that the real wage rate for urban workers has remained more or less stagnant over the past few years. The real wages are not linked to productivity, mainly because of the near-famine of the workers' bargaining powers. Gross casualisation of workforce, dearth of trade unions, near non-implementation of labour laws, and the perpetuation of the power structure existing in the villages have contributed to this situation collectively.

Section 4: State of Rural Workers' Earnings in Gujarat

In rural Gujarat too the workers' wages are lower compared to the All India average. The NSSO data shows the daily rural wages in Gujarat to be lower than the All India average both for regular and casual workers, with the exception of female casual workers. The average All India wage for rural regular workers (both male and female) compared to Gujarat is 1.18 times higher and for the rural casual workers it is 1.23 times higher.

The All India average was higher for rural wages compared to Gujarat in 2007-08 as well, with the exception of female casual workers (Table 5). The All India average rural wages for regular male workers were 1.15 times higher than for their Gujarat counterparts. For female regular rural workers, on the other hand, the wages in Gujarat were on par with the rest of India. For the casual rural male worker, the gap was narrowed further while the state paid more wages to female rural casual workers compared to the rest of the country.

Table 5: Average wage (Rs.) per day for Regular and Casual Rural workers of age 15-59 years, 2011-12

S. No.		*Regular*			*Casual*			*Gender Gap (male/female wage)*	
		male	*female*	*person*	*male*	*female*	*person*	*Regular*	*Casual*
1.	Gujarat	268.69	173.13	254.42	115.77	104.96	112.84	1.55	1.10
2.	all-India	322.28	201.56	298.96	149.32	103.28	138.62	1.60	1.45
3	The Gap (S.No. 1/2)	1.20	1.16	1.18	1.29	0.98	1.23		

Source: NSSO 2011-12

Table 6: Average wage (Rs. 0.00) per day for Rural workers of age 15-59 years, 2007-08

S. No.		*Regular*		*Casual*		*Gender Gap (male/female wage)*	
		male	*female*	*male*	*female*	*Casual*	*Regular*
1.	Gujarat	152.07	107.6	68.53	58.97	1.41	1.16
2.	all-India	175.3	108.14	75.3	51.17	1.62	1.47
3	The Gap (S. No. 1/2)	1.15	1.01	1.10	0.87		

Source: NSSO 2007-08

It is clear from the above tables (Tables 4 and 5) that Gujarat workers received lower wages compared to the rest of India between 2007-08 and 2011-12. The wage increase (at All India level) too, was higher compared to Gujarat. Yet there is one silver lining: the gender gap in rural wages in Gujarat is lower relative to the rest of the country. However, the rate of increase in gender disparity for rural workers has been higher in Gujarat than the All India average.

Agriculture dominates the sectoral composition of Gujarat's rural employment with 74.5 per cent of rural Gujarat workers (usual status) employed in agriculture, whereas, in the rest of India, the share of agriculture in rural employment is 64.1 per cent (2011-12). In other words, agriculture is predominantly responsible for providing rural employment. Agricultural output too, in a break from the past, has grown at a much higher rate compared to all of India in the last decade. And yet, there is an increasing rural wage gap between Gujarat and All India workers, which indicates that benefits of agricultural growth have not percolated to the rural workers, including a large section of agricultural workers, to any great extent. Besides, the agricultural mode in vogue in the State is predominantly capitalistic comprising non-food grain crops. As a result, agricultural surpluses getting concentrated in the hands of large land holders. The Schedule Tribes, who primarily work as agricultural labourers with large-scale agriculturalists, are concentrated within a few tribal districts of Gujarat. They migrate to other parts of the State during the agricultural sessions and possess less bargaining power compared to the locals.

Gujarat has had a Rural Labour Commissionerate in place since 1981, under which the Rural Workers' Welfare Board has been working. The activity list of this board has been getting truncated from the list since inception. The activities, like, the enforcement of certain labour laws pertaining to rural workers and encouraging rural workers' organisations has been omitted now. Only the helping workers to access the benefit of various welfare schemes has remained. The activity list of the Rural Labour Commissionerate includes the implementation of the Minimum Wages Act 1948, Bonded Labour (Abolition) Act 1976, Equal Remuneration Act 1976, Child Labour (Prohibition and Regulation) Act 1986, and the Inter-State Migrant Workers (Regulation of Employment and Conditions of Services) Act 1979.

According to Hirway's study (2011), the rural labour commissionerate is dogged by three problems. First, it is severely understaffed. Second, acute violations of the aforementioned acts notwithstanding, the number of inspections carried out under the various acts is very low. Third, post-inspection prosecution too is very low.

The above-mentioned situation is expected to increase rural inequality in Gujarat, a fact suggested by the Planning Commission data as well. Rural inequality (measured in the same way of previously calculated urban inequality) has grown in Gujarat at the rate of 7.2 per cent between 1993-94 and 2009-10. Compare this to the inequality growth rate of 3.19 percent in the rest of India.

To sum up, this section argues that despite Gujarat's high growth of agricultural output, the situation of rural workers is no better than that of their urban counterparts. The same reasons are attributable to both: lack of organisation between the workers and the State Government's inadequacies regarding implementing the labour laws. The result? Rural workers are denied the benefits of agricultural growth with a fast-growing rural inequality being greater than the national average.

Section 5: Conclusion

Both regular and casual urban and rural workers take home substantially lower wages compared to their counterparts elsewhere in the country. Moreover, the gap keeps widening, Gujarat's higher per capita income notwithstanding. The State's outputs in agriculture, industry, and services have expanded faster compared to the rest of the country. Its per capita income too, has been growing at a faster rate compared to other parts of India. This means that the State's profit share too, has been accelerating, resulting in growing inequality. The real wage rate for workers has remained more or less stagnant over the last few years and is not linked to productivity. This is because of the workers' low bargaining powers that may be ascribed to gross casualisation of the workforce, scanty presence of trade unions, near non-implementation of labour laws, and the perpetuation of the power structure of the villages and its continuity in the factories.

REFERENCES

Guha, A. and Tripathi, A. (2014). Linkage between food price inflation and rural wage dynamics. *IRMA Working Paper #253*. Anand: IRMA.

Hirway, I and Shah, N. (2011). Labour and employment under globalisation: The case of Gujarat. *Economic and Political Weekly*, xlvi (22), 57-65.

Nagaraj, R. and Pandey, S. (2013). Have Gujarat and Bihar outperformed the rest of India? A statistical note. *Economic and Political Weekly*, xlviii (39), 39-41.

Unni and Ravikiran (2014). Gujarat's employment story: Growth with informality. In Indira Hirway, Amita Shah and Ghanshyam Shah (eds.), *Growth or development: Which way is gujarat going*. Delhi: Oxford University Press.

NOTES

1. NSS Report No. 554(68/10/1): Employment and Unemployment Situation in India, 2011-12, p. 196
2. Calculated by the author.
3. Unni & Ravikiran (2014).
4. Source: http://planningcommission.nic.in/data/datatable/1612/table_98.pdf. The consumption figure of Uniform Recall Period is being used.
5. http://www.paycheck.in/main/salary/minimumwages/gujarat.
6. A more detail survey of this reasoning can be found in Guha & Tripathy (2014).

18

Brahmanism, Liberalism and the Postcolonial Theory

Ajay Gudavarthy

The common belief is that Brahmanism, liberalism and postcolonial interventions are not only mutually exclusive frames, but that they were inaugurated to displace one another. In India, Western liberalism was a response to undo the social hierarchies put in place by Brahmanical proclivities, including those of purity and pollution and gender discrimination closely linked to caste, all found in a programmatic form in *Manusmriti*. In turn, postcolonial theory was inaugurated to displace the 'imperialism of categories' introduced by Western modernity in our society which was originally communitarian, religious, and traditional. However, a closer look at Brahmanism, liberalism and postcolonial theory, and the way this triangular entanglement works itself offers us a possibility to read all the three frames as belonging to the same 'epistemic community'. The social and political effects of the three frames operate within the limits of a 'politics of accommodation', and of incremental and additive change.

Brahmanism's core philosophical propensity is not only to justify social hierarchy and untouchability but also to allow porous changes that will disallow the building of contradictions. Brahmanism is a philosophical system that co-opts and accommodates moments that emerge in opposition to it and tones them in its own colour. This is how Buddhism and innumerable other reform movements within Hinduism came to be co-opted into the Hindu fold as 'dissents' internal to Hinduism. Thus, even though core practices have a certain fixity, 'truth' becomes contextual here. Gandhian praxis is symptomatic of this practice, oscillating between claims that are non-negotiable and the idea that truth (God) itself needs to be unearthed through an ethical praxis, such as that of a *satyagrahi.* If seen in a deeper sense, liberalism reflects a similar kind of propensity to accommodate and arrive at consensus and dialogue without radically altering the structural power relations, or the equation between the hegemonic practices of the dominant over the dominated.

Adjusting Dissent

The inextricable link between these two epistemic systems in Indian social and political reality lies in its centrist nature. The much lauded idea that Indian democracy is essentially centrist, and that it remained democratic because it was centrist in nature reflects this convergence between Brahmanism and liberalism. Centrist polity, as Susanne Rudolph, Lloyd I. Rudolph and many other political scientists have noted, accommodates all that grows into dissent, hence not allowing dissent to fructify into a moment of throwing an open challenge. Liberalism allows incremental change as well, and believes truth to be contextual—thus the importance of dialogue since truth is never arrived at but only socially constructed. In this framework, old is not displaced but adjusted into the new, and polar opposites are not contradictory but two sides of the same coin. D.D. Kosambi captures this in his classical formulation that history and social transformation in much of South Asia moved through "adjustment and not displacement."

The history of Indian post-independence politics and democracy is a demonstration of this. Nehruvian politics was an accommodation between the private and public sectors: socialism with right to property, village as the soul with heavy industrialisation. The accommodation was captured in Nehru's inimitable statement that "dams are the modern temples of India." This centrist character is the defining feature of Indian politics, from the extreme right to the left. Bahujan Samaj Party had to move from *bahujan* to *sarvajan* and could seamlessly think of an alliance between the Dalits and the Brahmins in Uttar Pradesh; Arvind Kejriwal could announce that he is neither left nor right but practical, where on a given day he campaigned against Ambanis, and on another, had no qualms in announcing in a meeting with the Confederation of Indian Industry (CII) that he had nothing against capitalism. It is therefore not unthinkable for the Bharatiya Janata Party (BJP)–Rashtriya Swayamsevak Sangh (RSS) combine to think of appropriating Ambedkar as a symbol of Hindu nationalism. Someone who tirelessly campaigned all his life against the infirmities of Hinduism and its unalterable core character seems pliable to be co-opted as a Hindu nationalist. What we have in India in essence is an oscillating or a swinging public sphere that can seamlessly accommodate explicitly self-contradictory practices. This is all a part of the popular culture that lends support to *Love–Jihad*, *Ghar Wapsi* and the language of hyper-nationalism, while the stupendous success of Hindi films such as PK and *Bajrangi Bhaijaan* is also a reality, even as we are witnessing a rightward shift of the centre.

Postcolonial theory was a relatively newer moment in this accommodative and pragmatic turn which is internal to the centrist character of Indian social and political reality. Postcolonial theory opposes without challenging. It exalts the ability of traditions to assume modern forms and purpose. It engulfs the idea that parallel streams can co-exist—adjusting without displacing. In the process, it results in projecting the subaltern classes as in need of modernity, and Western liberal democracies as the missing community; both of them—modernity through higher education, and community life in all forms, including its hierarchical nature—are repositories of caste Hindus (*Bhadralok*) in India. In a sense, the superiority of the Bhadralok remains unchallenged in the postcolonial framework. In this frame, the category of a 'subaltern' becomes loose enough to include a Dalit in a ghettoised colony, and a professor in the South Asian department in the United States.

The Elite as Subaltern

Similarly, Gandhi can become a symbol of elite nationalism within the context of anticolonial movements, which is what the 'subaltern studies' project began with, but also a symbol of indigenous and postcolonial knowledge in the context of global knowledge systems, which is what Sumit Sarkar refers to as the "decline of the subaltern in subaltern studies." Gandhi becomes a symbol of postcoloniality and therefore his idea of the "ethical self" becomes central to much of the postcolonial project, like that of Ashis Nandy, Akeel Bilgrami and others. But the postcolonial frame also appropriates the politics of Dalits, and their claims to exclusive lived experience are accommodated within the same frame as spaces that give birth to an organic subaltern culture and perspective. There is no discussion on how to approach the continuing rejection of Gandhi by Dalit politics. The endemic tension between Gandhi and Dalits could have been used to conceptualise the missing link in Indian history: that of 'internal colonialisation,' and the story of 'our modernity' or stepping 'outside modernity.'

Similar is the accommodation of Ambedkar within the same postcolonial frame, which papers over his tryst with high modernism and the fact that for Dalit emancipation, Ambedkar reposed faith in the modern state and not in community. Such an approach significantly fails to note that these modes of accommodation shroud the emerging nexus between traditional forms of power found in community, religion and the local with modern governmental mechanisms. This process was best captured in the idea of "glass war" that P. Sainath reported regarding caste practices in Andhra Pradesh, iterating that modern technology, which allowed for the use of disposable glasses, in fact accommodates and does not displace untouchability in wayside hotels. Similarly, the project of vegetarianism can be couched in the language of science and new environmental concerns. These cases are not about subaltern counterculture and traditions subverting the hegemonic effects of modernity, but about how modern forms of power can sit well with traditional modes of power relations.

Instead of altering politics of patronage, a certain invisibilisation of power relations is effected, along with the absence of a political language that can capture prejudice. In essence, centrism comes to represent this nexus, notwithstanding the microscopic changes it allows for. All these three frameworks—Brahmanism, liberalism and the postcolonial—focus more on the microscopic changes that the accommodative and centrist nature of the social allows for, largely ignoring the larger grids of structural domination that continue unabated.

The Global Subaltern

This elasticity and accommodative character of postcolonial theory in India is also visible in the intriguing shifts it has made in consonance with the shifts in global theoretical frames. Postcolonial theorists of India began as Althusserian-structuralists, and then alluded to Gramsci; they moved on to Heidegger, to Laclau and Mouffe, and to Foucault, post-structuralism and autonomist philosophers. If one looks at it, the theorist's history of the subaltern in India, notwithstanding all the emphasis on difference, is strangely in alignment with the renderings of global political moves—beginning with structural explanations of peasant rebellions in Ranajit Guha's *Elementary Aspects of Peasant Insurgency*, to discursive contests over hegemonic articulations in the later volumes of the *Subaltern Studies*, to Heidegger in Dipesh Chakrabarty's *Provincializing Europe* and to more contemporary versions of poststructural politics of contingency, contextual negotiations, molecular change, politics of the possible and politics of the everyday in Partha Chatterjee's notion of "political society." Indian subaltern is, ironically, local and very global at the same time.

Such moves make it necessary to reason the relation between capital on the one hand, and social identities and hierarchies on the other. Here, capital has worked itself both ways: by definition, it could work itself independent of social hierarchies. In fact, capitalism's unique feature was that it was based on a wage labour system for extraction of surplus, and did not depend structurally on an extra-economic force. However, functionally, capital draws from all existing social and cultural resources to augment the production process, and to extract surplus through cheap labour and raw materials. This particular duality of capital renders history complex and in a sense, indeterminate and different. Yet, this indeterminacy occurs within the structural context of capital's drive for profits and extraction of surplus, which has the capacity to iron out cultural differences and undermine the capacity of societies to stand outside its machinations. This fact of capital's capacity—its 'double movement'—allows for a global history of capitalism, with and without differences. This stands doubly true with the nature of neoliberal capital that seems to have abandoned the enlightenment project of freedom, autonomy, and dignity. It could provide women with new opportunities in the market, yet reproduce caste differences within a factory; it could intensify commodification of religion, astrology and Ayurveda, whose mere existence should not be taken to signify 'the limits to capital.'

Politics of Patronages

This is akin to the subaltern theorists' understanding that mere use of religious forms makes the subaltern radical, different, and belong to an 'autonomous domain' without being hegemonised. This understanding occurs without considering the nature of demands the religious forms are put to. Even here, the attempt by the subaltern scholars has been to dignify the practices of the subaltern as they exist, instead of accounting for how their agency is determined by the way power is structured, and how resources constrain their choice of political action. While dignifying the practices of the subaltern holds some value when social and communitarian prejudice against them run high, for the very same reason, it falls into reifying the 'ethnicisation of the subaltern' in opposition to the modern.[1] For instance, consider Chatterjee's formulation of "political society," where he seamlessly assumes that there is a classical bourgeois "civil society" in India that is grounded in the rule of law, citizenship and rights as against an ethnic subaltern located in paralegal practices.

A similar issue is that of social separatism. Brahmanism is essentially a philosophy of separating and segregating social collectives along caste by birth. Brahmanical ideology separates groups through ritual practices, symbolic valuing of cultural lifestyles, food habits, and colour of skin, justifying spatial segregation of groups. Spatial separation is found not only in villages but at the heart of hypermodern urbanisation and in 'smart cities.' This separation is deeply biopolitical, castigating touch along the notions of purity and impurity. Liberalism, while it discounts ascriptive identities and privileges in the name of choice and autonomy, nevertheless institutionalises a similar worldview through individualism, which views freedom as the capacity to distance from social collectives, responsibilities and mutual obligations. Here, freedom as hyperseparation from the social is a given, while obligations need to be justified. Freedom is to be found in the extent of separation possible, given the limits posed by the need for cooperative activity. Even in managing social and cultural diversity, liberalism promotes multiculturalism, which privileges social and spatial separation of collectives in order to maintain mutual harmony. Blacks, Hispanics, South Asian immigrants, Muslims and Whites co-exist by living in separate ghettoes that allow each of them to live a parallel life of their own, 'uncontaminated' by others. This is much like the *agraharas* that sought to remain 'pure,' untouched by 'outcastes.' Postcolonial framework does something similar, but which looks radical and oppositional in its initial avatar. It privileges an 'autonomous domain' of the subaltern and attempts to legitimise this separation as a moment of radical assertion of the subaltern. It carves out separate domains of operation along the lines of civility and legality, undermining the power relations that structure and operate these separations.

In celebrating the cult of the subaltern, the postcolonial celebrates the very separations on which these subaltern practices are grounded; in the process it neither investigates the continuities of how dominant discourses structure subaltern practices nor the hierarchical imaginations internal to the subaltern popular culture. In privileging subaltern popular culture without a critical interrogation, the post-colonial institutionalises politics of patronage. In other words, the postcolonial has a mere rhetorical engagement with how the subaltern gets imbricated in political power games, without engaging with the hard political outcomes that could be detrimental to their interests, even if those interests are 'constructed' and not pregiven.

Postcolonial framework, in avoiding to open subaltern choices for critical interrogation in a larger society which is caste-based and ladder-like, makes a rather synthetic and a sociological reading of politics without ever getting into the nitty-gritty of it. 'Community,' then, remains an imagination without an accompanying sociological understanding of it. The distant reading of community and the local, places them as binary opposites of civil society, individual and the global. Much of postcolonial theory has selectively foregrounded the 'creative power of community' without ever laying out the practices internal to the formation of such collectives. The fantasy of community, as Zygmunt Bauman would put it, has haunted the postcolonial project as an "empty category" that is necessarily made sense of only as the other of modernity. Postcolonial theorists have held on to this 'fantasy' even as they have increasingly grown critical of utopias of the left and Marxist variant.

Indian politics today is witnessing an implosion of internal hierarchies, visible in conflicts between Dalit sub-castes, in conflicts between Dalits and Adivasis, between Other Backward Classes and Dalits, and between all of these social groups and Muslims. Much of these intra-subaltern conflicts cannot be captured either through East versus West or subaltern versus elite kind of frames. It is in this context that post-Mandal politics in India, in a sense, has forced a steady decline in the impact of subaltern and postcolonial Bhadralok scholarship on Indian academia, since much of it spread without laying out dynamics internal to subaltern political culture. Much of the political imagination in Indian academic scholarship, and Indian politics have remained caught in a dialogue between these triangulate frames of Brahmanism, liberalism and post-colonial theory, displacing any available space to point either towards the commonalities between these frames or the consequential molecular changes that these frames cumulatively privilege. Neoliberalism and accompanying pragmatism have only further entrenched the modalities intrinsic to all of these frames. This now requires a fresh and a more intensive empirical and theoretical study.

NOTE

1. I borrow this argument from my review of Vivek Chibber's book (Gudavarthy 2013).

REFERENCE

Gudavarthy, Ajay (2013): 'De-colonizing Post-colonial Theory,' *The Book Review*, Vol. 37, No. 9, viewed on 21 May 2016, http://www.thebookreviewindia.org/articles/archives-1339/2013/september/9/decolonizing-postcolonial-theory.html.

List of Contributors

Editor

Dhananjay Rai is Assistant Professor at the Centre for Gandhian Thought and Peace Studies, School of Social Sciences, Central University of Gujarat, Gandhinagar.

Contributors

Sudipta Kaviraj is Professor at the Department of Middle Eastern, South Asian and African Studies, and Director of Graduate Studies, Columbia University, New York.

Randhir Singh (1922-2016) was a distinguished teacher and former Professor of Political Theory, University of Delhi. He was associated with the communist movement since 1939. Of his writings, Harry Magdoff, editor, *Monthly Review*, said: 'I admire the solidity of your analysis as well as the firmness of your commitment'.

Harbans Mukhia is Professor (retd) at the Centre for Historical Studies, Jawaharlal Nehru University, New Delhi.

Chaman Lal is Professor (retd), Jawaharlal Nehru University, New Delhi.

Savita Singh is Professor in the School of Gender and Development Studies, IGNOU, New Delhi.

Manindra Nath Thakur is Associate Professor at the Centre for Political Studies, Jawaharlal Nehru University, New Delhi.

Veena Ravikumar is Associate Professor at the Department of Political Science, Lady Shri Ram College for Women, University of Delhi, New Delhi.

Hilal Ahmed is Associate Professor at the Centre for Study of Developing Societies, Delhi.

Manoranjan Mohanty is the Vice President of the Council for Social Development, New Delhi. A former Professor of Political Science at the University of Delhi, he is Editor of *Social Change* and a former Editor of *China Report*.

Anand Teltumbde is a writer and civil rights activist with the Committee for the Protection of Democratic Rights, Mumbai.

Ravi Kumar is Associate Professor at the Department of Sociology, South Asian University, New Delhi.

Abdul Rahman is Assistant Professor, Tata Institute of Social Sciences, Hyderabad.

Rityusha Mani Tiwary is Assistant Professor at the Department of Political Science, Shaheed Bhagat Singh College, University of Delhi, Delhi.

Pavel Tomar is Doctoral Candidate at the Centre for Historical Studies, Jawaharlal Nehru University, New Delhi.

Yoginder K. Alagh is Chancellor of Central University of Gujarat, Gandhinagar, Gujarat.

K.B. Saxena is distinguished Professor at the Council for Social Development, New Delhi.

Atulan Guha is Associate Professor of Economics, Indian Institute of Management, Kashipur.

Ajay Gudavarthy is Associate Professor at the Centre for Political Studies, Jawaharlal Nehru University, New Delhi.